‘Spellbinding, unique, and original, *The Global Origin* me with this fresh look into the ancient study of *ps* *psyche* is also true of *logos*: word, reason, argument, laws to be discovered, the human capacity for acce penetrating to its underlying laws – all the senses of *logos* – predate Greek philosophy. The journey of *logos* through the Fertile Crescent, Ancient Iraq, Ancient Egypt, Ancient Israel, and Ancient China delineates a new world map so that we understand how we reason in our mind in different areas of the world, historically, and cross-culturally.’

Ruyu Hung, *Distinguished Professor,*
National Chiayi University, Taiwan

‘Valentine provides a readable, fascinating review of the psyche through time, a sweeping tapestry of cultural and historic shifts in understanding the laterality of the brain. He brings forward ancient views of the mind and offers a thought provoking and insightful perspective on the challenges humanity has encountered and still faces.’

Darcia Narvaez, *University of Notre Dame,*
USA, and author of Neurobiology and the
Development of Human Morality:
Evolution, Culture and Wisdom

The Global Origins of Psychology

This book offers a historical introduction to the remote origins of psychology, and is the first book in a series on the history of the subject. Combining a deep history approach with the study of ancient civilisations, it places psychology in a historical and global context using rigorous academic research.

The book begins by separating the Greek components of psychology – psyche and logos – in order to trace their histories, separate and together, through the global Neolithic and Bronze Ages. The author develops a toolkit by deconstructing the writing of history, modern psychology, and analysis of culture, and by introducing theories from neuroscience and cultural psychology that can be tested against the data. He then takes readers on a journey back in time, from the borders of our current climatic envelope (the Holocene) towards the present, through Ancient Iraq, Egypt, Israel, and China. Each chapter deepens the reader's understanding of psychology in its global context outside the boundaries of Western culture. In so doing, the book initiates a post-colonial re-narration showing that the story of psychology is wider and deeper than many contemporary origin stories suggest.

Presented in an accessible manner, this is an excellent resource for students of psychology, philosophy, history, linguistics, archaeology, and anthropology, as well as general readers who want to learn more about the origins of this fascinating subject.

Richard Valentine is a researcher and cultural consultant for the induction of international students into UK universities, and has extensive experience leading multimedia online education platforms. He has published essays, articles, and policy pieces for higher education in physics, psychology, and religious studies. He is a member of the British Psychological Society as an occupational consultant with experience in developing and applying intelligence and personality profiling products. Before moving into psychology, his academic background was in philosophy and the natural sciences.

A New History of Western Psychology
Series Editor: Richard Valentine

Books in the Series

The Global Origins of Psychology
Neurology, Language and Culture in the Ancient World

The Global Origins of Psychology

Neurology, Language and Culture in the Ancient World

Richard Valentine

Routledge
Taylor & Francis Group
LONDON AND NEW YORK

Designed cover image: © Getty Images

First published 2024
by Routledge
4 Park Square, Milton Park, Abingdon, Oxon OX14 4RN

and by Routledge
605 Third Avenue, New York, NY 10158

Routledge is an imprint of the Taylor & Francis Group, an informa business

British Library Cataloguing-in-Publication Data
A catalogue record for this book is available from the British Library

ISBN: 978-1-032-49945-1 (hbk)
ISBN: 978-1-032-49944-4 (pbk)
ISBN: 978-1-003-39614-7 (ebk)

DOI: 10.4324/9781003396147

Typeset in Times New Roman
by MPS Limited, Dehradun

Support Material can be accessed at www.routledge.com/9781032499444

To Rosie
without whom this book could not have been written

Contents

Further Information Online

To find out more about Richard Valentine and this book, please visit www.richardevalentine.com or scan the QR code below.

Further Support Material can also be found at www.routledge.com/9781032499444.

Acknowledgements

David Hume lamented that his *Treatise of Human Nature* 'fell dead-born from the press'. I would like to thank these people for helping me to bring this child to birth, in the hope that it may have a happier issue. If not, it is not their responsibility.

In order of contribution by order of contents, not by quantity:

- Introduction: thank you to Jeff Slater for some careful comments on the whole text, editing for clarity and style.
- Chapter 1: thank you to Richard Coulson and Abel Brooks as the rest of my 'millennial focus group' for specific, sensitive, and well-judged advice on detail.
- Chapter 2: thank you to Rudi Hayward for detailed reading under time pressure, reassuring me about some more esoteric interpretations of Continental Philosophy.
- Chapter 3: thank you again to Jeff as first reader, for encouragement that I was still making myself clear; and Tom Wright who first put me on to Iain McGilchrist.
- Chapter 4: this thing of darkness I acknowledge mine. Thank you to all on the Orkney Mainland and in Wiltshire for hospitality, education and book selection!
- Chapter 5: thank you to J. Richard Middleton for 35 years of inspiration, warmth and meticulous scholarship, from *Enuma Elish* through Jacques Derrida to *Bereshith*.
- Chapter 6: a big thank you to Bojana Mojsov my first reader, who brought her curiosity and scholarship to bear on my text and cheered me on with this *magnum opus*. I took your advice, and kept the politics in the footnotes!
- Chapter 7: thank you to J. Richard Middleton as for 5; and to Mark Roques, Richard Russell and the team. Thank you to Michael Eaton, my starting gun in Hebrew, and to Richard Zetter for some hot takes on Semitic lore.

- Chapter 8: thank you to Ben Odart, Steve Odart and the team at the ranch, as well as Eric Wang for his input.
- The series: thank you to Kevin Wilson-Smith, midwife and lightning conductor. I'm working on the back story.

Finally, thank you to my editors at Routledge: Adam Woods, who like Saint Peter let me through the gate; Zoe Thomson for exceptional midwifery and adroit advocacy on the boards; and Maddie Gray who could run the country if she wanted to.

Preface

You may already know that the modern word 'psychology' was made from two older words from ancient Greek, *psyche* (mind, soul) and *logos* (word, reason):

***psyche* + *logos* = psychology** (talking or reasoning about the human mind)

Both words have long histories, going back almost 3000 years: in this series we will take you back into this history, tracing the stories of these words and the ideas behind them until they are combined into the word 'Psychology'.

This was done in modern times by people we call 'philosophers'. Philosophy is another Greek word made of two words, love (*phileos*) and wisdom (*sophia*):

***philo* + *sophia* = philosophy** (loving and pursuing wisdom or knowledge)

The 'lovers of wisdom' have long discussed the soul or mind of human beings (*psyche*) and how to reflect on it, understand it and make theories about it (*logos*). Before the word 'psychology' was coined, something like it was practised, and ideas which led to modern science have deep roots in ancient philosophy.

We are going to travel back in time and return slowly to psychology as taught today through its history. By the time we reach it today, you will have a unique understanding of its vocabulary, methods, schools of thought – and much else.

Breaking things into parts is known as **analysis** and reconstructing as **synthesis**. Starting close up with our immediate experience, we attempt to reach behind it and to explain it through analysis of hidden dynamics. In history, this means going back to the **sources**, reconstructing 'from behind' by telling a fresh story.

Therefore, in this book, we will start with global sources, including a survey of alternative routes from these sources before turning to Greek ideas about the *psyche* and how it should be investigated (in Book Two). The Romans picked up on this heritage, and this will be the content of the next volume (Book Three). We will start a long way back in order to gain some 'leverage' in the present: to try to understand the dynamics behind each stage before we move on to it.

We will have to touch on many ancient **languages** and those who used them. Already in Greek alone, we have used *psyche*, *logos*, *sophia,* and *phileos* as well as theory (*theoria*), practice (*praktike*), method (*methodos*), analysis, synthesis, dynamics (*dunamos*), and centrally, history (*historia* = enquiry, **investigation**).

Introduction

How this book can help you

As you have chosen this book you may be considering studying – or are already studying – a course which includes psychology, either alone or in combination with another subject. There is a wide family of related subjects (which we will visit in Chapter 2). There is also a family of historical disciplines, covering different times and places. You may come to this book as a historian looking into psychology, or a psychologist seeking to learn its history; or you may not know, as yet, where you will belong.

Surely all that really matters is choosing a course which motivates you, getting your assignments in, ending it all with a decent grade, and having an optimum experience of student life in the process? But one thing psychologists, as well as grandparents for that matter, can tell you is that **motivation** is everything: you will struggle either to complete a course, to achieve your optimum grades, or to use it effectively afterwards and make it all worthwhile, unless you want it, even love it. As in karate, the athlete can *will* her muscle fibres to 'line up' and move together as one, giving her extra strength, so in your studies, an intrinsic motivation (one driven from inside) can cause your existing skills to line up and move together. This book and this series are intended to motivate your studies.

So: what can the ancients do for **you** as a budding (let's assume) psychologist?

1 A safe space

On your chosen course, you will soon find that there are multiple '**schools**' in contemporary psychology: your task on the course is to understand, compare and evaluate their claims against one another, or competing claims within one particular school. Your department – and your individual lecturers – will have a bias toward a particular 'school' to use a traditional term, or 'research programme' in more contemporary language. Each will have its own fundamental 'take' on what a human being is – for the purposes of psychological research – and with this, its own preferred methods for studying and describing human beings as defined.

In the ancient world, you will meet a huge variety of competing 'schools' with wildly different views on what we now call psychology. In this first book

DOI: 10.4324/9781003396147-1

there are entire civilisations with completely different conceptions of several things:

- what kind of thing a **human being** is
- what a **mind** is (that is, disagreements over *psyche*)
- what if anything can be **known** about it (disagreements over *logos*)
- why it **matters** within a larger view of society, the cosmos, the afterlife, etc.

With all the possibilities of strangeness in the answers, ancient psychology and philosophy offer a wonderful '**brain gym**' to learn the skills of accessing ideas, exploring them, comparing them, and then (finally) coming to your own view: these are exactly the skills you will be learning towards assignments and exams.

These debates are safe ground because they are so distinct from contemporary psychology, yet they are still relevant to its concerns. It is often said that 'The past is a foreign country: they do things differently there.'[1] Learn to skirmish in this foreign land, before you return to your homeland to face today's battles.

You will find in many cases that today's opposed armies are the descendants of those you will meet in these pages; so train yourself in the critical evaluation of relevant sources. (Along the way, decide whether this kind of study is for you.)

2 A mental 'map' (see Chapter 2 for more details)

It is easy to become disorientated in any subject, unable 'to see the wood for the trees' (to use a favourite English idiom). This is true not only for beginners but professional academics, who are forced to **specialise** in tiny areas of research as their condition of entry, and then find they have little time to regain a broader view of the workload. This is the experience of your lecturers and tutors.

As a student you have an advantage of less specialised knowledge, a window of choice between options: the enormous advantage of a **less defined** future. If you are ever going to 'think outside the box' it is now, or – for the lucky few – much further down the line, when you are successful and can reclaim that freedom.

Such a narrowing of interest is not only a practical matter, of the limited time available. Every department, every research programme, and every discipline is subject to **fashions** and **biases**, so the further you enter into the academic system, the less choice you have of **opinions** – and especially public expression of those opinions. Your research is not funded if you do not 'say the right thing'. Ideological pressure is at least as much a factor as workload pressure or the practical limitations of time and it suppresses any sense of detachment, orientation, and **openness** to debate. The very things that make academic life effective can also negate its purpose.

Again, you have the advantage of being permitted to **explore** your own views as a student – before you are inside the system and have to watch your back. The ancient civilisations reflect that **freedom**, with their fledgling 'theories' – often anarchic by modern standards. Almost anything goes. As a Roman critic was to put it, 'Nothing is so silly that it has not been said by one of the philosophers'.[2]

This is the time to get a set of 'maps' in your head, so you will know what you *do not* know, which boxes have *not yet been* ticked and which areas are unexplored. Starting as far back as we can, at the 'dawn' of psychological thinking, we can work towards the present, noting which paths were *not* taken, for visiting later. You need a '**concept map**' which includes territory forbidden or neglected, of which departments, lecturers and tutors are trained to say, '*Here be dragons!*'

3 A map of the world (see 1.5, then the first section of each chapter)

You will also need a map in the literal sense: the **geographical** distribution of the conceptual options. Today the world – even the academic world – is moving back rapidly to a sense of **interconnection** it has not experienced since ancient times. Then, the technologies of communication were basic but there were far fewer people in the world, far less of the thing called *psyche* (see below), and even fewer people talking about *psyche*. The human world was much smaller.

Today, as the human population is unimaginably larger than in the ancient world, we also have far greater opportunities to connect across **global cultures**. Early centres of civilisation have grown to become hubs of modern civilisation, with long roots in the past. Business and trade, law and government, education and entertainment move between these ancient 'hubs' with their different outlooks.

Major modern nations such as China and India, and globally important regions such as Europe, can trace their cultural roots back more than two millennia to the time before the beginning of the Common Era – before the year we call 0. This time saw the birth of most world religions, belief systems and moral codes, as well as philosophies (and psychologies) associated with these. Atheist as well as religious philosophies can trace their roots back to this highly creative period.

In this book we will trace the great civilisations down to their roots, always in search of our particular targets: beginnings of ideas about *psyche* and *logos*. It will give us a preface to the Greek ideas we will cover in the next book, which are generally seen as the origins of **Western** philosophy (and psychology), but also place this preface securely on the world map – a 'map' of who was where, which languages they used, what they already knew. If you start in Book Two you will be joining the party late, without introductions: a little disorientated.

Today, the communications revolution which has climaxed in the Internet and social media has brought us full circle, back to a **global melting pot**. In this new context modern psychology, being 'modern', has to face its identity as a cultural product of the period of European dominance, which is currently ending. It is obliged to place itself, and its dearest assumptions, back in a global context with ancient roots.

Popular psychology has embraced this context, following 'the market' without the constraints of academic discipline. Bookshops have sections entitled 'Mind, Body and and Spirit' advocating esoteric practices from multiple world cultures as forms of self-help. Publishers make much of those rogue academics – often converts within medicine – who are prepared to endorse any esoteric 'method'. The same goes for popular archaeology, Egyptology, and evolutionary psychology: serving up what people want to hear, for any reason, and are willing to pay for.

Academic Psychology as a guild generally disapproves of this and sees itself as a fortress of rationality, rigour, observation, professionalism, peer review and quality control. These hard-won criteria are not to be taken lightly: the product of long centuries of extracting ourselves from ignorance. On the other hand, the publishing market is clearly ahead of the curve in globalisation, which is a valid concern, to which popular markets are faster to respond. Multiple international conferences today are trying to catch up. These urgently need relevant history.

4 The limits of time travel (see Chapter 1, especially 1.3)

The history of psychology is naturally a battleground for the competing schools and their preferred conceptions of the subject. Modern histories of psychology often begin about 150 years ago, when those who study 'the human mind' first began to imitate the natural sciences successfully, with experiments and new medical knowledge in laboratories. Such a '**short**' historical timeline is a preferred story for some schools in psychology, which matches their take on the key questions outlined in (1) above: people are much like animals, primarily **physical** entities; the mind is a **function** of the body; **observation** is essential; **measurement** with **mathematical** analysis is a primary aim; theories are tested rigorously in **labs**; and this overall project was outlined in Europe during the nineteenth century.

In some departments this approach is taken for granted: it just 'is' Psychology.

Many professional psychologists, like many professional philosophers, have no great interest in the history of their subject. What matters is what works and not how we got here. The same is true for most physicists, chemists and so on. It is part of what makes science special that it looks forwards and not backwards; it refers to facts and not books. If we are scientists, then we do not need history. If there must be history, it should be restricted to proper scientists: people like us.

Other schools, aware that theories must be framed in terms of **concepts** with their own history, look a little further back and want to include the

history of philosophy as a past 'laboratory of concepts'. These, more generously, look back to early modern **'philosophy of mind'**, tracing its beginnings to Descartes (1596–1650) and Locke (1632–1704).[3] One influential book on neurology, for example, was called *Descartes' Error*: the author seeks to unpick some conceptual errors from that time, which still influence and limit his subject, in light of recent research.[4] Such histories deploy what can be called a **'medium'** historical timeline. For many, this is as far back as 'History of Psychology' is considered respectable.

There are, however, important schools and particular thinkers, who appear in every psychology curriculum, and look much further back. In fact, almost every area and school of psychology uses concepts with older roots than the medium timelines allow. Descartes himself had deep roots in much earlier philosophy.[5]

The desire for psychology to be 'scientific' is a double-edged policy. If concepts or methods can be assumed and can remain unexamined, this no doubt helps to drive a research programme forward. No plant can grow well if we are forever digging up the roots. Some blinkers are necessary. On the other hand – as the natural sciences themselves have often discovered[6] – we can become stuck in a conceptual rut, struggling to 'think outside the box' until someone digs deeper.

Those who grasp the **Greek roots** of the philosophical concepts in the second approach are also driven back this far, leading to a **longer** historical timeline.[7] **Clinical psychology**, especially, tends to appeal to much older models of mind and method, using Greek myths and metaphors to help in healing minds. Major thinkers – Freud, Jung, Jaspers, Heidegger might be some names you have met already – have typically travelled in these corridors of time, back to the beginnings of our Western civilisation, especially its roots in ancient Greece.[8]

Like everything else produced by people, the 'History of Psychology' itself has a history. Without going down too far down this rabbit hole, we can simply observe that shorter timelines are quite a recent development, reflecting the dominance of certain schools. Go back a hundred years: you find books calling themselves 'A History of Psychology', taking the story back to the roots of Western civilisation and even a little further.[9] Go back two hundred years: this approach is first attempted.[10] Much of our effort in Part One will be to work out a suitable method by digging at the roots of modern history and psychology.

More recently, psychologists who cross over into archaeology have provoked a debate with the proposal that we can now go back much further.[11] The growing sciences of the past – evolutionary psychology and genetics, new movements in archaeology – offer us possibilities for capturing the development of human thought on a vastly **expanded** timeline. Something approaching 'psychology' is seen to evolve gradually in a continuous process, not only before the Greeks, or before the invention of writing, but before the production of food by farming, or further still, reaching ever further back into the recesses of human prehistory.[12]

Modern psychology was born alongside 'evolution' as it appeared in Darwin's theory (1859), and emerging sciences of the remote past such as archaeology.[13] Its sense of its own history is suddenly catching up, bridging the divide between the short, scientific history of modern psychology and the much longer story of human origins implied by Darwin's theory: catching up with the programme for psychology on evolutionary terms, which Darwin himself began to explore.[14]

In terms of the timeline we have gradually been stretching in this section, we have moved from 'short' and 'medium' to 'longer' timelines, and then suddenly shot back to '**deep time**' – as demanded by the logic of evolutionary thinking.[15]

This book can be read as part of this current movement to expand timelines.[16] The bridge between archaeology and psychology is still under construction, as methods on both sides are developing rapidly – hoping to meet in the middle of the river. This book is situated as an island in the stream, facilitating a crossing.

This book will focus on the **Bronze Age** – from five thousand to three thousand years ago – and to do this it starts with a common origin in the **Stone Age** (1.4).

We can summarise these approaches in a brief list, to locate this book's range:

• Short	back to 1850	Modern History
• Medium	back to 1650	Early Modern History
• Longer	back to Ancient Greece	Classical Civilisation
• **Long**	**back to 5000 years ago**	**Chapters 5–8**
• **Deeper**	**back to 12,000 years ago**	**Chapter 4**
• Deep	back over 12,000 years	The Ice Ages[17]

Having taken the timeline back beyond the ancient Greeks into previous ancient civilisations in Part Two, we must stretch the timeline back further still, dipping into the past as far back as 12,000 years, before moving forwards again through the invention of writing. This reduces the gap between evolutionary psychology – which can come as close to us as 30,000 years ago[18] – and the timeline of our narrative.

The day may come when we can close the gap entirely, but the variety of views in current evolutionary psychology suggests that we are not quite at this point.[19] We will touch upon the findings of evolutionary psychology, at the horizon of this book's narrative, but remain within the limits of currently reliable history.

A good argument for this longer timeline is from our previous sections above. If we seek to take a global perspective, as argued in the previous section, then this entails tracing global origins. In order to gain a wider perspective, we must go further back to our common origins, which means a longer timeline.

5 The role of philosophy (see Chapter 2 for more details)

Philosophy is content to trace its roots back to ancient Greece. One reason why old histories of psychology imitated this pattern is that psychology was seen as **a branch of philosophy** until they separated in Victorian times. As the branch grew further from the trunk, it developed its own methods, its own language, its own university departments, and its own journals. Like any teenager it was devoted to defining itself apart from its parent: this attitude endured and became fixed.

As we will discover at length in Chapters 2 and 3, most of the founders of modern psychology were well aware of their debt to philosophy and placed the new 'Experimental Psychology' alongside valid alternatives: 'Descriptive Psychology', which continued the traditional task of philosophy as a laboratory for concepts and methods; 'Social Psychology' as the context for behaviour, or 'Cultural Psychology', including the study of psychology itself as a cultural product.

All of these have been pursued diligently, if not in psychology departments and under that label, then in related subjects. In Chapters 2 and 3, we visit multiple methods in contemporary psychology which are openly **indebted** to pioneering developments in twentieth-century philosophy, as well as the other sciences developed from these beginnings. As psychology proliferated into its multiple 'schools' each has maintained dialogue with **other sciences** if not with other schools. We will attempt to draw this extended family back together (2.7).

Philosophy, the common parent of all, has also evolved. **Philosophy of science** has informed methods in experimental psychology,[20] as Cognitive Psychology is in intense dialogue with the **philosophy of mind** and Artificial Intelligence, as well as stretching into historical enquiry with evolutionary psychology and Cognitive Archaeology.[21] All of these are also in conversation with **philosophy of language** and linguistics, the study of spoken languages; and most recently with neuroscience, the study of our brains and nervous systems. **Continental philosophy** is increasingly allowed back into some of these discussions in the English-speaking world and never left the psychology discussion outside it.[22]

Philosophy, as practised today in university departments, has split into schools: the most fundamental split is between Analytical Philosophy, which dominates this subject in the English-speaking world, and Continental Philosophy, which has its roots in Germany and France.[23] We will be obliged to step between these as they are talking to different sciences, all of which we will be using in this investigation. A good rule of thumb is that the first talks to the natural sciences and the other to the historical or human sciences.

Finally, other new sciences have emerged from the nest of philosophy such as **anthropology** (Greek: study of human beings, usually in social groups without writing), **sociology** and the various kinds of **linguistics**. Historical studies have advanced and specialised, studying different regions and periods, in dialogue with philosophy, which given its parenting role, still tends to talk to everyone.

This book is intended to give you a fresh synthesis of these new sciences with psychology and philosophy today. The separation is vital to their development; their **integration** or **synthesis** is also vital. They can help explain each other.

6 Language and concepts in psychology

The idea of a 'map' is not exhausted by **geography** and **history**. Language is an essential feature of science. The vocabulary of psychology, even its name – as we saw in the Preface – is indebted to the **Greek** language of classical **Athens**:

- Psychology
- Theory
- Method
- Analysis – and thus 'psycho-analysis'
- Synthesis – and thus 'psycho-synthesis'

There are many more Greek terms we will meet in psychology and in this book:

- Logic, ethics, politics, economics – 'ics' ending from Greek *ikos*, 'about', coupled with *logos, ethos* (character) *polis* (city-state) *oikos* (household) respectively
- Biology = study of life, from *bios* (life) and *logos* (study, discussion)
- Physiology = study of bodily function, from *phusis* (nature)
- Neurology = study of brain and nervous system, from *neuros* (string)
- Pathology = study of illness, from *pathos* (suffering)
- Theology = study of God, from *theos* (god or God)
- Therapy = healing art, from *therapos* = healing, as in 'psychotherapy'

Where it is not in Greek, psychology is indebted to the **Latin** of classical **Rome**:

- Science from *scientia* = knowledge
- Concept from *conceptum*, a metaphor for an idea *conceived* in the mind
- Cognition from *con-gnosco* (originally Greek) = capacity for knowledge
- Intelligence from *intelligere* = to understand
- Personality from *persona* = mask, role, public presentation
- Ego = 'I am' in Latin, converted to a noun meaning 'the sense of oneself'

This language debt will be explored in this series. It is good for a student of the subject to start with an awareness of these languages. Rather than adopting such ancient languages blindly, on trust, you can come to psychology with a grasp of the **original meanings** – often lost to today's students. This will get you off to a flying start, 'owning the lingo', even anticipating the meanings of fresh terms.

The Greeks, as we will find, were not the only essential sources. They inherited many of their ideas from **older civilisations**, clothing them in a new language. All the senses of *psyche*[24] – the human mind, soul, heart, consciousness, feelings, personality, behaviour – had been considered, and beliefs about these debated and developed, for at least two thousand years before this also happened in Greek.

What is true of *psyche* is also true of *logos*: word, reason, argument, language, theory; the laws to be discovered, the human capacity for accessing experience and penetrating to its underlying laws – all the senses of *logos*[25] – predate Greek philosophy. There had thus been '**psychologies**' before the Greeks under other names, before *psyche* or *logos* or the Greek alphabet were even written down.

The discovery and deciphering of ancient languages have expanded our grasp of ancient history well beyond what was known from Latin and Greek. We can now read texts from ancient Sumer (Iraq) and ancient Egypt as well as Hebrew and Chinese. These have their own versions of *psyche*, *logos* and 'psychology', which we will begin to explore in Part Two and continue in subsequent books.

Reading the series will give you a 'map' in the sense of a **lexicon**, a **dictionary** of psychological terms – learnt most effectively, through narrative. As any child will tell you, a story is easier to learn than a list: it gives the mind an **embedded** and **contextualised** understanding, using metaphor as a chain on which to hang the pearls.

7 Learning scientific methods (see Chapters 2 and 3)

The format of this book is designed to provide a model of scientific procedure, which you should learn as you **follow the argument** from chapter to chapter.

You can **transfer** such a method to other sciences and other kinds of enquiry.

Part One is like the introduction to an **experiment**, which clearly sets out the concepts and methods before laying out the results and drawing conclusions.

Part One also introduces two main **theories** to be tested as part of this method.

This book is filled with theories and **hypotheses** (usually two interchangeable words meaning the same thing) about a wide range of topics, and it constantly introduces and **evaluates** new ones; but only two – which we call Theory One and Theory Two – are introduced specifically to compare with the evidence in Part Two: to see whether they match it, to see whether they can be **confirmed** by the available evidence, or to suggest ways in which they could be **revised**.

If a theory needs constant revision, then it will eventually be **abandoned**. Any revisions which change its fundamental assumptions are really fresh theories.

Part Two lays out the **data** that has been found and is subjected to the method.

Each of the five chapters ends with a **review** of each main theory, which sets out meeting points between the theory and the available evidence, then offers an evaluation judging the results of this encounter, reflecting on the implications.

During this series of reviews, we will gradually get 'inside' each theory as its strengths and weaknesses are exposed. In this respect, the five separate reviews of each theory are really one long review broken into five sections. These two 'strands' begin to interact and blend as the theories are compared to each other.

As well as the overall 'shape' of this book as a model of **scientific procedure**, the way in which it is written is also intended to set a model for your essays and assignments on a university course. There are several different styles of writing:

- Paragraphs studded with **references** to demonstrate careful research.
- Paragraphs offering a sequence of points to support a valid **argument**.
- Prose using **metaphors** that is designed to be evocative and memorable.
- Less cautious, more **speculative** passages especially in theory reviews, to provide a model of the free use of scientific **imagination** forming theory.

The intention is that in both structure and detail, this book will provide a model to support your studies. You should end the book having learnt some science!

8 Linking psychology to related subjects (see Chapter 2)

Your course may be a mixed one (such as Joint Honours) with psychology as a component, in which case you might need help connecting these components. Even on a pure psychology course, just as understanding the vocabulary in its original historical context can be a great help right at the start, understanding the links to other subjects helps to **embed** the knowledge and point to **applications**.

Ancient philosophy is ideal for this because psychology emerged alongside the rest of early thought. Philosophy has often been compared[26] to the **trunk** of a tree, with the special sciences including psychology as **branches** off this trunk. If we start with the young branches closer together, we can see their relations and connections, before increasing specialisation will drive them further apart.

Psychology is naturally connected to **medicine** and human **biology**, and ancient cultures – as we will see – sometimes tied their versions of psychology closely to the human body, while at other times they emphasised a separation. Modern psychology has several strongly materialist schools, which understand human beings as sophisticated animals: as evolutionary theory has greatly encouraged scientists to see human beings in this way over the past century. Books Two and Three will show how evolutionary and biological theories were already options for psychology in Classical Greek and Roman thought. In this book, those with the best medicine – the Egyptians – were the *least* materialist in psychology.[27]

The ancients also linked psychology – as they linked everything else – closely to **religion**, **spirituality** and **theology**: these too were a major aspect of ancient philosophy and psychology. We will explore this in Chapters 4–8. Among ancient sources, it can be hard to separate psychology from theology, or science from religion. As in modern psychology, there is a tension in ancient psychologies between models which seek to **reduce** us to the *purely invisible* and those which seek to **reduce** us to the *purely visible* aspects of our nature.

As well as connecting the study of the mind to the study of body and spirit, the ancient approach emphasises **social** context: aspects of humanity we now associate with **anthropology**, **ethics** – even **politics**. As we will discuss in Chapter 3, the study of ancient thought forces us to place contemporary Western tendencies to **individualism** in context, as ancients tend the other way – toward **community**.[28]

Indeed, you may feel when reading this book that there are so many branches off *from* psychology – so many links and connections – that you cannot 'see the wood for the trees': **'Where is the psychology?'** The best answer to this comes from the first historian of this subject in English: 'history alone can adequately unfold the content of the idea denoted by the word "*Psyche*"'[29] We have to be patient, and allow psychology to emerge as a branch from the cultural tree. This does not end with the Bronze Age: we will find the same in subsequent books of this series. We have to be prepared to revise our **preconceptions** of the subject, and to loosen up our definitions in order to understand its history. We will begin this process with an attempted 'deconstruction' of psychology as it is studied today in Chapter 2 (see 3.6 for an explanation of this term) to prepare us for significant challenges to the same preconceptions throughout Part Two.

9 Linking psychology to everyday life (see section 2.3 and Chapter 3)

Our theorising is only one activity alongside sleeping and waking, housework, relationships, travelling, eating, budgeting, entertainment, commitment, illness, loving and longing, fearing and avoiding, enjoying and hoping. It was always so for previous generations, who developed psychological language and theories, as it is for teachers, tutors, lecturers – or even authors of introductory histories.

Once again, ancient psychology – especially from the global perspective taken in this series – is a perfect place to start, before the barriers between ordinary life and scientific theory were erected, let alone before they developed into social divisions between professional academics and mere trainees.

The issues of life needed no specially constructed bridges to issues of scholarship; there was easier intercourse between the two. Just as the branches of 'philosophy' were closer to one another, they were closer to their common roots in ordinary life.

It was, of course, in most cases the ordinary life of a comfortable elite. Those who had time to spend on psychological reflection, and the skills to record it, were few and formed a more or less exclusive club. Yet within these limits, the gap between 'life' and 'thought' was smaller, and not all were exclusive elites.

By beginning with the ancient thinkers, we start a little closer to our common experience. The very thing that makes ancient content far from contemporary academia also makes it closer to our common starting point; so it seems a natural place to begin.

Notes

1 Martin, Thomas R. p.3; an allusion, but it originates in the first line of a novel: L.P. Hartley's *The Go-Between.*
2 Cicero, quoted by Descartes in *Discourse on Method* (a foundational text for modern philosophy) Part 2 p.39.
3 See Farrell 2014 for a good contemporary example of this approach.
4 Damasio 2006 (recommended).
5 As Brown p.50, Desmond Clarke p.189 and Stephen Menn's entire book (see Bibliography) can demonstrate.
6 Thinking of the role of Einstein in twentieth-century physics; Johnson Ch.1 pp.1–11; or Kant 1998.
7 See Leahey 2018 for a good example of this more inclusive approach.
8 We will cover some of these 'readings' of Greek myth by modern psychologists in Book Two of this series.
9 See for example George Brett's history, reviewed in 1.10 and 3.1.
10 See Hegel's pioneering studies reviewed in 1.8, 1.9, 2.3 and 3.5.
11 See for example Henley 2020 p.213 and commentary from Jordan in Henley and Rossano pp.41–4,49–51.
12 See 1.3,2.2,2.4,3.4, 3.8 and the whole argument of Chapter 4.
13 This was not simply coincidence: a major figure in archaeology, who popularised terms used to this day such as 'prehistory', 'Neolithic', 'Palaeolithic' and so on, was Darwin's friend John Lubbock: see Mithen 2003 pp.5–6.
14 Cole pp.27–30,98ff.; Farrell pp.216–8,245–6,269–271,288–290, 314–6; Henley and Rossano p.27; McVeigh p.2.
15 Smail pp.1,21,26,202.
16 For example, Henley 2020 and Henley and Rossano 2022 and the Recommended Reading for Chapter 1.
17 Pyne and Pyne p.3; see also Mithen 1994,1996,2003.
18 For example, Bellwood pp.28–33; Harari pp.22–3; Mithen 1993 p.32; Mithen 1999 p.22.
19 See notes to point 13 above; several papers in Henley and Rossano 2022 suggest this cautious conclusion.
20 Farrell 2014 Part 1 is an excellent account of this.
21 See 2.3,3.4 and Chapter 4.
22 Chapter 2 will give a survey of the interactions between psychology and these traditions in philosophy.

23 Friedman 2000, Magee 1997 and Solomon 1988 are all different attempts to build bridges over this divide.
24 Peters pp.166–176.
25 Peters pp.110–112.
26 For example, Bacon 1605 *The Advancement of Learning* II.9.1 and Descartes' Preface to his *Principles* p.183.
27 See Chapter 6, especially 6.8 and 6.9; also see the contrast with the Hebrew view in 7.5 and 7.8.
28 To be explored in Chapter 3 (for example 3.2, 3.4,3.5) and throughout Part Two.
29 Brett p.5.

Part 1

Toolkit

1 History

1.1 Parallel learning journeys

If you have read the Preface, you will know that 'Psychology' means 'study of the *psyche*' and that, whatever *psyche* means, it is a word from ancient Greece.

The name of this discipline is a time capsule, taking us back over millennia, and it has reached us like a message in a bottle, carried over a wide ocean of time.

The other component of the word 'Psychology' is the word *logos*, which means 'word, thought, meaning, understanding' and has come to mean 'the study of' in the names of sciences, such as biology (*bios* = organic life, *logos* = study of):

- anthropology (study of *anthropos* = mankind, usually in other cultures)
- archaeology (study of *arche* = origins, through digging up lost artefacts)
- philology (literally 'love of words', just as philo-sophy = love of wisdom)

All of these disciplines are 'sciences', in the broadest sense. As the meaning of *psyche* has evolved over the centuries, the meaning and nature of the *logos* in '-logy' (or to say it in Latin, the meaning of *scientia*) has also evolved. By the time the combined word 'psychology' was coined in modern times, each of its two components – *psyche* and *logos* – had a long parallel history, each evolving in meaning since the ancient Greeks who had used them as separate elements.

Western culture has been on a learning journey about its own sources in parallel with the development of modern psychology. Just as psychology was making its bid for freedom as a distinct science in the late 1800s, our historical roots were being rediscovered. The growth of historical sciences such as archaeology has uncovered the **non-European** roots of European civilisation – which became 'Western' civilisation through worldwide European colonies in modern times.[1]

This journey of Western culture has affected its descriptive frameworks for:

- historical time (1.2)
- historical periods (1.4)
- global geography (1.5)

DOI: 10.4324/9781003396147-3

- dynamics of history (1.6)
- imagined audience (1.7)

History is founded on the physical reality of places, times, and circumstances. This is as true of the history of psychology as that of anything else. Throughout Part Two we will set the historical context and boundaries for each chapter at the start. These **Orientations** set the foundations and framework for our story.

1.2 Dating apps: What the numbers mean

As any history book is organised into chapters as the 'frame' through which we look at the historical sequence, the time sequence itself is also organised into an agreed dating system. Look away now and move to the next section if this is too obvious, but some readers need orientation to understand these frameworks:

- Centuries and millennia
- BC and BCE
- AD and CE
- *circa* or *c.*
- The relationships between the dates and how to handle them

The ancient world used many different systems of counting. The one adopted by our civilisation is the *decimal* system, or base 10: we count years in units of 10, 100, and 1000 using the Roman names – *decade, century* and *millennium.* The word 'millennium' is made from two smaller Roman words, *mille* for 1000 and *annus* for 'year'; as 'century' comes from *centum* for 100 and 'decade' from *deca-ade*, 'set of ten'. In the plural, we describe these time intervals in the language of *centuries* and *millennia.*

When you measure something – in this case, time – you need a measuring unit and a zero point. We have covered the units but the zero point is what gives us the actual numbers. When history was first written by modern Europeans, they were Christian, so they set the zero point at **the birth of Jesus Christ**. Ancients had often restarted the dating system – reset the zero point – with the birth of a new king or emperor; as Christians believed that Jesus Christ was the 'king of kings', the ruler of the universe, they permanently reset the dating of history by his birth.

In this system, ancient dates count **backwards** towards the birth of Christ; and once Christ is born, we count **forwards**. *Before Christ* was abbreviated to 'BC'; from his birth, each year was 'the year of the Lord', in Latin *anno domini* or AD. As Europeans and their colonies have dominated the globe so completely over the last few centuries, this Christian system was **globalised** and is used by many nations today to give a common standard for calendars around the world. Within Western nations, and Westernised cultures, it is simply taken for granted.

To avoid direct references to Jesus Christ, for those who are not Christians, an alternative wording has developed, so that the two millennia since Christ are called the **Common Era**. Thus 'Anno Domini' (AD) becomes the more neutral 'Common Era' (CE) and 'Before Christ' (BC) becomes 'Before Common Era' (BCE) without changing the actual system. We will use this new standard form throughout the current series, working through the millennia BCE in the first two volumes and then moving from BCE to CE in Book Three.

All of this explains why we **count 'backwards'** in ancient history: 2000 BCE is before 1000 BCE, 5000 BCE well before 500 BCE, and so on. Later history is more straightforward when we begin to count forwards: 2000 CE comes after 1000 CE; with specific dates, 1627 CE comes after 1486 CE. Ancient history requires a little more calculation – and this can be a barrier to certain students.

When we label a **century** we use its end-point, so 'the twentieth century' leads to the year 2000, the nineteenth century leads to 1900, the first century to 100 and the fifth century to 500. When we label a **millennium** we do the same: the first millennium leads to 1000, the second millennium led to 2000, and we are now right at the start of 'the third millennium', leading towards the year 3000.

Ancient history – rather confusingly – has to **reverse** this system of labelling, so that the fourth millennium *starts* from 4000 BCE, the third millennium *starts* from 3000 BCE, and the important first millennium runs from 1000 BCE to 0. The same goes for centuries: the sixth century – which will be central for Book Two – *starts* from 600 BCE, the fourth century from 400 BCE, moving through annual dates such as 384, 347 and 333, in that order, running down towards 0.

The main difficulty comes in calculating **intervals**: if you learn that philosopher Réné Descartes lived between the years 1596 and 1650, you can quickly calculate his lifespan by crossing the century boundary, adding 4 years (1600–1596) to 50 years from 1600 to 1650, to make 54 years. If you learn that Plato's dates were 427–347 BCE, however, it takes a little longer to calculate his lifespan, because it is done in reverse. You must add 27 years to 50 and 3 (or similar) to yield 80 years.

This will not normally be important to understand the *psychology in* this book, but it will come up in every Orientation dealing with historical background. It is helpful for following the different ways of referring to time in any text about the ancient world (BCE) because there is a constant '**correction**' of 2000 years. It is easy to confuse '5000 years ago' with '5000 BCE', by missing that correction.

For example, the Sumerians invented writing – including numbers – around the date 3000 BCE – in fact probably a little earlier, in the late fourth millennium, perhaps 3200 BCE.[2] We can refer to this date as '5000 years ago', or '5200 years ago' (ignoring our own growing distance from the year 2000). If we want to relate an ancient date to ourselves and emphasise the distance in time we use 'ago'; but in this book – as a rule of thumb – we will stick to the absolute dates.

If we are giving approximate dates in any period the abbreviation is c. for *circa* in Latin, meaning 'roughly', 'about'. As ancient people did not share our dating system, many birth dates and not a few death dates are estimated. Even Plato's birth date could be 427 or 428; we are often obliged to give an approximate date such as c.427, 'about 427' BCE. Some major figures such as Zoroaster and Lao Tze have no definite dates at all: even Jesus Christ – the zero point of the whole global dating system, whatever our preferred terminology – is in this category.

Now that we have defined the language used, let us apply this to our narrative.

The ancient Greeks, who are normally considered the source of our 'Western' civilisation,[3] experienced their glory years 500–300 BCE; there are c.2500 years between these Greeks and ourselves, by adding the years BCE to the 2000 years CE. The oldest civilisations in Iraq and Egypt can trace their stories back to the invention of writing, cities and trading in bronze c.3000 BCE or 5000 years ago.

Half of the recorded history of humanity therefore occurred before the ancient Greeks: the 'first half' from 3000 BCE to 500 BCE, or 2500 years; the 'second half' from 500 BCE until today: another 2500 years. As Western civilisation looks back to its origins in ancient Greece, Indian and Chinese civilisation also trace their origins to a similar time period. Each of these 'great rivers' took its rise at the same time, from the common streams of the oldest civilisations: the start of the second half appears orchestrated across the planet. Karl Jaspers christened this 'turning-point' in his native German as *die Achsenzeit*, which translates into English as **the Axial Age** or the Pivotal Age.[4] We will cover this in Book Two, as the halfway point between the first invention of writing and the present day.

As we go further back into history and the numbers become larger, a correction of 2000 years becomes less and less significant. As these extend to 20,000 and beyond, the correction of 2000 years becomes a smaller fraction. Rather than BCE, when we go this far back, it is normal to use 'ybp' = 'years before present' or the larger units kya = 'thousand years ago' and mya = 'million years ago'.[5]

In Chapter 4, we will double the timescale again to around 12,000 years ago: 12,000 ypb, 12 kya or 10000 BCE. This period is the matrix (Latin for 'womb') from which civilisations appeared, and it provides the preconditions on which all civilisation rests, in which we can locate the roots of all global traditions.[6]

Finally, note that this whole framework for describing historical time has evolved entirely within Western civilisation, yet it is applied globally.

1.3 Stretching the timeline

Genetic and fossil evidence currently agree that our subspecies *homo sapiens sapiens*, defined by a new intellectual capacity, appeared in Africa before / c.

50kya, and then some found their way out of Africa to re-colonise the globe.[7] This was before the last Ice Ages, which lasted for tens of thousands of years,[8] and the final sudden burst of climate change, named after a hardy plant which survived it, *Dryas Octopetala* (Greek: eight-petalled): so the Younger Dryas.[9] This was followed by 'a springtime of environmental rebirth' worldwide, which can be dated with remarkable accuracy to 11,650 ybp or 9650 BCE.[10] As the last Ice Age ended in the temperate regions, ocean levels and climates finally began to stabilise; homo sapiens sapiens was at last permanently liberated to settle the globe.[11]

This historical envelope defined by a relatively stable global climate is called the **Holocene** (Greek: *holos* = entire, *kainos* = new, thus 'entirely new').[12] It comes at the end of the **Pleistocene** (Greek *pleistos* = most, *kainos* = new, 'most new' or 'newest') starting 2.6 mya, in which our species has evolved from a group of hominids or great apes until the appearance of our present sub-species, *homo sapiens sapiens* ('wisest of wise ones' in Latin).[13] There is a debate about whether we have now entered a new climate phase, the **Anthropocene** (*anthropos* = human, *kainos* = new, thus 'human-made') due to human action.[14] Sea levels and zones of climate have varied inside the Holocene 'envelope', but relative stability has given *homo sapiens sapiens* a clear theatre of action, and it is within this theatre that the rest of human history has occurred, thus defining the scope of this book.

Writers who have pioneered the 'long view' include **Daniel Smail** in his *Deep History and the Brain* (2008) and **Jared Diamond** in *Guns, Germs and Steel: A Short History of Everybody for the Last 13,000 Years* (1997). They argue that, in order to practice history in a scientific manner, we must go further back:

> ... for people specifically interested in the shaping of the modern world, a history limited to developments since the invention of writing cannot provide deep understanding ... the roots of western Eurasian dominance in the modern world lie in the preliterate past before 3,000 B.C.[15]

Smail argues for the replacement of the outdated category of 'prehistory' by a 'deep history' investigating the 'deep past' or 'deep time', acknowledging that 'the bottom dropped out of time' with the publication of Darwin's theories.[16]

Another pioneer of such thinking is the archaeologist **Colin Renfrew**, who has pioneered an argument – using a combination of early genetics, linguistics and archaeology – that the distribution of global languages today can be explained by stretching the time envelope back toward the Holocene boundary.[17] In his *Archaeology and Language* (1987) and many subsequent publications Renfrew has inspired teams of geographers, geneticists, linguists and archaeologists to pursue this as a worldwide research programme (2.4, 3.2 and Orientations).[18] A recent summary is Bellwood (ed.) *The Global Prehistory of Human Migrations*.

An archaeologist who has studied the Pleistocene 'backstory' and its impact on the Holocene is **Stephen Mithen**, with *The Prehistory of the Mind* (1996) and *After the Ice* (2003). He argues that 'the emergence of the modern mind' about 60–30 kya is the key event in deep time, taking the horizon back further still.[19]

Most recently, as noted in the Introduction, psychologist Tracey Henley has challenged psychologists to take the story back at least as far as the Holocene.[20] We will thus deliberately stretch the boundaries of standard Western historical timelines, to explore a much deeper context for more familiar developments in what is called 'deep time'. For those willing to undertake the journey this turns out to be necessary. At the end of Chapter 3, we will explore *psychological* reasons for seeking the broadest possible context at the horizon of ancient history.

Once again, along with understanding the framework, note that it has evolved entirely within Western civilisation but is still applied globally.

1.4 Ages and stages of ancient history

In addition to the dating systems used in ancient history, there are standardised terms used to describe the sequence of periods or ages within the Holocene. We have already met 'the Axial Age' as a label within the first millennium BCE. In order to set out our framework we need a 'potted history' of the system of ages.

The encounters of the ancient Greeks with older civilisations were the original lens and funnel through which Europeans received their lasting ideas of a more distant past. The Greeks gave us lasting impressions of their parent civilisations in Iraq and Egypt, as well as our traditional classifications of ancient history:

- The Stone Age
- The Bronze Age
- The Iron Age

An early Greek poet, **Hesiod**, tells the story of humanity up to his time with a myth of five 'ages' in a sequence: the Golden Age, the Silver Age, the **Bronze Age**, and the Age of Heroes – using bronze weapons, as in his fellow poet Homer – and finally the uglier **Iron Age** of his time.[21] His contemporary the poet Homer also looks back to the Bronze Age and the Age of Heroes. Inhabiting the Iron Age, both poets look back on the Bronze Age with nostalgia, as a shared cultural memory. It is this memory of a change of era which became the germ of a historical system.

The Latin poet **Lucretius**, in Augustus' time at the beginning of the Roman Empire, created an update on this Greek idea in his evolutionary epic *de rerum natura* (On the Nature of Things). The evolution of Lucretius' cosmos climaxes in the story of mankind, and then the forging of **a sequence**

of metals, in much the same sequence as Hesiod, which defines the first 'ages' of human history.[22]

Early in the history of archaeology, Europeans who were soaked in this Classical literature applied this idea to the technologies and tools they found from the past. Danish archaeologists found that the 'Bronze Age' and 'Iron Age' of the poets applied to the evidence: they added a 'Stone Age' because the most primitive tools they found were made of stone, and prepared in different ways.[23] Beyond the confines of Europe the same sequence still applied.[24] We, therefore, have 'Stone Age, Bronze Age and Iron Age' as categories for organising early history, now known as the **'three-age system'**.[25]

With these labels, there is a fixed **succession** but not a fixed timeline. Each 'age' is not a period but a way of life defined by its **economy** and **technology**. These labels based on the tools found are markers of the economic basis of a society, and their progression forms a sequence of economic development.[26] In this sense each 'stage' has continued in certain parts of the globe down to modern times.[27]

When Europeans first started to discover the rest of the globe, encountering a range of different civilisations, they surmised that some remained at stages their own culture had passed through earlier. In particular, one anthropologist points to 'the tremendous self-consciousness which the discovery of the New World aroused in Western thought'.[28] Europeans imagined a scale of human societies from 'uncivilised' to 'civilised', with their own ancestors at the other end of that scale: with Native Americans, they became conscious of looking back in time.[29]

For example, in the USA Declaration of Independence (1776)[30] future President Thomas Jefferson refers to 'the inhabitants of our frontiers, the merciless Indian **savages**, whose known rule of warfare is an undistinguished destruction of all ages, sexes, and conditions'.[31] In the same year the Scottish moral philosopher Adam Smith classified Native American culture as 'the **lowest** and **rudest** state of society'[32], 'the **savage nations** of hunters and fishers', as contrasted with the '**civilised** and thriving nations' seen in contemporary Europe and its colonies.[33]

Smith also describes 'a **more advanced** state of society, such as we find among the Tartars and the Arabs' (as travelling shepherds), and 'a yet more advanced state of society', the farmers or 'husbandmen'[34] While Smith was writing, other Europeans encountered the Maoris of New Zealand: here they believed that they found societies at Smith's second and third stages of civilisation.[35] In Australia, Europeans found the Aborigines still living comfortably as hunter-gatherers, like the American tribes, if perhaps moving very slowly towards farming and starting to gather in larger settlements.[36]

The same language of less advanced and more advanced, lower and higher on a scale (defined by Europeans and their descendants), **'Savagery'**, **'Barbarism'** and **'Civilisation'**, has persisted until quite recently in the historical sciences.[37] The question is whether such a sequence marks an ascent up a scale of **values** from worse to better or simply a value-free scale of

complexity. Even when the language is adjusted to appear more respectful, the attitude of superiority can persist in subtler forms. Even **inversion** of this scale – so that 'more primitive' becomes 'more noble' or 'more wholesome' – is still a projection of Western values, a classification by the more powerful partner.[38] Whether projecting its triumph or its guilt at their subjugation, it does not allow the subjugated a voice.[39]

There is, therefore, a political and ethical dimension to the writing of history in terms of the relationships between nations today, and their relationships within recent centuries, which were often defined by colonisation, subjugation, and (either accidental or deliberate) genocide.

At each age or stage, there is a debate between those who see a single point of origin somewhere on the planet, spreading out into other regions – by **transmission** or **diffusion** – and those who claim an independent appearance (whether from the same set of causes or not) in at least two regions. Even in the latter case, however, there is still a dateable **first appearance**, after which it is hard to prove 'no transmission' elsewhere.[40]

The Stone Age began when modern humans first appeared on the planet, so its start is defined by biology – or more specifically, the historical part of biology called 'palaeobiology' (study of oldest living things) or 'palaeontology' (study of ancient beings).[41] The Bronze Age comes much later in time and is defined by archaeology (study of human origins) and literary history, as is the Iron Age.

A tweak on the idea of 'the Stone Age' came in 1856 with the term '**Neolithic**' (Greek: *neos* = new, *lithos* = stone) for the most recent part of the Stone Age in the Holocene, starting from c.9000 BCE, marking the division of hunters from shepherds and farmers.[42] It corresponded to Smith's second and third stages of economic development. Another term 'Mesolithic' (Greek: *mesos* = middle) was soon added to capture a further gradation observed in the European record, in which hunting tools were improved, dogs recruited to the hunt, and sledges invented.[43]

The Stone Age was thus divided up: the much longer period, stretching back to the first evolution of *homo sapiens*, was called the Palaeolithic (Greek: *paleos* = old and *lithos* = stone) or Old Stone Age. This stretched forwards, either all the way to the Neolithic or New Stone Age (a much shorter, more recent period) or as far as an intervening period, known variously as the Ice Age, the Mesolithic or the Middle Stone Age.[44]

The prehistoric data had therefore expanded the poets' model of ages backwards in time:

- The **Stone Age** as an overall stage includes:

  1. A Lower Palaeolithic Era in which hominids evolved (Old Stone Age)
  2. The **Upper Palaeolithic** Era in which we reached full mental capacity
  3. The Mesolithic Era or 'the Mesolithic' for short (Middle Stone Age)
  4. The **Neolithic** Era or 'the Neolithic' for short (New Stone Age)

- The **Bronze Age** (the early civilisations, the main period for this book)
- The **Iron Age** (the next development, covered in Books Two and Three)

The term 'Neolithic' can thus be defined as 'a period between the end of the hunting way of life and the beginning of a full metal-using economy, when the practice of farming arose and spread through most of Europe, Asia and North Africa like a slow-moving wave'.[45] Chapter 4 will be devoted to this period and the subsequent Orientations to Chapters 5–8 connect this to the birth of Bronze Age civilisation in Iraq, Egypt, Israel and China. The original definition of the Neolithic in terms of stone tools and weapons has been supplanted by farming, but the label is still used for continuity and convenience.[46] The 'three-age system' is still the basic working framework for archaeologists. As with the number system and longer timelines, this framework is very much a product of Western civilisation: it has begun to break down under the pressure of growing evidence from global archaeology, as we shall see in Part Two, especially 4.1 and 6.1.

1.5 The geography of ancient history

The third element of orientation, after dating and ages or stages, is geography. When introducing the stages of 'prehistory' we have already touched upon the human geography of ancient settlements; we have not focused on **locations**. Just as we have to settle on time frameworks to describe historical developments, we have to agree on shared physical descriptions – maps, locations, landscapes and climates – and the human geography of resources, societies and relationships to other settlements. These descriptions also express a certain history and inevitable politics.

It is generally agreed that our species first emerged in **East Africa**,[47] travelling up through Egypt into the Near East, spreading out from there to the rest of the globe. Outside Africa, therefore, the narrow corridor from Egypt to Iraq is the source point for *homo sapiens sapiens*, our biological species.[48] Egyptologist James Henry Breasted coined the term '**the Fertile Crescent**' for the region[49] where humanity first appeared outside Africa: in Neolithic times it was indeed more fertile in its climate than it is today, and many settled there from Africa.[50]

There is little disagreement about this part of the story – the geography of our biological origins. The geography of the next breakthrough is more complex: between five and ten sites have been proposed for the independent invention of food production, but the *first* was near the top of the Fertile Crescent.[51] Farming is generally agreed to have spread from there throughout the great land-mass of Eurasia – as above, 'like a slow-moving wave'.[52] The next wave built upon this one with the invention of the city, writing, and other elements of civilisation in a new Bronze Age 'package' – again in this Fertile Crescent region, but around its curve in southern Iraq, or ancient Sumer.[53] Each breakthrough is built on the last. But this is a narrative based on the debt of European farming to the Fertile Crescent: if there are there are other independent starting-ponts for farming, on other continents or in other parts of Eurasia, then other sequences have been played out, modifying this picture.

From this centre and others successive waves spread, as ripples spread outwards from rocks dropped in a pond. In some places, the last wave had barely arrived when the next one caught up with it: in others, it only arrived at later times. In **Australia** and much of America, humans arrived as a species but stayed in the first state of wandering tribes – hunting and gathering – without agriculture or domesticated animals: the Neolithic or farming wave missed them entirely. In others, such as **Central America** and **Chile**, people arrived and the Neolithic or farming revolution followed, but not the further Bronze Age breakthrough.[54]

The Fertile Crescent region (from the European point of view, and only from the European point of view, 'the Near East') had the huge advantage of belonging to the largest land mass on the planet, Eurasia, with a unique **East-West axis** so that people, practices and inventions could travel in both directions along lines of a similar climate. For the second, Neolithic 'wave' especially, this continuity of climate was crucial, as the domestication of plants depends on the climate, which in turn depends on latitude (distance from the Equator, North or South), whereas for the continents on a **North-South** axis – Africa, the Americas, and in terms of human access, Oceania – any change of latitude would, and did, slow down the transmission.[55] The shape of the land affects the species of plants, which in turn affects animals further up the food chain. Once people were dependent on plants their history was tied to the land.

This helps to explain why the civilisations studied in this book are almost all in **Asia**. As humans spread out in both directions from the new centre in Western Asia to the periphery of East and West in the first wave, the Neolithic and Bronze Age achievements could also be exported rapidly to both ends of the Eurasian land-mass, in what has been labelled 'the Fertile Crescent package', including seeds from the original centres as well as later the wheel, writing, metalwork, and other ingredients.[56] These *eventually* resourced **China**, but not *originally*: China had evolved and exported its own indigenous package throughout South-East Asia.[57]

The best places and climates for farming were naturally the densest centres of population: these are always near freshwater sources such as springs or rivers. The metaphor of streams and rivers of civilisation is appropriate because all of the first civilisations arose on great rivers: in Iraq (Tigris and Euphrates), Egypt (Nile), Pakistan (Indus) and China (Yellow River).[58] Each of these also had a similar climate, at a similar distance from the Equator, that is, in a narrow range of **latitudes** 25°–35°. (To give a brief taster of Chapter 5, the reason we use degrees, minutes and seconds to measure angles – as well as hours, minutes and seconds to measure time – is that Sumer, the first civilisation in Iraq, used a base 60 number system rather than the decimal system, to measure the movements of the night sky. With anything circular we are children of the ancient Sumerians.)[59]

Everything so far has been the story of Europeans discovering their own history. The same applies to geography. The terms used for **regions**, normally used in English, such as 'the Near East' (1.1, even 'Hither Asia') and 'the Far East' (or 'the Extreme Orient') are the inventions of Europeans and reflect their perspective. '**Australia**' was Latin for 'southern' ('Southland'), invented by quite modern Europeans.

Europeans labelled the rest of their land mass and the neighbouring continents using the names of provinces from the old Roman Empire.

'**Asia**' once meant approximately modern Turkey, a fraction of the continent we call Asia today: the label was gradually expanded eastwards to cover everything as far east as China, Japan, the Philippines (named after a Spanish king) and Indonesia. '**Africa**' was a Roman province along the Mediterranean coast, including parts of Tunisia, Algeria and Libya; but it was expanded southwards, as the continent was 'discovered' (by Europeans) as far as South Africa. When speaking in English, Africans today still locate themselves using this vocabulary invented by Europeans.

The **latitudes** we have mentioned in this section are angles measured from the Equator, a system which could have been devised by anyone, from anywhere; but the **longitudes**, the East-West angles, have their zero-point set in London, because Britain was the most powerful nation when the system was adopted.

From all of the above, it should be clear that the geography which is the basis of this book – as of all history – is not neutral ground, but it is heavy with past and present baggage: politicaland cultural baggage, concerned with the relationships of power and justice between groups of people. We cannot escape such a reality in our search for scientific objectivity. As in politics, journalism and social media we always have to **check our sources** and allow for agendas, 'Who is writing this history?' is always a valid question. Someone must hand us the spectacles in order to see the view, and we should always have more than one pair available.

Once we consider geography, we find ourselves asking 'Who said this?' This leads on to 'Where were they?' and eventually to 'Why did this voice prevail?'

To take one important example, the story of **Africa** does not end with its role in simply producing *homo sapiens sapiens*, the 'first wave' with humans travelling north into Asia. There was a long evolutionary history **before** this migration, a history restricted entirely to Africa, which we will not cover in this book – as we will start with the Neolithic, after our species left Africa – but there is also a long history **after** the migration continuing in Africa to the present day. We will begin this story in Chapter 6.

By starting with the Neolithic, we also exclude the story of Australia, most of Indonesia, and the American continents outside Mexico, Chile, (perhaps) the Great Lakes and the Amazon basin.[60] What matters is that we give a reason for the exclusion which is better than 'These are not Europeans'. The new questions and answers in the sciences today are building on the story as constructed by Europeans and their 'Western' colonies, but it is quickly becoming an international enterprise. The writing of history today needs to take this back-story into account.

1.6 Dynamics of history: From 'Where?' to 'How?'

A further tweak on the 'three-age model' came more recently with the idea of a **Neolithic Revolution** by an archaeologist, Gordon Childe, who used the same economic mindset as Adam Smith.[61] When he coined this term, Childe was well aware that it referred to 'the end of a long process' but claimed that 'it had to be presented as a single event because archaeology can only recognise the result'.[62] Another archaeologist has pointed out that such a fixation on **events** and **results**, over the processes leading to those results, is only a reflection of our ignorance: and to label the end result of a long historical process a 'revolution' is no more meaningful than calling it a 'phenomenon'.[63] Living in times of rapid change we are tempted to project this situation onto the past - just as stable societies project stability onto the past and see very little change. The general rule seems to be that we normally expect the past to conform to our present experience.

Similarly, the development of the current human intellectual capacity mentioned in 1.3 is often referred to now as the **Cognitive Revolution.**[64] Given the enormous range of 30–40,000 years allowed for this development, it is worth interrogating the label. If it is the product of tens of millennia, then it stretches the meaning of 'revolution' even further: arguably, stretching the term well past its breaking point.

The American archaeologist Sally McBrearty has suggested that 'the search for revolutions' in this case is driven by the need to define humanity against other species: 'a search for the soul, for **the inventive spark** that distinguishes humans from the rest of the animal kingdom'.[65] Revolutions indicate qualitative change, a jump to **a new level**, rather than gradual emergence. One historian advocating 'deep history', Daniel Lord Smail, similarly suggests that this language of dramatic upheavals is a 'ghost theory' – a Western cultural echo of the Bible's history, where a cataclysmic Flood and a confusion of human languages were sent as sudden, unexpected judgements on humanity.[66]

Taking this point back to 'the Neolithic Revolution', this assumed a neat line of succession from one period to another, **punctuated** by sudden changes, which in the case of its inventor (Childe) was driven by a particular theory of history: the **Marxist** theory, involving a sequence of historical revolutions.[67] The neat line of **succession** entailed by this theory has gradually been undermined by the historical evidence, to the point where it is now accepted that mixed economies of farming existed side by side with hunter-gatherer sources of nutrition.[68] We can retain Childe's idea of a 'package' but discard his language of 'revolution' with its implication of dramatic, **irreversible** change from one state to another.

On the other hand, there are some cases where historical change is surprisingly rapid. The sudden start of our current climate window has already been mentioned (1.3). Just as we should beware of projecting modern 'revolutionary' rhetoric onto the past, we should also beware of projecting the exact opposite: gradual, incremental change, often rooted in complacency about the present day [69] The common lesson here is **to avoid projections** of any kind: to be alert to data as our object and alert to our own prejudices as subjects, staying open to evidence. Psychologist Tracey Henley suggests that 'one specific part of the deep history argument concerns **shifting away from metaphors** such as 'birth of', or even terms such as 'new' and 'revolutionary', to alternatives that create a more accurate and sober narrative framework'.[70]

1.7 Turning the ship of history writing: From 'How?' to 'Who?'

The 'Who?' of this section title is about three groups of people: not only who is producing the history but who is consuming it (the readers) and who it is written about (the historical subjects). These three categories naturally interact. Some readers are so accustomed to a hidden 'violence' which unconsciously excludes them from the texts they encounter, their lack of power to be heard, that they are equally unconscious of its effects on them; while others are so preoccupied with such things – with examining, polishing even smashing the lenses used to look at the past – that they never get beyond this: which is a new kind of injustice. If learning is a human right, then anticipating and addressing barriers to learning is a basic responsibility of the teacher.

One key aim of the historical project in this history of psychology is to subvert **ethnocentrism** – the blinkers we all tend to wear due to prejudice and ignorance of nations and cultures other than our own (Greek: *ethnos* = national or social group, 'tribe'). In earlier stages of economic development, human loyalties would stop at the biological unit: the extended family or clan. This soon expanded to the tribe, a more political unit in which people could be treated as 'family' even if they were not literally so. The expansion to national and cultural units has created new forms of ethnocentrism, less closely tied to biology, and often increasingly tied to users of some particular **technology**.

If you are an international student, for example, or encountering this text outside the usually identified orbit of 'Western culture', it is designed to bring you into the room – or better, to enter yours – by identifying and addressing traditional assumptions. Its very concept ('Global Origins') is intended to be inclusive. Yet, as we shall see in the next section, sometimes the best-intentioned attempts to be 'universal' and 'comprehensive' can end with the worst kinds of exclusion. It is a work in progress, a cross-section of a journey caught in print.

Aside from exclusion and prejudice **between** societies, regions and civilisations, which can be easier to notice and avoid, a major source of exclusion is **within** each society. As well as ancestry, class and wealth, it is often related to races and languages. There was almost always a division of **elites** from the rest of each society, especially after the onset of the Bronze Age – which is the main story in this book. Xenophobia (Greek = fear, *phobos*, of the outsider, the alien and the stranger, *xenos*), various forms of racism and 'tribalism' were normal;

and so were patterns of internal domination. With the invention of writing came opportunities to exercise elitism and tribalism in new forms. Part Two will explore some of these forms, which affect literate societies to this day. This is one example of exclusion through access to particular technology.

One critical group who have been persistently 'voiceless' is **girls** and **women**. The majority of the history written so far in the Western cultural tradition was not only written by European or Western *people*, but mainly by European or Western **men**. Just as a great 'rebalancing' has begun in terms of the geography, languages, regions and races involved in producing the history we read, a separate rebalancing is also underway in terms of gender or more specifically, biological sex, in terms of the production of scholarship, within wider social patterns of education and employment. Today we take it for granted that *psyche* is **gender-neutral**; many ancients downplayed or denied this assumption.

The psychological assumption in the framework of Chapter 2 is that cultural functions of *psyche* are anchored in biological functions: this implies continuity in some sense between biological sex and gender. On the other hand, growth in complexity at the cultural level and looseness of coupling allows varied gender. We will find grounds for distinguishing sex and gender in ancient Hebrew (7.4) as well as explicit discussions in the Neolithic (4.9), Sumer (5.10) and Egypt (6.7,6.11,6.12). Normal practice is followed in terms of mixed gender pronouns (2.2,4.6) and gender roles (5.4,5.6), where historical data permits such freedom.

Improving openness and inclusion for any institution or any tradition cannot be done overnight. It is more like **turning a moving ship** onto a new course: there is massive **inertia** to overcome, and progress is achieved incrementally. As new 'global voices' must build on a European and Western tradition which was previously closed, we are dependent on a long Western tradition forming our approach and method, a tradition made up almost entirely of white European males inhabiting the more privileged social niches of their respective societies. Further back, in the primary sources of 'the extended past' this is even more the case as women were not writing, nor was there any concept of such inclusivity. Contemporary 'course corrections' in the sciences need time to sort for quality of contribution, and this is a slow process.

To illustrate many of these points, let us turn our gaze backwards to an earlier phase of Western history writing.

1.8 Sampling previous history: Georg Wilhelm Friedrich Hegel

The theme of this chapter has been the European/Western journey of discovery: first of Europe's own history and then the world's. This book must be located in this larger journey. In 1.3 we have already begun a dialogue with recent revisions of history writing.

In 1.4 we touched upon Adam Smith's treatment of global economies in his day and his proposed scale of development from 'Savagery' through

'Barbarism' to 'Civilisation'. We have seen how this scale was transferred to the past evidence of human development, in terms of the three-age model of the archaeologists: in Smith's work, contemporary reports about non-European peoples were related to a common past. What became anthropology was connected with archaeology: foreign cultures were exciting because they represented time travel. One early, enthusiastic reader of Adam Smith was a German philosopher, Georg Hegel.[71]

In his famous lectures, published as *The Philosophy of History* in 1830, Hegel offers a philosophical history of the world.[72] It begins with China, India, Persia, Mesopotamia, Judea and Egypt, under the label 'The Oriental World' – Hegel's organisation of his history and its subdivisions are similar to those in this book. His account also moves through 'The Greek World' to 'the Roman World', then on to Europe in the same sequence as this series – at least to that point in time.[73]

His theme, which propels his account, is the growth of human **self-awareness**: 'The Sun – the Light – rises in the East ... by the close of day, man has erected a building constructed from his own inner sun ... the Sun of self-consciousness'.[74] The sun is treated as a symbol of movement from Asian dominance in ancient history – 'rises in the East' – moving slowly to the dominance of a Romantic German culture in his day. Expressing himself more literally, Hegel concludes that 'the history of the world is nothing but the development of **the idea of freedom** ... the process of development which the idea has passed through in realising itself ... the **consciousness of freedom**'.[75] Hegel believes that human beings are and always have been at least potentially the free, self-determining agents of his modern, German culture, but that they had to learn this about themselves, through a slow and painful history.

There is something valid about the general idea of the growth of 'consciousness': in Chapters 4, 5 and 7, we will see human self-awareness expressed subconsciously in a variety of ways; in Chapter 6 the states of consciousness, from sleeping to waking, dreaming to highly alert abstraction. Our Theory One (3.8) will depend closely on these distinctions: on the theme of a growth of consciousness.

Hegel's history, therefore, parallels this one in its basically **psychological** theme as well as in its clearly marked **geographical** basis and its focus on the **ideas** in a series of successive civilisations: 'in the history of the world, the idea of Spirit appears in its actual embodiment as a series of external forms, each one of which declares itself as an actually existing people'.[76] The word translated as 'Spirit' here is ***Geist***: like English 'ghost' or 'ghastly' it is the German word for 'invisible intelligence' or 'active mind', so it can be translated as 'mind' and is one German word for *psyche*. Hegel is looking for 'the spirit' of each civilisation, as a particular expression of a deeper human nature that is slowly being revealed.

Unlike this book and this series, however, it was also written two centuries ago before the modern historical sciences emerged and uncovered their independent **evidence**. In the absence of evidence Hegel substitutes **theory** and

speculation: and these substitutions often tell us much more about the author and his setting than about his subject matter. Notoriously, Hegel treats his own employer (the Prussian state in the 1820s) as 'the end of history', as the necessary climax of the long learning process undergone by the whole human species up to that point.[77]

There is a warning here for all historians, and all histories. We may use history to *explain* our present circumstances, but that is different from using history to *privilege* our circumstances: to claim that 'it was always leading us towards this point'. Hegel's history is blatant in this respect, but the same danger lurks for every historian. In explaining how psychology appeared as a discipline, we are not claiming that it *had* to happen in this particular way, nor that psychology, as practised today, is an *ideal* outcome: only that this is, in fact, **what happened**, in the one corner of human experience (Western civilisation) which has happened to dominate world affairs over recent centuries.

Historians have largely spent the two centuries since Hegel learning this lesson under various guises: it is now called **presentism**, a bias towards the present.[78] One form of presentism in history today is a tendency for history to be divided according to current university departments. The philosophers have their history and the psychologists and anthropologists their history; economists and political historians their history and the 'scientists' (meaning natural sciences) their own. But **the past is innocent** of these current divisions: we may analyse and isolate those aspects of the past that we consider relevant to our area – in practice, to our funding and the approval of our peer group, our academic tribe[79] – but we also need general histories to keep this in the context in which everything has happened, innocent of such divisions.

1.9 Exorcising Hegel's *Geist*

Hegel's history at least aspires to be global. By starting out with 'The Oriental World' before 'The Greek World' and 'The Roman World', he was expanding the European view beyond its traditional obsession with Greece and Rome: in this sense, his was a 'progressive' history in its time and this distinctive feature lent his history enormous prestige, because it was (or then appeared) so 'universal'.

Yet in practice the attempt to include 'all nations' only exposed the limitations of knowledge currently available. Hegel excluded most of the globe, confusing 'I don't know' with 'nothing to know', and setting this exclusion into a lasting form. In this series we take this lesson: instead of attempting a Global History of Psychology, we accept our limitations and attempt *A New History of Western Psychology* within its global context.

Another warning to historians – which has proven even harder to learn – comes in the **consequences** of an obsession with the historian's own setting.

When we get down to the detail of these lectures, we find that ancient Greeks and Romans – whom Hegel knew very well and loved – are the true formers of world history, '**world-historical peoples**': 'humanity in general is summoned to self-knowledge. This mandate was given to the Greeks, for in **the Greek spirit** humanity exhibits itself in its clear and developed condition', and 'Among the Greeks … we are in the region of *Geist*'.[80] The Greeks then hand over the torch of history-making to the **Romans**, 'the succeeding organ of world history', who in turn hand it to the **Germans**, who go on to lead the unfolding of freedom.[81]

In contrast to these 'world-historical peoples', the rest are mentioned only as commentary. Hegel dismisses and omits peoples of which he is ignorant, in a way typical of most Western history writing up to that point (and not a little since). In keeping with his metaphor of 'the Sun of consciousness' travelling from East to West, East **Asia** is 'the childhood of history', central Asia is 'the boyhood'; so 'it is the necessary fate of Asiatic empires to be subjected to Europeans'.[82] **America** is now 'an emanation from Europe', its First Nations 'physically and psychically powerless' in the face of Western vigour; and it is only 'the land of the future' because Europeans have arrived.[83] This echoes Jefferson and Smith as well as emerging ideologies from the USA in Hegel's lifetime, such as the Manifest Destiny movement.[84]

Hegel's most dismissive comments, however, are reserved for **Africa**: 'the land of childhood … lying beyond the day of self-conscious history, is enveloped in the dark mantle of night'[85]; '**the African** in the uniform, undeveloped oneness of his existence … exhibits the natural man in his completely wild and untamed state … capable of no development or culture; and as we see them at this day, **such have they always been**'.[86] Africa is 'the unhistorical, undeveloped spirit, still involved in the conditions of mere nature'.[87] **Egypt** cannot be African, as it displays 'a thoroughly **rational organisation** characterising all institutions, and most astonishing works of art'; surprising 'in the vicinity of African stupidity'.[88]

Hegel's racism is generally shocking today, but it was normal for its time – part of an ideology created to justify slavery and console the European conscience. He even writes that slavery is the natural state for the African, and many would be better off as the slaves of Europeans in the Americas than living in their own continent.[89] The African-American philosopher Olúfemi Taiwò argues that such attitudes still shape perspectives on Africa. With effective wit and rhetoric, he plays on the etymology of *Geist* as 'ghost': that '**The ghost of Hegel** dominates the hallways, institutions, syllabi, instructional practices, and journals of Euro-American philosophy … this is **one mean ghost** that will be tough to exorcise'.[90]

As Taiwò states with complete accuracy, Hegel's claims are 'the rantings of the uninformed … dilettantish glosses on the information available to him'; in other words, are practically indistinguishable from popular prejudices of his time.[91] Yet this 'collective libel against Africa'[92] was perpetuated and absorbed by the elites of Western countries, including their new rising star, the United States.[93]

A measure of this persistence is the ongoing **obsession with the ancient Greek** achievement and a fixed tendency to stop there, despite all the Greek tributes to older civilisations (see Book Two).[94] Positive interest in the Greeks often has a negative underbelly in a relative lack of interest and investment in other ancient civilisations – especially African studies – in the academic world. Hegel's vision outside his own borders was taken to be definitive: a door could be closed, and Europeans, Americans and all shaped by Western education could stay inside it.

In Chapter 2, we will see that there is more to Hegel than his prejudices. His *Philosophy of History* was derived from an earlier, more psychological project of lasting interest and value. Even as a historian, his emphasis on beliefs and ideas at the expense of particular social circumstances has come full circle, as archaeologists, anthropologists, sociologists and others have increasingly come to acknowledge the **leading role of beliefs** in forming human culture.[95] We will follow several arcs of development since Hegel in Chapters 2 and 3. As a human being, he was qualified to examine humanity; but as a European, he was far less qualified to pronounce on other cultures.

Even if he had no positive features, Hegel would have to be taken into account as he 'has influenced posterity as very few philosophers … intellectual history during the past 150 years [in 1979] cannot be understood apart from him'.[96] One German critic suggested that 'the vices of a thinker are more influential than his merits … one can concede the dangers of Hegel's thought without denying his greatness: distinction and danger are twins'.[97] Hegel's influence resembles the Palaeolithic and Neolithic shamans – including those of Africa – who thought they saw the truth of the cosmos but generated it from within themselves (4.4).[98]

In Chapter 6 (on Egypt) we will seek to exorcise Hegel's ghost by addressing the African heritage in the light of the wealth of knowledge since his time: not to react blindly by stating an opposing set of prejudices and repeating the mistake. The lesson from Hegel is to avoid cultural racism, not to repeat it in reverse, as Taiwò rightly suggests.[99] This is one example of the changing face of Western academic life, the transition towards 'a postcolonial globalisation of thinking'.[100]

1.10 Sampling previous histories: George Sidney Brett

Hegel's was a general history of human ideas, which happened to resemble this series in its conception. Now we turn to the invention of 'history of psychology' as an academic genre.

Stepping forward one hundred years, the first history of psychology written in English was by a Canadian psychologist, George Sidney Brett (1879–1944). His first volume *A History of Psychology: Ancient and Patristic* covers exactly the material we will cover in our first three volumes: (1) Before the Greeks; (2) Greeks; (3) Romans.

(The word 'Patristic' refers to the 'Early Church Fathers' in Roman Christianity from Greek and Latin *pater* = 'father' and *ics* = Greek 'study of' as in 'phys*ics*'.)

Brett is working in a tradition of history shaped by Hegel and his successors. It is purely **a history of ideas** rather than of individuals within particular societies, reflecting Hegel's model. There is plenty of **philosophy**, and plenty of religious speculation, but no equivalent to our Orientations to anchor it in a wider history. Our Orientations are intended precisely to correct this tradition of ideas detached from their origins.

More importantly, the **selection of material** by Brett echoes Hegel's a century earlier. Like Hegel's lectures *The Philosophy of History*, non-Europeans are included in the story to give a sense of completeness but are treated very briefly, against an extremely thorough treatment of **Greek** philosophy and then **Roman** theology.

The proportion of the non-Greek and pre-Greek material in Brett's treatment is almost exactly ten per cent. More important, **emphasis** and relative **evaluation** give greater contrast. Brett gives a brief account of 'Primitive Thought' – like our Chapter 4 in this book – and a longer account of 'Eastern Writings' with brief visits to Egypt and Persia, and a little more coverage of Israel and India.[101] In terms of **chronology**, most of this is located in the first millennium BCE as an international context for Greece in its golden age, covered in enormous detail. As in Hegel's treatment, other regions are *contrasted* with the glories of ancient Greece; Greek progress from them compared to 'the genesis of the world out of chaos'.[102] Even when it looks outside fifth-century Athens this history is written from a position inside that world, as though sitting on the Acropolis looking out. We will expand on this metaphor of 'sitting on the Acropolis' throughout this series.

Just as in Hegel, this is very much **the Greek viewpoint** on the ancient world, only with a greater emphasis on Jewish and Christian input than Hegel allows, presumably for a church-going (or at least 'culturally Christian') readership. In all of this it is typical for the period, and long after. English-speaking history today is often written in more or less the same framework as in the nineteenth century; in terms of texts and priorities, even as established in the thirteenth century.[103]

Bertrand Russell's *History of Western Philosophy* (1946) allows a few pages of ancient history context in a volume of almost 800 pages before informing us that 'philosophy' began with the heroic Greek civilisation of the sixth century BCE.[104] This mirrors the practice of ancient Greek historian **Diodorus of Sicily**: a few remarks on Egyptians, Sumerians and their successors, before focusing on the Greeks and Romans, where the real history lies.[105] Like Brett, like Hegel, Russell is 'sitting on the Acropolis': locating the home of Western thought here in Greece.

In one sense, it is entirely reasonable for **histories of Western thought** to start in Greece. The Romans absorbed Greek culture and they exported it throughout Europe; Europeans then spent centuries digesting this imported package before themselves exporting it worldwide to their colonies. But there are a few issues:

a The Romans also absorbed and exported the heritage of the Hebrews in the form of Christianity: this heritage has to be included, because it has formed Western thought alongside Greece and Rome. (**Chapter 7**)
b The Greeks inherited ideas from older civilisations to the east and south but we cannot check the accuracy of their account, or the extent of the debt to these, unless we know more about it than they did: an accurate initial account of these civilisations is needed. (**Chapters 5 and 6**)
c Europe and its Western 'impact zone' have developed an awareness of world history beyond Classical texts. As well as gaining leverage on what Greeks and Romans thought about themselves and their sources, we need a wider global context for our reorientation. (**Chapters 4 and 8**)

Brett's treatment allows for (a) but only gestures in the direction of (b) and (c).

Some histories since – such as Russell's – have dropped (a) as well; while others have explored combinations, though rarely all three together.

d The definition of the West has shifted significantly since Brett published: led by the **USA** rather than Europe; losing its **colonial** presence globally; defined by different **allies** and perceived enemies; the European Union expanding to include **Eastern Europe**; expansion of **global democracy**; a greater balance and distribution of **academic** communities worldwide.

The challenge is to tell the European and Western story while keeping this in a global perspective. This series is intended to reflect our changing perspective on global history and culture, collecting insights from across disciplines to give the history of psychology an adequate foundation in contemporary scholarship.

Discussion questions (tied to chapter sections):

1 Would you locate yourself as 'Western'? If not, which is your culture?
2 Are you comfortable with the dates? Millennia? Centuries? Intervals?
3 Can you sketch a timeline with a fixed scale for the content of this book?
4 What images do you associate with 'civilisation'? What kind of people?
5 What would be a fair principle for naming nations? Naming continents?
6 Where do you think the word 'revolutionary' is justified and overused?
7 Whose stories in the past would you like to investigate, if you could?
8 What if anything is admirable about Hegel's project? What is less so?
9 What other lessons can we learn from Hegel for our practice of history?
10 Where do you think the history of psychology could or should begin?

Recommended Reading (see Bibliography for details)

- Melanie Challenger *How to be human*
- Vere Gordon Childe *What happened in history*
- Vere Gordon Childe *Man Makes Himself*

- Jared Diamond *Guns, Germs and Steel: a short history of everybody for the last 13,000 years*
- Yuval Noah Harari *Sapiens: a Brief History of Humankind*
- Stephen Mithen *After the Ice: A Global Human History 20,000–5000 BC*
- Stephen Mithen *The Prehistory of the Mind: the Cognitive Origins of Art and Science*
- Colin Renfrew *Archaeology and Language*
- Daniel Lord Smail *On Deep History and the Brain*
- Michael Wood *In Search of the First Civilisations*

Notes

1 Wood p.11–12.
2 Kriwaczek p.61; Roberts p.50; Wood p.29.
3 Leahey p.71; but Wood pp.171–6 points out the competing claims of Israel, Rome and Islamic civilisations also.
4 Armstrong xii ff.; Jaspers pp.8–29,60–71; McGilchrist p.241.
5 Bellwood (ed.) p.5; Henley and Rossano pp.5,24, who also talk helpfully of better 'chronological resolution'.
6 Roberts p.31; see also Diamond pp.30–31, 85–113 for a narrative account; Roberts pp.30–36; Wood pp.16–17.
7 Bellwood 9–10, 15–16, 26–31,38–9,115–16,148,153; Diamond pp.36, 50–51; Harari pp.6,15; Roberts pp.10,20.
8 Oppenheimer p.115.
9 *ibid* pp.116–7,142,153–5.
10 *ibid* p.16.
11 Clark pp.11–17; Diamond p.35; Roberts pp.7–8.
12 *ibid* p.154.
13 Pyne and Pyne pp.3,266.
14 *ibid* pp.239ff.
15 Diamond p.10.
16 Smail pp.1–7,31–39.
17 Renfrew 1987 pp.123ff.,146ff.,277–289.
18 Bellwood pp.80,93,153,161 for example; but the entire volume of Bellwood (ed.) assumes this hypothesis. It will be compared to alternatives for a particular case in the next volume.
19 Mithen 1996 pp.11,13,15,22,151ff.
20 Henley 2020 p.213.
21 Hesiod *Works and Days* lines 105–202 pp.62–65.
22 Lucretius V.1241–1307 pp.94–99; Roberts p.24.
23 Daniel pp.55–61; Renfrew 1976 p.25.
24 Piggott p.50.
25 Renfrew 1976 pp.25,125.
26 Childe 1954 pp.29-32 as the summary and then throughout the same text as a single argument.
27 Diamond pp.14–15; Roberts pp.30–1.
28 Lévi-Strauss 1963 p.19.
29 Eriksen p.7.
30 Jefferson p.1; Paine pp.110,124,138.
31 Jefferson p.3.
32 Smith V.1.1 542–3.

33 Smith 'Introduction and plan of the Work' pp.1–2.
34 Smith V.1.1 p.541–2.
35 Childe 1981 p.80; Clarke pp.501–2.
36 Clarke pp.463,483; Diamond pp.155,297ff.
37 For example, in Childe 1954 p.33ff. and p.55ff. but also Lévi-Strauss 1978 p.13.
38 Eriksen pp.7–8; 171–6, 178, 182,186,201, 207–8.
39 This is a basic point from Derrida 1967 p.80 which we will expand a little in 2.6.
40 We will find such a debate concerning the origin of farming in Africa, writing in Egypt, and cities in Pakistan.
41 Turner 2011 pp.1–2,7.
42 Childe 1954 pp.50–52; Daniel p.62; Mithen 2003 pp.5–6.
43 Daniel pp.102–3.
44 Renfrew 1976 p.69.
45 *ibid.*
46 Darvill pp.29,50,70,90; Grabbe pp.7–8; Lewis-Williams and Pearce pp.23,33, 140,148,171.
47 Bellwood 9–10, 15–16, 26–31,38–9,115–16,148,153; Diamond pp.36, 50–51; Harari pp.6,15; Roberts pp.10,20.
48 Clarke pp.14–15; Haywood pp.19–21; Leakey pp.117–21; Lewis-Williams and Pearce p.18; Roberts pp.25–7.
49 Daniel p.178.
50 Diamond pp.410–11; Roberts pp.32–3.
51 Diamond pp.98–99, 177; Haywood p.20.
52 Lewis-Williams and Pearce p.20; Roberts pp.32–4; Roux p.56ff.
53 Diamond pp.85–113 for a narrative account; Kramer pp.3–5,33; Roberts pp.30–36; Wood pp.16–17.
54 Clarke pp.361–9,442–6.
55 Diamond pp.29,176ff.
56 *ibid* pp.80–83,90.
57 *ibid* pp.186,189; Piggott p.43.
58 Wood pp.16–19.
59 Kramer pp. 90–93.
60 Diamond pp.99–100.
61 Childe 1954 pp.52, 55ff.; Childe 1981 p.68ff.; Lewis-Williams and Pearce p.18.
62 Childe 1981 p.94.
63 Van der Leeuw in Renfrew and Zubrow p.135.
64 Harari pp.23,36–7,41–4.
65 Quote in Challenger p.44.
66 Smail pp.2–3,19,33–39,42–3.
67 See Childe 1954 pp.28–32,52,55,77,193,270–286; Daniel p.162; Lewis-Williams and Pearce pp.18–23.
68 Mithen 1996 p.226 (global); Mithen 2003 pp.413–14 (India),495–8 (Africa); Henley and Rossano p.170.
69 Roberts p.1097 makes this point.
70 Henley p.216.
71 Althaus pp.19,75; Beiser 2008 (ed.) pp.14,51; Taylor pp.432–3.
72 Hegel 1956 pp. xv-xvi,110,456–7.
73 *ibid* pp.xv-xvi, 111, 225, 278, 341. This entire series can be read as an answer to Hegel, although this is only one reading option. It was conceived and planned independently of Hegel and Brett.
74 *ibid* p.103.
75 *ibid* pp.456–7.
76 *ibid* p.79.

77 Althaus pp.158,259; Fukuyama pp.xii, 56–69, 143–56; Hegel 1956 pp.103, 108–10, 342, 442, 456–7.
78 McVeigh p.48; Smail p.9.
79 Henley and Rossano (eds.) pp.3–7.
80 Hegel 1956 pp.80,220,223.
81 *ibid* pp.221,224,279,341–6.
82 *ibid* pp.105–6,116,142.
83 *ibid* pp.81–2,86.
84 Brogan p.305.
85 Hegel 1956 p.91.
86 *ibid* pp.93,98.
87 *ibid* p.99.
88 *ibid* p.204.
89 *ibid* p.96,98.
90 Taiwò pp.3,11.
91 Taiwò p.8–9; Valls (ed.) p.208.
92 Taiwò p.5; see also Diamond pp.377–81,393 and Kathryn Bard in Lefkowitz and Rogers pp.103–11.
93 Heinemann pp.85–6; 89 n.49, 89 n.50; Kaufmann p.171; Russell p.775.
94 See Diop (1974), Howe (1998), James (2017) and Lefkowitz and Rogers (1996) for the debate on Egypt's role.
95 Most of the key sources for Chapter 4 on cognitive archaeology reflect this recent trend back to beliefs.
96 Kaufmann p.171; also see Hegel 1956 p.i;.
97 Kaufmann pp.65,158 within a longer appraisal pp.163–71.
98 Bourdieu in Fowler pp.33–5 and Kaufmann p.378; but Hegel owned this role, for example Beiser (ed) p.249.
99 Taiwò p.10; see Diop for a tendency towards a reversed cultural racism, so that only Black Africans are the creative source of 'civilisation', and internal racism between regions and tribes of Africa.
100 Smart p.11.
101 Brett pp.3–15 ('Primitive Thought'), 200–236 ('Eastern Writings').
102 *ibid* p.3.
103 Celenza pp.72–81; Copleston pp.64–72 Caputo pp.85,92,96–8.
104 Russell pp.8,14,25ff.
105 Van de Mieroop 2017 p.3.

2 Psychology

2.1 The spectrum of *psyche*: Levels of explanation

Now we have looked at the dating system, age system, geographic basis and politics of history, we have generic tools for any history of the ancient world, provided by historical disciplines outside psychology (especially archaeology). Chapter 1 acts as a meta-orientation: an orientation for all the Orientations, which form the historical foundation for our study.

These form the hard shell for the soft tissue, which is our central focus in each chapter in Part 2. Inside the brackets of Orientation, we seek the relevant content from each civilisation to the questions set in the Preface: tracing *psyche* and *logos*.

One historian of global *philosophy* noted at the outset: 'The word, after all, is a Western word, and there is no guarantee that it has a clear equivalent outside of the West'.[1] We could say exactly the same thing about psychology. If we take our *definition* of either philosophy or psychology outside its borders and attempt to find it, we will not match it precisely, because it is Greek; it is Western. There are ancient Greeks who describe the Sumerians as 'philosophers', which helps us to stretch that word beyond their borders.[2] They could not do the same for 'psychology' or 'psychologists' as those words were not yet coined; but what we call psychology was for them a part of *philosophia*, the search for wisdom.[3]

Having made this point, the same historian of global philosophy continues with another point: 'Actually, even in its home territory, the word is **controversial** and **confusing**'.[4] In other words, nobody is entirely sure – or, more accurately, no consensus can be reached – what we even mean by 'philosophy' in our own culture, and so we are not entirely sure what are looking for if we look outside its borders for the same thing. Again, the same is true of psychology: a plurality of schools in contemporary psychology each define it differently, so a global history of psychology – as of philosophy – must start with this identity problem.

If 'the past is another country',[5] then what are we looking for when we seek to investigate the history of *psyche*? If we do not know what it is, then we will not know when we meet it, perhaps being explored by unfamiliar means.

DOI: 10.4324/9781003396147-4

We could restrict our search at the outset and stay within the familiar boundaries of known methods and vocabulary to avoid this problem. But as we have seen (1.8) we will not then be good historians open to evidence: this is the fallacy of presentism. In Brett's words (1.10) 'history alone can adequately unfold the content of the idea denoted by the word "*Psyche*"'[6] – so we could jump straight to Part Two, follow the unfolding of psychological ideas and redefine our subject along the way; but once again, without a principle of selection, how will we know what to include?

In order to reach back over the millennia with a clear framework, we must look much closer: at the **recent** history of psychology, anticipating the final volumes of this series. We must survey the foundations of contemporary psychology, at least in outline, so that our grasp of what we are looking for in the distant past is more secure. We need an **'extended present'** to study a more extended past.

When psychology was first growing as a professional discipline, there was talk of a crisis in its identity as it rapidly fractionated into different 'schools'.[7] This was partly due to the deaths of its **founders**: James in 1910, Brentano in 1917, Wundt in 1920, Titchener in 1927, Freud in 1939.[8] It was also a result of their philosophical training, which (positively) had given them an **overview** beyond the new science, which their followers failed to absorb; and (negatively) had introduced philosophical **disputes** with deep roots in the history of philosophy into this new science.[9]

Finally, the professionalisation of the whole academic world, disputes over the boundaries of disciplines, and the crisis in Europe leading to the transplantation of leadership from Germany to the USA, all encouraged a loss of roots.[10] Although the subject needed to fly the nest of its parent discipline (philosophy), turning to the evidence with rigorous methods on the model of the natural sciences, it also became somewhat **disorientated** and fragmented; and these divisions endured.

When we are lost, it is often a good idea to retrace our steps; if disorientated, to go back to our roots. In this brief sketch, necessarily anticipating future volumes of the series, we return to **philosophy** to help organise and build our framework.

Historians of the natural sciences – physics, astronomy, chemistry and biology – have claimed that as each has developed and matured, one crucial mark of each coming to maturity was the achieved dominance of a single theory.[11] If this is true for all science, including psychology, then the continued presence of many competing theories, and even competing understandings of what psychology is and should try to study, is a sign that psychology is **not yet a mature science**.

But should this criterion (Greek: rule of judgement) be applied to all sciences? Should previous observations of the **natural sciences** provide the pattern for psychology? Should it be classed with them or it is a different species? Should psychology try to imitate physics, astronomy, biology or chemistry by seeking a single theory to explain all of its data, even if only temporarily? This introduces a question we must revisit throughout this chapter: whether the methods used in and suited to natural sciences are also suitable for **other sciences**, as studied in separate departments and faculties, including psychology and the historical disciplines.

On the first question – whether psychology can and should have one dominant, overarching theory to qualify as a mature science – let us answer this question with a parable. In the next book, we will look at the man now called the Buddha. He told a story about a group of blind men who found an elephant: as each one explored a different part of the animal – the trunk, the tusks, the legs, the ears, the sides – they described it differently, and each gave a different definition of the animal. Yet it was the same animal.

This is a helpful way to understand the current diversity within psychology, and its wide range of schools with totally different methods and definitions of *psyche*. Perhaps the complexity of its subject matter – the nature of *psyche* – means that it will **always** generate a wide variety of theories; and perhaps no single theory can ever explain all the data. Perhaps the current diversity is thus here to stay.

On this argument, the various competing schools in contemporary psychology do not have to yield a single winner of the competition or a dominant theory. Each claims its own definition of the subject, has its preferred methods and its own answer to the question, 'Should psychology resemble a natural science?'

We already have a potential key to this complexity in the sequence of history.

In the last chapter, we saw that **genetics**, **linguistics** and **archaeology** combine their evidence to give us increasing levels of insight into prehistory and ancient history (1.3).[12] We also noted that these kinds of evidence arrived in a certain order (1.4,1.5,1.6).

Human impact on this planet was compared to successive rocks thrown into a pond: first the arrival of *homo sapiens* as a **species**, then the apparent growth in **intellectual capacity** later in the Palaeolithic; third, the innovative 'package' of new **societies** based on agriculture, domestication and finer tools, labelled 'the Neolithic', on the basis of the last item in this list. Finally, a new 'package' of cultural and technological innovations arrived which, once again focussing on material technology, has been labelled 'the Bronze Age'.

These four 'rocks' could be taken to yield four different **levels of explanation**, corresponding to the several meanings of *psyche*, in a sequence or spectrum based on our history and origins:

- Biological *psyche* - body, brain, environment - *Lower Palaeolithic*
- Cognitive *psyche* - language, belief, wonder - *Upper Palaeolithic*
- Social psyche - society, mythology, building - *Neolithic onwards*
- Cultural *psyche* - states, systems, sciences - *Bronze Age onwards*

The idea of a hierarchy or order of functions, it should be emphasised, is not an order of value, only one of complexity. We could, therefore, start by suggesting that *psyche* (whatever it is) functions continually at **all** of these levels – perhaps also at gradations **within** every level, broadening into a rainbow-like **spectrum**.

Just as the Lower Palaeolithic, Upper Palaeolithic, Neolithic and Bronze Ages succeeded and built on one another, there is a **hierarchy** of roles or functions in psychology, in which every level supports the next. A spectrum can be found in the description and understanding of human beings, indexed to successive ages.

Each level of *psyche* will have its appropriate *logos*, with methods matched to the object in each case. A new level of psyche requires a new approach. The first level is part of the natural sciences, but there are also independent levels, outside their orbit, to be studied in distinct ways:

- Psychology as **natural science**: rooted in the Lower Palaeolithic outcome
- Psychology as **cognitive science**: rooted in the Upper Neolithic outcome
- Psychology as **social science** rooted in the breakthrough of the Neolithic
- Psychology as **cultural studies** rooted in the Bronze Age breakthroughs

The essentially biological, medical, and animal level of the subject is a foundation for everything else. It includes **neurology** (study of the nervous system) and **physiology** (Greek: study of nature like *physics*; as 'study of body functions'). Archaeologists, palaeontologists, and other scientists working alongside them can confirm that the first humans had bodies and brains more or less similar to ours. Despite whatever distance separates us from them in mental and cultural terms, by the time we reach the Mesolithic (let alone the Neolithic) we are the same biological species, with the same 'hardware'. This gives us a clear bridge: in Section 2.2 we will focus on this bridge and on this first level of explanation.

The next level is built on this foundation and includes thought, language, social interaction and emotional states, in a complex web. Here we move from brain to **mind**. One of the founders of modern psychology, Wilhelm Wundt, coined the term 'cognition' (Latin: thought and its processes), and this has developed into 'cognitive sciences', '**cognitive psychology**' and 'cognitive neuroscience' (2.3), especially in combination with linguistics (Greek: the study of language; see 2.4).[13]

Another of the fathers of modern psychology, Franz Brentano, initiated the study of experience using descriptive methods developed in the biological sciences, but developed further to match the material:[14] As one historian observes: 'Brentano cautioned against simply importing methods and techniques from other fields of science into psychology – one had to adapt one's method to fit the subject matter that was under investigation'.[15] Brentano thus re-established a discipline known as **phenomenology** (Greek *phenomena* = appearance), a very influential programme for many sciences, with a deep and lasting impact on psychology.[16]

A third area of contemporary psychology which overlaps with these studies is **psychometrics** (Greek: *metros* = measurement of *psyche*) – intelligence testing, personality testing and forensics. Careful design of tests and rigorous methods of statistical analysis used on test results yield reliable measures of cognitive and other functions, which can be related to biological and neurological data.[17]

In 2.3 we will look in more detail at these separate divisions of psychology, for what they can contribute to our investigation. In particular, we will look at the attempts of phenomenology to define itself against the natural sciences, and the growing relevance of cognitive psychology to the historical sciences. Here, we simply note that they were all born of **independent methods** from the natural sciences, as Brentano proposed, and operate independently of them, whatever their interpretation. We have only covered two levels of a spectrum, but have established this principle in the relations between the first two levels.

Wundt, as a pioneer of modern psychology, not only coined the term 'cognition' and opened the first laboratory for experimental psychology in 1879, but also 'conceived of psychology as necessarily constituted of *two* parts, each based on a distinctive **layer** of human consciousness and each following its own laws using its own methodology'.[18] As well as 'scientific' psychology, in dialogue with biology, physiology and the natural sciences, Wundt promoted a '**second psychology**', comparing different global cultures in terms of languages, myths and customs – using descriptive methods, allowing for collective purposes and beliefs.[19] This is similar to what we now call **anthropology**, the cross-cultural study of human lives, or **sociology**, the analysis of Western societies;[20] and indeed, it was students of Wundt's 'second psychology' who pioneered these new social sciences – Adolf Bastian in anthropology and Emile Durkheim in sociology.[21]

As Brentano's 'descriptive psychology' became the possession of **philosophy** departments (in the form of phenomenology), but has gradually re-entered the mainstream of psychology, Wundt's 'second psychology' was initially absorbed into the developing **social sciences**, but has re-emerged in part as **social psychology**.[22] This area of contemporary psychology is connected to cognitive, individual and language psychology – that is, in terms of our spectrum, to the level below – but also connects to economics, sociology and **social anthropology**, without a direct link to the natural sciences (except through evolutionary psychology).[23]

We therefore begin to see a spectrum emerging in which each level is linked to those adjacent to it (on either side), but only indirectly to those further away, in the manner of links in a chain. We have social anthropology (UK) and cultural anthropology (US);[24] and in parallel with these, we have both social psychology and **cultural psychology** marking another step up the spectrum, a fourth level.[25]

As we distinguish simpler Neolithic societies from more complex Bronze Age civilisations, while acknowledging their continuities, the social sciences began to distinguish the basic processes of **society** from more sophisticated realms of **culture** built on these processes: religion, art, business, law, education, politics, public media. This has been compared to the relation of geometry to physics, for example, or the **foundation** of a building under its visible **superstructure**.[26]

Returning to two of our original questions – 'Can *psyche* be explained in terms of a single theory?' – and closely related, 'Can psychology be treated as a natural science?' – we have reached a provisional answer to both: in the negative. In a direct line from Wundt and Brentano, and their insistence on the distinctive character of psychology, we can quote the anthropologist Claude Lévi-Strauss:

> … when we are confronted with phenomena **too complex to be reduced** to phenomena of a lower order, then we can only approach them by looking to their relationships, that is, by trying to understand what kind of original system they make up. This is exactly what we have been trying to do in linguistics, in anthropology, and in different fields … it is the same kind of problem arising at two **different levels of reality**.[27]

Our sketch of the recent history of psychology (which we will cover in greater depth in later books) has shown that a '**spectrum**' of function and explanation was recognised by the pioneers and founders of the subject in its present form, as we note that it can also be represented in terms of the major stages of human development. Our **inclusive** approach is justified by the 'extended *then*' of past development as an object of study, and by the 'extended *now*' of modern academic disciplines.

When we begin to discuss boundaries between academic disciplines and their assumptions, we are entering territory traditionally assigned to **philosophy**. In the history of philosophy, many thinkers have moved from the natural sciences to the human sciences, via a consideration of how we can know anything about either. The Greek philosopher Socrates was an early member of this 'club' including Descartes, Locke, Hume, Kant, Husserl and many others.[28] Modern psychology has followed, by gradually moving from a 'natural sciences' model to something more complex.

Philosophy has often been divided for convenience into three main parts:

- the study of 'what is out there' independent of us: **natural philosophy** (Greek *phusis* = nature, from which we have physics and physiology)
- the study of **how we know** about either nature or ourselves, at different times called logic, semiotics (Greek *semiotike* = science of signs) or epistemology (Greek *episteme* = knowing)
- the study of **practical philosophy** (Greek *praktike* = action, the ultimate origin of what are now the social sciences including *ethics* and *politics*).[29]

This traditional division of philosophy is a good match to our three-fold division of historical disciplines introduced in Chapter 1: **genetics** matches to *phusis*, **linguistics** to logic or *semiotike*, **archaeology**, of both prehistoric societies and literate civilisations, to *praktike*. The added evidence of **literacy**

and writing during the Bronze Age sub-divides *praktike*: thus, a spectrum of three becomes four – and the possibility of other gradations and subdivisions becomes clear.[30]

Now, we have overlaid a proposed spectrum of *psyche* which also corresponds to the historical evidence *and* to the traditional division of philosophy. An increase in complexity matches an increase in proximity to our own time; everything is anchored in a genetic, biological, neurological and evolutionary base, but such anchorage is a loose coupling, as yet unspecified, and resistant to **reduction**[31] – that is, we do not assume at the start that everything can be explained in terms of this base and can therefore be reduced to it, even in principle, let alone in practice.

This insistence on variety and, conversely, resistance to reduction could be called the first principle; the second is that 'neighbouring' levels have direct and intimate connections – those from the cognitive to the genetic, or from the social to the cognitive, or from the cultural to the social – whereas non-neighbours have indirect and remote connections, like non-neighbouring colours in the rainbow; perhaps functioning best as analogies and metaphors.

All of this is provisional, conjectural; awaiting confirmation, awaiting details. Let us work through this 'spectrum' in order – both of time and of complexity.

2.2 Bridges to the past (a) Natural sciences: Anatomy, genetics, neurology

As we saw, one foundation for 'time travel' in our investigation of the human past is that human skeletons dug up by palaeontologists and archaeologists are recognisably similar to our own. Whether inside a cave or inside a pyramid, the same bone and skull structure signals to us that we are dealing with the same species. In the Palaeolithic era, humans appeared that we would recognise as *homo sapiens* (Latin: 'wise ones') with the same innate capacities as ourselves.[32] While other things about us continue to develop, the biological basis appears stable.

Recent developments in the natural sciences have made human remains much more informative, giving us more insight into prehistoric lives. The **isotopes** of two chemical elements (oxygen and strontium) in bones and tooth enamel of a skeleton can tell us remarkably precise details about where a person spent the first and the last years of her life – how warm each place was at the time – even how far she lived from the sea; and also, whether she lived mainly on plants or animals, and if she was carnivorous whether this was seafood or land animals. We can therefore trace the '**biography**' of a skeleton, in extraordinary detail.[33]

We can also trace **ancestry** using breakthroughs in the science of **genetics**, and relate this to people living today, using the 'fingerprints' or 'silent messengers' of mitochondrial DNA.[34] This information can group people into clans and trace their movements, to distinguish *maternal* from *paternal* ancestors as well as to estimate dates for common ancestors, providing a whole 'genetic landscape'.[35] Combined with the isotope evidence, this brings clarity and precision to the construction of prehistory, independent of the evidence of human artefacts.[36]

More importantly for our purpose, it confirms the biological continuity, which was previously inferred from the bare anatomy of the skeletons. If the DNA is shared and is continuous between human remains and people today – and we know which genes determine the structure of the brain and nervous system – it confirms the assumption that people in the past had neurological 'equipment' much like our own.

We also know, with more confidence than ever before, that 'the neurological functioning of **the human brain**, like the structure and functioning of other parts of the body, is a human universal.[37] Not only is it universal across global cultures today, but it is also universal across all the different stages of human history. The study of Palaeolithic and Neolithic cultures today can tell us a lot about those in the past because they share both a universal genetic blueprint and a common cultural setting. If 'the human mind is an experience that is created by the working of the brain'[38] we can have greater access to **the ancient mind**. In the following chapters, we will explore this '**neurological bridge** to the Neolithic'.[39]

Our genes do not simply *determine* the shapes of our minds, however. Since the total inherited information in each human cell (the entire human genome) was described or 'mapped' 23 years ago, neuroscientists have recognised that each brain develops into something far more complex than its biological base: 'the genetic shadow looms large but it is not complete'.[40] The brain has a fixed '**neural architecture**' determined by its genes, from individual neurons (brain cells) to more complex systems, just like the rest of the human body; but at the top level – in the 'supersystem of systems'[41] and thus the mind – there is greater **flexibility** in the ways that it can develop. The whole body, natural and social environments work together to contribute to the development of the brain.[42]

The genetically **determined** element in the human brain can therefore help to explain the common features found between different cultures, including the ancient cultures we will soon begin to visit and explore; while the **flexibility** of brain development can help to explain the (sometimes enormous) differences. Both have a basis in natural science. Archaeologists looking back into the past, and anthropologists looking around us in the present, study the products of the complex '**interaction** between neurologically generated universals and cultural specifics'.[43] Culture or civilisation 'cannot be reduced to biological mechanisms and, even less, can they be reduced to a subset of genetic specifications. Their comprehension demands not just general biology and neurobiology, but the methodologies of the social sciences as well'.[44] The brain itself points us past the world of the natural sciences, because human brains **develop in societies**, their most complex structures moulded by, and dependent on, those societies, just as Wundt had insisted. One of the greatest moulders of human brains – as we shall see – is language.

In terms of individual **human development**, humans are born much earlier in their trajectory than most mammals. Studies of the 'species-typical development' demanded by human neurology, and exhibited by certain societies more than others, have built up a portrait of the Evolved Development Niche (EDN) that involves responsive breastfeeding, holding and related interactions, in balance with release to whole-body, self-directed free play, to optimise brain function, lifelong stress response, decision-making, and many other aspects of health.[45] The EDN requires not only a primary caregiver but the whole local community including **alloparents** – a range of trusted alternative caregivers – to share the care.[46] A much-quoted African proverb says: 'It takes a village to raise a child'. The EDN articulates this in scientific language.

Beyond motherhood and the early years, the plasticity of our inherited neural functions means that the opportunities for **education** and formation by wider culture are unique.[47] Archaeologists can find evidence of apprenticeship and training in Palaeolithic and Neolithic societies;[48] in Bronze Age civilisations this was extended to reading, writing, mathematics and other disciplines with the invention of the school: these societies could afford teachers, because there was a sufficient food surplus organised to spare people for specialised jobs, with teachers just one 'guild' among the many new specialist professions.[49] In the following chapters we will touch on evidence of educational 'psychologies' in the ancient world.

Whether starting from neurology or evolutionary dynamics, therefore, human biology *creates* **human society**. When we think of human psychology as a description of each of us as an individual, we have to *abstract* (Latin: stretch or pull away) not only from our cultural circumstances, but from our neurology, both of which start with us already embedded in networks of relationships. It is part of our human biology that we are social beings: and we can now see, with the advantage of hindsight and improved scientific knowledge, that this is why Wundt placed his 'second psychology' alongside experimental, natural-scientific psychology as an equally essential component.

This insight is foundational for this book, which has to start with communities: **human communities** are biologically generated and neurologically embedded. Archaeology, anthropology and linguistics, which study these communities, depend on this neurological foundation.

2.3 Bridges to the past (b) Cognitive sciences: Tools, equipment, artefacts

Are there other universals besides the medical or biological base? Since at least the eighteenth century, this has been a key question for Western thinkers and it has cropped up repeatedly as the various human sciences have developed.

In periods when the natural sciences are advancing with notable success, the search for universal features such as 'innate ideas' or 'laws of human nature' is often renewed. Diversity of personality, language, culture and historical period is always a challenge, and as each programme progresses it often finds that the human universals are not of the same kind as initially expected. This debate has to be repeated again and again, but in the process, progress occurs as new sciences are created, uncovering fresh data. We will see this unfold up to 2.6 in a spiral pattern, discussed at the conclusion (2.7) and in the next chapter (3.5).

In Section 2.1, we introduced **phenomenology** as description of experience. The Greek word *phenomena* signifies 'that which appears to us, that which comes into the light, which reveals itself'. It will become a very useful term in our investigation, as basic as 'facts' or 'data'. The history of phenomenology is a good example of the debate about how **scientific** a discipline can be and it is woven into the story of psychology. Here we will introduce this theme, which we can trace – through various interruptions – to the end of this chapter.

Originally, the term 'phenomenology' was used for the *phenomena* studied in natural sciences. It originally meant 'the method of the **astronomer**': taking observations from the night sky and attempting to explain these observations in a coherent way: what has been called 'saving the appearances'.[50] One astronomer and mathematician, Johann Lambert, having coined the term (in German) soon shifted its meaning to psychology, to a general discussion of how our minds process the observed data to make sense (*logos*) of the *phenomena*.[51] A friend of Lambert's, inspired by this project, envisioned a science of 'the most universal laws of sensibility' called 'general phenomenology'[52]: this was **Immanuel Kant**, who developed Lambert's idea of phenomenology into his *Critique of Pure Reason*, rethinking the origins, construction and limits of human knowledge.[53] Already we are on the way to Wundt's **cognitive psychology**, which was inspired by Kant's project.[54]

Although it began with a discussion of natural science, and it has had an enormous impact on physics, mathematics and astronomy, **Kant's 'phenomenology'** has also had a profound influence on the human sciences – psychology, sociology, and anthropology (the study of human origins).[55] Just after Kant's death his project was developed in this direction with Georg **Hegel's *Phenomenology*** *of Geist*, which describes 'the education of consciousness' through a 'detailed history'[56] depicting 'a slow-moving succession of spirits, a gallery of images'[57] marking the gradual, painfully achieved progress of our species. He wrote it up later in his *Philosophy of History* (1.8).[58] More explicitly that work confuses the learning process of one individual (Hegel) with the history of humanity.[59]

We already looked at Hegel's project as history (1.8, 1.9): here, we consider it as psychology, and from this angle, the outcome is actually more positive. Hegel's *Phenomenology* contains a fascinating description of the learning process of his 'consciousness' as an internal dialogue or debate (3.5): what philosophers since Aristotle have called **dialectic**.[60] Hegel defines his experience as a 'dialectical movement, which consciousness exercises on itself and which affects both its **knowledge and its object'**.[61] Finding that its answers do not exactly match its questions, consciousness is continually facing and **overcoming contradictions** in a dialogue with itself.[62] Even philosophers who reject most of Hegel's ideas admit that this is a reasonable description of the history of science and philosophy itself.[63] Kant had portrayed the history of philosophy to his time in this way in the *Critique*.[64] As already hinted, the process of working out the relationship of psychology to the natural sciences could itself be described in dialectical terms.

Most recently the psychiatrist and philosopher Ian McGilchrist has seized upon Hegel's dialectic as an intuition which matches discoveries in neurology today, even as 'an extraordinary instance of the mind by introspection [Latin: looking inward] "**cognising itself**"'.[65] In Hegel's synthesis of history and psychology, the history may be – upon reflection – 'the rantings of the uninformed'[66] (1.9), but the psychology has some lasting value if we focus on process, not the product.

Unlike Kant, who assumed human nature as a universal potential developed to different degrees in every individual, Hegel believed that 'Human nature only really exists in an achieved **community** of minds'.[67] In other words, the mind is reduced to the surrounding society and culture, rather than to its biological basis: a different form of reduction, reducing 'up' the spectrum rather than 'down'. Marx called the *Phenomenology* 'the true birthplace and secret of Hegel's philosophy' and he built a complete system on this theory, the basis of 'Marxism'.[68]

It appears that the attitude of the natural scientist, which seeks out generalised descriptions from the pattern of our shared biological nature, has given way to the citadel of the human sciences, in which our higher functioning floats free of those tethers. The concept of a 'phenomenology' which began with the natural sciences and moved into psychology has ended up in the human sciences. From Kant to Marx, phenomenology has 'changed masters' and changed its meaning. Nevertheless, the work of more recent psychologists such as Vygotsky, Luria and their followers, working inside the frame of Marx's thought, has been fruitful for educational psychology and cultural psychology – including, ironically, the teaching of natural sciences.[69]

The transition from Kant to Marx was found an echo in the twentieth century. A revival of Kant's thinking together with an enormous growth in the natural sciences (the era of Einstein) led Edmund **Husserl** to move, just like Kant, from physics and mathematics to a consideration of their foundations in human cognition.[70] Husserl developed a fresh version of phenomenology, seeking to uncover the universals in human experience, once again independent of its historical setting. He gave credit to Kant's original project but sought to expand it in light of the development of experimental psychology and the flowering of many other human sciences.[71]

One of Husserl's students, Martin **Heidegger**, took a similar role to Hegel in the previous century by developing the new phenomenology in a new direction, to make it a more supple instrument suited to the emerging human sciences such as psychology, anthropology and archaeology: in each of which it has proven fruitful.[72] Heidegger, like Hegel and Husserl, gives credit to Kant as a source for his phenomenology.[73] His findings – like Hegel's, but more so – match those in **neuroscience**, confirming these more recent findings of biology and medicine 'from the inside'.[74]

As phenomenology can work alongside clinical psychology and neuroscience, it can work alongside sciences of the past such as **archaeology**, and those of the remote such as **anthropology**, to uncover and explain past human experiences. These sciences, Heidegger suggests, can contribute in turn to phenomenology, telling us basic things about ourselves because their 'primitive phenomena are often **less concealed** and **less complicated** by extensive self-interpretation'.[75] This bridge carries goods in two directions: from data to theory and vice versa.

Heidegger points out that the Greeks had a term, *pragmata*, for things around us that we use. (It becomes 'practical', 'practically', 'pragmatic', 'pragmatism'.) An English equivalent for it is '**equipment**' or simply 'tools'.[76] In everyday life we use such tools as 'extracorporeal organs',[77] surrounded by and immersed in our equipment, and not distinguishing it functionally from ourselves – until we suddenly become aware of it by its not working[78] – like a part of our own body, which we inhabit with very limited awareness while it is doing what we want, because we remain focussed on the task in hand. Thus, our consciousness is **extended** into this wider environment of our equipment, to the extent that we – quite routinely and normally – fail to notice where the body ends and tools begin.

A key difference between the 'me' that is actually a part of my own body and the extended 'me' that is not, is that tools are **cultural artefacts**. We owe both to our ancestors, of course: each of us is physically the legacy from our parents as our surrounding tools are a legacy from them or from our wider society. But as the evidence shows, bodies have changed little in many thousands of years, whereas tools have changed beyond recognition, and are constantly developing – as some would say, are **historically conditioned**, as bodies are not. 'Our species ... has succeeded in surviving and multiplying chiefly by improving his **equipment for living**' – as the archaeologist Gordon Childe has observed.[79]

Another key difference is that we owe all the tools we use to a wider society: they are **socially conditioned**, as well as historically. They each point towards a larger world, in which they make sense to a group, and were devised by that group. I rarely, if ever, experience a tool alone; even if I invent it I will share it.

This has significant implications for historical sciences, such as archaeology and anthropology, and for our project in this book. When we look at a tool that has survived the centuries, we are – in phenomenological terms – looking at part of **an ancient mind**: the 'mind' of that society. Heidegger argues that each tool points beyond itself to 'that referential totality within which the equipment is encountered': to an entire **culture** or civilisation to which it refers ['referential totality'] and in which its intended function would make sense.[80]

This is precisely how the thinking of archaeologists has progressed over recent decades, from encountering material remains to encountering 'the societies of which these artefacts are the relic'; and then, with much greater confidence, to 'the perceptions and beliefs of the society'; and even to 'the cognitive maps of their inhabitants'. A whole sub-discipline calling itself **cognitive archaeology** has appeared, locating itself as a bridge between the historical sciences and the cognitive sciences.[81] The independent growth of the theory of 'embodied cognition' with minds 'spread through' their equipment, inhabiting it like inhabiting the body, has led archaeologists to make bolder claims: for example, that they routinely '**excavate minds** ... there is no self or mind *behind* the tool ... Mind exists inside the material expressions ... Tool making and using are ways of thinking, not the results of thinking ... [for example] thinking *with* and *through* stone'.[82]

This conceptual shift clearly has enormous implications for our investigation. It means that we can talk coherently about seeing and touching 'the ancient mind' which is the object of a cognitive archaeology.[83] If a hand-held stone tool, with its marks of manufacture, could be described as the 'thoughts' of a prehistoric person, then how much more so a stone building? In Chapter 4 onwards we will look at ways of 'reading' Neolithic structures for their cognitive content.

Finally, in the initial survey of 2.1, there was mention of **psychometrics**, which is the measurement of intelligence, personality and tendencies in our behaviour. *Intelligence* testing has an unexpected role as a bridge to the past of our species.

Other species display *modular* intelligence: they can function to high levels in certain *modes,* domains, activities – outperforming us in *specific* aptitudes and skills. What is distinctive about *homo sapiens* is management or government across modes, creating communication between these (usually called 'access' or 'accessibility'), and an internal structure or '**architecture**' which organises these into various **levels of function**.[84] This unique balance of modular and general intelligence is reflected in the findings of intelligence tests across the globe: we each have strengths and weaknesses in our profiles of intelligence, useful for matching each of us to suitable work, but across these specifics, we display reliable performance measures of general intelligence (labelled *g*).[85]

This contemporary evidence has been found to match past evidence for human evolution, or rather to offer a good explanation of the archaeological evidence. The metaphor of neural 'architecture', with modules and general intelligence, is taken further with 'an analogy of the mind as a cathedral' with side chapels (the specialist domains) built around a central nave (general processing capacity) according to archaeologist Stephen Mithen.[86]

The breakthrough of the late Pleistocene (1.3) or Upper Palaeolithic (1.4) came with a breakdown of boundaries between these areas: 'full cognitive fluidity' with unrestricted access and communication between the different modes.[87] The orchestration of separate domains under a general governing intelligence is the key to 'the emergence of the modern mind' which (for example) made metaphors possible and explains the appearance of art, religion and science in the historical record, as well as the topography of individual intelligence observed in psychometrics.[88]

2.4 Bridges to the past (c) Linguistics

Spoken language seems to be as old as tool-making: if correct[89] this takes us back to the hunter-gathering period (Palaeolithic) and human origins. Indeed, rather than considering language to be 'as old as tool-making', we can consider it as one tool among others.

Given all that we have said already about tools, this one is also a medium that we use, inhabit and experience in an immersive way in everyday life, without reflection: we experience the world through it, as part of a group. Language, if used unselfconsciously, becomes **fused with experience** and inseparable from it. As Heidegger notes, 'for primitive man, the sign coincides with that which is indicated ... the sign has not yet become free from that of which it is a sign'.[90] Like all tools, it is historically and socially conditioned: it develops over time, ties us to a social group, and functions as an expression of the shared 'mind'.

Unlike other tools, however, until a writing system is invented – and this was of course a rare occurrence – language is invisible: it remains, in the words of one archaeologist, 'spiritual equipment'.[91] As such, it is a tool more intimately tied to the functioning of our brains than any other: it **reveals** more about our brain's functioning and, in turn, also **shapes** our brain functioning more than any other. The interaction of language with brain functioning is now studied in a variety of disciplines such as **psycholinguistics** and neuro-linguistics.[92] (As with so many other areas, Wundt is now recognised as a founder of the first of these two.)[93]

We know that **spoken languages** had become extremely diverse by the onset of the Bronze Age, because when they start to become written, we find enormous diversity in their structures.[94] A single writing system was often used to record several spoken languages. It is not plausible that these all suddenly became so diverse at the time they were recorded – or just because they were recorded – because the 'grammar' and organisation are already so diverse. We are clearly getting a cross-section of a much longer oral language development at the point where a few languages were captured by the new technology, the invention of **writing** and literacy. All other languages continued to evolve uninterrupted as spoken instruments until much later on, closer to our own times when literacy has become widespread.

The study of world languages has progressed enormously over the last century with their classification into '**language families**'. Indo-European was the first of these to be identified,[95] but since then this insight has expanded to the entire globe, such as the enormous complexity of Africa.[96] Once the 'map' of world languages was in place the next step was to **explain** these distributions, as we find them today. One key to this has been found in the history of **food production**, that is, the Neolithic, and its effect on population (1.3). The massive growth in human fossils after the advent of farming[97] can be likened to **waves of denser populations** moving outward, from generation to generation, to support larger families from new land. These 'waves of advance' carried the original languages of farming tribes to ever wider areas, as a by-product of the natural population expansion, often **replacing** or **absorbing** the tongues of those remaining in the old, Palaeolithic way of life.[98]

As with language families, this was first proposed for Europe and then found to apply worldwide.[99] Various efforts to provide a reliable dating for languages have been tried, but the best historical 'anchor' for this data is by matching it to the evidence of global **archaeology**, which can be tied to absolute dates.[100] With these advances in method, as one historian comments, his profession 'shall have to consider beginning their histories ... with the invention of language, not writing'. This moves the historical horizon back from 5 kya to at least 50 kya.[101]

As with genetics and neurology, the best bridge into the past is in continuity of structure and function: and here there have been big advances in linguistics. A branch of psychology which has stayed close to the scientific base, and which is also useful to our investigation, is that of the American linguist Noam **Chomsky**.[102] His work, like Wundt's, looks back to Kant's phenomenology of experience;[103] and just as Wundt coined the term 'cognitive', Chomsky has launched a whole range of new cognitive approaches from the stronghold of his science-based linguistics – eventually coming into contact with archaeology, as explained above (Section 2.3).[104]

Chomsky views linguistics as part of **psychology**, rooted in **neurology**, seeing a genetic basis for our language-learning abilities, just as psychologists seek this for human perception.[105] As the huge variety of global languages suggests, he views our ability to learn language as **innate** (Latin: born in us) and universal.[106] The different language families traced by comparative and historical linguists he compares to outcomes of different switch settings in an identical **network**, with early choices guiding later possibilities, and the early choices decided by parents, alloparents and the cultural environment.[107] All 'serious psychology', in Chomsky's view, should study 'higher mental functions' such as language; as all psychologists have a working theory of language, whether or not this is articulated; and the variety of human language is part of the history of the human mind:[108]

> I believe that in specific domains such as the study of language, we can begin to formulate a significant concept of "human nature", in its intellectual and cognitive aspects ... I would not hesitate to consider the faculty of language as part of human nature.[109]

2.5 Bridges to the past (d) Anthropology

We have begun to move through the spectrum of *psyche* and *logos* proposed in 2.1, each time exploring the appropriate *logos* (suitable vocabularies, concepts, metaphors and methods) to match each level of functioning of *psyche*. This is to find the tools we will need to approach our search for **ancient beliefs** including those about *psyche*, in other words, ancient psychologies. We have an essential foundation from the natural sciences (2.2) then through telling the stories of phenomenology and cognitive sciences (2.3) we have derived a promising **toolkit**. As it happens, we can continue the dialectical spiral introduced in Section 2.3, as we progress through the spectrum.

Heidegger's suggestion of a fruitful dialogue between phenomenology and the historical sciences, such as archaeology and anthropology, proved prophetic.[110] It was **anthropology** which rescued phenomenology from its next ditch. Much as phenomenology become detached from its anchorage of the natural sciences, on its journey from Kant to Marx, it did so again after the Second World War – this time in France.

One enthusiastic reader of Heidegger was Jean-Paul **Sartre**, who developed a phenomenology of consciousness, embedding Heidegger's theory in everyday life with an emphasis on human responsibilities, decisions and freedom.[111] This new moral phenomenology was called **existentialism**.[112] Slowly moving his focus from individuals to societies, Sartre sought 'the universal method and universal law of anthropology'[113] in the dialectic that Marx had taken over from Hegel's phenomenology, accepting that this had become detached from the natural sciences, but accepting this state of affairs.[114] This matched his total denial of any such thing as 'human nature' as described by Kant, Husserl or Chomsky: Sartre insisted that we create ourselves by our moral decisions.[115] Sartre was, in effect, practising **social psychology**, not only through philosophical prose but also through **fiction**, drama and other forms: his approach to 'existential questions' is a helpful model for our investigation, as early cultures often explored this subject through similar means (see for example 4.3, 5.7, 6.4, 6.6, 6.8, 7.4, 7.7).

The story and the dialogue continue - but this time led by an anthropologist,[116] Claude **Lévi-Strauss**. He answered the 'armchair theories' of existentialism by re-asserting a science-based approach, aiming to uncover evidence of a human nature common to all societies and cultures.[117] Fifty years earlier, Husserl had revived a scientific approach – one modelled on natural sciences – by appealing to Kant as the founder of phenomenology; Lévi-Strauss led his fresh 'scientific' revival in dialogue with the new **linguistics**, or the science of language.[118] As with Hegel, phenomenology broadens from the individual to social experience, its social equivalent labelled '**ethnography**' (Greek: *ethnos* = nation or social group, *graphos* = recording or writing down), defined as the 'observation and analysis of human groups considered as individual entities'.[119] Sociology is then a subset of this discipline, focussing on more complex Western societies.[120]

Linguistics had taken a step forward with the realisation that, underneath any everyday spoken language, there was a social equivalent of a 'grammar' which (like grammar) was a **static** feature.[121] The analogy with a structure in building, with anthropologists 'reverse engineering' the visible manifestations to identify the underlying patterns, led to the name for this programme: **structuralism**.[122] (Chomsky's theory could also be called structuralist.[123]) For the native speaker grammar is an **unconscious** feature, but some 'reverse engineering' can reveal general laws, applying to other languages.[124] Everyday speech, as spoken and heard, is the tip of the iceberg; what lies beneath it exists only in the mind.[125]

Using this analogy, Lévi-Strauss saw a way for psychologists, sociologists, and anthropologists to join together in 'a very pale and faint imitation of what the hard sciences … have been doing all the time … though, of course, the cultural is much more **complicated** and calls upon a larger number of variables'.[126] In 2.1 we noted that Wundt's 'second psychology' had inspired anthropology in Adolf Bastian and sociology in Emile Durkheim; these children had since separated – from each other, and from psychology – but Lévi-Strauss believed that he had found a way to reunite these endeavours to understand the human condition.

The structuralist programme is based on the creed 'that notwithstanding the cultural differences between the several parts of mankind, the human mind is everywhere one and the same and that it has the same capacities'.[127] This has been the common creed of most anthropologists, from the nineteenth-century pioneers to today's professionals, entitled 'the **psychic unity of mankind**'.[128] Structuralism has been well described (by a critic) as 'an explicit search for the **permanent structures of the mind** itself, the organisational categories and forms through which the mind is able to experience the world'.[129]

We can recognise this as the original project of Kant and Husserl; as an update of the programme they labelled '**phenomenology**'. The main difference is that rather than starting with individual experience, and then considering the social applications, we begin at the **social** and **communal** level, already containing a group of individuals. It is, therefore, very similar to the moves made by Hegel and Heidegger in their versions of phenomenology. This time, however, there is less tension with the natural sciences, as we move up the functional scale, because Lévi-Strauss points (as Hegel and Heidegger could not) to **neurology** as the foundation of this creed, anticipating the recent growth of this science.[130]

Brought into anthropology by Lévi-Strauss, this has proven a fruitful approach for almost all the human sciences and social sciences, including archaeologists, some of whom identify as structuralists.[131] The assumption of a common nature as a bridge between societies can apply **across time** as well as across space, as 'man has always been thinking equally well; the improvement lies, not in an alleged progress of man's mind, but in the discovery of new areas to which it may apply its unchanged and **unchanging** powers'.[132] This approach empowers us to compare and combine the insights of anthropologists and archaeologists, where cultures today appear to resemble the cultures of the distant past.[133] On both sides of this divide there is a recognition that different cultures will shape the development of neurological capacity, but that total **capacity is constant**.[134]

For our purposes in studying Neolithic and Bronze Age cultures, the method of structuralism, moving as it does 'from the study of conscious content to that of unconscious forms', seems very suitable.[135] Archaeology deals with material remains, but 'if the unconscious activity of the mind consists in imposing forms upon content, and if these forms are fundamentally **the same for all minds** – ancient and modern, primitive and civilised … it is necessary and sufficient to grasp **the unconscious structure** underlying each institution and each custom, in order to obtain a principle of interpretation valid for other institutions and other customs'.[136] The method is to analyse each phenomenon, identify the underlying structures, and then make inferences about related phenomena.

The archaeologist and the anthropologist both deal with people 'without writing' whether or not writing was present elsewhere, so there is a major advantage in the structuralist method.[137] Even if we had written records, unconscious forms would be sought to explain them – as with all outward, surface manifestations – and the psychological content will be located in the subconscious of the group.

Most useful of all – for our purposes – is the approach to **myth** in structuralism. One thinker in dialogue with Husserl and Heidegger, Ernst Cassirer, pioneered a 'phenomenology of the mythical consciousness', based on Kant's first model of phenomenology, in which mythical thinking lies at the boundary of waking and dreaming.[138] It has a 'grammar' made up of contrasts and contradictions, and is an important clue that consciousness is not the whole picture in psychology.[139] Lévi-Strauss fully agrees, and suggests that myth is **the language of the *psyche***, communicating at a deeper level than rational discourse, with music as its twin sister.[140] Myth has its own code that **must be decoded**, and has a static quality underlying its expressions, as music can be heard, but also read off a stave.[141]

Mythos, thinking in images as in dreams, was traditionally opposed to *logos*, a sequence of conscious reasoning, in ancient Greece.[142] In ancient psychologies we will meet a great deal of mythical thought, so we need a 'grammar' to read it effectively. A key element of the unconscious structure is **binary opposition**: pairs of opposites such as life/death, male/female which reveal simply 'how the brain works' underneath language, the '**deep grammar**' of human minds.[143] Lévi-Strauss's proposal is that binary oppositions do not necessarily – or even usually – function to *resolve* these contrasts, but simply to *place* two poles side by side to mark an opposition: it is thus a mythic form of **classification**. A third category is then typically added to function as a bridge and to bring these two opposed or contradictory categories into a stable and structured **relationship**.[144]

Lévi-Strauss's claim that mythical thinking reveals the language of the *psyche* is similar to the claim of Marx, that there is a hidden economic basis to culture, its **infrastructure**, of which it is only the expression or **superstructure**;

as also to the claim of Freud, that there are hidden, unconscious drives behind all social behaviour and civilisation in general.[145] As the mind is a product of the brain, this claim makes culture (shared 'mind') a product of something else, the underlying and unconscious structuring processes. Where Marxists identified these with the economic base of society, and Freudians with our basic animal instincts,

> … so deeply does anthropology of the kind propounded by Lévi-Strauss probe into the 'encoding' or structuring capacity of the human mind, that one of its conclusions must be that it has encountered the human mind in its fundamental form, **regardless of the particular society** in which it appears.[146]

In other words, structuralist anthropology is not only a method for analysing different cultures, but **a form of psychology** in the tradition of phenomenology. It starts from the social or communal level but it moves to psychological claims, which are then applied to other communities.

In keeping with the dialectical patterns traced so far, structuralist anthropology generated various schools and reactions – some of which are also of help to our project. All began by reacting against Lévi-Strauss, just as he had against Sartre: one historian observes of European thought and especially French thought, that 'rejection of the tradition is, perhaps, the heart of the tradition'.[147] Such attempts at post-**structuralism** (Latin: post = after) generally accept structuralism as a method for Palaeolithic and Neolithic cultures, but seek to build on it for cultures beyond the Bronze Age, including – ultimately – our own, extending this approach to much more complex contemporary civilisations.

Historian Michel **Foucault** has brought archaeological methods into historical enquiry for literate cultures, emphasising **unintentional** survivals and finds so that this kind of 'history' becomes more like genetics, historical linguistics and archaeology.[148] A written document is treated like other kinds of historical evidence, avoiding bias by avoiding intention. The other kinds of evidence are 'valuable checks on the written word' for this reason: 'the author, in effect, disappears, and you are left with **a text** that must be decoded in a different way'.[149] The other kinds of evidence are called 'texts' in a deliberate analogy with a written document: a helpful way of thinking for our investigation of ancient evidence.[150]

Besides Michel Foucault, the most influential successor to Lévi-Strauss is Pierre **Bourdieu**.[151] He turned the methods of anthropology towards modern France, as many anthropologists began to do the same, engaging in 'field studies' in a developed society, reflecting on the contrasts between France and Algeria, as well as urban and rural society, tribal and society culture in both countries.[152] As Foucault's work points to our historical methods, Bourdieu's points more directly toward the **psychology of transitions** from Palaeolithic to Neolithic, and especially from Neolithic to urbanisation in the Bronze Age. We will draw on it for our final synthesis and applications in Chapters 3–5.

2.6 Bridges to the past (e) Grammatology

For our purposes, perhaps the most useful response to Lévi-Strauss is the work of Jacques **Derrida**. Born an Algerian Jew, later moving to the USA,[153] Derrida remained sensitive to marginal voices and to power dynamics: witnessing the **end of the colonial era** between France and Algeria, he sought to update the human sciences to match this, by engaging in a productive examination of the **roots of Western thought**, some of which will be useful in our investigation.[154]

We saw in 1.3 how the 'deep time' approach to the history of languages and cultures was pioneered by the archaeologist Colin Renfrew, geographer Jared Diamond and historian Daniel Smail, among others. Derrida had already taken this journey back 'beyond the Greeks', even beyond the **alphabetic writing systems** which have dominated the 'second half' of (at least Western) recorded history, to explore **older writing systems** such as the Sumerian, Egyptian and Chinese.[155] Derrida acknowledges their appearance in the Bronze Age as 'an extraordinary leap in the history of life' and seeks to use them as leverage for his project of escaping the assumptions of Western civilisation.[156]

He looked, in fact, beyond even this horizon, towards 'the Neolithic, to which in fact may be attributed the creation of **the deep structures** upon which we still live'.[157] Much as Lévi-Strauss had looked beyond the confines of Western civilisation to what he called 'savage' or 'primitive' people, inhabiting different versions of what he called '**the Neolithic complex**' in the present or the recent past,[158] Derrida transferred this argument to the remote past: to the formation of 'social, economic, technical, political, and other structures' achieved in Neolithic cultures in the absence of writing, and especially the first writing systems of the Bronze Age.[159] Like historians of 'deep time', he saw the invention of farming as the origin of permanent features of our culture such as **hierarchies** of status and power, intensified by writing.[160]

Although he understood himself as responding to Lévi-Strauss's anthropology, Derrida also saw himself as working in the tradition of **phenomenology**, again expanding its range from individual experience to group or social experience. Like Heidegger, Husserl and Hegel before him, Derrida gives credit to Kant as a source for his phenomenology and recognises its ultimate origin in Lambert.[161] He placed himself firmly in this tradition with a long intellectual apprenticeship to Husserl and his phenomenology, in early publications[162] and a fruitful dialogue with the thought of Heidegger.[163] Like Foucault and Bourdieu he builds consciously and critically on the anthropological work of Lévi-Strauss;[164] but he situates this more firmly in the long dialogue we have outlined within phenomenology, from its earliest origins in Lambert and Kant, through all its subsequent modifications.

Derrida proposed a science, philosophy or **theory of writing**, which he named **grammatology**.[165] He sought to *correct* what he saw as the neglect of writing, the outer 'clothing' of thought, in favour of speech, which Western philosophy had seen as a more direct expression of the soul. Aristotle and others had seen spoken language as the symbol of the mind and its thoughts; written language only as a symbol of the spoken language: as a symbol of a symbol, and thus only giving indirect access to the *psyche*.[166] Derrida sees the parallel with neglect of the **body** in favour of the **soul** in Western thought, a theme we will encounter many times: in Chapter 6 and Book Two (the Greeks) onwards.[167]

The simple point is that this assumption about ourselves and the world around us is shaped by our writing technology: Western philosophy and psychology are written in alphabetic, that is, **phonetic** (Greek: sound-based) languages, which are not the only option. Decipherment of **non-phonetic** scripts from Egypt, Iraq and elsewhere, as well as the Western encounter with Chinese, can liberate us from the limitations of working inside a closed circle of phonetic scripts, which he also calls **linear**: 'Writing in the narrow sense – and phonetic writing above all – is rooted in a past of **nonlinear** writing'.[168] He sees this as the link back to pre-literate myth in Lévi-Strauss, to the dream world of Stone Age societies.[169]

As with the study of historical linguistics (2.4) Derrida believes that making this distinction and looking outside the limitations of our phonetic written language has enormous implications for the way we think, including the basic categories and concepts of philosophy which are basic to Western psychology.[170] We will see in this book and in the next that 'the concept of the 'soul' … is tied up with the whole character and orientation of a language'.[171] Grammars and writing scripts affect psychology, because they create the categories for practising it.

Looking beyond these cultural limits, grammatology can be a general theory of writing encompassing all cultures, straddling the divides created by our scripts:

> Since individual markings reveal the particularities of the mind of those who write, the national markings should permit to a certain extent researches into **the particularities of the collective mind** of peoples.[172]

This theory, which Derrida also calls '**cultural graphology**' (Greek: the study of writing), connects writing to other areas of a culture such as mathematics, art, science, politics, economics, religion, technology and law; it can be 'renewed and fertilised by sociology, history, ethnography and psychoanalysis'.[173] As a theory it should include writing systems used before and alongside the invention of the alphabet: ancient Egyptian, Sumerian and Chinese.[174] Theory needs to catch up with the history of writing: this is another example of the Western mind 'de-centring', as Western people are exposed to new sources of data.[175]

2.7 Conclusion

In our survey of the spectrum of *psyche*, we have moved from a historical sequence of the 'extended past' – the major stages of human development, as introduced in Chapter 1 – to another historical sequence of the 'extended present', giving a survey of the development of modern academic psychology in its wider context. We have had to stray beyond the bounds of 'psychology' into other disciplines, but we have always found justification for this in the vision of the founders of psychology. In effect, we were seeking out the lost relatives and bringing them back together an act of **family reunion**, of **family reorientation**. We have located psychology in this extended family.

We have also moved up a spectrum of **complexity**, from lesser to greater. The different methods, vocabularies, categories and disciplines encountered in this survey (kinds of *logos*) were each matched to the multiple meanings of *psyche*. To return to Buddha's elephant parable, we have examined the answers given by psychologists (with apologies, our blind men) as they examined the same elephant from different angles. In the process we have found a range of methods used in contemporary psychology which can be useful in our investigation of ancient psychology.

Now consider your own training in the academic subculture. You are taught which **categories** and **methods** are acceptable for public use. Cognitive psychologist J. Scott Jordan refers to 'the **ontologies** at work in contemporary psychology'.[176] The philosophical word 'ontology' (Greek *ontos* = being, that which exists, and *logos* = studying, talking about, examining) is an alternative to 'metaphysics' (Greek *meta* = after, *physics* =study of things). Jordan therefore means **'What people believe exists'** in contemporary psychology, in other words, their range of answers to the question, **'What is the *psyche*?'** as the basic object of study.

We have deliberately loosened up and expanded the range of possible answers to that question through our tour of contemporary psychology and its histories in this chapter. This has equipped us for a journey well beyond the borders of our academic subculture, indeed beyond the borders of a much larger cultural unit which contains it: what we have called **Western culture**. Chapter 1 was an equivalent treatment of the writing of history, to loosen up our European or Western perspective on history, reflected in our many ways of describing it. In this chapter have engaged in a parallel 'deconstruction' of academic psychology (Deconstruction itself will be explained at 3.6).

We are almost ready to catch the flight on our global tour of the ancient world. Part One of this book is your orientation exercise before the flight. Now we are critically aware of 'the history of history' in the larger envelope of our Western culture, and the recent history of psychology in the smaller subculture of the Western universities, all we need is to examine the central concept of culture, before passing through the gate.

Discussion questions:

1 With what kinds of psychology do you usually feel most comfortable?
2 How does our genetics lead to our need for education and nurture?
3 Can you relate to the idea of cognitive extension, of tools as the mind?

4 Which parts of your spoken language are learned and which are innate?
5 Is there such a thing as human nature? Which parts of us do we choose?
6 Do you find it plausible that writing media can affect psychology?
7 Can you give a definition – in a single sentence – of what psychology is?

Recommended Reading

- Francis Bacon *The Advancement of Learning*
- Andy Clark *Supersizing the Mind: embodiment, action and cognitive extension*
- Antonio Damasio *Descartes' Error: Emotion, Reason and the Human Brain*
- Réné Descartes *Discourse on Method and the Meditations*
- Martin Farrell *Historical and Philosophical Foundations of Psychology*
- Thomas Kuhn *The Structure of Scientific Revolutions*
- John Lyons *Chomsky*
- Jonathan Smith (ed.) *Qualitative Psychology: a practical guide to research methods* (2nd edition)
- Thomas Leahey *A History of Psychology* (8th edition)

Notes

1 Smart p.2.
2 Van de Mieroop 2017 p.3.
3 Everson pp.1–12; Irwin pp.98–101,130–1.
4 Smart p.2.
5 Martin, Thomas R. p.3; see first note in the Introduction.
6 Brett p.5.
7 Cole p. xiii.
8 Farrell pp.216–8, 245–6, 269–271, 288–290, 314–16.
9 *ibid* pp. 233–41 (Freud), 263 (Wundt), 271–5 (Titchener), 286–94 (Brentano), 319–28 (James).
10 Leahey Ch.8 pp.219–53 narrates this in some detail.
11 Kuhn pp.11–22,163,178.
12 Bellwood pp.3,45,94,100,103,107,140,175; Renfrew 1987 pp.76–7,123,141, 158,216,234,238.
13 Henley and Rossano pp.27–37 for an excellent, clear and brief summary of the history from Darwin to today.
14 Farrell pp.287–94; Sajama and Kampinnen p.27ff.
15 Farrell p.288.
16 Leahey pp.239, 251,275; McCumber pp.128ff.; Smith (ed.) pp.26–80 for methods today; Solomon pp.129ff.
17 For example: accounts in Cooper Ch. 11 pp.171–89; Sternberg (ed.) Ch.1 pp.1–48, Ch.16 pp.445–72.
18 Cole p.7.
19 Cole pp.27–30.
20 Lévi-Strauss 1963 p.2: his point is that this is what 'sociology' often means in an English-speaking context.
21 Eriksen pp.22–3,25–9,39–41.
22 Cole pp.30–35; 98–109; Farrell pp.251,261–2; Leahey pp.227–35.
23 Hogg and Vaughan pp.4–5.
24 Eriksen pp.58–9,61,92,94,120; Grabbe p.4; Lévi-Strauss 1963 p.3.

25 Cole pp.1,35.
26 Childe 1954 pp.22–4,29–32; Eriksen p.26; Inglis pp.112,165; Marx pp.164,167,389–90; Simmel pp.5,19,28–9.
27 Lévi-Strauss 1978 p.7.
28 Plato *Phaedo* 96a-c p.83 in Cooper; references to the rest can be gathered throughout this book (see Index).
29 Bacon *Advancement* VII.6-IX.1 p.105; Kant *Critique* A xxi PP.104–5, B viii P.106, B 868–9 P.695–6; Heidegger *Letter on Humanism* 1978 pp.195–6,232; Locke *Essay* IV.XXI p.385.
30 Bellwood pp.3,45,94,100,103,107,140,175; Renfrew 1987 pp.76–7,123,141, 158,216,234,238.
31 McGilchrist 2021 pp.5–7,39,45,440–443,1043–7.
32 In Chapter 1 the full subspecies name *homo sapiens sapiens* was used; from here, we will abbreviate this.
33 Darvill p.151; Haywood p.15; Lewis-Williams and Pearce p.283.
34 Haywood pp.6,12–13, 19–20,26.
35 Sykes pp.18, 121–40; Oppenheimer pp. xiv,15,122,208,211–2,284f.,488–97.
36 Oppenheimer pp.112–13,183.
37 Lewis-Williams and Pearce p.6.
38 Lévi-Strauss 1978 p.11.
39 Lewis-Williams and Pearce p.40.
40 Lévi-Strauss 1978 p.7.
41 Damasio p.30.
42 *ibid* pp.xvii, 252.
43 Lewis-Williams and Pearce p.10.
44 Damasio p.124.
45 Henley and Rossano (ed.) pp.56–9; Palmer (ed.) pp.34–40,44–52.
46 *ibid* pp.56,58.
47 Harari p.11.
48 Childe 1981 pp.58,65; Henley and Rossano pp.105–8; Mead pp.25–44 (Ch.3); Renfrew and Zubrow pp.162–4.
49 Hung pp.44–83 (Ch.3); Kramer pp.229–48 (Chapter 6); Kriwaczek pp.187–95; Murray pp.105–9; Roux pp.331–2; Van de Mieroop pp.59–61,80; see also Childe 1954 pp.83–8 on the new guilds of metallurgists.
50 See Lewis pp.14–15 and the book of the same name by his friend Owen Barfield (Barfield Press, Oxford 2011).
51 Derrida 1967 p.49; Lambert to Kant 13.10.1770 pp.117 in Kant 1999.
52 Kant to Lambert 02.09.1770 pp.108 in Kant 1999.
53 Kuehn pp.xiii,196,201,231–2,234,241,254: the *Critique* was originally dedicated to Lambert for this reason.
54 Farrell pp.246–63.
55 Eriksen p.17; Farrell pp.246–63; Inglis p.5; Leahey p.171; Simmel pp.xxxvii,3–22.
56 Hegel 1977 #78 p.50.
57 *ibid* #808 p.492.
58 Hegel 1956 pp.xv-xvi,110,456–7.
59 Hegel 1977 #28–9 pp.16–17.
60 Aristotle *Topics* 104b,105a p.148.
61 Hegel 1977 #86 p.55.
62 Hegel 1977 #2 p.2; #53 p.32; #73–89 pp.46–57.
63 Popper pp.315,335 in a larger essay entitled 'What is dialectic?' pp.312–35.
64 Kant 1998 B500 p.501, B881–5 p.702–4 (two traditions).
65 McGilchrist 2009 p.205; *also see* pp.198, 203–7,230.
66 Taiwò p.9.

67 Hegel 1977 #69 p.43.
68 Marx p.98; Popper pp.331–5 and Sartre CDR pp.29–34 on the weakness of Marx's scientific basis.
69 Cole pp.104–21.
70 Husserl 1980 p.49; McCumber pp.128–9.
71 Husserl 1970 pp.91–104,114–20; Husserl 1980 pp.27,116; Husserl 2012 pp.31,120; McCumber p.130.
72 Heidegger *Being and Time* Intr. II.5 p.37; I.1.9 p.71; Smith (ed.) pp.27–8,53–4.
73 Heidegger *Being and Time* Intro I #3 p.31, Intro II #6 pp.45–6, I.3 #20 p.134, I.6 #43 p.247, II.3 #64 pp.366–8.
74 McGilchrist 2009 pp.149–58 (Heidegger) and pp.203–7 (Hegel).
75 Heidegger *Being and Time* I.1.10 p.76.
76 *ibid* I.3.15 p.99.
77 Childe 1954 p.15.
78 Heidegger *Being and Time* I.3.16 p.102.
79 Childe 1954 p.13.
80 Heidegger *Being and Time* I.3.68–70 pp.97–99.
81 Darvill pp.16,29; Lewis-Williams and Pearce p.171; Renfrew 1976 pp.277–9; Renfrew and Zubrow pp.3–5,10–11, 18,22.
82 Henley and Rossano pp.xii–xiv.
83 Renfrew and Zubrow p.5.
84 Mithen 1994 pp.29,31,35,116.
85 Roth pp.338–340; Sternberg (ed.) pp.64–5,450,459,462,467–9.
86 Mithen 1996 pp.61,65–72,151–4.
87 *ibid* pp.178–184,195,217.
88 *ibid* pp.154ff.,174ff.,192–5.
89 Childe 1954 p.18.
90 Heidegger *Being and Time* I.3.17 p.113.
91 Childe 1954 pp.21–22.
92 McGilchrist 2009 Ch.4 pp.93–132 is a primer, although these disciplines are not mentioned by name.
93 McVeigh p.29 n.11.
94 Childe 1954 pp.26–7.
95 Diamond p.91; Eriksen pp.27,35.
96 Bellwood pp.88–9; Muksawa pp.31–5.
97 Childe 1954 p.73; Childe 1981 pp.70–1.
98 Renfrew 1987 pp.124–31,145–52,269–73,281–9.
99 Bellwood pp.79–84,92–4,161; Renfrew 1987 pp.124–31,145–52,269–73,281–9.
100 Clarke p.xix; Diop p.128; Renfrew 1973 p.68; Renfrew 1987 pp.146–9.
101 Smail p.57.
102 Chomsky pp.106–8,175; Magee 1997 p.92.
103 Magee 1982 pp.175,191; Magee 1997 pp.197,202.
104 Henley and Rossano pp.31–2,37–8.
105 Chomsky pp.43–53,98; Lyons pp.83,86,96; Magee 1982 175—9,184–7.
106 Lyons pp.11,15,42–6,99–101,105–6; Magee 1997 pp.339–341; Mitchell and Myles pp.2,9–10,32–3,52–7.
107 Mitchell and Myles p.70.
108 Chomsky pp.50–1,99.
109 *ibid* p.77.
110 Heidegger *Being and Time* I.1.10 p.76 from 2.5 above.
111 Solomon p.178ff.
112 Heidegger 1978 pp.191,204,208; Solomon pp.172ff.
113 Sartre 1960 p.18.

114 *ibid* pp.29–34.
115 Sartre 1996 p.26ff; Solomon p.178ff.
116 Eriksen pp126,130–5; Hawkes pp.32–58.
117 Solomon pp.194–7.
118 *ibid* plus Lévi-Strauss 1963 pp.20–21,31–34,209.
119 Lévi-Strauss 1963 pp.1–2,16–17.
120 *ibid* p.2.
121 *ibid* p.209.
122 Eriksen p.132.
123 Chomsky pp. 97–8,156; Lyons pp.29,34,37,79–81.
124 *ibid* pp.33–4.
125 Hawkes pp.20–21.
126 Lévi-Strauss 1963 p.31,1978 pp.7–8.
127 Lévi-Strauss 1978 pp.4,6,15.
128 Eriksen pp.22,27–9,45,96,207–8.
129 Hawkes p.18.
130 Eriksen pp.205–9; Lévi-Strauss 1978 p.5; Smail p.30; see McGilchrist 2009 Part 1 for a recent summary.
131 Lewis-Williams and Pearce pp.150–2; Renfrew and Zubrow p.3; Whitley pp.6,22,49.
132 Lévi-Strauss 1963 p.230.
133 Lévi-Strauss 1963 p.103; Renfrew 1976 pp.273–7.
134 Lévi-Strauss 1978 pp.14–15; Lewis-Williams and Pearce pp.8–12.
135 Lévi-Strauss 1963 p.23–4.
136 *ibid* p.21.
137 Lévi-Strauss 1963 pp.16,25,101; 1978 pp.11–14.
138 Heidegger 1929 pp.180–1,186.
139 *ibid* pp.181–5,187–190.
140 Lévi-Strauss 1978 p.47.
141 *ibid* pp.6,34,40.
142 Peters p.111.
143 Lewis-Williams and Pearce pp.151,157; Van de Mieroop 2017 pp.124–5.
144 Lévi-Strauss 1963 p.161.
145 Hawkes p.33; Inglis p.109; Lewis-Williams and Pearce pp.18–19,37–9.
146 Hawkes p.54.
147 Solomon p.153.
148 Eriksen p.133,174.
149 Smail pp.59–63.
150 *ibid* pp.46–56.
151 Eriksen p.133,159,174; Fowler p.2.
152 Eriksen p.168; Fowler pp.1,3,13–22,31,175.
153 Powell pp.9–13, 16–19,37,41 (Derrida's origins); pp.99–102,121f–7,150 (USA).
154 Eriksen pp.174–9.
155 Derrida 1967 pp.74–31–87–93; Hung pp.vii,2–8,19,23,144; Van de Mieroop 2016 pp.78,235 n.61.
156 *ibid* p.131.
157 Derrida 1967 p.129.
158 Lévi-Strauss 1963 p.116.
159 Derrida 1967 p.129.
160 *ibid* pp.130–1.
161 Derrida 1967 p.49 (Lambert); Derrida 2001 pp.49–50,147–9,168,171,175; Powell pp. pp.9,21,225 (Kant).
162 Derrida 1967 pp.40,48–50,64n.,121 n.,290–1; Powell pp.25–7,42–6,49–54,74,77.

163 Derrida 1967 pp.10,19–24,21,72; Powell pp.6–8,20,30,33,62,128,134–40,162–8,196,205,216–17.
164 Derrida 1967 pp.101–40 (the whole of Part 2 Ch.1); Powell pp.61,65–7,71.
165 Derrida 1967 pp.74–5,83,93.
166 *ibid* pp.11,29.
167 *ibid* pp.34–5.
168 *ibid* p.85.
169 *ibid* pp.68,87.
170 Derrida 1967 pp.3–4,25,32–3,52,76–87,90,314; Hung pp.vii,xvi,2–3,89–94;Van de Mieroop 2017 pp.77–80.
171 Snell p.15: a major source in Book Two.
172 *ibid* p.87.
173 *ibid* pp.87–8,92.
174 *ibid* pp. 3,25,30,33,74–93 (Part 1 Ch.3).
175 *ibid* pp.79,83–4.
176 Henley and Rossano p.44.

3 Culture

3.1 Applying the second psychology

We now need specific tools for this investigation: a global history of *psyche* and *logos*, tracing their separate developments before the Greeks. The tools found in Chapter 1 were generic to any **global history**; and the tools in Chapter 2 were specific to **psychology**, clarifying what we are looking for in the past. In this chapter we complete our framework by turning to the specific units of this book, which are separate ancient cultures examined in Part 2: Chapters 4–8.

Throughout the last chapter, we met Wilhelm Wundt's pioneering vision for a psychology in two parts, working – as he insisted – at two independent levels:

- **Experimental psychology**, working close to the natural sciences in both its object (*psyche*) and its methods (*logos*), studying 'cognition' among other things; today's **cognitive psychology**[1] and **psycholinguistics**.[2]
- **Cultural psychology**, with distinct objects and methods, working further from the model of the natural sciences and closer to the Humanities:[3] this has impacted **sociology**, **anthropology** and **educational psychology**.[4]

Wundt recognised that a history of psychology can be a work of psychology, in the second sense: 'the development of the mental objectifications [theories] of psychical activity during the course of history'.[5] Data from the historical record can interact with contemporary psychological theory, as they will in this series.

The argument of Chapter 2, however, was intended to demonstrate that we can and should use tools from all levels of the discipline, including those closer to the natural sciences: in other words, use results of experimental psychology. Wundt's two-fold division of the subject approximates our proposed spectrum.

Wundt's death coincided with the publication of the first history of psychology in English (1.10),[6] including coverage of 'Primitive Thought' and 'Eastern Writings'. The latter included Persia, Egypt, Israel and India.[7] A glance through this book or its Contents will show you that it will cover very similar ground:

DOI: 10.4324/9781003396147-5

• Primitive Thought	>	4. The global Neolithic
• Persian Beliefs	>	5. Ancient Iraq (before it became Persia)
• Egyptian Beliefs	>	6. Ancient Egypt
• The Hebrew Tradition	>	7. Ancient Israel
• Indian Writings	>	See Book Two

One key difference will be that we cover these in much **greater detail**, because each area of study has seen a century of growth since then, and because the extension of our historical awareness has deepened significantly, as seen in Chapter 1. We have also **added China** to Brett's original list, and postponed India. Most importantly, this book is only the introduction to a much longer story of each culture. Each regional narrative will continue as a global background for comparisons to European developments, **throughout the series**.

In this book, we are dealing with **people** in the largest unit possible, at the level of nations, cultures and civilisations. These large units need particular methods.

Wundt's 'second psychology' shows that these are not entirely remote from the methods of psychology, but they are loaded at one end of our **spectrum**: we are analysing *psyche* in languages, cultures, societies, belief systems and practices.

Each chapter has a similar (though not quite identical) structure in its sections:

1 Orientation to place each culture firmly in the stream of history
2 Portrait to capture the particular individuality of each culture
3 Analysis to extract *psyche* and *logos* content to take forward
4 Reviews to compare that content with two chosen theories
5 Questions to stimulate engagement with the chapter content

Our careful study in the last chapter has given us a framework for the Analysis of their psychological content, as Chapter 1 equipped us with the Orientations.

In this chapter we will add methods to capture the 'mind' (that is, the **culture**) of each civilisation in a Portrait. In order to practice the scientific method, we will need at least two **theories** which cover as much of our spectrum as possible so that we have rival models in dialogue, to compare with the evidence and with one another. We also need to consider the relationships between the levels of **society**, from the smallest unit (the individual) to the largest units; the relations of society to culture; their **development** over time; and our role as participants.

We will end the chapter with a presentation of two relevant and related **theories** which connect all the levels of *psyche* outlined in Chapter 2.

3.2 Patterns of culture

Much of contemporary social psychology converges on the concept of culture.[8] The simplest of characterisations is to consider it as **the plural form of *psyche***.

In her classic study *Patterns of Culture*, the anthropologist Ruth Benedict wrote:

> The life-history of the individual is first and foremost an accommodation to the patterns and standards handed down in his community ... By the time he can talk, he is the little creature of his culture, and by the time he is grown and able to take part in its activities, its habits are his habits, its beliefs his beliefs, its impossibilities his impossibilities.[9]

The word 'culture' originally meant '**growth**' (for example in *agriculture*, Latin = growing fields, and *cultivation*) and our culture is where each of us grows. The German *Kindergarten*, 'garden of childhood', captures the same idea; and 'education' is from the Latin *educare* = **draw out** or lead out, from an undeveloped state.[10] A close relationship with individual growth is built into the language of 'culture'.

Benedict's two stages mark an important distinction – between reception and participation, absorbing and contributing, in passive and active modes, young to mature, child to adult – which is very clear in most of the societies studied by anthropologists, with 'rites of passage' marking the artificial border between these modes, with each culture choosing a point to define every youth's entry into adulthood.

Consider your own upbringing: you learnt to speak by hearing and imitating a spoken language – or perhaps more than one – from parents and 'alloparents' (other primary caregivers). You learnt a range of *feelings* and *habits* before you learnt to speak: cultural and educational psychologists, who like to speak Latin, call this *affective* development (Latin *afficere* = to cause to feel, as 'passive' is from *patior* = to receive) and *conative* development (Latin *conatio* = purposeful behaviour, attempt) – both usually coming ahead of *cognitive* development (see 2.2).[11]

In other words, our culture teaches characteristic **habits**, **feelings** and **beliefs** in a seamless **package** that we absorb without conscious control or awareness. In each of these areas, we absorb **norms**: a range of **normal** (or 'normative') ways of behaving, experiencing and thinking, and a parallel sense of the **abnormal**.[12]

If we as individuals are **shaped** by a wider culture through our upbringing and different forms of education, from adulthood we become **shapers** of culture. A key question for anyone moving between cultures is why they have turned out one way rather than another, and how each developed its particular character.

Let us briefly look at one example.

Learning styles are routinely discussed in modern classrooms, especially child-centred environments such as primary schools and elementary schools: a child is labelled a 'visual learner', an 'aural learner' (by ear), a 'kinaesthetic learner' (learning through movement) and even taught to recognise their own learning preferences.[13]

One startling feature of the two oldest civilisations is that each one appears to display a contrasting sensory bias, which appears upon comparison. Sumerian culture, for all its pageantry, displays a discernible public emphasis on hearing and **the ear** – in what little they had of a 'psychology' – reflected in a variety of ways, as we shall see in Chapter 5. With ancient Egypt, it is obvious that **the eye** dominates (6.2). With all due caveats about what we do not know, all the evidence points this way.

How could this happen? Can we devise an explanation of **national character**?

From dealing with smaller human institutions, we know that the founders and those 'there at the start' have the most leverage. Neolithic peoples reverence their ancestors; kingdoms appeal to great past kings and lawgivers; empires to conquerors. At group level in 1.3 and 2.4, we saw the **language-farming** theory: that on each continent, those tribes who first discovered the production of food had spread their language – and presumably with it some of their culture – across huge regions, absorbing or replacing many of the others, then diversifying over the millennia, to yield the present global distribution of 'language families'.[14] If a single tribe can gain that much **cultural leverage**, simply by coming first, then this encourages us to consider other forms of leverage in the ancient world.

In modern states, with their infinitely greater complexity, the idea of a collective personality seems a highly artificial construct – and this is a matter of the actual data, not our modern reluctance to think in images and symbols. But the ancient states are much closer to tribal units, to which assigning **collective personality** seems more plausible. We should beware of comparing ancient and modern at the level of states; only at tribal levels does some comparison seem justified.

But how do languages come to diverge? Expanding on Chomsky's metaphor for the development of a natural **language** (2.4), it is 'a fixed network connected to a switch box … When the switches are set one way, we have Swahili; when they are set another way, we have Japanese. Each possible human language is identified as **a particular setting of the switches** – a setting of parameters … small changes in switch settings can lead to great apparent variety in output, as the effects proliferate throughout the system'.[15] Early choices have **cumulative effects** over the large scale of the millennia involved, with divergent outcomes.

Ruth Benedict makes the same point: from the infinite variety of possibilities '… each language must make its selection and abide by it, on pain of not being intelligible'. She then compares this to culture, to the choices of **customs** and institutions within the universal constraints of our inherited ancestry, or local constraints of environment: 'Without **selection** no culture could even achieve intelligibility, and the intentions it selects and makes its own are a much more important matter than any particular detail'.[16] The collective characteristics of a culture are the result of a mass of formative decisions in the past: 'a culture, like an individual, is a more or less consistent **pattern of thought and action**', more or less integrated, more or less successful;

and therefore we can study 'cultures as **articulated wholes**', as psychologists can study individual **personalities**.[17] Here is a provisional explanation of how ancient cultures could evolve distinct, identifiable 'personalities'.

This is a general version of what Derrida has called 'cultural graphology' (2.6): that 'the national markings should permit to a certain extent researches into the particularities of **the collective mind** of peoples'.[18] National character was a major theme in Wundt's second psychology and it is a persistent theme within anthropology. Benedict and her colleague Margaret Mead pioneered the study of collective **habits**, **feelings** and **beliefs**, and their associated norms, including differences in how these work at national levels.[19] Pierre Bourdieu picked up their study of these things as expressed in body language, calling it *habitus*.[20]

We now have at least **two levels interacting**. Culture as humanity on the large scale forms the habits, feelings and beliefs of individuals – that is, humanity on the small scale – through institutions, education and parenting. We also have a more limited contribution in the other direction: of individuals forming culture.

If we add a **third** or **intermediate level** of units such as tribes and **teams**, with their own simpler collective personalities, then we have a more realistic model of interaction. If the language families of the world could result from individual tribal discoveries and successes, then nations can be formed by the personalities of particular tribes. We will see something like this at work in the Neolithic, in Iraq, Israel, China, and perhaps most clearly in the case of Egypt (see 6.2–6.4).

We are now beginning to work at our '**target level**': at what Benedict called 'a bird's-eye view of human cultural forms'.[21] The Assyriologist Samuel Kramer called it approaching culture 'from the psychological point of view, that is, from a consideration of the character and **personality of the people** who created it'.[22] Egyptologist Margaret Murray called it 'understanding **the soul of a people**'.[23]

We are at the far end of our spectrum, and the largest social unit: civilisations. We are developing tools to sketch a portrait of each culture.

3.3 Worldviews

Although it involves habits and feelings, psychology primarily concerns beliefs: it is primarily **cognitive** in that we are evaluating theories and judging rational propositions, although they may be theories and propositions *about* habits and feelings as well as *about* beliefs. A wealth of reflection on collective beliefs has focussed on '**systems of meanings**', 'the life-world'. 'Models of the Universe', 'cognitive maps', and similar terms intended to capture community beliefs.[24]

As we only tend to notice our culture when we encounter another, we tend to become aware that our beliefs are simply *beliefs* and not certainties when they change. One relatively recent change in the 'cognitive map' of Western culture is the discovery of '**deep time**', a stretching of our historical timeline (1.3); but before that came the discovery of '**deep space**': that our planet moves around the sun, the sun belongs to a galaxy, and soon. The two astronomers, Lambert and Kant, whose conversation gave birth to phenomenology (2.3) wondered at this 'world-edifice', 'the starry heavens' and 'the Milky Way'.[25] Kant went on to coin a new German word for our ability to conceive an enormous universe all at once: *Weltanshauung*, **world-view**. Like his 'phenomenology' it has become tremendously popular in a broad range of disciplines, including psychology.[26]

In Part 2 we will use this term freely to capture the dominant outlook in each culture, normally set by 'those who got there at the start' (3.2). In Iraq it is the Sumerians who set the worldview so we will talk of 'the **Sumerian** worldview' and 'the Sumerian mind'; in Israel, we can focus on 'the **Hebrew** worldview'. There is even an identifiable 'Neolithic worldview'. Egypt had its worldview set in the Old Kingdom so successfully that we call it 'the **Egyptian** worldview'; and the point applies especially well to China, where the Zhou kingdom used a selection of sacred texts and a writing monopoly to establish a **consensus** (8.2).

Like the more general analysis of social *ethos* in Benedict, Mead and Bourdieu, a current analysis of worldview breaks it into **four components** which embody and underpin group beliefs: group **stories**, such as national founding myths and creation myths; the rituals and **practices** that, like *habitus*, embed beliefs; group **symbols** (totems, buildings, scripts) often created by ritual practice; and finally, a catechism of **questions** and **answers**, directly interrogating shared community assumptions. Together these form education, indoctrination and propaganda, as the various instruments of **collective identity** or shared **group consciousness**.[27] Worldviews can be extracted and reconstructed from the remaining evidence, but can also be deliberately built: designed and constructed within a society to provide it with coherence and continuity.

3.4 Correspondences

At this point, we must introduce another principle that will serve as a vital tool throughout our project. In contemporary Western society, **individualism** is the key concept in the dominant political and economic framework (**liberalism**), as '**the self**' (understood individually) is the concept around which much of social psychology rotates.[28] Modern liberalism assumes 'the **atomistic** principle': that each individual in society is a separate self-governing unit, like an atom.[29]

In the ancient world – from what survives – there is far less sense of **individual** identity, and a much more vivid sense of identification with a larger social unit. Most importantly, the ancients assumed a fundamental principle of **analogy** or **correspondence** between individual and **collective**: essential in understanding Neolithic societies and social psychologies onwards, through the Bronze Age.[30] It is pervasive in Neolithic cultures (4.4 to 4.6) and we will meet it repeatedly, for example, in Hebrew architecture (7.6), Sumerian legends (5.7), Egyptian ideology (6.4, 6.7) and Chinese philosophy (8.6). It is one of the basic principles of ancient culture.

A helpful source to grasp this principle is one of our key authors for Book Two: the Greek philosopher Plato. The argument of his *Republic* is based on the neat correspondence between individual's *psyche* and the *polis*, the Greek city-state. One is the **microcosm**, the other its corresponding **macrocosm** (Greek: *micro* = small, *macro* = big, *cosm* for cosmos; 'small world' and 'big world').[31] Plato's further assumption is that 'there are the same three elements in the *psyche* of the individual as there are in the *polis*'.[32] Socrates – as the leader of the dialogue – suggests that they '**read the larger letters first** and then compare them with the smaller': that is, that the group will enquire first 'on a larger scale in the larger entity … **then proceed** to the individual'.[33] It is assumed that both levels, both scales will be subject to the same basic rules and written in the same language.[34]

We will follow Plato's procedure when examining **the Neolithic** *psyche* in the next chapter: starting at the social level, where the patterns are clearer, then trying to identify the same patterns at an individual level, assuming this correspondence.

Beyond the analogy of self and society, the ancients (and not only the ancients) sometimes pursued a further analogy: the individual to the whole **human race**. The most obvious connection was **origin**: the Sumerians believed that humanity (*namlulu*) is all descended from the survivors of a catastrophic Flood (5.2, 5.4) who in some sense 'contained' all of their descendants; for Hebrews and Arabs *ha-adam* (the earthy one, known to European tradition as 'Adam') and *hawwa* (the living one, the source of life, who became 'Eve') were a historical couple at the dawn of history; as were Noah and his wife after the global Flood (7.3, 7.4).

This idea, which often seems so alien and strange to modern ears, has actually played an important role in the development of the evolutionary and historical sciences when transformed from static correspondence of *psyche* and humanity to a **dynamic correspondence**, displaying two parallel paths of **development**.[35] In the language of many biologists: **ontogeny** (from Greek *ontos* = individual being, *genesis* = beginning) corresponds with **phylogeny** (from Greek *phylus* = kind, species), or the individual development of each human body and *psyche* echoes the overall evolution of *homo sapiens*; in biological terms, and also in our psychological development.[36] We saw that Hegel considered his education a model for humanity as a whole (1.8); this is the same idea, accepted in the modern natural sciences.

A key difference between ancient peoples and our own perspective, therefore, is not the sense of analogy or correspondence, which we share in different ways, but a **static** versus a **dynamic** view of that correspondence. The static version of the principle appears repeatedly in the 'extended past' of Part 2; but closer to home in the 'extended present' of modern history and its sciences, the dynamic version appears.

Just in any static model of correspondence, we have **intervening levels** between the individual and the whole of humanity, as we saw in 3.2 with the intervening levels between individuals and whole civilisations, so in the dynamic model, we need not accept stark opposition between *individual* psychological development and that of the *whole species*, as studied by today's evolutionary psychologists. This leaves us with an enormous time contrast between a few decades and many millennia, a chasm which seems impossible for us to bridge.

Cultural psychologists have argued that 'Psychology needs to acknowledge a **third type** of time, a **mid-range** temporality, measured in centuries – or even several millennia'.[37] If we now have a growth of evolutionary psychology in Western universities, studying our 'phylogeny' and relating this to behaviour, (they argue) then we also need an intervening level of **cultural psychology**.[38]

This is, of course, exactly how **Wundt** saw the matter; it was in practice what William James and Sigmund Freud engaged in, at the birth of our psychology. They were all enthusiastic evolutionists, yet sought to add a study of culture, seeing the parallel between the education of an individual and that of the species, which – as noted at the outset in 3.2 – is implied by the vocabulary of culture.[39]

Finally, beyond even global society, there is the correspondence of self to **cosmos**: and this is extremely common in ancient thought. Again, Plato offers us a model in his dialogue *Timaeus*: the origin of '**macrocosm**' and '**microcosm**'. Here the human being corresponds to the whole cosmos, in a myth of creation which has had a deep impact on the formation of European civilisation.[40] Yet we will find it already a fundamental theme in the Neolithic worldview (4.3, 4.4) as well as in the later Hebrew worldview (7.6); and it will reappear throughout the series.

Rather than *psyche* and *polis*, or individual and community, this correspondence is of *psyche* and *cosmos*: somehow each of us, or more usually the experience of a single special individual, becomes – for a time – a mirror of the entire universe. This also can be understood by modern psychologists in terms of development, as a regression (Latin: going backwards) back to an early state of consciousness in babies in which self and world, *psyche* and *cosmos* are not yet fully distinct.[41]

3.5 Dialectic

We have now the tools to construct a meaningful 'portrait' for each chapter, to describe the content of the cultures and worldviews in Part 2. We will soon move to introducing our two main theories which we can test against this data.

The traditional discipline in which theories are proposed and tested is named '**dialectic**', from Greek *dialectikē* = argumentative use of language.[42] Theories in the **natural sciences** are not produced by this but it can provide a forum for criticism and debate.[43] These depend on the production of theories by other means: experiment and fieldwork are two examples. In the **human sciences,** however, some claim that it is more fruitful: 'We cannot discover the nature of man in the same way that we can detect the nature of physical things … Only by way of dialectical or dialectic thought can we approach the knowledge of human nature'.[44] This is why Plato chose the **dialogue** form, to further the project of his master Socrates, the 'first moral philosopher' in Greece, who had moved from natural sciences to human.[45] Heidegger presented his phenomenology as a **spiral form** of enquiry, circling towards the mystery of who we are.[46] The history of phenomenology from Lambert and Kant to Lévi-Strauss and Derrida seems to confirm the point that theory develops through the **cycles of debate**.

For much of the history of Western civilisation, a key source of theories has been transmission, especially from ancient Greece: when the huge collection of **Aristotle**'s theories came through Arab sources in the twelfth and thirteenth centuries, this gave the dialecticians plenty to discuss in the new universities.[47] Aristotle – who will become a major figure in Book Two – was an extraordinary scientist and producer of theories; his lectures provided what Bourdieu calls 'cultural capital',[48] but like any capital, it would run out without investment. About four centuries ago European universities began to run out of ideas.[49] It took outsiders, amateur scholars following Aristotle's example and producing **new theories** in dialogue with his own, to refresh Europe's cultural capital.[50]

Immanuel Kant has already appeared at the opening of phenomenology (2.3) as well as informing Chomsky's linguistics (2.4), much of anthropology (2.5) and Derrida's grammatology (2.6) plus inventing the concept of worldview (3.3); in fact, he was also a key figure in the move to dynamic, **evolutionary** thinking (3.4) and in both of these last his involvement in astronomy was decisive.[51] His **dialectic** is his last contribution to our framework. In his most famous work, he appraised two opposing theories – in psychological terms, nature and nurture – in a traditional dialectical fashion as **thesis** (Greek: proposal) and **antithesis** (counter-proposal), before seeking to find a middle ground: a new **synthesis**, allowing for what was true on each side, much like reaching a peace treaty.[52]

What was less traditional, however, was that Kant presented the two theories as historical traditions, so that his dialectic was a **movement through history**.[53] In an influential chapter he sums up his dialectical work as a historical invention.[54] As with the correspondence above, a static principle inherited from the Greeks was converted by modern Europeans into a dynamic principle for describing development in history.

In 2.3 we saw how Hegel turned this idea into a psychological history,[55] and in 1.8 how he projected this history outward onto the canvas of world history.[56] A tool for appraising theories had now become a description of the dynamics of **historical development**: an early appearance of the dynamic correspondence in 3.4, now assumed and explored in evolutionary psychology and (differently) in cultural psychology. But this is now *also* a theory, needing its own appraisal.

Our two theories below (3.8 and 3.9) – but especially the latter – will propose a pattern to cultural history involving the alternation and **dialectical interaction** between two poles: and these poles will stem from the two sides of the brain. They also assume interaction between the microcosm of the brain's functions and the macrocosm of the cultural structures built up from their interactions.

3.6 Deconstruction

We have not left culture behind: both theories we will introduce in 3.8 and 3.9 belong to cultural psychology as a discipline. We need briefly to consider the academic subculture of Western culture as the main forum for discussing and testing (if not producing) theories.

Considering Western culture as a whole, its academic subculture, or any culture, including those described in Part 2 (or modern psychology in Chapter 2), we must be alert to the ways in which cultures can make themselves **exclusive**.

Aside from the comments above (3.4) about a sense of larger humanity among some ancient cultures, the norm for every ancient people was **ethnocentrism**: a tendency for each *ethnos* (tribe, community, nation) as a unit to be at the centre of its own world, understanding itself as uniquely good, virtuous or privileged. In most ancient languages the word for 'humans' is the word for tribe or nation because 'Outside of the closed group there are no human beings', as Benedict summarises it neatly: 'the old distinction of the in-group and the out-group'.[57]

We can consider it in terms of the levels of social existence outlined in 3.4: the range of identities, from myself as an individual to ever-greater circles of 'we', from family and clan to tribe, nation and culture. Rather than units of identity in terms of self-perception, now we are considering them as units of social loyalty.

Each of us learns in infancy that we are not, in fact, at the centre of our family, but others also have rights, feelings and perceptions of their own' in childhood, we learn that our family is not the centre of our community; perhaps, as adults, that our community is only one among others incorporated into a wider culture. This is often where the learning process stops: *ethnos* becomes ethnocentrism.

Essentially, **tribalism** and ethnocentrism were pervasive in the ancient world. Once writing was invented, a new class of specialised scribes was created as its guild.[58] The Bronze Age had accidentally invented a new way of being tribal.[59] Derrida has alerted us to the manifestation of ethnocentrism in language (2.6) which he refers to as **logocentrism**: confusing the categories from our written language (Greek *logos*) with universal features of reality. He suggests that this is an **elite form of tribalism**: 'the most original and powerful ethnocentrism'; which in the case of alphabetic languages, from Greek to English,means 'privileging the model of phonetic writing'.[60]

As argued through Chapter 1, such tribalism is the result of a long history of cultural dominance of the globe by '**European man**' – often with a mixture of ignorance and violence.[61] European tribalism is labelled '**Eurocentrism**'. We met it in Hegel and his influence (1.8, 1.9). It often takes those on the margins, such as Derrida – an African and a Jew – to identify what others have struggled to see. In the history of psychology, this surfaces in statements from – otherwise reasonable – authors such as 'the rise of thinking among the Greeks was nothing less than a revolution … They discovered the human mind … In Greece, and **only in Greece**, did theoretic thought emerge without outside influence'.[62] This author (Bruno Snell, *The Discovery of the Mind*) is a subtle and excellent guide to his material, and we will use his work in Book Two; but the circular nature of the claim he is making does not occur to him. Western thought, from its Greek roots, is *equated* with truly 'psychological' thinking, and so psychology, by this definition, was invented 'in Greece, and only in Greece': the evolution of Greek thought from its own, local 'primitive' condition is expanded to all of humanity.

In Brett's earlier *History of Psychology* similarly 'the birth of scientific thought' comes in Greece, and Greece alone, after millennia of 'primitive ideas about the soul'; the treatment of these primitive ideas is respectful but clinical, in the tone of dissecting a corpse on a table-top. The thoughts of 'the primitive mind' are 'gigantic, crude, and unrefined' and 'the animistic mode of thought dies with a greater struggle in psychology than elsewhere'; he contrasts this with 'the **scientific** pursuit of actual **facts**' and 'a spirit of **exact enquiry**'.[63] This author was open and liberal for his time, but that time was the height of colonial Eurocentrism. More than just the condescending tone, it is the **selection** and **arrangement** of material (outlined in 1.10, 3.1) which displays this ethnocentrism most clearly.

Apart from the privileging of European cultural sources, ethnocentrism appears in more specifically **modern** ways. Arguably, any conception of psychology which is entirely restricted to 'individual *psyche*' simply reflects 'the atomistic principle' which Hegel correctly identified as the emerging centre of **liberal** Western culture, and thus reflects unintentionally ethnocentric assumptions.[64]

For us today, expansion of the self to a **collective** consciousness is an everyday occurrence: for example, under the heading of 'identity politics'. My personal identity is then an **intersection** of multiple group identities, as in Marx's model (2.3) where *psyche* is entirely socially constructed. 'I' become only a particular combination of 'we'-identities, without remainder, in terms of performing social roles.[65] This is the 'self' constructed on social media. We can identify ourselves with our bodies, genetic inheritance, family or ancestry; but we **choose** the rest. The leading principle of Western culture is self-governance and self-direction.

This affects psychology because our easy assumption that *psyche* is something we all possess individually and in equal measure – whatever it is – is not shared by most ancient cultures (7.8). There is less emphasis on **choosing** who we are, although people did align themselves with tribes and adopt fictional ancestries.[66]

It also affects psychology because, as Snell suggests, 'the concept of 'soul' … is tied up with the whole character and orientation of the language'.[67] (2.6) We have picked the Greek *psyche* as the ancestor and root of the label 'psychology' but both are tied to phonetic, linear, alphabetic languages. If Snell is correct, it will translate differently into non-linear scripts including the first Bronze Age writing systems, cuneiform and hieroglyphics, and the one survivor of these non-linear early systems, Chinese.

First on Western history (Chapter 1) and then Western academic psychology (Chapter 2) we have engaged in **deconstruction**: that is, patient, subversive, relentless, potentially unlimited application of historical criticism.[68] The method of Lévi-Strauss, directed at contemporary Palaeolithic and Neolithic cultures, is intended to dissect their surface manifestations and locate underlying structures in a process sometimes called reverse engineering. Like most post-structuralists Derrida is turning this method on our own culture, analysing Western tradition. Without this discipline, our own ethnocentrism meets ancient ethnocentrsm 'head to head', and understanding is impeded.

The aim is only negative in attempting to unpick ethnocentrism. It is positive in opening us up to learn something new, and to be open to evidence as historians. In such criticism, Derrida suggests a **twin strategy** for maximum effect: digging down into our own **familiar terrain** (that is, our own culture) to uncover, and then examine, the hidden assumptions and motivations behind our concepts and language; then also 'brutally placing oneself outside' the familiar – leaping off our own terrain into **the unfamiliar**. That is a neat summary of the two parts of this book. In Part 1 we focus on ourselves in the (Western) extended present; in Part 2 we brutally place ourselves outside the familiar terrain of modern, Western culture using deep history. By combining the two strategies in a dialectical spiral, we approach the truth.[69]

3.7 Neurology and culture

We will finish this chapter with **two theories** especially relevant to our central question. Both theories have enthusiastic followers today, though one was first developed fifty years ago, the other less than fifteen – by an author still actively promoting and developing it today. After an initial presentation below, as explained in 3.1 we will **review** each one against the data gleaned within each chapter, in Part 2.

Our two theories have the advantage of working at **many levels** of *psyche*: they are founded in neuroscience and brain anatomy; they include phenomenology, linguistics, and the psychology of perception; and they make clear statements about the functioning of ancient societies, common patterns and differences in ancient cultures, and the long-term cultural development of the ancient world.

It has to be admitted that each is a competing 'psychology of history' and not a history of psychology. They are both in effect theories of **cultural psychology** (2.1, 2.3, 3.1, 3.4), although only the author of the first theory has explicitly owned that label.[70]

In testing them against the data we are practising part of **scientific method**, with the dialectical procedure of theory appraisal outlined above (3.5).[71] Through subjecting each to criticism and debate, we are learning transferable skills for psychology and any other science. At the same time, however, we will also be processing the historical data relevant to the history of psychology. We hope to generate a history of psychology thoroughly informed by psychological theory of both of the kinds envisaged by Wundt: experimental *and* cultural psychology. The two theories themselves have some basis in experimental psychology, by using the findings of neurology, but apply this in cultural psychology.

In terms of the experimental and scientific basis, a basic feature of our anatomy as a biological species is our **symmetry:** our bodies are divided into two equal halves, left and right, almost but not quite mirror images of each other. This division includes the two halves of the human brain, described in Latin terms as **bi-lateral** (two sides) or **bi-cameral** (two chambers); in Greek **bi-hemispheric** (Greek: two halves of a sphere). When we talk of brain **laterality**, we mean its two-sidedness. In its **lateralisation** an activity can be balanced or unbalanced, using both hemispheres or mainly one. Normal life requires their cooperation.[72]

The brain you are using to read this text is divided into a left and a right 'half'. Just as the eyes you are using to see it – or the ears you are using to hear it, or the hands you use to turn the page or scroll down the screen – give **split input** which your brain integrates into a single stream, so your brain also operates in two separate **hemispheres** (Greek: half spheres) in processing the information it receives, which it integrates into a single experience to determine the response.

These left and right hemispheres have different modes of operation: there is a **'division of labour'** built into thinking, perceiving, remembering and deciding – the cognitive processes of our brains. The hard part is to capture and describe this division of labour and interaction: what does each half, side, or chamber of the human brain do? How are their two roles – if different – integrated into a single mind? How can they come into conflict? Why did we evolve like this?

Those who investigate these questions are called **neuroscientists** (Latin: *neuro* = stringed tissue of nerves, *scientia* = knowledge by division or analysis). This discipline is under constant development, with contributions from **experimental** research in the laboratory, **clinical** findings from patients with abnormal brain functioning, and studies in normal humanexperience from **phenomenology** and the **cognitive sciences**.

Growth in this science since the Second World War peaked during the 1990s, 'the decade of the brain'[73]: today, psychological theorists can traverse the full spectrum of *psyche* from its biological base to its most complex functions, and can seek to re-integrate all these levels in different, rival attempts at **synthesis**. Many of the Recommended Reading texts for Chapter 2 as well as this one are attempts at such synthesis.

If we can understand the functioning of the brain in a normal individual, this is likely to tell us something important about our **shared** brain activities, in the form of **culture** and its development. The study of these, in turn, could tell us something important about our brain functioning. We can read 'nature' into 'history' and vice versa, acknowledging the complexity of this interaction.[74]

3.8 Theory One (T1): The bicameral mind

One major theory which answers these questions is that of **Julian Jaynes** in *The Origin of Consciousness in the Breakdown of the Bicameral Mind* (1976): well received at the time, and still a provocative read almost half a century later.[75] He was a student of George Sidney **Brett** (1.10), whom he admired; he was also a close friend of Edwin G. Boring, another pioneering historian of psychology.[76]

With a fresh awareness of the history of the discipline, Jaynes reacted against the narrow focus on experimental psychology – Wundt's 'first psychology' (3.1).[77] He came to believe that modern psychologists are 'guilty of aping the physical scientist in their frantic rush to construct a scientific discipline'; in rebellion he spent some years in the UK as a playwright and actor before starting a career in academia, eventually receiving a PhD from Yale and moving on to Princeton.[78] Researching between the laboratory, the library and his archaeological studies, he rediscovered Wundt's second psychology (3.1) and generated a new theory.

First presented to the American Psychological Association in 1969, this theory proposes an alternative to 'the genetic hypothesis': that our brain function is determined by our **genes** and has therefore been the same throughout human history.[79] Instead, Jaynes proposed that consciousness, the phenomenological surface of our brain's functioning, its user interface, is determined by **culture**.[80]

He identifies and describes a period in human cultural evolution in which our brains functioned differently: same hardware but different user interface.[81] From the Neolithic to the Iron Age 'human nature was **split in two**, an executive part called a god, and a follower part called a man. Neither part was conscious'.[82] This is the period of '**the bicameral mind**' before consciousness as we know it appeared. Today we see various examples of the '**vestiges**' of this period of past evolution in our religion, art, hypnosis and psychosis as 'cultural antiques', 'the ruins of an **archaic mentality**' – phenomena left over from the bicameral age.[83]

Jaynes does not deny that our genetic blueprint was fixed long before this but he points to genetically inbuilt potential for 'neural reorganisation of **hemispheric relations**' – the way that our right and left brain hemispheres interact.[84] The two halves of the brain have differences in function today: for example, the left brain perceives the parts but the 'right brain sees parts as having meaning only within a context; it looks at wholes'.[85] Both halves are involved in the production and reception of language but in slightly different ways.[86] On the whole, they work together so smoothly that we are unaware of the process, at least in their current configuration, as experienced by today's consciousness; but Jaynes argues, from rare 'split-brain' cases, that 'the two hemispheres under certain conditions are able to act almost as **independent persons** ... almost as two individuals ... Two persons in one head'.[87] He argues from research on flexibility and **plasticity** of brain function, that the two halves can be trained to operate more independently by education and culture.[88] (This is an important foundation for our next theory also: the 'two persons in one head' can be trained to function apart and then come into conflict.)

From these two points, Jaynes argues that during the long bicameral period a split occurred, so that the right hemisphere functioned as 'the **god-side** of the bicameral mind', issuing the instructions, while the left hemisphere functioned as 'the **man-side** of the bicameral mind', receiving instructions as though from an outside source.[89] We were following ourselves, believing we were following **the voice of another**; and unable to perceive their identity – what he means by 'Neither part was conscious'. Jaynes explains that 'The gods were in no sense 'figments of the imagination' of anyone. They *were* man's volition. [His will.] They occupied his nervous system ... and 'told' the man what to do'.[90]

Other thinkers, since, have argued that after biological evolution was complete, people began to create shared fictions as social identity.[91] Jaynes builds on this point but offers a specific mechanism: 'The bicameral mind is **a form of social control** which allowed mankind to move from small hunter-gatherer groups to large agricultural communities. The bicameral mind, with its **controlling gods**, was evolved as a final stage of the evolution of language'.[92] It served this role throughout the Neolithic period and the Bronze Age, allowing a stable growth of villages into towns and cities; having served its purpose, it was then outgrown.

It began with auditory hallucinations, which were organised into a hierarchy of authority: invisible ancestors and gods reflecting a visible human leadership:[93] 'The only possible way there could be a bicameral civilisation would that of a rigid hierarchy, with lesser men **hallucinating the voices of authorities** over them, and those authorities hallucinating yet higher ones, and so on to the kings and their peers hallucinating gods'.[94] It helps to create a **hierarchical society**.

Jaynes places his '**bicameral age**' against our timeline c.9000–1000 BCE, while human communities are growing in size, from the onset of the Neolithic to the end of the Bronze Age; but he does not tie it geographically to the sequence in Iraq, seeing it manifested alongside **parallel** Neolithic developments in Mexico and Peru, India and China. The great similarities between early civilisations can be explained, not by transmission, but by his theory: 'I suggest that given man, language, and cities organised on a bicameral basis, there are only certain fixed **patterns** into which history can fit'.[95] In each setting, the same social dynamics came into play: people evolved a bicameral mentality **to facilitate the growth**, with a religious elite controlling every aspect of the life of a passive population. The 'unsuspicious meekness' of the Incas, remarkable to the *conquistadores* of the sixteenth century, was an abrupt meeting with their own bicameral past.[96]

Although Jaynes sees the Bronze Age civilisations as the peak of the bicameral mentality, he also traces the beginnings of its collapse throughout the Bronze Age, in the gradual '**advent of consciousness**'.[97] The invention of writing itself early in this age weakened the hold of auditory hallucinations, and thus marked the end of '**the classical bicameral mind**'.[98] The continual growth of the cities made the bicameral form of social control increasingly precarious and fragile, so that **sudden and unpredictable political collapse** became a possibility.[99]

It was a condition of stable civilisations that they remained isolated, avoiding the possibility of **competing** voices of authority confusing the social contract; and so increasing encounters with other civilisations through trade, travel, natural disaster and migration could easily **erode their stability**.[100] The resort to new forms of social control, such as legal codes and militarism, not needed within classically bicameral theocracies, further undermined their delicate balance.[101]

In the chaotic world of the late second millennium and the early Iron Age, we can see a transition: 'nonconscious early man', 'the absolutely social individual of bicameral societies', had to undergo a painful 'change towards subjectivity', today's 'conscious stage of mind'; re-learning, over a millennium, how to make **personal decisions** in 'the initiative vacuum left by the **retreating gods**'.[102] The breakdown of the bicameral mind is therefore the origin of our consciousness.

This theory gives us a promising candidate for discussion throughout this book. It covers exactly the right **period**, as well as stretching into later volumes with its account of the 'change towards subjectivity' and then the remaining vestiges of the bicameral age lasting until today. It gives a clear basis in our **neurology**, and was ahead of its time in giving a role to the right hemisphere in language.[103]

It questions the transfer of (our) **phenomenology** to the ancient world, offering a competing account of ancient mental experience, undermining our assumption of 'the psychic unity of mankind' as a bridge across the centuries (2.3, 2.4, 2.5).

It offers an explanation of the transitions between historical stages – Neolithic, Bronze Age, Iron Age – and their internal **dynamics**, to test against alternative explanations.

It has also received some support from subsequent archaeology. The cognitive changes of the Upper Palaeolithic have been depicted as a rearrangement of our neural architecture: between cognitive domains, rather than whole hemispheres, but supporting Jaynes's opposition to a 'genetic hypothesis' of fixed structure at the level of use and experience, and his alternative hypothesis that culture can affect this level.[104] The Neolithic itself has been explained using such a model of neural rearrangement: a point to revisit in our first review of theory (4.7).[105]

3.9 Theory Two (T2): The divided brain

Our second theory is also based on the bilateral or bicameral brain, with its left and right hemispheres; it also connects the right brain and left brain functioning to long-term cultural history. Where Jaynes was a psychologist with an interest in the ancient world, Dr **Iain McGilchrist** – the author of our second theory – is a psychiatrist, a medical doctor who has specialised in mental illness. He has researched neuro-imaging (brain scans) for understanding psychiatric illnesses.

Like Julian Jaynes he is also a scholar of literature with very broad interests, so his own thinking is unusually **balanced**, a model of lateral development in both directions, left and right.[106] Before medicine, he studied English Literature and has published, lectured and researched in this field around his other career. We have seen how Kant's unusual **breadth of competence** inspired breakthroughs in phenomenology – Hegel, Husserl, Heidegger – and McGilchrist shares such a range, including this very tradition. He is a **polymath**, that is one with multiple expertise and claims that his theory has been brewing for over twenty years.[107]

In his bestseller *The Master and his Emissary: The Divided Brain and the Making of the Western World* (2009) McGilchrist explains – as the subtitle suggests – first the divided brain, then a history of our civilisation as a product of the interaction between the two hemispheres over the centuries. In his view the **right brain** is the **Master**, the left brain its natural **Emissary**, its servant; but the servant has a constant tendency to **usurp** the Master and to take his place:

> In reality we are a composite of the two hemispheres, and despite the interesting results of experiments designed artificially to separate their functioning, they work together most of the time at the everyday level. But that does not at all exclude that they may have radically **different agendas**, and over long periods and large numbers of individuals it becomes apparent that they each instantiate a way of being in the world that is at **conflict** with the other.[108]

McGilchrist devotes half his book to a thorough grounding in **the neuroscience** of brain laterality and its agreements with **phenomenology** before he turns to **history** and **culture**. In the terms explored above (2.1) he moves steadily up the spectrum of explanation from the biological, through the cognitive, up to the cultural – at each stage anchoring his argument, before moving on to the next.

He compares our consciousness to a tree, with roots below the division of the hemispheres in our basic animal functions, a sense of 'self' that is already one and does not need to be integrated.[109] Echoing Julian Jaynes's language of 'two persons in one head', McGilchrist suggests that although 'hemispheres are not people', nevertheless 'they share an office'.[110] As they work together to inhibit, restrain and build on the animal functions – food, sex and survival – from lower down in the structure of our brains, they also inhibit and **restrain one another**, and have a remarkable degree of inbuilt **independence** of one another.[111] They are not perfectly symmetrical as there is a slight twisting effect which leaves the right hemisphere longer, wider, heavier, and dominant at the front, but smaller at the back.[112] When compared with their function in other mammals, the right has a **global** view and wide focus, looking for wholes and thinking in **teams**; the left has a **local**, **narrow** view focusing on the parts, which among our Palaeolithic ancestors can easily be interpreted as better suited to catching **prey**.[113]

It is easy to see, from this initial sketch, how the two can work well together. Their independence of function, which has a strong neurological base, means that they can divide the mental labour in creative ways, and their cooperation holds the key to the success of our species: 'the two hemispheres, as two vast **coherent neurological systems**, each capable of sustaining consciousness on their own, do have different concerns, goals, and values'.[114] Their potential for conflict – as with actually separate personalities – is the **price** of their creative interaction and their independence of one another.[115] McGilchrist believes that both sides are written in large letters through **human history**, as we shall soon see.

A team usually needs a leader; and with its dominance of speech and its less subtle functioning, the left was seen for a long time as the **natural leader**.[116] More recent research has shown that this assumption was the result of the left-dominated attitude of **scientists** asking the questions, analysing the data and trying to build models and systems – working only at a **conscious** level.[117] In fact, on most measures, it has come to be recognised that the natural leader is the **right** hemisphere, **the Master**, and that the Emissary is dependent upon it: 'the conscious left hemisphere **thinks that it is in control**, directing its gaze where it wants, bringing the world into being … while the reality is that it is selecting from a broader world that has already been brought into being for it by the right hemisphere'.[118] Just as our conscious life rests upon the unconscious processes below both of them, the activity of the left rests upon the right.[119]

In our short tour of the spectrum of *psyche* and its associated levels of *logos* we moved from the natural sciences to a completely different kind of science, and McGilchrist does the same. As he puts it: 'We can inspect **the brain** only 'from the outside' … . But we can inspect **the mind** only 'from within''.[120] Our present phenomenology, our inner experience of our own consciousness, is shown to be deeply rooted in our genetic and biological inheritance: 'the world we actually experience, phenomenologically, at any point in time is determined by which hemisphere's version of the world ultimately comes to predominate' in that experience.[121] McGilchrist is just as comfortable in this realm of thought as he is in neurology and understands the tradition of **phenomenology** (2.3), narrating its development in some detail.[122] He has a particular respect for Hegel and Heidegger, noting their extraordinary intuitive insights into the interaction of the two hemispheres in our thought processes.[123] His central **metaphor** of the Master and Emissary is taken from Hegel, from Hegel's mentor Goethe, and from Nietzsche, who had a huge influence on Heidegger's thought.[124]

In keeping with its tilt and enlargement towards the front of the head, the right hemisphere is 'in direct contact with the embodied lived world'[125]; as he also says, 'Only the right hemisphere is **in touch with primary experience**, with life; and the left hemisphere can only be a staging post, a processing house, along the route – not the final destination'.[126] The right therefore leads in any **learning** process, through its earlier development in children and its continued role as the 'face' of the team, turned with **openness** towards fresh experience.[127]

The right hemisphere deals with **unique** things: names, places, faces, memories of specific events in the past: 'actually existing things, as they are encountered in the real world' as opposed to more familiar categories, kinds, types, labels, copies, models and skills:[128] 'the right hemisphere deals with the world before separation, division, analysis has transformed it into something else, before the left hemisphere has **re-presented** it'.[129] The world of the left hemisphere is easier to control and use because it is created by ourselves: selected, **extracted**, organised, virtual, static, boundaried, frozen, certain; ready for **public** use.[130]

This gives us a very helpful guide for discerning the psychological implications and sources of the multiple cultural products we will examine in this book. We are studying specific places and times, but everything we will study has already passed out of private experience into a **public** form; that is, already processed by the left hemisphere. As we noted in the first theories about the dominance of the hemispheres, our enquiry is already biased towards the left hemisphere's perspective, not least because it is preserved in a **book** using literal language:

> Language enables the left hemisphere to represent the world 'off-line', a conceptual version, distinct from the world of experience, and shielded from the immediate environment …**abstracted** from the body, no long dealing with what is concrete, specific, individual, unrepeatable, and constantly changing, but with a **disembodied** representation of the world, abstracted, central, not particularised in time and place, generally applicable, clear and fixed. Isolating things artificially from their context brings the advantage of enabling us to focus intently on a particular aspect of reality and how it can be **modelled**, so that it can be grasped and **controlled**.[131]

Although language in general, has this character as used by the left hemisphere, it is also true that specific **written languages** can display the influence of both. The development of the ancient languages – for example,

Sumer, Egypt, China, Greece, Arabia and Israel – into modern usage in Europe and Asia has shown a great variety of possible **configurations**, due to the effects of brain laterality.[132]

Just as Hegel mapped individual experience onto history in his *Phenomenology* using the same mechanism (overcoming contradiction), McGilchrist assumes that his portrait of the higher brain functions and their wrestling match in our individual experience can map onto communal experience, becoming *culture*. Hence his subtitle, *The Divided Brain and **the Making of the Western World**.*

Julian Jaynes proposed that an entirely different configuration of the two brain hemispheres occurred during his 'bicameral period' – between the onset of the Neolithic and that of the Iron Age – led by language and culture, learned by the successive generations, and ultimately led by an adaptive pressure to conform in order to survive as a species in large groups beyond the tribe.[133] McGilchrist also argues, with the advantage of more scientific data, that **culture and brain** are symbiotic: 'Our experience of the world helps to mould our brains, and our brains help to mould our experience of the world ... changes throughout the nervous system of an individual ... **transmitted** to the next generation, culture and the brain shaping one another over relatively short time spans'.[134] If brains are trees and hemispheres branches, he moves up to the level of a whole forest.

As his model would predict, he believes that all major leaps forward in cultural history, at least at their beginning, are the result of 'symmetrical, bihemispheric advance'[135] finding a new depth of **cooperation** between the twin hemispheres, pushing one another to new levels of functioning and corporate achievement. His two main examples are the flowering of Athenian culture in the sixth and fifth centuries BCE, and the Renaissance led by Florence in Western Europe in the fifteenth century CE. Neither of these fits on the timeline of this book but the obvious comparison within this volume is the arrival of the Bronze Age.[136]

Although such breakthroughs are characterised as **symmetrical**, bihemispheric advances, McGilchrist also believes that there is an **asymmetrical** tendency in the relationship of the hemispheres, and that this is clearer at the cultural than at the individual level, due to the **reinforcement** of cultural pressures on the basic biological system. (Recall Socrates suggesting in 3.4 that 'the larger letters' are easier to read)

In his long narrative he detects 'a succession of **shifts of balance** between the hemispheres over the last 2,000 years',[137] and overall 'the story of the Western world is one of increasing left-hemisphere **domination**'.[138] He perceives Hegel (and contemporaries such as Goethe, Coleridge and Hölderlin), then Nietzsche and Heidegger, all identifying this problem in their different ways: the last saw not only the historical dialogue but even some hope for a self-correction.[139] It is in the nature of the right hemisphere to self-balance, like **homeostasis** in living organisms – a **negative feedback** loop which adjusts back to equilibrium – but the left hemisphere, being less self-managing, can instead become trapped in a **positive feedback loop**, where every increase only leads to another increase, and the whole process spirals out of control

> '... we have entered a phase of cultural history in which negative feedback between the products of action and the two hemispheres has given way to positive feedback in favour of the left hemisphere. Despite the primacy of the right hemisphere, it is the left hemisphere that has all the cards'.[140]

This yields a number of points to guide our approach in this book and series.

McGilchrist's view of a long **dramatic dialogue**, played out through historical developments, a troubled marriage between the brain hemispheres, provides us with a '**psychology of history**', a promising model for cultural psychology.[141] It can be set against Jaynes's psychology of history, from bicameral to subjective. Both can inform a history of psychology such as this, designed to incorporate the findings of psychology.

McGilchrist's affirmation of the insights of **phenomenology** has implications for such a project. If there is continuity to human nature across the centuries, we can share in dialogue with people from remote civilisations and cultures, and assume – within certain limitations, cultural and not neurological – that their experience matches our own. If certain particularly gifted modern people - he cites Hegel and Heidegger - are capable of grasping intuitively the inner complexities of their own brain functioning, and capturing this in words, then we can assume what the mystics have always assumed: there is a whole library of ancient texts, from all global cultures, long revered for their 'psychological insight' by enthusiasts, but not taken seriously as such by most, which can potentially yield equivalent insights into their own brain functioning, and therefore into our own. Where Jaynes and T1 creates a gap between then and now, them and us, McGilchrist bridges this gap.

McGilchrist provides a reason why behaviourism and materialism neglect and truncate the history of their subject. McGilchrist explains that they exemplify 'the left hemisphere's way of construing its own history',[142] in other words, a *psychologically* inadequate approach – linking to our first point. Jaynes's own account of his past trajectory within behaviourism confirms this conclusion.[143]

The history of psychology, if it is to reflect an adequate psychology of history, cannot be dictated by research programmes formed under the circumstances of **left-brain dominance**, but should reflect a deliberate attempt to **correct** this.

McGilchrist provides a reason why the long-term approach in this book and series has its place in such a correction. According to his characterisation, a **right-brain approach** seeks the **widest possible context** for understanding.

This history is intended, among other things, as a **right-hemisphere history**: one which takes the neurological correction of T2 into account.

McGilchrist's characterisation of the right hemisphere's approach to language involves a constant awareness of language as a tool, rather than a transparent window, and as a servant rather than a master; so the **etymology** (background and origin) of words, the diversity and even the contingency of languages, become features as aids to understanding. Rather than getting immersed in this tool, we constantly keep it in view, deliberately subverting its familiarity and looking to 'new shores', **alternative** perspectives and means of expression.[144] We saw this policy approach with Derrida (2.6, 3.6), who is a fellow student of Heidegger.[145]

In connection with this, we will not only emphasise the origins of psychological vocabulary and other academic language in our target language of English, but also emphasise the vocabulary of each ancient language, where appropriate. In every case, this means **transliteration**: the sounds of each language reproduced using the English alphabet. (The original forms would be meaningless to almost all readers, as well as harder to write and print.) In Sumer, we will not try to use cuneiform, nor in Egypt hieroglyphs, in Semitic languages the Arabic or Hebrew alphabets, nor Chinese characters; but will always transliterate, preserving the '**strangeness**' of the sounds, with the intention of **stimulating** our right-hemisphere curiosity. (Recall Derrida's deliberate strategy of confronting the alien and the strange in 3.6.)

Finally, his observations about **written languages** also have implications. If the **orientation** (direction of reading) and **scripts** of written languages reflect brain laterality and language as a tool forms brain activity (2.4), then we have a key to Snell's thesis that 'the concept of 'soul' … is tied up with the whole character and orientation of the language'.[146] (2.6, 3.6) Old scripts will represent different brain orientations to alphabetic scripts, with implications for their potential psychologies to be explored in Chapters 5–8 and Book Two. To some extent, the medium of the written language will affect, constrain or even dictate the message in the history of psychology.

Discussion questions:

1 What do you make of Wundt's idea of a second or cultural psychology?
2 How would you describe your culture? How did you learn to live in it?
3 Has your own worldview experienced any major shifts or changes?
4 With which collective identities do you identify at an emotional level?
5 How do you prefer to learn? Is it through debate? Or more solitary?
6 Has this book yet challenged any of your prejudices or assumptions?
7 How much do you already know about the two sides of your brain?
8 Is there anything in T1 (Julian Jaynes's theory) that excites you?
9 Can you draw and label a (Venn) diagram of brain functions using T2?

Recommended Reading

- Ruth Benedict *Patterns of Culture* Routledge 1935

- Michael Cole *Cultural Psychology: the once and future discipline* Belknap Press 1996
- Julian Jaynes *The Origin of Consciousness in the Breakdown of the Bicameral Mind* Houghton Mifflin 1982
- C.S. Lewis *The Discarded Image: an Introduction to Medieval and Renaissance Literature* CUP 1964
- Ian McGilchrist *The Master and his Emissary: the divided brain and the making of the modern world* Yale University Press 2009
- Brian J. McVeigh *The "Other" Psychology of Julian Jaynes* Imprint Academic 2018
- David Naugle *Worldview: the history of a concept* Eerdmans 2002

Notes

1 Henley and Rossano pp.27–37 for an excellent, clear and brief summary of the history from Darwin to today.
2 McGilchrist 2009 Ch.4 pp.93–132; McVeigh p.29 n.11.
3 Cole p.7.
4 Cole pp.30–35; 98–109; Eriksen pp.22–3,25–9,39–41; Farrell pp.251,261–2; Leahey pp.227–35.
5 Quoted in McVeigh p.25.
6 Farrell pp.216–8,245–6,269–271, 288–90, 314–16.
7 Brett pp.3–15 ('Primitive Thought'), 200–236 ('Eastern Writings').
8 Hogg and Vaughan p.620.
9 Benedict p.3.
10 Hung p.147.
11 Henley and Rossano p.76.
12 Kant 1996 6:313 p.457; his three *Critiques* reflect this triad as three faculties: as Kant 1928 8:197 p.39.
13 MacGilchrist, Myers and Reed pp.60–1.
14 Bellwood pp.79–84,92–4,161; Diamond Ch.19; Renfrew 1987 pp.124–131,145–152269–273,281–9; Smail p.57.
15 Mitchell and Myles p.70.
16 Benedict pp.16–17,171.
17 *ibid* pp.33–5.
18 *ibid* p.87.
19 Eriksen pp.28,49,77–9.
20 *ibid* pp.79,159–160,169.
21 *ibid* p.25.
22 Kramer p.249.
23 Murray p.xxi.
24 Henley and Rossano p.71; Husserl 1937 pp.111–116; Lewis p.11; Renfrew and Zubrow p.11.
25 Kant 1996 5:161 p.269; Kant 1928 8:256 p.105; Lambert pp.45ff.
26 e.g. Kramer p.33 (Assyriology); McGilchrist 2021 pp.8,624 (philosophy); Naugle pp.126–7 (psychology); Renfrew and Zubrow p.10 (archaeology).
27 Wright 1992 p.124.
28 Hogg and Vaughan p.113–14; Simon pp.xi,3.
29 Hegel 1956 p.452.
30 Brett p.201.
31 Annas p.150.

32 *Republic* 441c p.1073.
33 368d–369a p.1008.
34 *ibid.*
35 Lewis pp.220–1; Lovejoy pp.244–8,265–6,301–2,317.
36 Cole pp.146ff.,158ff.; Mithen 1994 p.31; Oates pp.29–33,50–4.
37 McVeigh p.13; see also Cole pp.149,163,167,185.
38 McVeigh p.13; see also Cole pp.149,163,167,185.
39 Cole pp.27–30,98ff.; Farrell pp.216–18,245–6,269–71 ,288–90, 314–16; Henley and Rossano p.27; McVeigh p.2.
40 36 d,e p.1240; 44d,e p.1248; Celenza p.73; Clark p.286; Lewis p.52; Lovejoy pp.54,59–66.; Tarnas pp.85,213.
41 Kiev pp.38–55; Lewis-Williams and Pearce pp.42–6,261–9.
42 Popper pp.313n.4, 314,328.
43 *ibid* pp.28,335.
44 Cassirer 1944 p.5.
45 Cooper pp.xviii–xxi; Irwin p.84; Plato *Phaedo* 96a–c p.83 in Cooper.
46 Heidegger *Being and Time* Intro I.2 pp.26–8; Intro II.7C pp.59–62.
47 Copleston p.64–5.
48 Fowler p.31.
49 Bacon 1605 I.4.6 p.27, II.3.5 p.148; Descartes p.33; McGilchrist p.285.
50 Bacon 1605 II.1.1 p.61, II.24 pp.208–9; Descartes p.78; Leahey Ch.5 pp.121–51; Whitehead pp.1–3,8–9,15.
51 Lewis pp.220–221; Lovejoy pp.244–8,265–6,301–2,317.
52 Kant 1998 A xii p.101, A84–6 pp.219–21,B779 pp.649–50 (tribunal metaphor).
53 Kant 1998 B454–88 pp.470–94 (thesis vs. antithesis), B500 p.501 (two traditions).
54 *ibid* B881–5 pp.702–4 (two traditions).
55 Hegel 1977 #2 p.2; #53 p.32; #73–89 pp.46–57.
56 Hegel 1956 pp. xv–xvi,79,103,110,456–7.
57 Benedict pp.5,8.
58 Eriksen p.44.
59 Henley and Rossano p.3.
60 Derrida 1967 pp.3,120.
61 Hawkes p.146.
62 Snell p.v.
63 Brett pp.17,20,23,201.
64 Hegel 1956 p.452.
65 Hogg and Vaughan pp.115–16; Simon pp.48–9.54–6.
66 Grabbe pp.18–21,105–7; a famous example is in the Hebrew story of Ruth.
67 Snell p.15.
68 Rothfield pp.32,97,99; Solomon pp.200–1.
69 Rothfield pp.10,13.
70 McVeigh pp.20–8; strictly speaking from Jaynes's student, but with good evidence from his life and work.
71 Popper pp.313n.4, 314,328.
72 McGilchrist 2021 p.35.
73 Smail p.7.
74 Eriksen p.204.
75 McVeigh p.2.
76 *ibid* pp.7,9.
77 Cole pp.30–35; 98–109; Farrell pp.251,261–2; Leahey pp.227–235; McVeigh pp.8,14,18.
78 McVeigh pp.8–9.
79 Jaynes p.380.

80 McVeigh pp.2,13.
81 *ibid* p.10.
82 Jaynes pp.84,228–9.
83 *ibid* p.360,446.
84 *ibid* p.374.
85 *ibid* p.119.
86 *ibid* pp.102–3,106–7.
87 *ibid* pp.106,113–4.
88 *ibid* pp.106,122–5,344–5.
89 *ibid* pp.305,342.
90 *ibid* p.202.
91 Harari p.42.
92 Jaynes p.126.
93 *ibid* pp.88–98,138–145.
94 *ibid* p.79.
95 *ibid* pp.155–163,169–173,202.
96 *ibid* p.160.
97 *ibid* p.428.
98 *ibid* p.228.
99 *ibid* pp.207,211.
100 *ibid* p.206–17.
101 *ibid* p.205,214.
102 *ibid* pp.79,135,154,231,432.
103 See Blakeslee pp.6,9,16,89–91,159–160 for an illustrative sample of the neurological consensus by 1980.
104 Mithen 1996 pp.11,15,61–72; Smail p.131 concurs as a historian.
105 *ibid* pp.11,217,221–6; Smail p.156 concurs as a historian, as does Henley, citing other psychologists p.211.
106 Albert Einstein's brain development was highly lateralised in this way: see Blakeslee pp.45–6,107–8.
107 McGilchrist 2009 p.x.
108 *ibid* p.91; in the sequel he writes of 'two distinct, entirely coherent visions of the world', 2021 p.30.
109 *ibid* pp.185,221, referencing and critiquing the essential message of Damasio pp.xxiii,27,249–52.
110 *ibid* p.214; see 2021 pp.27,36–40.
111 *ibid* pp.9,17–19,198,210–12; see 2021 pp.40–1.
112 *ibid* pp.22–4,33; see 2021 pp.25–6.
113 *Ibid* pp.27; this is expanded in 2021 pp.19–25, for which see exposition at 4.9 in this book.
114 *ibid* pp.226.
115 *ibid* p.210.
116 *ibid* pp.93,129; as seen in Jaynes pp.100,108, 119, 115; see also Blakeslee in n.102 above.
117 *ibid* pp.89,215,222,228.
118 *ibid* pp.6,176,191,200,236.
119 *ibid* pp.98,187.
120 *ibid* p.7.
121 *ibid* p.10.
122 *ibid* pp.143–158.
123 *ibid* pp.91,203–7,231 (Hegel); pp.149–158,314,449–50 (Heidegger); 527 (references to both).
124 *ibid* pp.14,204,234.

125 *ibid* p.199.
126 *ibid* p.219.
127 *ibid* pp.40,56,88,213.
128 *ibid* pp.50,51,56,59,61,75,78,79.
129 *ibid* p.179.
130 *ibid* pp.89,191,195,196.
131 *ibid* p.115.
132 *ibid* p.275–9,311,452–9.
133 Jaynes pp.13,66,106,124–9.
134 McGilchrist 2009 pp.245–51; Smail ch.3 pp.74–111 gives an illuminating account of this set of assumptions.
135 *ibid* pp.259,299.
136 And this phrase will crop up again for the Neolithic as well as the arrival of the Bronze Age in Iraq and Egypt.
137 *ibid* p.240.
138 *ibid* p.237.
139 *ibid* p.157–8,182,232–3.
140 *ibid* p.232.
141 In 2021 p.41 he makes the 'troubled marriage' metaphor explicit.
142 *ibid* pp.243,247,256,382–6; he elaborates on this point in 2021 pp.5–7,7–17.
143 Jaynes pp.3–18; McGilchrist 2021 has a comparable confession of the origins in his first book as a 'reaction'.
144 McGilchrist 2009 pp.275,381.
145 McGilchrist 2009 p.275 notes this point about Heidegger's constant uncovering of word etymologies.
146 Snell p.15.

Part 2

Workshop

4 New stones, new cosmos

4.1 Orientation: The new world

The purpose of each Orientation is 'to lead us in' with a historical narrative. In the case of the Neolithic, we simply need to draw all the elements mentioned in Part 1 together to give us a back story. The Neolithic will then provide this back-story for the following chapters.

In 1.3 and 2.3 we noted the theory of the proposed appearance of 'the cathedral of the modern mind' with side chapels around a central nave, achieving free-flowing mutual access in the late Pleistocene or Upper Palaeolithic era.[1]

This sudden burst into 'fully modern cognition'[2] during the Upper Palaeolithic had dramatic effects. Humans colonised new areas of the globe, leaving Africa and reaching Siberia, Oceania and the Americas. Boats of all kinds were invented, allowing for example a migration out of Africa across the Indian Ocean: what has become known as the Southern Route.[3] Once our species arrived, the evidence suggests that humans consistently **wiped out** most of the larger species in the new territories, as humans have done in every global territory they have populated.[4]

The new rate and range of learning capacity bore this fruit. We cannot mystify our ancestors as more 'connected with nature' than ourselves: it is easy to forget that humans have spent most of our history as the **prey** of other predators before reversing the relationship, and once it was reversed, we have rampaged across the globe in an orgy of killing.[5] In this respect, the Neolithic era was a **respite** for other species on this planet; one which lasted until industrialisation, the next great step forward in human presence, initiating a new wave of mass extinctions – still currently underway – and, according to some, moving us from the Holocene into a new Anthropocene era.[6]

After the 'cultural explosion' of the Upper Palaeolithic era,[7] the biggest single change in the story of our species was the change to producing our own food by domesticating other species.[8] When the earth's climate settled permanently into its present Holocene phase after the Younger Dryas, c.9500 BCE (11,650 ybp), farming was quickly discovered – or perhaps rediscovered – and it has continued to be pursued, spreading out from new centres all over the globe from then on.[9] Human populations rose steeply from their slow growth under

DOI: 10.4324/9781003396147-7

previous conditions , creating dense populations which had to spread out by land and sea, in many cases leading to permanent distributions.[10]

At the other end of the Holocene, the new world looked different from ours. In **Africa** people started moving towards farming on either side of the giant lake where the Sahara Desert is now;[11] to the west in Mali very early[12] and to the east in Sudan not long after.[13] Similarly, at the Western end of **Asia** in the Fertile Crescent region, food production was discovered i,[14] as well as far to the east in China (see 8.1) and Siberia, on Lake Baikal and the Aldan River.[15] From these some had crossed the land bridge across to the **Americas** just before farming developed: so it had to be rediscovered in Mexico, Peru, the USA and Brazil.[16] Each of these areas will make a contribution to the argument of this chapter, because these were the pioneering regions of the Neolithic and its culture.

This has affected everything about human lives: you are only reading this book because a whole series of steps have made this possible, and the production of food was the first step. It 'made the participants **active partners with nature** instead of parasites on nature', and not only in farming: 'The new aggressive attitude to the environment ... created **new substances** which did not exist in nature' such as pottery – which would lead on to metals – and woven fabrics such as linen.[17] It soon led to the construction of artificial landscapes, as we shall see in 4.2.

Our gradual education away from Eurocentrism in Western history (Chapter 1, 2.6, 3.6) can be seen in the use of this label. The Fertile Crescent was **Europe's Neolithic** as it spread north and west from this region, through Turkey and Greece, crossing the Aegean Sea into Europe, just as it would later cross the English Channel.[18] As Europeans were interested in their 'local' Neolithic in West Asia, it was given the most reliable dating, and the consensus is still that this was the earliest arrival of farming; but it is slowly emerging that we have **defined** the Neolithic so that it will start here, much as we defined philosophy and 'psychology' to start in Greece. Not only has it happened **more than once**; it has happened in more than one way.[19] Once this is admitted, several locations press close to the same time horizon, at the start of the Holocene.[20]

In a sense, 'the Neolithic' has only become part of history since the 1960s. The term itself was coined in 1856, to mark the stage just before the Bronze Age in the three-age system. (Just before this, the word 'prehistory' was first coined in 1851[21] to mark the undiscovered country of the past before 'history' began in written records.) For a century after this, all archaeologists had was the 'box' with this label, with little sense of its contents and no clear sense of a **timeline** to organise it. Now that we have these things, we are gradually finding it an inadequate label.

The discovery of the uses of **carbon dating** in the 1950s and 1960s opened up a new world: the world of the Neolithic. Suddenly, there was a timeline before the invention of writing: a new, alien world beyond the (more familiar) Bronze Age. It was found that the Neolithic period had begun **earlier** than anyone had expected, and that many of its monuments were older than any writing. A long stretch of human history had been opened up for investigation. As well as this extension of the time corridor, reliable prehistoric dates opened the possibility of an extension in space: a '**world prehistory**' stretching between continents.[22]

This scientific advance coincided with a rapid decline in European colonialism following the Second World War. Just as Europe began to recede from its peak of influence in the global order, and the United Nations began the formation of a new global order, Western science found a new window into the past shared with all other nations. Combined with the breakthroughs in genetics (2.2) and new archaeological discoveries, we have adequate tools to explore prehistory.

Much has been said about the Neolithic as a historical phenomenon between nations; we must also see it in terms of **geography** within nations today. We cannot ignore the presence of **rural** and **village** communities, dialects and cultures worldwide. Our minds are trained to make the contrast '**developed world = urban**' and '**developing world = rural**' – especially in the discourses of the city (broadcasting, printing presses, strong WiFi signal, bookshops) which dominate academic life – and to forget that not everyone, even in our own country, even today, inhabits the global city. Rural life worldwide can often reveal unexpected continuities with the distant past.

The geneticist Barry Sykes brought this out starkly in 1997, with the discovery that a schoolteacher in a small rural town in England was related to a skeleton from a local prehistoric site. His ancestor's community had migrated across a land bridge which still connected the British Isles to Continental Europe until the sixth millennium BCE. The land bridge closed before agriculture arrived so the ancestor arrived well before the Neolithic; his descendants **stayed local**.[23]

In the next chapters, we will move to the Bronze Age and the invention of city life, as a context for the first writing and the first explorations of the *psyche* in writing. The point about geography reminds us that until very recently most of the world's population lived in the countryside, was illiterate and saw only the modest habitations of the village: the Bronze Age had barely arrived.[24] It was confined to improved equipment, a money economy, and rumours of the city.

This point is important to give us a 'buffer zone' between Western civilisation and the Neolithic world – for both the remote past and the recent past. There has been growing embarrassment among anthropologists about the word 'primitive',[25] and the assumption that their findings could be applied to the extended past; but archaeologists have found clear matches of past and present Neolithic evidence, suggesting that there is a certain internal 'logic' to that kind of economy and the worldview of Neolithic societies, and common patterns of development.[26] If we take away the urban/rural barrier, the Neolithic becomes more approachable as an economic and geographical category.[27]

Our story begins in small social groups before the advent of 'civilisation': there was no writing, but there was building, burying, decorating, pottery, art, religion and a growing set of tools. The human mind could expand to fill a new **range of tools** within a **larger social unit** – affecting *psyche* and *logos* in different ways.

The first test of our theories and tools from Part 1 comes in their encounter with evidence from the Neolithic. If they can succeed here, they can succeed anywhere. If we can catch *psyche* out here in the ocean of prehistory, we can approach more familiar waters with more confidence, and the momentum we will have gained can help to take us forward into the Bronze Age civilisations.

4.2 Göbekli Tepe: A premonition

A good introduction to the themes of this chapter is in southern Turkey, on the hilly north of the Fertile Crescent between the headwaters of the Tigris and the Euphrates.[28] One *tepe* (Persian: hill) contains a massive stone structure dated to 9,600 BCE – that is, up against the far wall of the Holocene era. This resembles other megalithic sites, such as Stonehenge and the pyramids, except that this one is **much older**: it is the earliest of all built stone structures yet found anywhere.[29]

The locally quarried limestone blocks were moved, shaped and decorated with wild animal images, by people with no metals, no wheels and no domesticated animals to help.[30] Most important, there are no signs of habitation: it was just before the invention of agriculture anywhere on the planet, so far as we know to date, and the remains of the builders' food show that it was built by what we now call '**hunter-gatherers**'.[31]

The stone pillars with their relief decorations of animals seem to be models of people meeting in a circle, surrounded by wild animals: symbolic of a place of gathering. It seems to have functioned as an **outdoor temple**, a place of annual or seasonal worship, a place of ritual and pilgrimage: its discoverer called it '**a mountain sanctuary**'.[32] The building process would have involved an unusual size and duration of community, with cooperation, communication and organisation, as well as specialised skills for the stone carvings.[33] It therefore both created and represented a community: it is in this sense – like Egypt's pyramids (6.4) – an exercise in applied group psychology.[34]

A stream of similar inferences follows from its existence. The structure shows us something about the elements of cognitive and social skills involved in this kind of building project: the cognitive steps implicit in artefacts, and attempts to enter into the symbolic world of the builders (4.6).[35] The fact of priority in time shows that before farming came community and religion: 'a need that runs deep in the human *psyche*' as one commentator suggests.[36] Its discoverer even boldly claims that this site proves that '**civilisation** is a product of the human mind'.[37]

This may be true at another level, however. As well as coming just before the beginning of farming, it may even have *led* to farming. The nearby hills had the best species of wheat for domestication, which could be fully domesticated by selection in a couple of centuries. Wild sheep and goats were also suitable for domestication; so the whole Neolithic 'package' of West Asia, with its huge impact on the surrounding regions, was available to those building this site.[38] It is not inconceivable that domestication occurred during the construction itself, as 'no more than an accidental **by-product** of the ideology' that drove the building process:an unintended but seismic outcome.[39]

Whichever of these was the actual process, the association was certainly strong, and it involved belief, religion or worldview (3.3) – that is, a cognitive component as well as ritual, symbolism, narrative and *habitus*. In reach of the site are several others, and also related settlements in Syria, Lebanon, Jordan and Israel, which benefited from the discovery of agriculture in the same region just after Göbekli Tepe was first constructed.[40] Local populations soared after this discovery[41] and the seeds became a valued, probably magical commodity for trade, finding their way rapidly to Cyprus,[42] and eventually to Egypt.[43] The obsidian flints used at this site – having 'the sharpest edge of any stone … a truly magical material' – as part of the same niche cultural **package** - were soon being traded from Jericho, a settlement further south in Palestine.[44]

We can see a premonition of the later Bronze Age in this 'export package'; and Göbekli Tepe suggests that this package contained **ideological** and **symbolic** as well as material elements.[45] If the building project did not initiate the Neolithic, it would have become a major symbol for it. It not only pre-dated and resembled, but probably inspired, other megalithic structures along the Atlantic coast in the coming millennia, such as Stonehenge, as well as the stone temples on Malta.[46]

The site has recently featured in a debate about the history of psychology and a challenge to the definition of the subject, raising many of the issues covered in Part 1.[47] The definition of psychology as 'the study of individuals' has been challenged, as well as the ethnocentrism of borrowing categories of definition solely from Greek philosophy;[48] by the US psychologist Tracey Henley asking 'what **Neolithic architecture** … might contribute to the history of psychology', with Göbekli Tepe as his central example.[49] The rest of this chapter (at least to 4 4) can function as an extended answer to this question.

To avoid Eurocentrism, however, we should look beyond our 'local' Neolithic to other continents with the same question. Göbekli Tepe has been compared to gathering places in the jungles of New Guinea – another Neolithic centre.[50] A closer equivalent is **Nabta Playa** on Egypt's southern border with Sudan. Like Göbekli Tepe – though two millennia later – it was built by nomads and used as a meeting place and ritual centre with a stone circle. This too is like a Neolithic gateway, in time and place: just a few centuries before agriculture, on the cusp of a new way of life, and offering a monumental gathering space.[51] As Göbekli Tepe is at the beginning of a process that will end in Bronze Age Sumer, Nabta Playa was built at the beginning of a process that will end in Bronze Age Egypt.

In both cases, we are at the headwaters, not only of great rivers but of the first civilisations. When cities appear, they will be built around temples and shrines in both visible and invisible ways.[52] This underlines the lesson of Göbekli Tepe, which seems to be that 'the religious system of an early society can no longer be considered a secondary factor in the explanation of culture change'.[53] The beginning of the Neolithic includes evidence of an emergent worldview, from which it may be possible to extract some meaningful psychological content.

4.3 Inside the Neolithic mind: *Psyche* and cosmos

Now that we have a 'map' of the global Neolithic world (4.1) let us look at the functioning of these societies – especially their common cultural patterns – for insights into developing self-awareness and self-exploration of the human *psyche*.

Two South African archaeologists, based at the Rock Art Research Institute in Johannesburg, recently published a study entitled: *Inside the Neolithic Mind.* Comparing the findings of anthropologists with the archaeological record, they discover 'empirically established existence of commonalities. Certain beliefs and experiences crop up … around the world'.[54] They account for these using contemporary neuroscience, and from it they develop a theory of Neolithic culture.

Their particular interest is the role of the **shaman** in Neolithic societies. This word comes from a specific family of cultures in Siberia called the Tungus.[55] We noted in passing (4.1) the importance of Siberia as a hub for migration into the Americas, and indeed similar practices to those in Siberia developed, over the millennia, in North, South and Central America.[56] The land bridge was lost before farming began on the Asian side,[57] yet the societies are similar. This suggests that the role of the shaman is probably **pre-Neolithic** – a 'fossil' from the Upper Palaeolithic. Archaeologists have long inferred that those dealing in ritual and the management of the unseen world were 'the first specialists' who supported the hunt without direct participation, training each other in the role as '**the first profession**' fed from a surplus: a social wedge which would widen throughout the Neolithic.[58] Food production enabled this social niche to grow and develop; it is still found in the oldest human cultures in Africa and this was the starting point for the investigations of shamanism by the South Africans.[59]

The role has been found worldwide with such remarkable **consistency** that this word is now used routinely. Ruth Benedict applies the same category to tribes as far apart as the Americas and New Guinea: 'Shamanism is one of the most general human **institutions**. The shaman is the religious practitioner who … gets his power directly from the gods'.[60] The South African team agrees: 'there are **astonishing similarities**, which are not easy to explain, between shamanistic ideas and practices as far apart as the Arctic, Amazonia and Borneo, even though these societies have probably never had any contact with each other'.[61] It is not a precise social role but is a **loose cluster** of roles just in English, some equivalents are witch doctor, medicine man, wise woman, shape-changer, seer and especially 'walker between the worlds'. It is clearly one of the oldest specialisations.[62]

What the South African team have noticed is a set of **correlations** between the reports of **shamans** about their experiences, reports of patients with **psychotic** illness (that is, losing contact with reality) – both of these in what we have called the extended present – and Neolithic **artwork** and **architecture** in the extended past. They propose that a common thread connecting these is **exploring the limits of our neurology**.[63] It is based on the assumption (2.2) that human brains today are unchanged since the early Holocene period, so we have 'a neurological bridge to the Neolithic'.[64] As a complement to the new kinds of *intelligence* unleashed by access between mental modules during the Upper Palaeolithic, these authors propose a new spectrum of states of *consciousness*, in which the rationality of waking life is just one small part: and they have found that this offers powerful explanatory tools for both the archaeological and the anthropological data.[65]

The traditional shaman's laboratory is his or her own body and own *psyche*.[66] Techniques used include hallucinogenic drugs, sensory deprivation, sensory overload, exhaustion, terror, pilgrimage and others: all 'induction procedures' which 'may also lead to a breakdown of the higher integrative functions of the central nervous system', in other words one description of **psychosis**.[67] Typically the person falls into a trance in which they become 'dissociated', less recognisably human – temporarily forgetting **boundaries** of self and world learnt in infancy. They may be very still, even appearing 'dead' – and many shamans value this as a sign of the best visions – or they may have dramatic convulsions and fits.[68]

The strange thing is that the visions seen – expressed afterwards according to the language of the culture – reveal a fixed, stable cluster of patterns. These include vivid experiences of **flight** and travel through a **vortex**, both related to a specific point in the brain, the striate cortex: 'descent into a tunnel and flight to a realm above are both sensations wired into the human brain and activated in altered states of consciousness'.[69] Both interpretations appear universal in global shamanism, and the neurology can explain this fact.[70]

We now add the insight from structuralism (2.5) that these are interpreted as **opposites**, according to the subconscious 'binary logic' which the authors – in agreement with Lévi-Strauss – believe is wired into our neurology.[71] The two trance experiences are understood as up/down, and both as involving travel. The sensation of flight is categorised as 'up' and the sensation of moving through a tunnel as 'down'. Structuralist anthropology proposes a third category to **relate** the opposites[72] – here supplied at 'ground level' in everyday experience. Thus, a Neolithic logic applied to the vision of cosmic travel yields a mystical cosmos of **three levels**, tiers, layers or storeys: 'the Siberian shaman's soul is said to be able to leave the body and travel to other parts of the cosmos, particularly to an upper world in the sky and a lower world in the underground'.[73] Similar reports come from all Neolithic tribes with shamanic culture: we seem to have reached a **structure**.[74]

In Colombia, a Barasana shaman's vision can include transformation between different species on the three levels: 'the eagle is the predator of the sky, the jaguar the predator of the earth, and the anaconda the predator of the water, the underworld'. In his trance state, he imagines himself entering all three.[75] Here we can see an origin of the global phenomenon of different gods who **personify** the different regions of the cosmos. In Egyptian religion, they kept their animal character,[76] whereas in others the gods had human personalities – just for the sky, in this book and the next we will come across Anu, Enlil, Horus, Indra and Zeus. These gods are called **anthropomorphic** (Greek: in the form of men) as people have projected their own *psyche* onto the map of the cosmos;[77] the others, **zoomorphic** ('in the form of animals'); but – as the Barasana shaman found – there is a porous boundary between the two. Humans can imagine themselves transforming into animals. In the Amazon, the presence of other species is hard to forget, because there 'we are surrounded by a multitude of alternative psychologies'.[78]

Here we have a **worldview** – in its original sense of a world vision – emerging from deliberately induced out-of-the-body experiences, so that inner travel through the varying states of consciousness is **projected outwards** as 'astral travel' through the cosmos. It enables people to draw 'maps' of that cosmos, to create a **cosmography** (Greek: representation of the universe). In fact, on this interpretation, shamans are simply exploring their own **neurology**: 'the multiple realms, or dimensions, that are integral to the electro-chemical functioning of the human brain'.[79] A folk technique which formed part of 'native systems of psychotherapy'[80] was treated like modern science or astronomy.

The revelations of the shaman were privileged as true visions of reality, as we shall see in the next section. If this interpretation is correct, then at least in the sense of cosmography, 'Religion is, ultimately, embedded in neurology, as is pre-scientific cosmology: the two are hardly separable'.[81] These early technologies were in fact mirrors of the mind, **psychological** in nature; but all the psychological content was projected outwards onto the larger screen of an innocent universe. If the first farming was indeed an accidental by-product of religion, as was suggested in the previous section, the first psychology seems to have been also. Shamans explored the depths of the cosmos within the depths of their own minds, and in Neolithic societies, there was little or no perception of the difference between the two.[82]

The techniques of the shaman did not stop with the Neolithic but are found in later civilisations – among the Mayans, the Egyptians, the Greeks and the Japanese.[83] Chinese mythology betrays many signs of its Neolithic shamanic origins.[84] The **dreamlike** quality of much mythology and symbolism is a direct result of this persistence: simply put, their ultimate sources lay in dreams and in altered states of consciousness. Once we become alert to this aspect of ancient cultures, we suddenly find traces of it everywhere: a fact to be explored in 4.7.

4.4 Inside the Neolithic mind: Modelling the cosmos

Structuralism was described (2.5) as 'reverse engineering'; and indeed, this is literally what the South African team offer us: a Neolithic **architectural plan** based on their findings about the neurology of shamanism.

The *maloca* longhouse of the Barasana people in the forests of Colombia is an intricate **microcosm** of the shamanic universe, in which 'the roof is the sky, the house posts are the mountains that support the sky, and the floor-space is the earth'. The dead inhabit the earth beneath the tribe's feet, and thus fill up the three realms of the **dream-cosmos** seen by the shaman.[85] A **Bororo village** in the rainforests of Brazil has the same function: a cosmic map with an intricate arrangement, 'simultaneously dwellings and models of the cosmos'.[86] In the **extended present** of anthropology, the models built match the shamanic visions, which function, in effect, as the basis of architectural plans.

Anthropologists can interview shamans today for their reports of their visions; archaeologists only have mute sites. Yet we can infer what shamans *saw* in the remote past – according to the theory presented in 4.3 – if their tribes listened to them in the same way and *built* what they saw. Conversely, if surviving stone structures from the **historical Neolithic** resemble those of the Bororo and the Barasana in the extended present, we can infer that these involved a similar process. A direct link has been made between historical megalithic structures and recent Neolithic tombs in a single culture among the Merina people of Madagascar.[87] The Direct Historical Approach has also developed, linking Neolithic cultures in the extended present into the past in North and Central America, tracing the continuities.[88] Yet patterns are so consistent that remoter links, reaching back into early Neolithic cultures, appearvalid. As noted in 4.1, Neolithic culture displays fixed patterns and structures independent of its historical setting.

The senior of the two South Africans presenting the neurological theory (4.3) made a study of Mesolithic art, ***The Mind in the Cave***, arguing that during the Upper Palaeolithic 'caves had been part of a visible, and at the same time **invisible universe**. In the Neolithic, on the other hand, people constructed a model of the cosmos in which **'the cave in the mind'** played an ever more defining role … human control of the conceived cosmos increased markedly … There lies the real, innovative essence of the Neolithic: expression of religious cosmological concepts in **material structures** as well as myths, rather than the passive acceptance of natural phenomena (such as caves), opened up new ways of constructing an intrinsically dynamic society'.[89] If this is the case, then what did they build?

The first thought was to imitate: as the *later* ziggurats, pyramids and mounds – whatever else they may be – are clearly man-made mountains or hills, the *first* built structures were dug into the ground. Göbekli Tepe and those like it were built 'within circular structures that had been sunk into the hill to create what looked like cellars in the earth'.[90] These **artificial caves** were given meaning of course by the shamanic experiences, especially those of the vortex or tunnel. It was 'a simultaneously material and **psychic underworld**'.[91] But now it was the ordered and controlled world of human construction. The key transition in Neolithic construction is from underground – mostly tombs and graves – into much more visible **overground structures**. This peaks at the beginning of the Bronze Age when stone circles and artificial hills appear on the Atlantic coast, almost exactly contemporary with the Pyramids of Egypt.[92] Between the two levels, lower and upper, came impressive structures such as those in Malta.[93]

At **Stonehenge**, one archaeologist concludes that 'it may not be too far-fetched to imagine the structure as **a model of the world** as its builders saw things'.[94] As at Göbekli Tepe, the bluestones represent 'petrified guardians or ancestors keeping watch over a sacred place, or perhaps as pieces taken from one sacred spot to enhance the significance and special powers of another. One such power might be **to assist shamans** to make prophecies … as elements of a complicated structure with deeply embedded **cosmological references** … providing **metaphors** in its architecture that structure ritual'- we might say, rather like a service booklet in a modern Anglican church.[95]

The South African team find the same pattern at **Bryn Celli Ddu** on Anglesey as at other sites: the builders 'were constructing an '**existential diagram**' of their beliefs … death was conceived as a passage between cosmological realms. Cosmological transition, death and the structures themselves formed a conceptual triad', in which 'the tomb as an emblem of the overall cosmology *becomes* that cosmology'.[96] Most impressive is **Newgrange**, one of the tombson the 'Isle of the Dead' on the bend of the Boyne in Ireland: a massive Neolithic structure which is now read as 'a complex statement about **spiritual travel** through the cosmos'.[97] The authors conclude from the Neolithic evidence surveyed that 'When people of that time built structures, cosmology was never far from their minds'.[98]

We are beginning to answer the leading question from 4.2: 'What has Neolithic **architecture** to do with **psychology**?' From 4.3 we know that the 'cosmos' of which these buildings are intended as visible models was in fact a model of the shaman's *psyche*; and the middle term of the correspondence '*psyche-cosmos*-structure' is redundant. Structure is *psyche*. The revelations of the shaman were expressed in the architecture; cosmographic maps and dream reports functioned as **architectural plans** for the teams involved. We have the vision here in stone.

Therefore, we have a startling conclusion: some Neolithic archaeological sites *are* **Neolithic psychology** expressed visually in the language of earth and stone. As Plato could write a dialogue, or Aristotle give a lecture, and we might call it 'psychology' – with a few caveats, to distance it from current definitions – each Neolithic tribe produced a model of what its shaman saw in a **built structure**. If psychology is the use of *logos* – some kind of method and **agreed approach** – to investigate *psyche* (which we assume to be common to all humans) and we build theories which are invisible **models** of the *psyche* in words and concepts, consciously and intentionally, in the Neolithic we have visible structures, built in stone, which are the **unconscious**, **accidental 'psychology'** of their culture.

In terms of production, the difference is significant. In terms of **interpretation**, however, the difference is far less: we hear the lecture and read the treatise in a particular language, as we can 'read' each Neolithic site as a symbolic system, pointing like any set of symbols to its subject, showing us what they mean. We have to translate in both cases; in both, there is a distance from then to now. We can read both books and buildings as attempts at psychology, lacking later resources.

Arguably, through the Neolithic, there is a progression from the psychologically generated structures described by the archaeologists, towards a convergence on models of the visible universe.[99] There is a progression from **below ground** to **above ground**, symbolic of the move from **subconscious** to **conscious** experience. Socially, this marks an emergence from the **private** authority of the shaman to publicly held authority, an appeal to common experience: remotely akin to the modern emergence of **public science** from a monopoly on public belief by ecclesiastical elites.

This places Neolithic psychology, Greek psychology and ours on a single scale, from 'entirely subconscious' through to 'entirely conscious'. Presumably the cultures in Chapters 5–8 will reveal that progression. But this does not authorise us to assume only one such scale: that this tree only has one branch. From this Neolithic root, we will trace several divergent branches of global culture.

Here too we must note that the correspondence of buildings and monuments to the cosmos – and thus indirectly to the *psyche* – is another feature of global tradition which does not *end* with the Neolithic evidence. Here it was inferred from the evidence by archaeologists, but it also crops up in other contexts: an independent *confirmation* of this idea in the *continuation* of Neolithic culture.

Its most obvious expression is the **temple**. In Bronze Age settings the place of ritual is a model of the entire cosmos, at least during some ceremonies, and the purpose of the ritual enacted there is the cleansing of the cosmos. This is very clear in the Fertile Crescent region, where a whole civilisation is expressed through its sacred architecture.[100] The Neolithic principle is unchanged, simply expanded in scale, materials, number of staff and level of authority required.

In ancient Israel, the threefold correspondence *psyche*-cosmos-structure had a particularly precise form, described in Chapter 7 (7.6). More important, it is *consciously understood* there as a correspondence, at least by certain writers, from a remarkably early point in that nation's history. **Tabernacle** and **temple** are not only cosmographies – maps of the cosmos – but can also function as a symbol for the individual *psyche*. Construction becomes the first psychology in the sense of building models and metaphors. We cannot know how far back it became a **conscious** metaphor, but it becomes one soon after writing appears.

An attentive reader may have noticed the **convergence** of this proposal with our starting metaphor of 'the **cathedral** of the modern mind', first introduced from Stephen Mithen's work (in 2.3) as 'an analogy of the mind as a cathedral'.[101] Mithen writes:

> When I look at the evidence about the modern mind provided by the psychologists in the previous chapter, I am reminded of our work at the South Church at San Vincenzo – or indeed any modern church or cathedral.[102]

This author intends his metaphor to explain the appearance of art, religion and science in the historical record during the Upper Palaeolithic[103] through a novel breakdown in barriers and opening up of **access** between neurological systems, creating something like the 'full cognitive fluidity' we experience today.[104] But he goes on to extend this explanation to the Neolithic itself as a further stage in the same process, with deeper **integration** of the functioning of the specialised neural systems: in terms of his metaphor, with the side chapels of the cathedral operating simultaneously, combined with particular **climactic** circumstances.[105]

The convergence of this neurological metaphor with our argument on Neolithic architecture is not entirely a coincidence[106] but the fact that it occurred to him at all is suggestive.[107] It also makes sense of the claim (also in 2.3) by archaeologist Lambos Malafouris that archaeologists '**excavate minds** … [that] Mind exists inside the material expressions … thinking *with* and *through* stone'.[108] We will return to these themes in our first review of Theory One against the data, towards the end of this chapter (4.7).

4.5 Neolithic society: Macrocosm and myth

If the visions of a shaman functioned as architectural plans at megalithic sites, there was still a need for builders and for significant leadership of the builders: a site foreman. All who encounter and reflect on ancient construction – whether Neolithic or Bronze Age – are struck by the **organisation** of labour required. In many cases, we are also confronting by-products of a more invisible building process, which was the building of **community** and shared group identity. In both senses we are witnessing a premonition of larger-scale **leadership**.[109]

In Palaeolithic societies and their Neolithic successors, treating the visions of a shaman as a source of truth carried great dangers. The office could function as a social niche for people whom we would now describe as **mentally ill**. The deliberate induction of a psychotic state can help those already tending that way but it is a dangerous game – as are hallucinogenic drugs – for individuals who are not.[110] A greater danger is to the society itself, which is highly vulnerable to individual input: unhelpful traits can easily become permanently **embedded** in group culture.[111]

One balance to the dangers of the shaman's role was the distinction between **shaman** and **priest**, which emerges in many Neolithic societies: 'The priest is the depository of **ritual** and the administrator of cult activities … Every prayer, every cult act, is performed at an **authorised** and universally known season, and in the **traditional** fashion'.[112] This is a description of the

New Mexico Pueblos priesthood, for example, as contrasted with the role of a shaman in most of the First Nations, where **personal authority** and private experience are only normal in 'a person whose instability has marked him out for his profession'.[113] This distinction has also been identified in Siberia, the Amazon, and the Pacific islands of Polynesia.[114]

One difference is that the priest represents the **community speaking to itself**, whereas the shaman is **an individual voice** speaking into the community as an independent source of authority: potentially innovative, but at higher risk.[115] In Israel the latter role will become that of the **prophet** (*navi*); a translation into familiar terms, for *us* to grasp the role, though we must be cautious in applying it to Neolithic society.[116]

A distinction has been made between two kinds of shamanism: a hunting and gathering community had a **horizontal** (or 'classic') **shamanism** focussed on private experience, bodily experience, personal authority, and **individual** *psyche*; whereas farming tribes normally develop **vertical shamanism**, essentially the priestly role, focusing on the transmission of tradition, correct ritual, community memory and **collective** *psyche*. As with the difference in economy, this is not necessarily a sequence with replacement of one by the other, but rather a **further specialisation**, creating twin, parallel paths; but it was the vertical form which reflected or facilitated larger settlements.[117] The evidence worldwide points to the continuation of Palaeolithic bands into the earliest Neolithic societies, with no hierarchies; but eventually the new economic basis becomes reflected in a **new society**.[118] Horizontal shamanism points back to Palaeolithic roots; whereas vertical shamanism points forward to the Bronze Age. Let us attempt to construct a plausible narrative of this process in the extended past.

Slowly the implications of the new economy worked themselves out; a tribe could afford for some people to come off the land to specialise, in leadership and crafts, as the shaman had long been a specialist. The specialisms became interdependent and 'symbiotic' (Greek: cohabiting or mutually supportive): some tribal leaders became tribal **chiefs** commanding a larger territory, able to sponsor full-time craftsmen; crafts adding dignity and mystique to leaders.[119]

The role of the shaman evolved in step with these changes: like the craftsman the shaman could develop a 'symbiotic' relationship with the tribal leader or chief, adding the prestige of the unseen realm. There was potential for **conflict**, because a horizontal shaman represented an independent source of **authority**. The two could become 'poles apart', or else mutually **reinforcing**; either way, the stakes were higher. Chiefs might often prefer a 'chief's priest' for a quiet life but even this refuge had the potential to shift to the prophetic. An obvious ruse for a leader was to **combine** these roles in himself and become a priest-king.[120]

We therefore have a spectrum of **social authority** emerging: the classic (or horizontal) shaman, the priest (or vertical shaman) and the chief. In this triad, the first and second, or the second and third could be combined in various ways. Weavers, potters and metallurgists could easily be considered to have powers comparable to those of the shaman in the transformations of materials; powers which a chief or a shaman might also possess, or claim to possess.[121] These were different kinds of status.

As the *psyche* of a shaman was projected onto the division of the cosmos, and human personalities projected onto the inhabitants of each cosmic division, a third act of **social projection** is extremely common in the ancient world. Here, instead of the individual *psyche* in the personalities of gods, the **collective *psyche*** – or if you prefer, **political** self-awareness – of the society was projected into the heavens, so that the community of gods and their various relationships were essentially a **mirror image of the society**, in the symbolic language of myth.[122]

We will see this in Sumer, Egypt, India, Greece and most ancient worldviews: 'people did not read the spirituality of an institution straight off from its outer manifestations. Instead, they projected its **felt or intuited** spiritual qualities onto **the screen of the universe**, and perceived them as cosmic forces reigning from the sky ... In the ancient worldview, a seer or prophet was able to sense the ... spirituality of an institution or state, and then bring that ... to awareness ... Our task today ... is to **withdraw** that projection from on high and **locate** it in the institution in which it actually resides'.[123] This is exactly what we have done with Neolithic cosmography, expressed in Neolithic architecture: withdrawing the projection and locating its origin in the neurology of the shaman. Here, the idea is applied to social psychology (or political theology) but the procedure is the same. It is what anthropologists call an **etic** or imposed interpretation, one contributed by the observer.[124]

We, therefore, have at least three kinds of psychological projection: traditional (long recognised) anthropomorphic and zoomorphic projection of *psyche* onto the heavens, so gods become mirrors of **individuals**; a projection of social or political **group** self-consciousness; and to locate these within a mythical cosmos, the **frame** of neurological structures identified by the South Africans. None of these projections are conscious, and all have to 'withdrawn' – referred back from the canvas on which they are projected, locating their projector closer to home, in the brains of contemporary people. If Neolithic architecture can be characterised as psychology, then so can Neolithic religion and mythology, as expressed in artwork and sculpture. These ancient people are **exploring themselves**, but in the language of myth.

It is important to keep this worldview and our own located on a spectrum; not simply facing one another in stark opposition. That spectrum is provided by the sequence of history as well as geographical distance. What the South Africans have done is a form of 'deconstruction' (3.6): examining a **conviction** of access to privileged knowledge, by not looking through the lens of the projector or the telescope, but standing back and looking at it 'sideways on'. As Jacques Derrida has initiated the deconstruction of Western **logocentrism** – privileged access by one particular language family – the archaeologists have been 'deconstructing' Neolithic cosmology. As we move through the subsequent evidence, we can recognise at least three phases of symbol: the **mythic** symbols of the Neolithic, the almost equally alien symbols of **non-phonetic** writing systems (Sumerian, Egyptian, Chinese) and the more familiar **phonetic** writing we share with other Bronze Age cultures such as Hebrew, Arabic, Sanskrit and Greek. The final list is a reminder that the last category hides its own 'spectrum' from the unfamiliar to the more familiar. The Bronze Age can 'loosen us up' to read the Neolithic, just as Neolithic insights can underpin study of different Bronze Age cultures.

We have now explored the correspondence of *psyche* and *cosmos* in Neolithic culture, but not yet the other kind of correspondence (3.4) we found in Plato's *Republic*: that of self and society, *psyche* and *polis*. Following the advice of Socrates, we started with the larger of the two before moving to the smaller unit. Let us turn to this form ofcorrespondence.

4.6 The neolithic psychologist

The new discipline of '**cognitive archaeology**' (2.3)[125] builds on the conviction that we can 'make inferences about ancient mental worlds from the material manifestations and representations of those worlds'.[126] Using clues from living Neolithic cultures in the extended present, we applied the idea of a 'cognitive map' of a similar kind as an explanation of historical Neolithic structures.[127] Its source, then and now, seems to lie in the vision of the shaman, like a playscript or a screenplay; but we know that this is only the starting point for any production.

Let us apply the insights of cognitive archaeology to the Neolithic community. We will start with extensive quotations from this subdiscipline with a focus on cognition and **tools**, but then transfer its ideas to the wider society and differentiated social roles outlined in 4.5.

The builders of Göbekli Tepe and other structures did not mainly engage their 'thinking mind', but their '**doing mind**'.[128] What was needed was a 'practical or procedural know-how';[129] not only, or even mainly, 'pure reason', but '**practical reason**'.[130] This would be in two respects: knowing how to handle the materials and knowing how to handle the people, both a 'techno-psychological axis' and a 'techno-sociological axis'.[131] Anyone with experience in **project management** knows that skills in both of these areas are needed to produce anything with a team. The 'material manifestations and representations'[132] of the cosmological vision are with us today because someone succeeded at bringing that vision into reality.

Whoever exercised leadership – an individual, a core team or the whole group – had to convert the shaman's 'cognitive operating system' (the 'map') into a 'conceptual operative schema' when selecting the **site**, the **objective** and the **materials**.[133] At Göbekli Tepe and early Neolithic settings, given its Palaeolithic social context, the leadership was probably informal or personality-based; later there would be formal leadership.

Up to this point, we have called our species ***homo sapiens*** (*sapiens*), translated 'wise one' to be more inclusive than the traditional 'wise man'; but in building projects, those involved were also ***homo faber*** (Latin: making ones).[134] This distinction matters, because in the words of one cognitive archaeologist: 'The inherent superiority and interest of the 'thinking mind' has been shown, time and again, to be often a matter of cultural prejudice and **academic ethnocentrism**'.[135] Those of us with expertise in one function – the thinkers – have redescribed human identity in our own image. This is comparable to the privileging of waking experience over other, alternative states of consciousness.

What is clear at the level of the group is also true at the level of an individual **carver** – let us say, of the wild boar relief sculpture at Göbekli Tepe – by acting out a parallel sequence at the **microcosmic** level: the choice of the objective, the tools, the dialogue with the limestone surface. For this craftsman, 'Mind exists inside the material expressions … Tool making and using are ways of thinking, not the results of thinking … [for example] thinking *with* and *through* stone'.[136] To **guide** him he has what Heidegger calls 'that referential totality within which the equipment is encountered'[137]: first the pillar which is to be carved, then the stone circle, the site, the setting, the original guiding vision.

For the **team leader** and the carver, the ability to hold their whole task in mind and then to plan 'a series of operations, rigorously chained, each conditioning the other and supposing rigorous foresight'[138] requires 'accessibility' between mental modules for carrying out different functions, especially a deliberate 'hierarchization of mental processes', which requires working at full capacity in their 'technical intelligence'.[139]

For the individual stone-carver and site leaders, there is what we might call a **legislative** (Latin: law-making) capacity and an **executive** (decision-actioning) capacity.[140] The first is delegated entirely to the group, and through the group to a trusted source of truth, such as the shaman: it has become **'group mind'**. But the executive function is also delegated – by the group to the **individual** – at a level of responsibility. At the larger levels of the pillar, the circle, the site, the setting, executive function can be delegated, or negotiated via discussion. Some such delegation and allocation of roles must have occurred, in order for the finished product on the Turkish hills to appear.

At the level of the community these roles are shared by the **division of labour** between the shaman or priest and the tribal leader: someone **embodies** each mental function. The modern political idea of a legislative supposes that laws take priority over leaders and that leaders are subject to those laws; but in the Neolithic, religion takes on some of that crucial role in restraining executive leadership. It is hard to say with Göbekli Tepe but if we move forward halfway to ourselves, to the project at Stonehenge, then we have a full chiefdom and a priesthood.[141] The'brain' of the community in terms of its **legislative** function is now the priestly class with its monopoly on tribal tradition; in terms of the **executive** function, it is the local chief now evolving towards the role of king.

Finally, let us turn these analytical tools from leaders and carvers on a building project - more traditional subjects of archaeology - to **the role of the**

shaman in a different way. Aside from intellectual leadership, her main craft is not leading a community; the role is extremely flexible and varies from culture to culture,[142] but helping individuals in a therapeutic, even a medical way is normally part of the cluster.

If we apply to this the stone carver's 'series of operations, rigorously chained, each conditioning the other and supposing rigorous foresight'[143], we have the remote beginnings of **clinical practice**. Faced with a tribe member in distress she needs some kind of 'conceptual operative schema' to seek a resolution.[144] Here as with any skill, 'practical or procedural know-how'[145] is required and especially the 'techno-sociological axis'[146] of interpersonal discernment, just like the project manager or the tribal leader. She, too, must be ***homo faber***.[147]

Archaeologists have pointed out that the jungle lore of the hunter-gatherer must be the remote roots of today's botany and zoology, astronomy and climatology; as 'the control of fire and the manufacture of tools initiate the traditions that emerge as physics and chemistry'.[148] The **complexity** of the mental processes involved in baking, pottery, and especially the forging of bronze, presuppose a 'conceptual operative schema' in each case significantly greater than those in stone carving, which have themselves been found to be surprisingly complex.[149] If this is the case, then it serves as a comparison: we cannot underestimate the complexity of mental processes involved in the work of the shaman, in her clinical roles among individuals, nor indeed also in her more public and formative community roles.

The role of the shaman as **the seer**, the one who sees into the invisible realm, seems to have evolved continuously in several directions. As one of the earliest 'divisions of labour' in humanity, other than that between mothers and fathers, the shaman seems to be the **common ancestor** of the priest, the doctor, the scientist and yes, the psychologist and psychotherapist. We have noted that the Neolithic is the most important change since the start of the Holocene and its social patterns have proven remarkably stable. As noted in 4.1 , it is not only in remote history, but in many world communities today that these patterns of Neolithic culture can be found: the role of the shaman is still used and still valued, in many such societies and in rural cultures worldwide, over the claims of Western medicine and its psychologies.[150]

With the shaman, therefore, we have found something just as essential to our story as any depiction or description of *psyche* or of *logos*: we have found the remote origins of the social role of **the psychologist**. As with Göbekli Tepe we are at the hilly headwaters of two streams: one of the two streams, starting with the site foreman or the tribal leader, will become something like the entity we recognise as government; the other stream, which begins with the equivalent of the shamans observed today, will be the 'truth industry' – including science and psychology.

As we turn to our first Theory Reviews in this book, you may want to re-read 3.8 and 3.9 beforehand to remind yourself of these two theories, which will now be discussed in the light of our findings in this chapter. As noted in the Introduction (Section 7) we will change our style in the Reviews, from the focus on careful references and clear exposition in the body of each chapter, to a somewhat less disciplined, more speculative, and - you may find - more demanding style. The intention is to capture the relative freedom of the dialectical method (3.5).

4.7 Review of Theory One (T1)

- Can we make any connections between the data and argument of this chapter and Jaynes's theory?

An obvious point of connection is the leadership 'division of labour' described immediately above (4.6). The legislative role of the shaman in Neolithic society closely resembles the guiding role of the right hemisphere in the bicameral age. When Jaynes writes about 'an executive part called a god, and a follower part called a man'[151] he means that the god-side of the brain *guided* the executive in the way that a modern legislature guides a government and regulates its actions. Each community projects its neurological division of labour onto these public roles. It seems that, on this point, subsequent archaeological theory and evidence have 'fleshed out' the framework of T1 in context of the Neolithic.

The right hemisphere in T1 has the role of the shaman in Neolithic societies, depicted from 4.3 to 4.6, as the left hemisphere has the role of leaders, and the people under these leaders, actioning the shaman's visions. It is certainly a possible meeting point, assuming a prominent public role for the shaman. Given this connection, we should be alert to the development of these two kinds of leadership in Bronze Age societies: can these also be interpreted in terms of a division of brain hemispheres? We can explore this idea further.

- How well does T1 match 'the shamanic hypothesis' outlined in 4.3?

Jaynes offers us a definition of the bicameral mind as 'a form of social control which **allowed mankind to move** from small hunter-gatherer groups to large agricultural communities'.[152] This does resemble the 'consciousness contract' proposed by the South African team for Neolithic communities, as well as the transition from the 'horizontal shamanism' of hunter-gatherers, with their more democratic social structure, to '**vertical shamanism**' in which the community projected authority onto particular members. Esoteric training enabled shamans to see and travel the cosmos on behalf of the community, ensuring the stability of a shared belief system, reflected in a system of government and in shared construction projects acting out the visions of the seer.[153] For Jaynes, this was a significant shift in the expression of our neurological inheritance, sufficiently flexible to allow growth from villages to cities, with the hierarchy of visible authority and invisible authority both somehow managing to keep in step.[154]

Jaynes's bicameral period thus **corresponds closely** with 'vertical shamanism' in both origin and structure. He emphasises the **irrational**, **mythological** and ideological elements in Neolithic societies, seeking their basis in neurological structures. This is very similar to the South African team and their hypothesis. Whereas Jaynes locates the source of the irrational experience and output in a whole brain **hemisphere**, the South Africans locate this (at least for Neolithic shamanism) in at least one **specific region**: the visual or striate cortex at the back of the human brain.[155] As their theory and findings are independent of T1, we can see the hypothesis of 4.3 at least as independent confirmation of Jaynes's theory. In terms of the distinction of the two basic kinds of shamanism, T1 picks up the story at the transition to vertical shamanism.

One of the two South Africans acknowledges the connection explicitly in the epilogue to his first book presenting his theory. He welcomes Jaynes's pioneering focus on altered states of consciousness, and residual 'fossils' of a more bicameral phase in modern culture; but he also radically alters the timeline, placing the origins of something like the bicameral mind much earlier in the Upper Palaeolithic, suggesting that it is a built-in feature of the human condition rather than a phase restricted to the Neolithic and the Bronze Age. This is such a complete revision of T1 that it represents a new theory. In its longer-term evolutionary approach to the historical narrative, it actually takes us closer to T2.[156]

- How well does T1 match 'the construction hypothesis' outlined in 4.4?

A particular connection to the hypothesis in 4.3 and 4.4 concerns the origins of psychological language. Jaynes sees the origin of most psychological words or 'psycho-lexicons'[157] in metaphors which transfer outside, **spatial** experience to an imagined 'interior space' (new words such as 'introcosm' and 'psychoscape' have been coined by Jaynes and his followers to try to capture this notion).[158] It is this interiorisation of the *psyche* into spatial images, 'a metaphorical build-up of consciousness and **mind-space**'[159] that is a key facet of T1. If Snell is right when he suggests that 'the concept of 'soul' … is tied up with the whole character and orientation of the language'[160] then early psychology will vary from language to language, Different metaphors from the spoken language, and different aspects of the writing technology, will both enable and restrict what can be said in each language about the invisible, intangible realm of the *psyche*.

This is a very good fit for the hypothesis of Neolithic archaeology as a 'script' for psychology. Before there was any written language, the spatial experience was organised through **architecture**, and so the first 'metaphors' for psychological experience – what became 'interior space', as described in written languages – were expressed in visible terms. One is a whole building in three dimensions, the other a picture in two. David Lewis-Williams traces both forms of symbolic communication right back to the shamanic visions of Upper Palaeolithic cultures.[161]

In this sense T1 can actually **strengthen** the (otherwise bizarre) hypothesis in 4.4: writing is then a new technology to capture Jaynes's process of interiorisation, on a continuous scale from architecture and other three-dimensional forms through to written characters in a script. Following Jaynes's lead, we can also trace this as an inward journey from unconscious expression through subconscious to conscious. Once again, the good match of T1 to recent Neolithic findings can be taken as a partial confirmation of theory.

It seems, from these reflections, that T1 was indeed well ahead of its time as a cultural interpretation. It can survive subsequent developments of **archaeology**, **anthropology** and **linguistics**, at least in Neolithic settings – even if it does not survive the development of neurology, where T1 now seems a little 'primitive', and the expansion of timelines, where it is hampered by its restriction to the Holocene.

- Does Jaynes's view of early religion match the portrait in this chapter?

Jaynes's focus on religion as fundamental to Neolithic societies – which was made in the teeth of more **materialistic** explanations in his time, and before cognitive archaeology – has been vindicated and supported by the evidence. Schmidt's interpretation of Göbekli Tepe is a good example of this change in thinking since Jaynes's time, as indeed is the emergence of the whole subdiscipline of cognitive archaeology.

There is also a strong thematic link here with Jaynes's conception of bicameral minds anticipating what we would now call **psychosis**: what is now abnormal – hallucinated voices and visions – was once healthy and normal, even creative. Jaynes's theory of religious and spiritual phenomena as '**regressive**', reaching back towards the bicameral era, correlates with the ongoing public fascination with **shamanism** as an enduring ecological niche on the margins of modernity. That is certainly how Jaynes would have understood this global phenomenon, although of course, this is open to more positive, less secularist interpretations. We will visit diverse religious systems further on in this enquiry.

- How does T1 fare when placed against more recent archaeological data and theory?

A potential problem for Julian Jaynes's theory (3.8) is the fact that it is 'dated' within the history of archaeology and the 'history of prehistory' in general by its **emphasis** on Bronze Age developments, at the expense of the Neolithic. It was developed when the Neolithic was only just becoming securely dated, especially with carbon dating, which detached prehistory from its previous dependence on Bronze Age literature.[162] Jaynes saw this but was too early to trace implications.

Nevertheless, as indicated in 3.8, subsequent archaeological theory has far from outdated Jaynes's theory but has instead 'caught up' with it in some respects. T1 successfully anticipated the trajectory of archaeology towards the

cognitive. We have already found a continuity from one current theory of Neolithic buildings as psychological models to Jaynes's theory of the Bronze Age 'psycho-lexicon' in terms of a smooth development from one form of public metaphor to another.

We have noted Stephen Mithen's 'cathedral of the modern mind' (first introduced 2.3) with its separate side-chapels as the domains of older, specialist intelligence in the evolving human brain, and the **breakdown** of their separation into a free-flowing mutual communication.[163] This is a more complex version of Jaynes's theory, in which modern consciousness results from the breakdown of the bicameral mind. As noted in 4.1 and 4.4, Mithen extends this explanation to the Neolithic as the deeper **integration** of neural functioning across domains.[164]

Mithen classifies the previous, Upper Palaeolithic transition with the Neolithic as 'the two really dramatic transformations in human behaviour', of enormous cultural significance; but he considers the first the more important of the two.[165]

- Could Mithen's cathedral theory of the evolution of intelligence offer T1 an explanatory back-story and integrate with it?

They share a spatial metaphor of mental 'containers'; but that in T1 is grounded in our anatomy, where the anatomical, neural basis of the other is not specified.

They share the notion of a breakdown between these neural barriers, but that in T1 is on a large scale with the two brain hemispheres, which seems primitive by comparison with Mithen's theory. On the other hand, the intelligence 'domains' in that theory line quite well with T1: linguistic and technical intelligence with the left, social intelligence with the right.[166] This seems promising: it could offer a possibility of seeing Mithen's theory as a 'higher resolution' expansion of T1.

It is a weakness of T1 that the bicameral mind simply appears in the Neolithic, and there is little attempt to reach further back in evolutionary terms, because carbon dating was so new: Mithen's theory, or an updated version of it, could outflank and encompass the earlier T1. Lewis-Williams, the senior South African archaeologist, implies something like this at the end of his earlier publication on the Upper Palaeolithic. Havingoffered his spectrum of consciousness theory as a supplement to Mithen's cathedral of intelligence theory from the start,[167] he ends by introducing Jaynes and T1 explicitly, as noted above, but he then immediately moves the timeline much further back.

This is just the kind of help we need when comparing theories. Here we have an informed reader of both Mithen and Jaynes, suggesting that their two theories are compatible and could even be integrated in principle. As noted above, however, so many elements of T1 would have to be sacrificed in the process that it would only have a contributory role, perhaps by adding its interpretations of the Bronze Age data.

- Are there any problems with Jaynes's view of Neolithic development?

The biggest problem, and where Jaynes looks most dated, is his insistence on a **single line of development** – like Marx's or Childe's view of history, a single track towards the present state (1.6). Almost everything in archaeology has moved away from this recently, towards many poles and geographical **diversity**, even some **reversibility**. There is no longer a single fixed path leading in one direction. T1 could be rescued from this, but it may require considerable revision to do so; which again, may mean that it will become less recognisable in its original form[168]

- Can we give an overall evaluation of T1 against the Neolithic data?

In terms of the lowest levels of our spectrum (2.1,2.2), in pure biology and in basic historical processes, T1 is weakened by its age, dated by advances in neuroscience; but in language and culture, it seems to hold up well. T1 and this chapter's hypotheses seem to confirm one another: Neolithic structures reflect an early stage of psychological self-expression, involving altered states of consciousness. It builds a much-needed bridge between long-term evolutionary psychology and the cultural psychology of the archaeologists. We may find many fruitful applications of T1 in Bronze Age civilisations, especially in its analyses of religion, government and written language.

4.8 Review of Theory Two (T2)

- How can T2 be applied to the evidence of this chapter?

In terms of history, the second half of T2 as presented in *The Master and his Emissary*, this chapter goes much further back than the original 'data set'. An advantage for T1 is its 'reach' in this respect as a history **designed** for the timescale we are covering, but such an advantage goes the other way as well. T2, being out of its 'comfort zone' in the Neolithic, can undergo a test *outside* its original data set, where it can be **falsified** by new evidence but also confirmed and extended. Scientifically, the stakes are higher.

A built-in advantage for T2 is its stronger basis in neurology and natural science – the first half of T2, in contrast to Jaynes with only a chapter or two at the start of his presentation. T2, as a cultural theory, is better grounded in **science**. Although its historical treatment does not stretch as far back as the Neolithic, in another sense it can 'overleap' T1 by using neurology which is still valid as far back as the Upper Palaeolithic. All that it requires is the same species; and this has been thoroughly confirmed, back to this point, by the scientific evidence (2.2).

Neolithic breakthroughs in each region, where they occurred, appear to be the first – or at least an early – example of 'bihemispheric advance', in the terms of T2: one distributed unevenly across the globe, because it needed the right environments as much as the right neurology to take place.[169] The fact that it occurred independently in several places can be **explained** more easily as a neurological advance from a capacity hard-wired into the human brain, led from within our biology and thus possible for humans anywhere, than in terms of diffusion from one centre with unique conditions. By grounding his cultural theory more securely in neurology McGilchrist has created a **robust** model, which can 'travel' with the evidence.[170]

- How does Stephen Mithen's 'cathedral' theory line up with T2 in the Neolithic?

Mithen's theory of the Neolithic is that the social, technical and natural history domains of fully evolved human intelligence rapidly integrated their functions, under the new circumstances of the Holocene.[171] T2 as a historical theory does not stretch to the Neolithic, but Mithen's theory might offer us a useful entry point to this data, given its inclusion of more recent neuroscience and cognitive psychology.

The intelligence domains in Mithen's theory line up better with T2 than they do with T1: with linguistic and technical intelligence on the left, and social and natural history intelligence on the right.[172] Although he talks of the breakdown and pooling of function between domains (more like T1's 'breakdown' of walls between halves) this can easily be understood as the cooperation or 'bihemispheric advance' in T2.[173]

T2 is also on 'this side' of Mithen's work, with the advantage of a much more sophisticated neurological basis and a yet more recent update; which includes a more explicit evolutionary account in terms of the adaptive advantages of brain lateralisation.[174] It seems that T2 could absorb Mithen's theory, as we have proposed that this theory could absorb T1: we appear to have a 'line of succession' with each theory outflanking the last. Certainly, T2 seems to perform well outside its original data set in this respect, due to its firm neurological basis and the historical continuity of that neurology.

- Given the lateralisation of leadership offered by T1, does T2 offer equivalent opportunities for such interpretation?

It was part of our argument in 4.3 that shamans and shamanic societies applied a subconscious 'binary logic' which the South African authors – in agreement with Lévi-Strauss – believe is wired into our neurology.[175] Could this binary logic be identified with the brain laterality of T2 and applied to the forms of Neolithic social leadership we have outlined?

The findings of 2.3 about the role of the shaman and the **multiple meanings** of Neolithic beliefs – that moving through a tunnel, for example, was at the same time an experience of bodily, psychological and cosmic travel – are suggestive of McGilchrist's **right-hemisphere** sensibility in the **leadership** role. Putting it too simply, **continuity** from unconscious through subconscious to waking states is characteristic of right-brain leadership according to T2, as is the directness and the **physicality** of the experiences signposted, even their **vagueness** of reference.

The findings of 2.4 about the role of the chief and the construction of **models** are more obvious indications of a sudden growth in **left-hemisphere** activity, which specialises in **hierarchical** relationships and in **second-order** response to primary experience. At least the 'project manager', whether chief, designer or architect, for at least part of the time, is exercising left-hemisphere functioning.

Again, this raises the intriguing possibility of the two novel divisions of labour within Neolithic **society** reflecting hemispheric leadership: the shaman from the right, and the chief (or project manager) from the left. We have proposed that *psyche* was projected onto one member of a clan in the shaman, and onto another as chief, so that the relationship of the two could be a **social microcosm** of lateral leadership in brain function.

If so, then McGilchrist's **normative** relationship between the hemispheres has a social counterpart, in the chief's continuing submission to the revelations of the shaman; the **'battle of the hemispheres'** is also played out in a social form, between these two forms of leadership.

That is, if hemispheric leadership can be embodied in respective social roles in a Neolithic group such as a tribe or a clan – with the shaman as right and chief as left – this raises the possibility of the same division of labour becoming embodied in larger social forms, the **institutions** derived from the original roles – so that shamanism becomes **state religion** and continues to embody right hemisphere leadership, while chiefdom becomes **government** embodying left hemispheric leadership. All we are doing here is taking the same principle and scaling it up.

As chiefs become kings, as shamans become priests in a state cult, everything depends on the representatives of the left hemisphere continuing in a public **submission** to the representative of the right hemisphere: state religion. This is a promising hypothesis as we move from Neolithic to Bronze Age societies. Everything so far has pointed to the centrality of religion: and this explains it.

This has an advantage over the simpler (and more explicit) social aspect of T1: instead of every member of the community, as an individual, displaying a more or less identical bicameral relationship, expressed on a larger scale, we have a looser arrangement – and a more testable theory – in which the division of two hemispheres is expressed **primarily at a social level**, leaving individuals under their respective forms of leadership, but their individual neural functioning only an **echo** of this social context, rather than the other way around. It seems ironic that a socially-led theory (T1) is obliged to dictate individual neurology, while a neurologically-led theory (T2) can yield a more flexible, observable prediction.

To take this 'scaling up' one level further: could different **civilisations** embody different configurations of the relationship between the two brain hemispheres?

We are getting ahead of ourselves – but also expanding the reach of the theory, tracing the trajectory of Neolithic developments and forming predictions to be tested in the Bronze Age. Let us find out in the following chapters if this works.

Do we find new left-hemisphere initiatives as it gradually discovers its powers? Do we see recognisable evidence of a re-balancing of hemispheric leadership? Can we identify such patterns at the level of **Bronze Age** social institutions? Or even at the level of relationships *between* different Bronze Age civilisations?

- Could you spot any **dialectical developments** growing in the Neolithic?

In terms of T2, what we seem to uncover in at least some examples of Neolithic culture and society is small '**forays**' by the left hemisphere, quickly re-absorbed and **rebalanced** by the right. We do not have the total or undisputed leadership of the right which seems to have characterised Upper Palaeolithic cultures, nor a serious challenge from the left. T2 predicts that the hemispheres will gradually 'experiment' with **independent** functioning, finding ways to operate at greater removes from one another, each time requiring a new re-balancing at a slightly **higher level**: a dialectical growth. This appears to describe the Neolithic data, which therefore begins to anticipate the narratives built on T2 for later history in *The Master and his Emissary*.

4.9 T2 and the role of the mother

T2 has one tremendous advantage: that it is from a living, active author who is busy developing his brainchild, for example in a recent sequel to *Master* – called *The Matter with Things* - and an ongoing social media presence. But T2 is also being developed by **other people** and providing an ongoing research programme for others – including, in some respects, this series.

A recent contribution came from Darcia Narvaez and Mary Tarsha at University of Notre Dame, Indiana.[176] One weakness of McGilchrist's presentation is that he barely connects the two **halves** of this book, named respectively *The Divided Brain* and *How the Brain has Shaped our World*, by outlining the **mechanisms** which **connect** the neurology of the first part to the larger cultural narratives of the second. The individual mind becomes 'communal mind' with only the briefest of arguments in support, and a general point: 'Our experience of the world helps to mould our brains, and our brains help to mould our experience of the world'.[177]

Narvaez and Tarsha propose a practical mechanism – through the processes of **motherhood**. They give positive and negative examples. A positive example is child-rearing practices in Palaeolithic hunter-gatherer societies, encouraging optimum nurture of a secure right-hemisphere leadership in a set of mothering behaviours they describe as the **Evolved Development Niche** – touch, attention and other factors (2.2).[178] This was maintained from generation to generation, with expectations of motherhood intricately matched to a child's neurological needs.

The EDN is largely only a redescription of standard **child-rearing norms**, in terms of evolutionary psychology: but the authors connect this explicitly to T2. Mothers nurture hemispheric balance, rearing children who will shape culture to stay in that balance. In particular, Narvaez and Tarsha suggest that the rearing of **boys** is vulnerable to the decline of the EDN and 'misraising of the species' brain', as a matter of biological input.[179] As their portrait is presented within the Palaeolithic era, it raises the question: 'How did the Neolithic affect the EDN?'

One proposal could be that the optimum nurture of balance in brain laterality does not **prevent** the left hemisphere from exercising its inbuilt creativity, but rather encourages it. Iain McGilchrist affirms the 'rights' of this hemisphere in his portrait of the Greeks: that 'it was through the workings of the emissary, the left hemisphere, that the 'empire of the mind' expanded in the first place'.[180] In the Neolithic we see the growth of hierarchies, cosmographies and models as legitimate expressions of this hemisphere, fully subservient to the right leadership.

In his latest publication, McGilchrist gives an evolutionary explanation of T2 as balanced representatives of the roles of predator (left) and prey (right): 'Every animal, in order to survive, has to solve a conundrum: how to eat without being eaten'.[181] The twin brain has evolved as a solution, with 'narrow-beam, sharply focussed attention … the kind paid by an animal locking onto its prey'[182] as the purpose of the left hemisphere, and 'broad, open, sustained, vigilant attention … designed to look out for all the rest – whatever might be going on in the world while we are busy grasping'.[183] During the Upper Palaeolithic 'transition' our basic position in the food chain was reversed (4.1) entailing a greater use for the 'predator' hemisphere, to the point where it was out of control for a time.[184] The link between this narrative (2021) and his sketchy historical account of Bronze Age origins (2009) is the Neolithic; the implication would be, if anything, more of a role for the right hemisphere, at least initially, as humans became more like their domestic animals in guarding their resources rather than seeking them; and another implication would be a need to find new cultural outlets for both hemispheres within the new societies.

Given McGilchrist's characterisation of the left hemisphere's central motivation as 'power', as an inbuilt predisposition,[185] presumably all that was needed was the right circumstances for domination of the *same* species to replace that of *other* species. The Neolithic created the **preconditions**, providing the right arena, and we see this in the transition from equal, democratic societies to patterns of hierarchy (4.5).

It is also possible, however, that changes to society *actively* disrupted the EDN and helped to 'nudge' the left hemisphere forwards, adding to its tendencies in that direction: that the Neolithic was an **active partner** in 'losing our balance', so that the left hemisphere sought to exercise power *over the other hemisphere.* In terms of McGilchrist's historical narrative, this was ultimately one consequence of the Neolithic.

In either case, whatever the dynamics, a loss of balance has followed. What was needed was a set of resources at the next stage – Bronze Age civilisations – to provide a **correction** and preserve lateral balance. In the following chapters, a series of such resources will appear, which we can examine along these lines. It may be that **some** Bronze Age civilisations preserve the lateral balance better than others.

Discussion questions:

1 Do you think that the word 'Neolithic' is still worth using as a label?
2 What do you think used to happen at Göbekli Tepe, and how often?
3 Why do you think people listened to trance visions seen by a shaman?
4 Do you find the association of subconscious with underground bizarre?
5 What myth or metaphor could capture your current educational setting?
6 Is there any valid role for the skills of the shaman in today's societies?
7 Do you find the interpretation of social roles in lateral terms convincing?
8 Do you think lateral balance could be applied to different civilisations?
9 What were the disadvantages to mothers in the Palaeolithic way of life?

Recommended Reading

- Peter Bellwood (ed) *The Global Prehistory of Human Migrations*
- Luigi Luca Cavalli-Sforza *Genes, Peoples and Languages*
- David Lewis-Williams *The Mind in the Cave*
- David Lewis-Williams and David Pearce *Inside the Neolithic Mind*
- Tracey B. Henley and Matt J. Rossano *Psychology and Cognitive Archaeology: an interdisciplinary approach*
- Claude Lévi-Strauss *Structuralist Anthropology*
- Colin Renfrew *Before Civilisation*
- Colin Renfrew and Ezra B.W.Zubrow *The Ancient Mind: elements of cognitive archaeology*
- Nicholas Thomas and Caroline Humphrey (eds.) *Shamanism, History and the State*

Notes

1 Mithen 1996 pp.61,65–72,151–4,178–184,195,217; we have dated this 70-50 ybp, from its global appearance out of Africa, within Africa it was earlier. See Lewis-Williams pp.96–9; 180–1; 189; 287.
2 Henley and Rossano p.160; Renfrew and Zubrow p.32.
3 Bellwood pp.39,52–9,294–7; Cavalli-Sforza pp.61,93,170–2.

4 Harari Ch. 4 pp.70–80 gives a brilliant account of this process; Lewis-Williams p.88 suggests that the extinction of the Neanderthal population was possible through simple biological competition.
5 Ehrenreich pp.22,47,121–2.
6 Pyne and Pyne pp.239ff.
7 Mithen 1996 pp.151–2; Lewis-Williams offers a sustained critique of this notion, in line with our own general critique of the language of sudden change in 1.6: see pp.40,82,96–9,180–1,189,287.
8 Bellwood pp.84,393; Lewis-Williams and Pearce p.6; Mithen 2003 pp.3,67.
9 Bellwood pp.5,79–81; Mithen 2003 pp.12–13.
10 Cavalli-Sforza pp.92-3,102-3,107,127-8; he explains the genetic technique of Principal Components Analysis which has enabled detailed tracing of human population histories pp.107-8,127–130.
11 Bellwood 101–3,109,135; Diamond p.390; Howe p.148; Muksawa pp.xxv,64,169–171.
12 Bellwood pp.97–8,100,121; Cavalli-Sforza p.123; Muksawa pp.36–42.
13 Bellwood pp.103,116,135; Muksawa pp.106–7.
14 Bellwood p.81; Diamond p.99.
15 Bellwood pp.63,71,191–4.
16 Bellwood pp.79080,83,354–5,370,392,397,406,410; Diamond p.99; Harari p.89.
17 Bellwood p.82; Childe 1942 pp.55–6; Childe 1981 pp.83–87.
18 Bellwood pp.32–3,139–144,153,168–172; it also contributed to Egypt's Neolithic (6.1) and Israel's (7.1), but the point here is specifically its relationship to Europe, and thus to Eurocentric history.
19 Bellwood pp.103 (Aquatic over Neolithic), 135 (Ceramic over Neolithic).
20 Mithen 1996 pp.217,219,226 assumes and explains it as 'near-simultaneous'; Mithen 2003 details its variety. Cavalli-Sforza pp.97–100 even suggests that if we used Ceramic rather than Neolithic as our primary label, then Japan would have the priority from a global perspective, and the African tribes in what is now the Sahara would have priority over West Asia. He also suggests that the cow is more likely to have been domesticated first in West Africa pp.121–3.
21 Renfrew 1976 p.22.
22 Renfrew 1976 pp.21,27,67–8 and Clarke's volume *World Prehistory*, which followed this breakthrough.
23 Bellwood pp.172,175; Norman Davies pp.3–5,7–9; Sykes pp.27–33.
24 Leahey p.93; we will see this in the case of Semitic nomads in 7.1; Cavali-Sforza pp.117–119,125 points out that Indo-European nomads also remained 'between' farming and hunter-gathering.
25 Eriksen pp.40,50,62,86,132,182,219.
26 Henley and Rossano pp.viii,2,75–6,97–108; Lévi-Strauss 1963 pp.101–117; Renfrew 1976 pp.174–182,200–4, 256–264.
27 Eriksen pp.207–9; Grabbe p.4 and Johnson p.33 also note this convergence of anthropology and archaeology.
28 Renfrew 1976 pp.172–3.
29 Harari pp.100–2; Lewis-Williams and Pearce pp.; Mann p.39; Mithen 2003 pp. 89–90,103,522 n.6.
30 Lewis-Williams and Pearce pp.; Mann pp.39,41,44–5,48–54; Mithen 2003 pp.65–6.
31 Harari pp.100–2; Mann p.48; Mithen 1995 p.226 – Eric Higgs was teaching this at Cambridge fifty years ago.
32 Harari pp.100–2; Lewis-Williams and Pearce pp.28–32; Mann p.39; Mithen 2003 pp.66.

33 Harari pp.100–2; Lewis-Williams and Pearce pp.; Mann pp.39,41,44–5,48–54; Mithen 2003 pp.65–6.
34 Mendelssohn pp.16,46,68,128,134–7,140,146; Lewis-Williams pp.229,266,269, 284–6 suggests a comparable role for Upper Palaeolithic cave art, strengthening the case for this interpretation.
35 Renfrew and Zubrow pp.3–11.
36 Mann p.57.
37 *ibid* p.58.
38 Harari pp.100–2; Mann pp.39,57; Mithen 2003 pp.38,67,77–8.
39 Harari pp.100–102, Lewis-Williams and Pearce pp.33,148; Mann p.41,49,56–8; Mithen 2003 pp.62,64,67,94–6.
40 Mann pp.40,42–4,49,56–8; Mithen 2003 pp.65,90.
41 Bellwood p.128; Childe 1954 p.73; Mithen 2003 p.71.
42 Mithen 2003 pp.67–8,104.
43 Bellwood pp.126–8,134,136–8; Diamond pp.386–7; Muksawa pp.33–4.
44 Mithen 2003 pp.67–8.
45 Kristiansen and Larsson pp.105–7,140–1.
46 Lewis-Williams and Pearce pp.81,167,176; Renfrew 1976 pp.161–6.
47 Henley pp.211–8; commentary in Henley and Rossano pp.41–4,49.
48 Henley pp.211–2,215–6; Henley and Rossano pp.42–3.
49 Henley and Rossano pp.43,49; with additional support on this point from historian Daniel Smail on p.43. This chapter was planned and researched before coming across Henley's publications.
50 Bellwood pp.79–80,83,93,284,305–6; Diamond pp.99–101,147–150,304–5,315,335; Harari pp.88–9; Mithen 2003 p.345.
51 Bellwood pp.103,116,135; Muksawa p.106; the link to the Egyptian Bronze Age is by no means direct nor as well understood as that to Sumer. See 5.1 and 6.1 for more detail of each as context.
52 Roberts p.41; Davies pp.3–5,7–8; Wood pp.16, 22–5,27,124.
53 Renfrew and Zubrow p.51.
54 Lewis-Williams and Pearce p.41.
55 Thomas and Humphrey pp.76–8,191.
56 Thomas and Humphrey pp.190ff., 105ff.
57 Bellwood pp.79080 83,354–5,370,392,397,406,410; Diamond p.99; Harari p.89.
58 Childe 1954 p.48; Lewis-Williams and Pearce pp.140–148; Lewis-Williams pp.131–5,205,225 argues this point about the far more remote origins of shamanism during the Upper Palaeolithic era.
59 Lewis-Williams and Pearce pp.118,124–5,141–4.
60 Benedict p.69.
61 Lewis-Williams and Pearce p.68.
62 Renfrew and Zubrow p.88; Thomas and Humphrey pp.6,76,192.
63 Lewis-Williams and Pearce pp.42–55,68–77,260–271 are the main expositions.
64 *ibid* p.40; Lewis-Williams pp.39,130,203,206 extends thatbridge back to the Upper Palaeolithic and its rock art, many millennia before the more accessble and complex structures of the Neolithic.
65 Lewis-Williams pp.9–10,107–112,121–9; Lewis-Williams and Pearce Ch.2 pp.37–59.
66 Benedict pp.30.191–1.
67 Challenger pp.123–4; Kiev p.40–42; Lewis-Williams and Pearce pp.42–6.
68 Henley and Rossano p.133; Kiev pp.39,43; Lewis-Williams and Pearce pp.124–5.
69 Henley and Rossano p.134; Lewis-Williams and Pearce pp.47–55,67–8.
70 Lewis-Williams and Pearce p.67; Renfrew and Zubrow p.88; Lewis-Williams extends the point further back between the Upper Neolithic transition and Neolithic pp.9–10,39,121–9,130,203,206.

71 Lévi-Strauss 1978 p.5; Lewis-Williams and Pearce pp.160–1; Van de Mieroop 2017 pp.124–5.
72 Lévi-Strauss 1963 p.161.
73 Lewis-Williams and Pearce pp.64–5.
74 *ibid* pp.65–6,92; Lewis-Williams pp.144-8,208–210 underpins this insight by tracing the same worldview with the same cosmos in Upper Palaeolithic cave art.
75 Henley and Rossano p.134; Lewis-Williams and Pearce p.93.
76 Watterson 1996 p.4.
77 Henley and Rossano pp.127,129.
78 Challenger p.33.
79 Lewis-Williams and Pearce p.255.
80 Kiev p.50.
81 Lewis-Williams and Pearce p.285.
82 Lewis-Williams and Pearce p.280.
83 Henley and Rossano p.133,5; Kiev 39–40.
84 Ball p.59; Gernet pp.45,85Thomas and Humphrey pp.191,207.
85 Lewis-Williams and Pearce pp.88–93.
86 *ibid* pp.93–4,126.
87 Renfrew and Zubrow pp.79–80.
88 *ibid* pp.56–7,71–2.
89 Lewis-Williams and Pearce p.167; a useful summary of the thesis for the period prior to the Neolithic can be found in Lewis-Williams p.282.
90 Mithen 2003 p.65.
91 Lewis-Williams and Pearce p.12.
92 Lewis-Williams and Pearce p.243; Renfrew 1976 pp.240,256,262.
93 Lewis-Williams and Pearce pp.81,167,176; Renfrew 1976 pp.161–6.
94 Darvill p.144.
95 Darvill p.145; Renfrew 1976 p.259.
96 Lewis-Williams and Pearce pp.182–4.
97 *ibid* pp.224–243.
98 Lewis-Williams and Pearce p.88.
99 Lewis-Williams and Pearce pp.176,196,201–2,248; Renfrew and Zubrow p.77.
100 Hoyland pp.175–183; Kramer pp.135–142; Roux pp.78–9,126,156–160,196–200 (structure),365–9 (ritual).
101 Mithen 1996 pp.61,65–72,151–4.
102 *ibid* p.61.
103 *ibid* pp.154ff.,174ff.,192–5.
104 *ibid* pp.178–184,195,217.
105 *ibid* pp.217–226; in his Epilogue.
106 Lewis-Williams and Pearce p.308 list Mithen 1996 and 2003 as sources and use the latter pp.33,148.
107 McGilchrist 2021 pp.584,630 on Lévi-Strauss's suggestion that myths and metaphors can 'think themselves'.
108 Henley and Rossano pp.xii–xiv.
109 Henley and Rossano p.48; Mendelssohn pp.16,46,68,128,134–7,140,146; Mithen pp.66–7.
110 Benedict pp.191–6; Kiev pp.32,39,53,103.
111 Benedict pp.13,20,23–5,179,186; Mithen pp.93–5 offers a possible example from archaeology.
112 Benedict p.69.
113 *ibid* pp.69–71.
114 Thomas and Humphrey p.18,22,24,26–7,32–5,38.
115 *ibid* pp.193,197,199.

116 Henley and Rossano p.127; Renfrew and Zubrow p.47.
117 Lewis-Williams and Pearce pp.86–7; Thomas and Humphrey pp.7,78–85.
118 Childe 1954 pp.53,73; Childe 1981 pp.91,114; Diamond pp.268–272.
119 Childe 1954 pp.94–5,251–2; Diamond pp.268–273,273–8.
120 Thomas and Humphrey pp.6,28,193,199,224; Renfrew and Zubrow p.50.
121 Childe 1981 p.114; Kristiansen and Larsson pp.51–5.
122 Renfrew and Zubrow p.50; this is very obvious for example in early Greek literature, to be studied in the next volume, where the Greek gods are straightforward mirrors of archaic Greek society.
123 Wink pp.7–8.
124 Lewis-Williams and Pearce pp.78,288–9.
125 Darvill pp.16,29; Lewis-Williams and Pearce p.171; Renfrew 1976 pp.277–9; Renfrew and Zubrow pp.3–5,10–11, 18,22.
126 Renfrew and Zubrow p.129.
127 *ibid* pp.3,10,51.
128 *ibid* p.144.
129 *ibid* p.149,154.
130 *ibid* p.149 n.3.
131 *ibid* p.154,163.
132 *ibid* p.129.
133 *ibid* p.154.
134 *ibid* p.144.
135 *ibid.*
136 Henley and Rossano pp.xli-xlv.
137 Heidegger *Being and Time* I.3 68–70 pp.97–99.
138 Renfrew and Zubrow p.145.
139 Mithen 1994 pp.31–2,35–6.
140 Henley and Rossano pp.49–50.
141 Renfrew 1976 pp.250–268.
142 Thomas and Humphrey pp.32–8,76–8,92,197–200.
143 Renfrew and Zubrow p.145.
144 *ibid* p.154.
145 *ibid* p.149,154.
146 *ibid* p.154,163.
147 *ibid* p.144.
148 Childe 1954 p.40.
149 Childe 1954 pp.56,65; Childe 1981 pp.85,101–5.
150 See Machinga and Marovic for a representative contemporary argument.
151 Jaynes pp.84,228–9.
152 Jaynes p.126.
153 Lewis-Williams and Pearce pp.40–42,59,86–7.
154 *ibid* pp.88–98,138–145.
155 Lewis-Williams and Pearce p.54.
156 Lewis-Williams p.287-291.
157 McVeigh p.46.
158 *ibid* pp.11,38,57.
159 *ibid* p.246.
160 Snell p.15.
161 Lewis-Williams *The Mind in the Cave* pp.60–68,192–6, 200.
162 Renfrew 1976 p.27.
163 Mithen 1996 pp.61,65–72,151–4,178–184,195,217.
164 *ibid* pp.217–226; in his Epilogue.
165 *ibid* pp.11,226.

166 *ibid* pp.67,69,92–4,96–108,132–142,222,224–5.
167 Lewis-Williams pp.9–10,107–112.
168 The whole timeline of his student McVeigh is still 'mono-linear', with a single date given for the Neolithic. The focus is more on saving the theory than on exploring the evidence; on the terms of T2, this is a very left-brain approach!.
169 McGilchrist 2009 pp.259,299; exactly the argument of Mithen 1996 p.226.
170 This is precisely the point Lewis-Williams makes for his own theory at pp.39,130,203,206.
171 Mithen 2003 pp.67,222–6.
172 *ibid* pp.67,69,92–4,96–108,132–142,222,224–5.
173 McGilchrist 2009 pp.259,299.
174 McGilchrist 2021 pp.20–26.
175 Lévi-Strauss 1978 p.5; Lewis-Williams and Pearce pp.160–1; Van de Mieroop 2017 pp.124–5.
176 'The Missing Mind' in Henley and Rossano (2022) Chapter 5 pp.55–69.
177 *ibid* pp.245ff.; 2021 p.43 repeats this almost word for word.
178 Narvaez and Tarsha pp.55–60.
179 *ibid* p.64.
180 McGilchrist 2009 p.296.
181 McGilchrist 2021 p.20.
182 *ibid* pp.21,24; in McGilchrist 2009 p.37 this is characterised more basically as 'focus and grasp'.
183 *ibid* pp.21,25.
184 Ehrenreich pp.22,47,121–2.
185 McGilchrist 2009 p.209; rephrased with added complexity and nuance for example in 2021 pp.43–5.

5 Ancient Iraq

5.1 Orientation: The land between the rivers

From their headwaters to the east and west of Göbekli Tepe in the Turkish hills, two rivers that have been called by various names by various peoples – once *idiglat* and *buranun*, today Tigris and Euphrates – flowed through the plains of Iraq down to the Persian Gulf.[1] The very early Neolithic breakthrough had led to population bulges moving in all directions; one moved south-east, between the rivers into dryer lands, using irrigation to support farming, creating a very high-density population as it reached the Gulf coast.[2] Settlements of mud-brick houses – with painted walls and frescos, stone carving and sculpture, property seals and irrigation for farming – gradually became the largest on the planet.[3]

One of these became, by most estimations, 'the first true city on earth'.[4] It was **Uruk**, now – 5000 years later – called Warka. It was inland of a coastal settlement named Eridu, where fish offerings to a water god had been offered for many millennia; and the shrine at Eridu was always considered the origin and source of the 'Uruk-culture' which became identified with **civilisation**.[5] It inspired the other settlements to imitate its model, so that by the end of the third millennium, some of the cities on this plain contained over 200,000 people.[6]

The Romans called this *Mesopotamia*, in Greek 'the land between the rivers' (*meso* = between, and *potamos* = river); but in ancient times it was first called Shinar or **Sumer**. It was later named after the most dominant city: Uruk, Ur and **Babylon** fought over the south, Asshur (hence **Assyria**; now Syria) over the north; and eventually **Persia** absorbed it from what is now Iran. With so many changes of name for this region we will simply use the most recent one: **Iraq**.[7]

When discussing its **culture**, however, we will focus on the first and the most creative leaders in the region: the **Sumerians**. In their big cities, they pooled so many cultural innovations from the Fertile Crescent region that they created a measure of what **civilisation** looks like.[8] Sumerian cultural dominance in West Asia lasted until the Greeks, halfway to ourselves; that is, for half of all recorded history.[9]

DOI: 10.4324/9781003396147-8

The logic of the Neolithic led to similar intensifications of human habitation on the Nile (6.1), the Indus and the Yellow River in China (8.1).[10] All involved a **melting-pot** of tribes and cultures – but in Sumer perhaps more than the others. One of its non-native groups, speaking a language which did not survive and does not belong to any recognised family – now called Sumerian – developed a **writing script** which became the voice of its culture, still speaking to us now.[11]

5.2 The Sumerian writing system

Given all that has been said about the relationship of linguistics to psychology in principle (2.4), and the importance of written language to it in practice (2.6), as well as the importance of the latter to both our theories (3.8,3.9) we are going to devote considerable attention to writing systems as the medium of thought in the Bronze Age. Our encounter with Sumerian is only the first of several more.

We know that Sumerian was not the original language of the region because the river names, most of the farming words, and even the main city names do not seem to belong to it.[12] It is possible that it was spoken by a Neolithic tribe long established on the coast.[13] When the script arrives it does not seem to match the spoken language quite as comfortably as we would expect if it simply emerged directly from it; there are signs that it was actually invented further along the Gulf coast, in southern **Iran**.[14] It evolved into full sentences during an intensive trade in the Gulf with Bahrain, Oman, Iran and Pakistan, strongly suggesting a **coastal** location for the original spoken language, which shaped the grammar of the script; but then the script itself outlasted the death of the spoken language.[15]

All of this suggests that this technology was developed in the context of local, national and international **interaction**. One scholar labels it as '**cosmopolitan**' (Greek = citizen of the world)[16] and this seems a fair description. It contained a word *namlulu* meaning 'mankind', '**humanity**', and understood all of *namlulu* as inhabiting the four *ubda*'s, the four corners of the earth, with one of its gods referred to as 'king of all the lands', not territorially but as shared possession.[17] Although we will meet this notion in Book Two, it was a very unusual outlook for the Bronze Age. In inventing the city in a bustling area, the Sumerians seem to have glimpsed something beyond the tribal ethnocentrism of the Neolithic.

Equally unusual was their lack of interest in either the past or the future. They had little interest in ancestors, except great kings and heroes, nor an afterlife, and thought of everything (including their writing system) as having arrived as it was from the gods – unchanged since the moment of creation if temporarily unsettled by the great Flood.[18] Here lay the source of the **new ethnocentrism**, not tribal but cultural, what Derrida has called logocentrism the assumption that this particular writing system was the language of creation, **the language of the gods**, and the source of all science.[19]

The Sumerians were a fertile source of **symbolic systems**: their images of gods, heroes and events in stone carvings and sculptures, like those at Göbekli

Tepe but more complex, had a hieroglyphic character – like a visual symbol system, which inspired other emerging cultures.[20] This could have evolved as in **Egypt** into a two-dimensional writing system, continuous with the three-dimensional surface.[21] The cylinder seals used to mark property could have developed into a script, as they seem to have done at around the same time in **Pakistan**.[22] As we have already seen in the previous chapter (4.4) their architectural inheritance contained its own symbolic system, shared with multiple cultures.[23] There are Chinese, Olmec, Mayan, Inca and other examples of independent systems.[24]

The symbolic system which became Sumerian writing was an invoicing and accounting code on clay tokens, inscribed using a piece of reed which made wedge-shaped, almost triangular marks. As Latin for 'wedge' is *cuneus*, it is called **cuneiform** = 'wedge-shaped'. These clay tablets survived better to the north, away from the sea salt, but hundreds of thousands survived, transmitting a wealth of insight.[25] Most of the early tablets are **inventories** and receipts for temple **accounts**, concerned with animals for sacrifices and staff wages, so it is closely tied up with the number system, and initially the business of priests.[26] As with architecture – and perhaps agriculture itself (4.2) – the beginnings of writing lay in **religion**, but in this case expressed in religious administration. Originally written from right to left, it gradually switched its orientation.[27]

Nevertheless, once the tool was discovered it could easily be transferred as an invoicing and accounting system for trade; and its presence rapidly accelerated trade. Just as the Neolithic is named (inadequately) after stone carving methods which accompanied it in certain parts of the world, because these were the first evidence unearthed, the breakthrough to civilisation is called 'the **Bronze Age**' for the good reason that this alloy of copper and tin had been discovered – no mean feat of chemical engineering, as many archaeologists insist[28] – and bronze artefacts survived to be discovered (1.4). For Iraq, this meant a growing demand for **raw materials** from outside its borders, especially Iran to the northeast and Oman down the Gulf.[29] For this purpose, as well as temple accounts, the new writing tool provided an extension of human ability; in this case, human memory, constituting what we would now call a **data-processing system**.[30]

The core elements of such recording systems were already very old: a team of archaeologists has identified a proto-writing system in the Palaeolithic caves of Lascaux, France, formally not very different from the clay labelling system used in Iraq before the cities.[31] What made the difference was bringing such a system inside the city environment, where its uses could diversify quickly, and adding the crucial phonetic (sound-based) and semantic elements to express speech.[32]

The Sumerian script spread widely: first through trade, later through conquest to expand, maintain and control trade networks.[33] It had begun as a cooperative, outward-looking technology and had probably been adapted to its first spoken language; similarly, it proved **adaptable** to other spoken languages.[34] The script travelled with the city, each 'prototype' forming part of a single package throughout Western Asia.[35] The largest neighbouring language family was the Semitic group, closely connected to the start of the Neolithic (see 4.2 and 7.1), and the first big jump in the use of Sumerian cuneiform script was to embrace **Akkadian**, an early Semitic language, when Sargon the king of Akkad invaded Sumer.[36] From now on the city-states were caught in a wrestling match, slowly growing in extent, with the south initially fought between Babylon and Ur.[37]

Akkadian was incorporated into cuneiform, following the victory of Semitic-speaking cities and the first empires: first the Akkadian, then finally the Babylonian.[38] Spoken Sumerian disappeared but the status of the Sumerian cuneiform script survived,[39] adapting to Semitic phonics and grammar as (we infer) it once had to Sumerian phonics and grammar.[40] This led to significant new writing genres beyond the dominance of lexical lists, and it greatly enriched its expressive potential.[41]

The relevant dates for this language history can be captured on a short timeline:

c.3200–2100	Sumerian culture (southern Iraq) with cuneiform script
c.2500	Sumerian cuneiform develops into a full written language
c.2330–2000	Akkadian (Semitic) culture competes with Sumerian
c.1800–1600	Akkadian adopts cuneiform; spoken Sumerian disappears
c.1300–600	Assyrian culture (Semitic, northern Iraq) dominates region

What held it together was the **Sumerian culture** – cities and writing – which outlasted the end of Sumerian as a spoken language.[42] In every city there was a library with a catalogue, listed by the opening words.[43] As with the system of Chinese characters (8.3), cuneiform became less of a language and more of a system of public representation like a digital 'app', capable of great flexibility and ability to absorb an ever-wider family of spoken languages needing a script. From its humble beginnings as an accounting tool, it became for more than a millennium a great medium for epic poetry and myth.

5.3 Scribal training: The *é-dubba*

Studying Sumerian is a useful exercise in breaking down our reading habits and associated cognitive style: what Derrida called our 'logocentrism'. In engaging with cuneiform we can continue the 'mental gymnastics' of Chapter 4, the effort of deconstruction (3.6) and the understanding of the global background to our Western legacy in Book Two. Sumer is particularly important for this, as its direct descendants in Babylon and Persia interacted with Greece during the birth of that philosophical tradition, including its experiments in written psychology.

Sumerian texts show, as soon as writing appears, that reflection had long been occurring. People were not unintelligent. As with the complexity of the languages, as soon as we have access to ancient minds, we find that they mirror our own. Let us enter the world of the **scribe**.

For us in the extended present – the generations since modern psychology first began – the invention of writing marks the division of 'prehistory' from history. We have seen plenty of reasons to update or simply abolish this distinction.[44] For those in the extended past, however, there were enormous continuities and writing was just another technology: except for those who specialised in it. In the common patterns of the global Neolithic (4.5) we traced the emergence of the first specialisations: the classic **shaman** in early Neolithic tribes, then the vertical shaman or **priest** in later Neolithic, evolving opposite the tribal **chief**, and diverse **crafts**, some of which seem to have overlapped with the shaman.[45]

Scribes in Sumer were not all priests but an entirely **new specialism** – emerging from the guilds of **crafts**, rather than the line through priests back to shamans. Sumerian cities continued the division of labour between priest and chief – *en* and *ensi* respectively – and the scribes could serve either, for temple or palace accounts, the justice system, diplomacy and trade abroad, or training future scribes in one of the cities: that is, education.[46] The *ensi* was seen as the steward of the city god's estates, advised by a bicameral assembly (that is, two-chambered, with an upper and lower house) but able to act independently;[47] he evolved into a traditional chief role, *lugal* (literally 'big man') under the pressure of competition and conflict.[48] The *en* was the leading priest and guardian of the god's temple,[49] and many scribes were supported from the temple income.[50] As the Egyptian scribes had Thoth as the god of writing, Sumerian scribes had Nisaba; they would sometimes end a piece of work, especially a temple script, with *nisaba zami* = 'O Nisaba, praise'.[51]

As soon as there was a new craft, there was always training or **apprenticeship**. There is evidence of teaching and learning stretching as far back as Palaeolithic cave art and flint-breaking.[52] Contemporary skills with their own evidence of training and apprenticeship included the forging of bronzes in northern Iraq, the cutting of exact measuring weights in Pakistan's emerging cities, and the very different form literacy was taking in Egypt – alongside the scribes of Sumer.[53]

Scribal training evolved with the writing system. As early as 3000 BCE, some scribes were already thinking in terms of **teaching and learning**; and by 2500 schools had multiplied in the fast-growing Sumerian cities. Cuneiform developed into a full written language, moving from simple public inscriptions to full written sentences – exactly contemporary with the same development in Old Kingdom Egypt (6.2).[54]

To be able to write *dubsar*, 'scribe', after your name was the equivalent of **BA** or **BSc**. There was no thought of a distinction between school and university, and indeed the training centre was most like a tertiary **technical college**.[55] It was called *é-dubba*, literally 'house of tableting', and laid out very much like a school or college today with a **principal** called *ummia*, a **deputy** *adda é-dubba* (father of the tablet house), and even a **secretary** (*ugula*).[56] The *dubsar nishid* was the scribe of accounting, the *dubsar zaga* the scribe of measuring, and *dubsar ashaga* the scribe of surveying; this was the **faculty** or staffroom, often with a young **trainee** or junior scribe, a recent graduate: *dubsar tur*.[57] These parallels even stretch to a college **nurse**: though *mash-mashu* is also translated 'exorcist', such dramatic language often masked a more rational approach to medicine.[58]

Whether or not we can find much evidence of psychological content in Sumer, we can already see the importance of this more generic contribution to the story of academia. We noted that there would be no **academics** today without their beginning (however remote) in the specialised role of the shaman during the Neolithic; it is equally obvious that without the Sumerian *é-dubba* there would be no **academy**. This interpretation is guilty of 'presentism', but from the facts it is clear that a permanent **template** was set for all classical, literate education. There would be no psychology, nor any other collective, literacy-based academic activities today, without this Sumerian template.

The *é-dubba* was 'the centre of culture and teaching in Sumer',[59] and also from Sumer to the whole of Western Asia. Scribes were **exported** like missionaries of civilisation.[60] The civilisations of the Mediterranean, including eventually the Greeks, were indebted to Sumer for this and the city, as the great Assyriologist Samuel Kramer observes: 'From the point of view of the history of **civilisation**, Sumer's supreme achievements were the development of the cuneiform system of writing and the formal system of **education**'.[61] The link between the two key Sumerian cultural innovations – the city and writing – was here in the *é-dubba*.

For the apprentices at the new craft, the whole business of **literacy** as we know it has begun: 'Regardless of the writing system, the visual, cognitive and motor processes of reading take months or years of repetitive effort for normal children to master, whether with alphabets or logo-syllabic scripts like Chinese' – or cuneiform.[62] In Sumer the reading was the main focus; whereas in Egypt and China writing had the higher status. Writing on clay tablets was not as demanding as hieratic (6.2) or especially hieroglyphics and Chinese. It is fair to say, however, that at the *é-dubba* there was a very long school day for a remarkable number of years because this civilisation set such a high priority on producing written records.

In Derrida's grammatology (2.6, 3.2) he suggests a 'cultural graphology' – that 'the national markings should permit to a certain extent researches into the particularities of the collective mind of peoples'.[63] What portrait can we derive from cuneiform literature 'from the psychological point of view, that is, from a consideration of the character and **personality of the people** who created it'?[64]

From his studies in Greek, Snell suggests that 'the concept of 'soul' … is tied with the whole character and orientation of the language'.[65] What is the match of cuneiform to **psychology** in the modern sense, as the collective study of individual *psyche*?

We started our general introduction to culture (3.2) with Ruth Benedict's idea of a child becoming 'the little creature of his culture' through the long process of induction.[66] In most of this book we work at the level of a whole culture; let us, at least in this case, take the **child's eye-view** to explain this central question.

In keeping with our promotion of the needs of the right hemisphere, inspired by T2, we will use fiction. There were a few women in the scribal elite; therefore, there were girls at the *é-dubba*, and women called *dubsar*.[67] Let us pick a Sumerian girl at Uruk c.2400 BCE, and call her Namtar. She is ten years old; her brother Lulu is eight.

5.4 A day at the *é-dubba*

Namtar sits on a shaded bench in an open courtyard, beside boys and girls of her age. Her brother is in the neighbouring yard and she sometimes hears his voice, typically quarrelling with other boys when the *dubsar nishid* has gone inside.[68]

She has the younger *dubsar tur*; both classes are engaged in *lishanu*, copying lexical lists, their main school activity.[69] They have both endured a long lecture followed by hours of rote copying, with memorisation of their lists and tables and clusters of syllables: there are beatings at the discretion of the supervisors and – whether it is Lulu's temper or the *dubsar* 's – Namtar hears it regularly.[70]

She smiles as she hears the *dubsar nishid* explaining her brother's exercise: it is an old favourite, *urra* = *hubulla* ('loan with fixed interest');[71] every item copied out from the left hand of the tablet to the right. Lulu is proud of the fact that he can already recite most of this list – learnt at home from his big sister – and can write some of it with his eyes closed.[72] As well as muscle memory Lulu is being conditioned to associate, substitute, match and contrast these words; as he has already learned many of the letters, and how to prepare his tablet.[73] Then he will be given a new tablet multiplying to find the final numbers in the list: he and his teacher know the answer, but the problem is to find the way to it.[74] Lulu loves to talk, but he has already learned that writing is the superior art.[75] Like a *dubsar* he already believes that activity is the source of order, and laziness of chaos.[76]

Namtar's text is more demanding – but much more interesting. It is a founding myth of the city from before the Flood: the story of Inanna and Enki, when the arts of civilisation were brought from Eridu to Uruk. Inanna, the goddess and embodiment of Uruk, visits Enki, the god of Eridu and guardian of all wisdom; they feast together; he becomes drunk; he offers her the **Tablet of Destinies**, containing the secrets of civilisation which govern Uruk, Sumer and *namlulu*:

> 'By the name of my power, by the name of my power,
> To holy Inanna, my daughter, I shall present the divine decrees'.[77]

When sober, he regrets this decision and tries to retrieve the tablet, but the goddess eventually reaches the harbour of Uruk and unloads the cargo. Each decree, called a *meh*, represents the divine laws, regulations or norms for a part of human experience:

- a role in society (shepherd, king, eunuch, priest, *en*, *ensi*, god)
- a specialism or craft (building, basket-weaving, smithing, scribing)
- a virtue (wisdom, heroism, honesty, cunning)
- a mental capacity (attention, judgement, decision)
- an emotional state (fear, joy, weariness, worry, anger)[78]

Namtar has to copy out the list of more than 100 items as *lishanu*, like a lexicon or a dictionary.[79] But the story plays in her head, to flavour her task.

She has had the same kind of task (*lishanu*, lexical lists) for multiple topics such as (in modern language) anatomy, zoology, botany, geology and astronomy.[80] There is *lishanu* for every topic under the sun. In each case, her wedge-shaped marks move from right to left over a clay tablet, from top to bottom on one side; then she turns it over and continues from bottom to top on the reverse side.[81] In terms of neural formation, both sides of her brain are stimulated: the right hemisphere prefers to work top to bottom from the right, but the left enjoys bottom to top on the reverse, as well as the whole business of using abstract symbols.Most of all, her left hemisphere is emphasised and its activity cultivated by the systematic reduction of the whole of creation to *lishanu*, to lexical lists.[82]

Namtar's daydreaming on the story behind this list is an escape and a relief for her right hemisphere, while her left is absorbed in a linear, instrumental task. If she learns little about civilisation from this task, she can brood on the fatherly character of Anu (literally 'sky') as a divine legislator and source of these laws;[83] on Enki, the lord of sweet waters, under the earth at Eridu[84]; on the 'Tablet of Destinies' she is copying, in its mythic role;[85] or – perhaps best of all – on holy Inanna, the local goddess and heroine of the story, the lady guardian of Uruk.

5.5 Sumerian *psyche* (1) The tablet of destinies

Our short visit to the *é-dubba* has given us some potential content for 'Sumerian psychology' and its possible sources. The obvious place to start is the Tablet of Destinies.

This list has been called the 'first recorded attempt at culture analysis'[86] and it does seem to be on the same territory as Chapters 2 and 3 in this book:

1. Plato's assumption: that individual and social *psyche* can be found on the same scale.
2. The assumption that both of these are subject to underlying norms or laws.
3. The assumption that norms of the same kind apply to both technical skills and morality.

They have been characterised, by one scholar, as 'a set of rules and regulations assigned to each cosmic entity and cultural phenomenon ... devised by the gods to make the cosmos run smoothly and effectively'.[87] They suggest reflection on the recent development of Bronze Age civilisation, human thought catching up with its technology by matching the innovations of city, school and scribe with '**an entirely new cognitive concept** ... divine decrees which are the basis of the culture pattern of Sumerian civilisation'.[88] Despite a general tendency to think of culture with a fixed origin, they also represent laws for growth and change.[89]

This is promising. The first objection is that it is **just one hint** – perhaps from a single author – and not a major theme of the curriculum. It seems a dead end, an unexploited flash of insight. The second objection is that it is **simply a list**. One scholar observes that Sumerian 'never quite escapes from the fact that it was originally designed for the purposes of practical **book-keeping** rather than to express abstract ideas'.[90] The written language is perfect for the classification of a range of phenomena because it was originally designed for administration. It struggles to move beyond that initial task because it lacks flexibility of thought. We can propose that one key problem here is with the language as a **medium**.

The other problem is symbolised in the story itself: it is a ***Tablet*** of Destinies. It shows the mysticism associated with written language, the tendency with any new technology to exaggerate its significance – and of those who control it to exaggerate their own. Derrida opens *Of Grammatology* with this quotation:

> 'O Shamash, by your light you scan the totality of lands as if they were cuneiform signs.'[91]

This is in order to introduce his concept of **logocentrism** in Western culture: it is easy to see the Sumerian confusion between written script and reality, but he immediately turns it on our own European prejudices about the alphabetic and phonetic alternative.[92] In an attempt to apply Derrida's programme to Sumerian literature in reverse, Marc van de Mieroop notes that – in contrast to European prejudice in favour of phonetic and alphabetic scripts as 'access to reality' – the Sumerians saw their own cuneiform writing as possessing an independent reality, its own system of meaning, so that reality must actually conform to the script, not vice versa.[93] As in the Shamash quotation, 'Reality had to be interpreted as if it were a text'.[94]

The Taiwanese educator Ruyu Hung has helpfully applied Derrida's programme to Chinese literacy and coined the term '**graphocentrism**' for this tendency in his own scribal tradition, its own form of logocentrism, which is the exact opposite of the Western prejudice: instead of a bias in favour of speech, or phonocentrism, Chinese culture has the '**cult of the written word**'.[95] The same phenomenon with Sumerian cuneiform writing, combined with its rigidity of form at the early stage represented in the story, seem to explain its limitations as a medium for psychology. (We will explore the possibilities of written Chinese as a medium for psychology in Chapter 8 and its continuation within Book 2.)

In each culture, in the same spirit of neologism (creating new words from Greek *neo* = new) inspired by Derrida, we could say that these idolatries of the script, whether ethnocentric, Eurocentric, logocentric, phonocentric or graphocentric, forms of tribalism by scribes, ancient and modern, can be labelled collectively as '**scribalism**'. This, whatever we choose to call it, was an invention of the Bronze Age. Bacon used the far more elegant term *idola tribus* (Latin: idols of the tribe) for Derrida's notion.[96]

We see in Namtar's task at the *é-dubba* that there were two sides, however: a **left-brain** dominated, linear and meticulous 'official' task alongside the more **right-brain**-friendly context in a story with characters, humour, playful details and emotional connections to her community. Perhaps here, in myth, is the potential for a more adequate start at Sumerian psychology? Let us briefly continue our little story.

5.6 A warm evening in uruk

Namtar and her brother step out of the courtyard into the sunny street. They can smell the quayside, can hear the seagulls and the merchants. They turn inland, their minds and their hands tired from labour. Some of the houses now have two storeys – their father says these are the great merchants, some from Meluhha – but the one outstanding feature of the city, towering above all of them, is the temple of Inanna, the lady of Uruk.[97] The whole city looks to her house as their own.[98] This year it resembles an enormous building site, a great workshop: they can smell the evening sacrifice along with much else on the offshore breeze.[99]

Invigorated by the smell, the noise and the steady walk, Namtar recites from one of her favourite stories: 'Approach Eanna the dwelling of Inanna, our lady of love and war … Climb upon the wall of Uruk; examine the masonry. It is not burnt brick and good? The seven sages laid the foundations'.[100] Lulu chimes in: 'One third of the whole is city, one third is garden, and one third is field, with the precinct of the goddess Inanna. The parts and the precinct are all Uruk'.[101]

When they reach home, they nag over dinner to hear their father continue it: '*adda*, tell us the story of Gilgamesh and Enkidu' as he is the best storyteller.[102] With wide eyes and wild gestures, high voices and low, he takes them there.

He tells them of the man to whom all things were known; who knew all the countries of the world; who had been king in Uruk in his great-grandfather's time.[103] He was two-thirds god and one-third man; strong as a wild ox like Enlil, but given a thirst to know all that could be known by Ea. Nothing would hold him back and none was his equal.[104] With Enkidu his servant he travelled far to the forests of Lebanon, cut down the cedars, and defeated the giant Humbaba.[105]

But Enlil was angry that they killed his servant, the giant. Enkidu, who had slain Humbaba, became ill: on his deathbed, he saw a vision of the land of the dead: 'I entered the house of dust and I saw the kings of the earth, their crowns put way for ever; rulers and princes, now turned into servants. Priests and slaves'. When his heart ceased to beat, Gilgamesh cred out and would not let Enkidu be buried, until his body began to rot away.[106] 'Despair is in my heart, for what my brother is now, that shall I be when I am dead. I thought my friend would come back because of my weeping. Because of my brother, I am afraid of death.[107]

The hero travelled far, went to the eastern mountains, and even to the place of the dead. All who met him told him, 'You will never find the life for which you are searching'.[108] And so it ends: 'Gilgamesh, son of Ninsun, lies in the tomb'.[109]

5.7 Sumerian *psyche* (2) Myth as mirror

Much of Sumerian character, concern and reflection is poured into Gilgamesh – 'a surprisingly **complicated** individual: chivalrous, daring, tyrannical, loyal, plaintive, oracular, and inquisitive'.[110] The Sumerians 'were firmly convinced that man was fashioned of clay and created for one purpose only: to serve the gods ... so that they might have the full leisure for their divine activities'.[111] So Gilgamesh is sent into the underworld, and on long adventures, to confirm this view: an 'adventurous, brave, but tragic figure symbolising man's vain quest for fame, glory and immortality'.[112] This hero embodies the Sumerian world-view and expresses, in myth, the Sumerian's view of themselves.

We saw in the last chapter (4.3,4.5) that Neolithic communities projected their own brain functioning – their own *psyche* – onto selected individuals, or projected their collective identity onto a mythical cosmography, as a means of self-reflection by proxy, like a mirror. Here in Sumerian myth, we seem to have the collective identity finding itself in the largely fictional character of Gilgamesh, *as well as* in the Tablet of Destinies.

It seems that the **poetic** curriculum is where the richer psychological content is found. Namtar's day at the *é-dubba* showed that the Sumerian writing system was highly '**lateralised**': left and right brain functions were highly 'segregated' and given quite different tasks. We have a glimpse of this in the different cultures in Western psychology today: we have both a scientific approach to psychology which (it is often said) imitates other sciences, and a humanistic approach, often using metaphors and claiming 'psychological insight' among novelists.

Samuel Kramer observes that 'Sumerian men of letters were the direct heirs of the illiterate minstrels, and **poetry** came to them more naturally than prose ... Intellectually speaking, the Sumerian myths reveal a rather **mature** and **sophisticated** approach to the gods and their divine activities; behind them can be recognised considerable cosmological and theological **reflection**'.[113] This is a more developed tradition than the mere hint and list in the Tablet of Destinies.

Thorkild Jacobsen takes this further, portraying the poets as psychologists:

> '... since the myth-maker sees these forces as 'Thou's', as members of a society, his endeavour is to understand them through **psychological analysis** of their character and through their **corresponding** reaction to the laws which govern the state of the universe ... in the Mesopotamian [that is, Sumerian] universe **understanding means psychological insight**'[114]

Insight developed down different channels. It is possible to trace projections of human psychology in the personalities of Anu, Enki, and Inanna – as suggested in Namtar's daydreaming. Even more promising was the popular and relatable deity **Enlil** (literally 'lord air'): just as Anu was a projection of human authority and legislative capacity, and Enki of human intelligence and inventiveness, Enlil the unpredictable 'divine **executive**' seems a clear projection of the human **will.**[115] People were projecting both government and self-government onto the heavens.

This was usually **subconscious**, implicit, and broken into separate elements. If Neolithic shamans, builders and leaders could play with *psyche* in the medium of stone, then it seems perfectly possible – and a sign that significant progress has occurred – if Bronze Age Sumerians could play with *psyche* in the medium of written myth, carved into tablets. If Kramer is right about their 'mature and **sophisticated** approach', if Jacobsen is also right about 'psychological analysis and psychological **insight**', we always have the possibility (as in the Neolithic) that some were more conscious and **knew** what they were doing, in something more like our own perspective.

Surely the best example of this narrative 'playground' for Sumerian *psyche* is with **Gilgamesh** 'the supreme hero of Sumerian myth and legend', and indeed beyond Sumer eventually 'the hero par excellence of the ancient world'.[116] We may recognise him as 'like Odysseus'; in fact, it works the other way around.[117]

His legends and stories appear a very clear example of the Sumerian collective *psyche* looking in the **mirror**. Just as Palaeolithic art and sculpture often show imaginary figures who are half-human and half-animal (a theme elaborated in Egypt) Gilgamesh is introduced as 'two-thirds divine and one third mortal'.[118] Like the 'entirely new cognitive concept' of a *meh* for each area of civilisation in the myth of Inanna and Enki[119] but more clearly and fully, Gilgamesh is the collective attempt to process the new way of life and what it told them about themselves; a group effort to rethink their **identity** after a momentous shift.[120]

The story emphasised the hero's highly competitive and aggressive nature, as these are collective characteristics of Sumerian culture noted by all scholars.[121] Sumerians instinctively desired the rule of law as a form of **self-restraint**.[122] In the epic the people cry out: 'Is this the king, the shepherd of his people?'[123] It was recognised as a shared national character trait in the mirror of Gilgamesh, with a subconscious awareness that it was a potentially **self-destructive** trait.[124]

Gilgamesh befriends the 'wild man of the woods' Enkidu,[125] and then mourns his death: this is normally taken as a clear symbol of Bronze Age civilisation or even the earlier Neolithic settlements of the plain, coming to terms with their own ancestral past – or their troublesome uncivilised neighbours – or both.[126]

As this myth was extremely popular in its time and long afterwards, travelling like a meme through the European hinterland of the Sumerian achievement, it seems almost certain that it was the ultimate source for Homer's *Odyssey*.[127] It is also fair to say that Greece saw a successful revival of the Sumerian model, not only in its city-states, but in the same creativity, competitiveness, and highly extraverted cultural personality.

The eye of Sumer was turned outwards; you cannot look inwards for long while making all this outward change. The myth seems to have been the national mirror, and within that reflection, some individuals were surely able to see themselves.

5.8 Review of Theory One

Careful study of Bronze Age civilisations was the original evidence base of T1 so it should be on very safe ground in Iraq: the theory was evolved precisely to explain this data. Jaynes has a section on the bicameral mind in Sumerian and Egyptian culture, noting that these are two different kinds of 'theocracy' (Greek: rule by gods or their representatives): both involve auditory hallucinations that images of the gods can talk, but the Sumerian model has a **steward-king**, Egypt a god-king.[128]

Jaynes makes the point that in Sumer the temple was considered the house of the god: her statue (in the case of Inanna) was heard speaking to the priest, by **projection** of his right-hemisphere activity onto the statue. Jaynes sees this as the only plausible explanation for the sustained **illusion** that she was alive.[129] In this bicameral arrangement 'It is not the human beings who are the rulers, but the hallucinated voice of the gods'.[130] The Sumerian belief that free people had the same relationship to their gods that slaves had to free people can thus be explained.[131]

T1 can also explain the strong association of **hearing** with intelligence, to the point where the sense of hearing is equated with **thinking**, or *psyche* itself:[132] Jayne's former student Brain McVeigh notes that *ĝizzal* meant 'understanding' and 'wisdom' as well as 'ear' and 'hearing', and demonstrates statistically that in the millennium 2600–1600, there were more Sumerian psychological words created by combinations with the sign for 'ear' than those for 'eye' or 'head'.[133] The double use of *ĝizzal* suggests that the Sumerian approach to *psyche* was not anatomical (that is, where *psyche* resides) but mainly social, functional: we might even say 'behaviourist'. Outward, observable behaviour was the central focus.

Jaynes proposes a mechanism for this classic bicameral civilisation to function with the 'personal god' (*ili*) representing the private auditory hallucinations of the ordinary Sumerian.[134] The obvious bicameral interpretation is that this was a Sumerian's right hemisphere, whether he was a king or a commoner; Jaynes adds the detail that personal **names** were often a **compound** of a given name plus the name of a person's *ili*, 'thus making obvious the bicameral nature'.[135]

All this data makes sense under T1: could there be **alternative** explanations? A theory is not **confirmed** by data that it was originally constructed to explain. It needs new data by which it can be falsified: as we saw with T2 in the Neolithic. T1 survived exposure to more recent research on community psychology in the Neolithic, despite appearing early in the development of this new area; but its successes further back with the Neolithic may simply be due to **extrapolation**; that is, working backwards logically from better-known data in the Bronze Age – which was Jaynes's central focus – to the lesser-known data of the Neolithic.

Can it work forwards? Jaynes describes the bicameral mind as a mechanism to allow the growth of 'large agricultural communities'[136] climaxing in the great civilisations, in which the invisible realm reflects visible political leadership.[137] This certainly describes Sumer, with its heavenly councils mirroring the earthly councils, and its passion for social stability in the midst of so many destabilising forces. Ideally, what a bicameral society needs is isolation from any competing influences, from competing voices.[138] Sumer achieved this through a social system which could – and did – outlast political change. The complexities of the later history can be interpreted as the gradual unravelling of a previously stable bicameral civilisation; but there are other factors, other possible interpretations. T1 appears much too simple and schematic.

A clear weakness of T1 is in the area of **writing systems**: Jaynes developed his main linguistic ideas from his own study of ancient Greek,[139] which in the light of **Derrida**'s grammatology – with which T1 was contemporary – [140] is likely to be problematic. Jaynes suggests that reading cuneiform was more like hearing: 'hallucinating the speech from looking at its picture-symbols, rather than visual reading of syllables in our sense'.[141] This seems a more appropriate account of **Egyptian** hieroglyphics, however; and it is also impossible to **verify**. He dismisses cuneiform as 'a clumsy and ambiguous communication system', but criticises the cuneiform translations of experts because they do not match his theory.[142]

Jaynes recognises that 'The very words that might be relevant to tracing the metaphorical build-up of consciousness and **mind-space** are precisely those that are extremely **difficult to translate** with precision'.[143] But is this asking too much of one of the earliest writing scripts on earth? His former student Brian McVeigh tried to demonstrate that early Sumerian (2600–1600 BCE) has more religious than psychological words in its lexicon, displaying 'an insistent and robust religiosity' alongside 'a weakly developed psychologicality' – matching the prediction from T1 that a bicameral civilisation knows no 'consciousness' so it will not need that vocabulary.[144] Yet, for a writing system that was under development with no supportive models, this distribution could be explained not by the absence of consciousness, but by the newness of the technology; and (as we have observed in 5.5 above) its **mismatch** with psychology as a writing technology. T1 needs another system for comparison; such as Egypt's (6.11).

It is an irony of Jaynes's theory that although he had developed it in response to Bronze Age data for the most part, it is a better match to Neolithic data (4.7) on this issue of finding a 'script' to capture the gradual interiorisation of language: at the unconscious level of architecture (4.4). When brought forwards to its data set, T1 appears hamstrung by its logocentrism: that is, its limited view of language, its 'scribalism'. Although Jaynes had read Snell, he also needed to read Derrida.

Overall, T1 has some insights to offer in its account of Sumerian spirituality and religion, but as a wider account of Sumerian political history it lacks grip on the data, precisely because it starts directly with culture and applies exactly the same framework to all Bronze Age civilisations. It lacks recognition of the individual character of Sumerian culture, and potentially other Bronze Age cultures, which are increasingly divergent. It appears - from this first foray beyond the Neolithic - that it lacks sufficient complexity and nuance to explain Bronze Age data adequately. Finally, it offers a disappointing account of Sumerian literature, because it shares in the Eurocentric prejudices of much Western scholarship: in effect, Julian Jaynes's logocentrism (his bias to the alphabetic languages since Greek) confronts Sumerian logocentrism, without any critical mediation.

5.9 Review of Theory Two

The first thing Sumer seems to offer in terms of T2 is an outstanding example of '**bihemispheric advance**' outside its initial data set.[145] McGilchrist says of the Greek advance: 'This was marked not by some sort of compromise, a holding back, of both hemispheres in relation to one another, but on the contrary by a going further than had ever been gone before in both directions at once'.[146] Like the brains of Kant, Einstein, Jaynes and McGilchrist himself, Sumerian *psyche* at the collective level somehow developed strong hemispheric lateralisation.[147]

McGilchrist also notes that 'it was through the workings of the emissary, the left hemisphere, that the 'empire' of the mind expanded in the first place'.[148] Sumer, with its numbers, lists and representations, is clearly marked for left-hemisphere functions and represents an advance in this direction: the clearest and most rapid to this point in the human story.[149] It taught the world this new way of thinking.

With this comparison in mind (and especially Egypt which was contemporary) this can reveal 'what is wrong' in Sumer: only the **left hemisphere** has a voice in terms of a matching 'script'. The right hemisphere, lacking such an outlet, is forced to fall back on older resources: hence Namtar's daydream, and *adda*'s storytelling. We fell into fiction to capture that need for an outlet. Therefore, Sumer's 'bihemispheric advance', by increasing the hemispheric lateralisation of the culture, generated a need to rebalance the functioning of the hemispheres at a cultural level. We have seen something like this played out within Neolithic societies, before literacy (4.5-4.9), in terms of their differentiation of leadership; now it is played out in the new forum of a literate culture, between the new symbolic systems of writing, which are both more complex and more rule-based.

Should any culture be obliged, however, to offer its **own** internal integration? In Ruth Benedict's theory of culture, there are different **kinds** of civilisations, with different quasi-social personalities: 'oriented as wholes in different directions … lack of integration seems to be as characteristic of certain cultures as extreme integration is of others'.[150] Rather than offering its own internal consolidation as an 'introvert', a civilisation can offer half of the picture, then lean on **others** for balance. Egyptologist John Baines contrasts 'highly interconnected and inward-looking' Egyptian culture with the plural, **extravert** civilisation based in Iraq.[151]

As a result of this contrast, Baines observes, Egyptian civilisation was 'basically **non-expansionary**', while Sumer and the successors influenced other cultures. 'Egyptian cultural traits did not travel well', while Sumerian culture 'travelled'. Like China, but very unlike Sumer, 'Egypt offered a dominant model of a large-scale society that confronted that outside world in relative **isolation** while also interacting with it'.[152] Our observation of a complete 'brain' with two balanced halves in public systems of representation in the social macrocosm of Egyptian and Chinese culture, in Chapters 6 and 8 respectively,will match this profile of the introverted civilisation well; the contrast with Sumer helps us to understand its gift of spread and influence.

Finally, after everything that has been said about Sumer, the 'extraversion' of its civilisation and 'one-sidedness' of its symbolic system, this was only true of its earliest, purely **Sumerian** phase (which has been the focus of this chapter). In fact, there *was* a correction to the limitations of Sumerian cuneiform; but unlike hieratic in Egypt, which arrived almost as early as hieroglyphics,[153] this arrived *later* when **Akkadian**, a Semitic language, was incorporated into cuneiform.[154] Much of what is now known and studied in cuneiform comes from this post-integration period.

The same writing system and script were now used for a completely different and unrelated spoken language: cuneiform was said to be '**twin-tongued**' and the fiction maintained that the two languages hidden inside the writing were entirely interchangeable, mutually intelligible '**mirror images**' of each other.[155] It led to significant new writing genres beyond the dominance of lexical lists, and eventually to a rich and colourful literature of myths and legends including the final versions of the Gilgamesh epic, which would breed many children.[156]

In the long run, therefore, with the arrival of Semitic Akkadian and its adoption of cuneiform, the writing system was transformed and it became a comfortable 'home' for the human brain. Both hemispheres could operate within it, and the literate culture (like Plato's *polis*) could become a macrocosm of normal individual *psyche*. The arrival of Akkadian greatly enriched the expressive possibilities of Sumerian cuneiform.

We can see this dynamic in the **orthography** (writing conventions) of cuneiform script. A significant element of T2 is its thesis about scripts reflecting the shifting leadership of brain hemispheres: that writing and reading from left to right reflects left-hemisphere leadership, and from right to left reflects right-hemisphere leadership.[157] Cuneiform began, as most scripts begin, reading from right to left, reflecting the preference of the right hemisphere; and this continued as the standard practice in public monuments and cylinder seals into the middle of the second millennium, that is, the end of the Sumerian period which is our focus; but in its ordinary use on clay tablets it switched quite early in its history, almost as soon as full sentences were being written in it, to a left-to-right orientation, at around the time of the first appearance of Akkadian political rivalry.[158] From then on the standard form was left to right. In orthography, once again Sumer acted as the mirror image of Egypt (6.2).

Given the logic of the technology itself, with its origins in accounting, this is a predictable move: the left-hemispheric bias of the form led to a left-hemispheric bias in the direction of script. It is interesting, however, that this move seemed to concide with the appearance of Akkadian, a Semitic language, which we have taken to have opened up the more right-hemispheric possibilities of Sumerian cuneiform. In accordance with McGilchrist's notion of 'bihemispheric advance', we seem to have the two hemispheres jostling for leadership and reaching a new compromise.

Empire is also a factor. The arrival of the Akkadians represented an incursion of the imperial mentality and its obsession with administration. In our account of the Neolithic, we have tentatively associated tribal leadership and the emergence of chiefs with left-hemispheric dominance in a new social form (4.5–4.9). In a Bronze Age context, with ever-larger political units, this association would presumably become stronger. A political leader would naturally turn to a system such as cuneiform for its administrative potential: as the Sumerian *ensi* and *lugal* had already discovered (5.3). The fact that cuneiform finally settled into a left-to-right orientation at a time of growing imperialism could well reflect this.[159]

It is an oddity of T2 that it contains no acknowledgement of 'Grammatology'; McGilchrist shares so much of Derrida's tradition in German phenomenology, especially Heidegger, that despite this explicit connection, there is substantial agreement on the central points. McGilchrist agrees with Derrida, for example, that all writing is political and that empires and writing are twin 'children of the left hemisphere' involving a certain degree of control and implicit violence.[160]

He distinguishes non-phonetic from phonetic scripts, which he labels 'syllabic' and 'phonemic', because he is independently so well informed in linguistics.[161] Without Derrida, he avoids 'logocentrism' better than Jaynes, because he has much more sophisticated linguistics and grammatology (from his immersion in phenomenology) and also a great interest in an alternative civilisation and writing system: Chinese.[162]

Our findings in Iraq, therefore, complement and do not contradict Theory Two. In specific respects, they strengthen it by offering a wider pool of evidence, like the Neolithic, prior to its author's central example. They simply extend its reach backwards in time. It is an interesting irony that a theory such as T2, based strongly as it is on neurological data from the natural sciences, seems to fare better than another such as T1, based on direct investigations of ancient culture through archaeology and literature, when both are applied to cross-cultural contexts. By starting outside culture with our shared biology, T2 seems to achieve greater flexibility in its applications to the variety of cultures.

5.10 T2 and the impact of the city

We ended the last chapter with a proposal from two researchers in Indiana.[163] They gave a positive example of child-rearing practice in Palaeolithic society in terms of evolutionary psychology. Their negative example is **their own** society, the contemporary USA: where, they believe, child-rearing practices are tending to reinforce the dominance of left-hemispheric functioning – caught in that '**positive feedback**' loop identified by McGilchrist. They simply provide a mechanism to explain the cultural theory in T2, especially the dialectics of positive feedback.

Cultural pressures, they believe, distort the roles of US mothers, who are rearing children with an unhealthy, disbalanced hemispheric function biased to the left; these grow to become culture-formers, mothers, fathers, and alloparents in the same mould, creating positive feedback in an ever-more-distorted pattern. The cumulative 'intergenerational effects' are amounting, they believe, to a 'snowball effect'.[164]

This is suggestive of a general **application** of T2 involving the education of young, adult education and public information. Mothering practices can be the starting point for a wider theory of **how brains are formed** by a culture, in the early stages of childhood when the right hemisphere is ahead of the left in its natural development, and is therefore especially vulnerable; and then through socialisation and schooling when the hemispheres are learning to interact.[165]

The positive example of Narvaez and Tarsha in the Palaeolithic contrasts with **Bronze Age** cultures – less starkly than with contemporary USA but including a measure of urbanisation and increasing specialisation. Their negative example has suggestive connections with Sumerian culture at some points in its history.

A particular connection is their observation about the vulnerability of **boys** to the 'misraising of the species' brain'.[166] With the cultural importance of Enlil and especially **Gilgamesh** as wayward yet admired characters mirroring social developments, we seem to glimpse a Sumerian **crisis in masculinity** which fits these observations about the consequences of disrupting the evolved patterns of nurture. In the Gilgamesh myth, we learn that 'his arrogance has no bounds by day or night ... His lust leaves no virgin to her lover ... yet this is the shepherd of the city, wise, comely, and resolute'.[167] It portrays a city tormented by restless masculinity, familiar from any age – but this from the first cities on the planet.

Tentatively, then, we are dealing with fixed patterns related to **urbanisation**: the social psychology of 'the city', which was born with it and travels with it. Bourdieu called private land ownership **'the death sentence of the tribe'** – a major disruption to traditional patterns noted in his field studies in Algeria.[168]

This would include child-rearing. It suggests that the novel disbalances of brain laterality developed in Sumer could simply have been a fairly fixed symptom of the interaction of **mothering** practices with the invention of **cities**. From Sumer to today is an enormous leap in historical terms, but perhaps it is comparable in terms of geography and social psychology: and perhaps clearer, because it is the first appearance of an urban environment out of a tribal culture. What we find in Sumer implies that in order to address our **contemporary** loss of hemispheric balance as diagnosed in T2, one element of the treatment has to be a rethinking of the city and retrieval of what was lost in terms of EDN, mothering and *psyche*.

Discussion questions:

1. Do you feel confident about locations and dates in the Bronze Age?
2. How would your life be different without technologies of memory?
3. What was your response to the first portrait of a Sumerian school?
4. Which tasks demand your attention in one way but leave your imagination free? Which do not?
5. What could the *meh* of study look like? What are its main norms?
6. What does the story of Gilgamesh tell you about Sumerian society?
7. Does it make any sense to you that psychology could be practised through myth?
8. What, in your view, are the emerging strengths and weaknesses of T1?
9. Is it meaningful to claim that a whole civilisation has a personality?
10. Do you agree or disagree with the argument about urban life? Why?

Recommended Reading

- Stephanie Dalley (trans.) *Myths from Mesopotamia*
- Henri Frankfort *Before Philosophy*
- Samuel Noah Kramer *The Sumerians*

- Paul Kriwaczek *Babylon*
- Andrew Robinson *Writing and Script*
- Andrew Robinson *The Indus*
- Georges Roux *Ancient Iraq*
- N.K. Sandars (trans) *The Epic of Gilgamesh*

Notes

1 Kramer p.40.
2 Bellwood pp.125–6; Mithen 2003 pp.438–440; Van de Mieroop 2007 pp.7,10–14.
3 Roux pp.88; there are claims to larger settlements at this time in Central Asia and East Asia, but none in such a situation of population density and intensity, that is, none leading into the first cities.
4 Kriwaczek pp.20,37,41; Wood p.24.
5 Kriwaczek p.37; Roux pp.61,71,77,90.
6 Kramer pp.88–9; Wood p.27.
7 Following the example of Georges Roux.
8 For example: in Renfrew 1976 p.212; Wood pp.11,29.
9 Kriwaczek pp.10–11.
10 Wood pp.16–19.
11 Bellwood pp.125–8.133–4; Kramer 264,285–6; Roux p.89; Van de Mieroop 2017 pp.15–16 bb.
12 Kramer pp.40–1.
13 Roux pp.61,71,77,90.
14 Walker pp.17–19,22,25,51.
15 Hoyland p.14; Kramer pp.147–9,269–279,284; Robinson 2021 pp.98–104,135, 142; Van de Mieroop 2017 p.71.
16 Van de Mieroop 2017 pp.15–16.
17 Kramer pp.264,285–6.
18 Kramer pp.33,74,129,262–3; Kriwaczek Ch.4 (pp.66–76).
19 Derrida 1967 p.3; Hung pp.xiv–xvii,16–7; Van de Mieroop 2017 pp.77–84, 184,221.
20 Renfrew and Zubrow pp.40–44,176ff.; Roux p.82.
21 Davies pp.84–9; Putnam p.86.
22 Kramer pp.37,290; Robinson 2021 Ch.10 (pp.144–170).
23 Hoyland pp.175–183; Kramer pp.135–142; Roux pp.78–9,126,156–160 (ziggurats),196–200 (internal),365–9.
24 Harari pp.140–2; Renfrew 1976 pp.192–5,199,203–4; Wood pp.145, 158.
25 Kriwaczek pp.59–65; Roux pp.46,76,80–82; Walker pp.21,25,30,33; Yurco p.96.
26 Walker p.30.
27 *ibid* p.24; a fact to be explored in some detail in 5.9.
28 For example: Childe 1954 pp.83–93; Childe 1981 pp.100–5.
29 Hoyland p.110,112; Kramer pp.267–276; Van de Mieroop 2007 pp.53,139–142.
30 Harari p.137; Walker p.17.
31 See Bacon, B. et al. (2023); Lewis-Williams, in his treatment of Lascaux, notes the conjunction of geometric and reprepresentational images as a symbolic system which lasted many millennia, with indications of equivalent processes to speech, writing and grammar, much like later written languages, pp.60–68,192–6,200; but the new study uncovers a literal meaning of some of these conjunctions.
32 Robinson 2009 pp.3–6,15–16.
33 Sandars p.83.
34 Hoyland pp.13–15; Robinson 2021 pp.90–91; Sandars p.47; Walker pp.50–3.

35 Kramer p.289.
36 Bellwood p.126; Van de Mieroop 2007 pp.63–73; Walker pp.26–7.
37 Van de Mieroop 2007 pp.74–106.
38 Bellwood p.126; Van de Mieroop 2007 pp.63–73; Walker pp.26–7.
39 Hoyland p.14; Kramer pp.147–9,269–279,284; Robinson 2021 pp.98–104, 135,142; Van de Mieroop 2017 p.71.
40 Van de Mieroop 2017 pp.12–14,38,56–8,63.
41 *ibid* pp.87ff.,144ff.,195.
42 Van de Mieroop 2017 pp.70–1; Walker p.27.
43 Walker pp.48–9.
44 See Smail Ch.2 (pp.40–73) for a critique.
45 Lewis-Williams and Pearce pp.86–7; Thomas and Humphrey pp.7,78–85.
46 Kramer pp.86,230–1.
47 Jacobsen p.203; Kramer pp.74,77,186–9,274.
48 Jacobsen p.203; Kramer pp.74,77,186–9,274.
49 Jacobsen p.204.
50 Roux p.128.
51 Roux p.332; Walker p.43.
52 Childe 1981 p.65; Renfrew and Zubrow pp.162–3.
53 Childe 1981 p.87; Murray pp.105–9; Renfrew and Zubrow p.27.
54 Davies p.81; Harari p.142; Jacobsen p.229; Kramer p.229.
55 Walker p.43.
56 Kramer p.230; Walker p.43.
57 Walker p.45.
58 *ibid.*
59 Kramer p.231; Roux pp.338–342.
60 Kramer p.5.
61 Kramer p.229.
62 Sandars p.45.
63 *ibid* p.87.
64 Kramer p.249.
65 Snell p.15.
66 Benedict p.3.
67 Van de Mieroop 2017 p.7.
68 Kriwaczek p.190.
69 Sandars pp.49,84.
70 Kramer pp.98,236–7,241–3; Roux pp.331–2; Sandars pp.40,45–6.
71 Sandars p.84.
72 Kriwaczek p.63.
73 Renfrew and Zubrow pp.168,174.
74 Walker p.45.
75 Van de Mieroop 2017 p.19.
76 Jacobsen p.187.
77 Told by Kramer pp.160–161.
78 Kramer pp.115–6,150–161.
79 *ibid* p.116.
80 Kramer pp.232–5.
81 Walker p.24; noting the fictional date of this story, it is before the switch of orientation mentioned in 5.2 and discussed in 5.9.
82 McGilchrist 2009 pp.276–7; Roux p.128.
83 Jacobsen pp.150–3,156,162.
84 *ibid* p.159.
85 Kramer 175,182.

86 *ibid.*
87 *ibid* pp.115,125.
88 Kramer p.161; Kriwaczek pp.30–1,34 (partly quoting Kramer but enlarging on his interpretation).
89 Kramer pp.33,74,129,262–3; Kriwaczek Ch.4 (pp.66–76).
90 Walker p.25; Jean Bottéro agrees, as quoted in Van de Mieroop pp.79,235n.64.
91 Derrida 1967 p.3.
92 By placing this beside a contrasting quotation from Hegel.
93 Van de Mieroop 2017 pp.9,78–82.
94 *ibid* p.10.
95 Hung p.xiv.
96 Bacon 1620 Book I.XLI p.41 and the Latin text ed. Fowler, Clarendon Press 1889.
97 Kramer pp.73,104; Robinson 2021 p.90; Roux pp.77,80.
98 Kramer pp.140,260; Roux pp.73–4,78,90.
99 Kramer pp.137,140–1; Kriwaczek pp.40–1.
100 Sandars, N.K. 1972 Gilgamesh prologue p.61 p.117.
101 *ibid* p.117.
102 Kramer pp.78,256–7.
103 Dalley p.40; Sandars, N.K. 1972 p.61.
104 From the epic and the national profile in Kramer pp.3–4,249,261,264–5; Kriwaczek pp.20–22; Roux p.87.
105 From the forest journey in Sandars, N.K. 1972 pp.76–83; this is the role of Enkidu in early versions, but this role was altered later, in Assyrian and Babylonian times, to become more of a rival.
106 *ibid* pp.91–6.
107 *ibid* pp.97–8.
108 *ibid* pp.100,102,106–7,118.
109 *ibid* pp.119.
110 Kramer p.185.
111 Jacobsen pp.123,203,218.
112 Kramer p.45.
113 *ibid* pp.128,144.
114 Jacobsen pp.170,172,175.
115 Jacobsen pp.146,149, 155,157,207–8,211.
116 Kramer p.45; Lewis-Williams and Pearce p.153.
117 Kristiansen and Larsson pp.39–57 do not quite say this, but do acknowledge the influence of Gilgamesh.
118 Dalley's translation, Tablet 1 p.51.
119 Kramer p.161; Kriwaczek pp.30–1,34 (partly quoting Kramer but enlarging on his interpretation).
120 Kriwaczek pp.20–22.
121 From the epic and the national profile in Kramer pp.3–4,249,261,264–5; Kriwaczek pp.20–22; Roux p.87.
122 Kramer pp.266–8,295.
123 Sandars, N.K. 1972 p.62.
124 Jacobsen pp.201,210; Kramer p.268.
125 Sandars, N.K. 1972 pp.62–9; skipped in the telling because some of this is from the later, Akkadian version.
126 Kristiansen and Larsson p.316; Lewis-Williams and Pearce pp.153–8 for an excellent analysis.
127 Dalley pp.48–9; Kramer pp.183–5; Sandars, N.K. 1972 pp.45–6.
128 Jaynes pp.177–8.

129 *ibid* p.180.
130 *ibid* p.181.
131 Jacobsen p.163; Jaynes p.178.
132 Jacobsen p.146.
133 McVeigh p.58.
134 Jaynes p.183.
135 *ibid* pp.183–4.
136 *ibid* p.126.
137 *ibid* pp.88–98,138–145.
138 *ibid* p.79.
139 McVeigh p.57; so did McGilchrist 2009 pp.276ff.; leaning heavily on Kerkhove see p.500 n.84 to n.91.
140 Derrida 1967.
141 Jaynes p.182.
142 *ibid* pp.176–7.
143 *ibid* p.246.
144 McVeigh pp.46–8,51–2.
145 McGilchrist 2009 pp 259,299.
146 *ibid* p.296.
147 Albert Einstein's brain development was highly lateralised in this way: see Blakeslee pp.45–6,107–8.
148 McGilchrist 2009 p.296.
149 Van de Mieroop 2007 pp.19–20,23.
150 Benedict p.161.
151 Baines pp.33–4,43–4 in Lefkowitz (ed.)1996.
152 *ibid.*
153 Davies pp.84,95–6, Murray p.290; Robinson 2009 pp.25–6; Watterson p.xviii.
154 Bellwood p.126; Van de Mieroop 2007 pp.63–73; Walker pp.26–7.
155 Van de Mieroop 2017 pp.12–14,38,56–8,63.
156 Dalley pp.48–9; Kramer pp.183–5; Sandars, N.K. 1972 pp.45–6; Van de Mieroop 2017 pp.87ff.,144ff.,195.
157 McGilchrist 2009 pp 275–9,311,452–9.
158 Walker p.24.
159 In Book 2 with the short-lived Athenian Empire, and Book 3 with the longer-lived Roman Empire, we will explore this dynamic, in which both set the Western orthography in a left-right direction.
160 McGilchrist 2009 p.278.
161 Davies p.103; Hooker p.8; McGilchrist 2009 p.273,275,278.
162 McGilchrist 2009 pp 277–9,311,455,457–8,502n.1,516n.95.
163 'The Missing Mind', in Henley and Rossano (eds.) Chapter 5 pp.55–69.
164 *ibid* pp.60–65; see Challenger pp.77–81,137–158,219–229 for a sobering portrait of how far this has gone.
165 Two helpful examples of such policy: Sue Palmer's *Play is the Way* and Suggate's *Reclaim Early Childhood.*
166 *'The Missing Mind'*, in Henley and Rossano (eds.) Chapter 5 p.64.
167 Sandars, N.K. 1972 p.62; this part may be later than Sumerian leadership, but dating is not central here.
168 Fowler p.15; note also Eriksen p.168 and Fowler pp.1,3,13–22,175 on this issue.

6 Ancient Egypt

6.1 Orientation: The gift of the Nile

Egypt is recognised as the second oldest 'civilisation', in the sense of a literate, increasingly urbanised Bronze Age culture.[1] As Mesopotamia was named 'the land between the rivers', a different group of tribes settled along another river a thousand miles to the west, in what was later to be called Africa. They called their land *Kmt* (the black land) and the river was a god.[2]

Egypt had, of course, been the **land corridor** for the migration of *homo sapiens* into Asia in Palaeolithic times: both the first waves of hominids and the second wave of *homo sapiens sapiens*, who came through here in the Upper Paleolithic c.50kya to colonise the globe.[3] When the period of Holocene stability arrived it was also in position to receive traffic in the opposite direction: agriculture and other inventions from the Fertile Crescent came south-west across the same bridge, back into Africa.[4]

There was more than one Neolithic, however, and a larger African background. During this time northern Africa was very different from our familiar picture of a narrow river passage beside the world's largest desert. Early in the Holocene and for more than half of it, the Sahara became fertile grassland, watered by a system of lakes and rivers supporting an '**Aqualithic culture**' of hippopotamus and elephant-hunting, intensive fishing and experimental plant domestication.[5]

Farming was discovered at several locations around the margins of the Sahara by tribes living with suitable plants, all north of the Equator; these populations expanded as the desert grew again, their tongues overwhelming all others and becoming the major **language families** of Africa.[6] As noted in 4.1, a new diet was developed in Mali in West Africa, which became the homeland for the **Niger-Congo** family of today (including Wolof, Igbo and Yoruba), travelling east along a southern belt in tropical climates, then becoming the Bantu expansion from Cameroon: a second, independent innovation in food production, which slowly travelled through Africa during all the royal periods of Egypt.[7] Closer to Egypt, two millennia before in the Sudan another new set of crops led to a separate population expansion westward along a belt just south of the Sahara, and expansion south-east

DOI: 10.4324/9781003396147-9

down to the Great Lakes region, to become the **Nilo-Saharan** family (today including Dinka and Maasai) which in its early form, would enter and influence ancient **Egyptian.**[8]

To add to this complexity, the genetic and linguistic evidence suggests a flow of people from Arabia across the Red Sea and the Gulf of Aden into what are now Somalia, Ethiopia, Eritrea and Sudan, associated with another Neolithic crop in the Ethiopian highlands and the **Cushitic** languages of that region, moving into the Sudan and through it to Egypt.[9] Finally, and relatively late in the Holocene, around 4000 BCE those living in Egypt imported the Asian Neolithic package of wheat and barley; and with it, more components of the **Afro-Asiatic** language family.[10]

This wider context, which seems remote from our purposes, will turn out to be important for the specifically **psychological vocabulary** of the Egyptians (6.3), which seems to be particularly embedded in wider Africa and thus emblematic of the role of wider Africa in Egypt. The story of ancient Africa is still 'under construction' using the materials outlined in Part 1, and it is intimately tied up with the recovery from colonialism and the slave trade.[11] As noted in 1.8 and 1.9, one of our key aims in retrieving this story is the exorcism of Hegel's ghost (or *Geist*); as it happens, the retrieval of the psychology of ancient Egypt is an excellent tool for such an exorcism, as its origins seem to lie further south.

The Nile Valley as a whole was therefore a **meeting point** of many influences in the mid-Holocene, especially as the Sahara expanded, forcing many tribes into the same hotly contested area.[12] The lakes to the west and to the south were shrinking, and the river Nile became a moving oasis, a natural paradise for the hunter-gatherers from the Aqualithic world. Ancient Egyptians have a number of hieroglyphs for species we would *now* associate with the jungle, savannah and safari regions further south: the Egyptians knew (and hunted) rhinoceros, elephant, giraffe, deer, ibex, gazelle, wild ass and ostrich, as well as hippos and crocodiles in the river.[13] Agriculture could co-exist with the older hunting and fishing of previous millennia.[14] Similarly, many tribes of different languages, cultures and beliefs had to **co-exist**.

In the densely populated, narrow corridor created by Neolithic climate change the axis of movement had therefore moved from east-west to **north-south** and it was on this axis that Egypt was formed. The tribes of Upper (southern) Egypt were first to organise themselves into a unit, and these pushed north into less advanced tribes with weaker unity, creating a single national unit c.3200 BCE.[15] Just as Sumer had established a pattern of competition between the city-states of Iraq inside a cultural container, ancient Egypt consisted of forty-two provinces called *nomes*, derived from localities of rival tribes, inside a national container.

The great division was between North (Upper Egypt) and South (Lower Egypt) with power oscillating between major centres of the one (Thebes, Abydos and Luxor) and the other (Memphis, Heliopolis and Giza) throughout a long history. There were about twenty *nomes* in each half of the kingdom, North and South. The central achievement of each of the great Kingdoms was to unify the two.[16]

With a population of several million people[17] acting as one organism under a single government, Egypt was able to build on a much grander **scale** and in much more **permanent** forms, with stone quarries and a stable and predictable river. In its isolation it became a cultural laboratory, testing and exploring inventions. The megaliths of Neolithic culture in the Fertile Crescent and even the Atlantic coast of Europe were already greater than any stone architecture in Egypt and Africa, and the temples of Malta were the largest stone structures in the world, until Egyptian engineers took the Sumerian idea of the pyramid to its spectacular conclusion.[18]

Instead of the restless innovation of Sumer, Egypt quickly settled down into a **static** form. The heart of the civilisation was a myth very like the biblical Eden, although it was more a symbol than a story.[19] Everything was designed to look back at this ideal, to celebrate it and maintain it forever. It functioned however as a symbol of something more recent than the creation of the universe – that is, the creation of the Egyptian state: 'centralised power, royal rituals and the cult of the dead intertwined to form **the ideology of the world's first state**'.[20]

With this difference, Egyptian civilisation developed in parallel with Sumerian civilisation: its history divides up into periods not unlike those in Mesopotamia and spreads over a similar timescale, beginning slightly later and ending slightly later. Both remained indebted to the great innovators who kick-started the two, around five thousand years ago, and worked within the parameters they set. A lot of contrasts can be drawn, but there is a shared timeline and an interaction.

How much did Egypt owe **Sumer**? The very fact that Egypt did not continue to innovate, but became 'static' after the first dynasties and the Old Kingdom, suggests an impulse from outside at the start rather than any built-in capacity for innovation. But was this from the **north**, or **south**, or **both**? Sumerian influence as far as Turkey and Pakistan, at its peak of innovation in the Late Uruk phase, and the late arrival of its Neolithic suggest that Egypt fell inside this orbit of influence;[21] but there is growing awareness of southern input into Egypt from **the Sudan**.[22] As with Iraq, these questions await the opportunity to access and gather more data on the 'weightings' of possible foreign influences.

Historians once talked of 'stimulus diffusion': that some technologies are not imported but spread as inspiration, where the basic idea is heard of and taken up in a new context, then developed in an original way.[23] This is only one **possible** explanation of pyramids and hieroglyphs but is unlikely in the case of Egypt.[24] Ancient and classical American examples show that both can evolve independently;[25] Chinese is another example with writing. The southern region up the Nile, which would become Upper Egypt, shows evidence of a fertile blend of creative talent, in the tribes of the fourth millennium, to form its own 'critical mass' independently of Uruk or Iraq.

When we think of 'Egypt', defined since that time as a single land, continuously existing separate from the rest of Africa and interacting with nations across the land bridge in Asia, or across the Mediterranean, we easily forget its larger **African** context. The Nile, as the longest river on our planet, starting halfway down Africa – below the Sahara, below the Equator in Tanzania – is a helpful symbol of the continuities with the continent, an anchor back into Africa, to prevent perceptions of Egypt floating free of African identity.

Egypt itself bears considerable responsibility for this common error, because it was so successful at forging a strong national identity so early in its history, and because it then became introverted, conservative – and not a little **xenophobic** (Greek = fearing foreigners). Egyptians, as the richest and most sophisticated nation on the planet, let alone Africa, and enjoying the delights of Bronze Age civilisation, treated those on their margins, in all directions, as lower down the scale. Their word *remeth* for 'mankind', also meant 'Egyptians' while Libyans, Nubians and Asians were all routinely dismissed as 'vile Kushite', 'wretched Bedouin' or 'barbarous Asian'.[26] It was **cultural racism**, as encountered in 1.9; Egypt was not the last nation of immigrants to develop a hatred of foreigners.

In Egypt, a **timeline** is needed to organise its history, even more than in Iraq because there is more political continuity, so time markers cannot be provided by invasions. A Greek historian wrote a history of Egypt organised in a sequence of about thirty royal dynasties: these, in turn, were organised into larger periods, by nineteenth-century European historians, after Napoleon's conquest of Egypt.[27] The relatively brief Neolithic period in Egypt from 4000 to 3000 is classified as '**Predynastic**', with competing tribes worshipping local gods, in continuity with the rest of the world; the first time these tribes were all brought together into a single container is called the '**Archaic period**', the first two dynasties around 3000 BCE; and the later periods when the state returns to this looser arrangement are called 'Intermediate'. The 'golden ages' when the Egyptian state is fully centralised and enjoys military and cultural peaks are as follows:

- **Old Kingdom** c.2686–2040 *aka* the Pyramid Age
- **Middle Kingdom** c.2006–1633 *aka* the Classical Age
- **New Kingdom** c.1550–1070 *aka* the Empire

In Iraq, we focussed on the Sumerians, the innovators who bequeathed their worldview and technologies to the region for millennia after their political rule, and on the Late Uruk phase behind this process. In Egypt, the equivalent focus must be on the Old Kingdom, beginning in the **Third Dynasty**: the century in which the cult of the sun was adopted, the scripts finished, and the pyramids built.[28] In our analsis we will also include some literature from the Middle Kingdom, which coincides with the transition from Sumerian to Akkadian and Semitic leadership in Iraq.

The Nile is a good metaphor for the timeline of Egyptian culture: just as it is the longest river in the world, the Egyptian cultural tradition was the longest (or at least the longest recorded) lasting from the fourth to the first millennium BCE, its hieroglyphics lasting more than 4000 years as a meaningful script: only Chinese can compete with this continuity, and even then only just, by starting much later and reaching to today.[29]

Extending the metaphor: after flowing halfway up the continent of Africa, the thin strip of water suddenly breaks into a delta almost two hundred miles wide feeding into the Mediterranean. This can be taken as a symbol of the *trajectory* of ancient Egypt: fertilising surrounding cultures, and spreading its influence before coming to an end. By the end of its story its capital, Alexandria, was actually on the coast, the second largest city in the Roman Empire, with its famous library and Museum, as the greatest intellectual and cultural **resource** in the Empire.[30]

The Nile Delta is an excellent metaphor for the fertilising impact of Egypt. The Middle Kingdom traded extensively with early Minoan civilisation on **Crete**;[31] during the New Kingdom there was an even closer relationship of trade, going further to reach the **Greek mainland** during its Mycenaean civilisation, which extended to influence on Greek culture.[32] There is much debate about Egyptian influence on the Minoans, including their hieroglyphic script.[33] What is clear is that in the brief golden age of Greek civilisation in the mid-first millennium the impact of Egyptian culture on **the Greek mind** was very significant.[34] Margaret Murray claims that 'In every aspect of life Egypt has influenced Europe ... Egypt was to the Greek the embodiment of wisdom and knowledge'.[35] In Book Two we will explore what this means – in kind and in extent – against a wealth of evidence.[36]

The impact of Egypt to the south – moving back up the river Nile – was equally transformative, as a series of **African kingdoms** and civilisations looked to the Egyptian model. The New Kingdom's empire reached halfway up the Nile to what is now Khartoum, at the junction of the Blue and White Niles.[37] It took over what was already in place: a Bronze Age culture of the **Sudan**, of slightly later origin than Egypt's, but with its own deep indigenous African roots in the Sudanese (Nilo-Saharan) Neolithic, with input from further east in the Cushite or Ethiopian Neolithic. Before the Egyptian invasions, then during and after them, this region operated as an export point for cultures elsewhere in **Africa** on the east-west axis that was established before the Egyptian Neolithic, and to the southern origin of the Nile in the Great Lakes.[38] This reached West Africa, the homeland of the Niger-Congo Neolithic. As in Europe, it was not people who moved – as a rule – but their practices, technologies, vocabularies and ideas.[39] As the first Bronze Age civilisation in Africa, Egypt set a template for imitation further south.

6.2 Sacred marks: Egyptian writing systems as media

The subject or discipline of Egyptology is slightly older than most disciplines we have used to this point. It is usually dated from Napoleon's conquest of Egypt, or from the decipherment of Egyptian hieroglyphics by Champollion in 1822–1824 which followed on from this.[40] Much like Assyriology, the academic study of Iraq and other areas of the Fertile Crescent, it combined the archaeology of a region with the philology of its written language, splicing the two together to form a growing body of knowledge; and like Assyriology it has been increasingly informed by the findings of other relevant subjects, such as modern genetics. Here, we seek to extend this well-established discipline into an enquiry into the sources of psychological thought in ancient Egypt.

The spoken language, as we have seen, was blended from the north and south, reflecting previous movements of people due to climate and food production: from West Asia and possibly southern Arabia it was dominated by **Afroasiatic** elements: it shared with the Semitic languages a triple-consonant root, as for example in the name for the land,*kmt*, in which vowels are added to make a transliteration such as *Kemet*, *Kimit* or *Kemit*.[41] The Ethiopian Neolithic, with Cushitic languages from the same broad family, could have brought this from the south to meet a related language from the north: this would explain the Afroasiatic dominance and it also gives a strong match to recent genetic evidence.[42]

In its psychological vocabulary, however – the focus of this chapter – there are clearly contributions from the **Nilo-Saharan** family, rooted in the (indigenous) **Sudanese** Neolithic, coming into Egypt from south and west.[43] It was a blended language, reflecting its circumstances of populations brought together from all points of the compass. A loose collection of villages, markets and shrines in the Nile Valley, each with its own language or dialect, was slowly converted into a state model, its monarchy and its ideology invented and imposed on this as an abstract idea.[44] Dominant settlements naturally promoted their gods and their tongues over the others, as a basic expression of their dominance.[45] **Cushite** leadership seems likely, given Afroasiatic language dominance and the south-to-north movement of the unification; the Egyptian ideal of the nation-state was distinct from Sumer's city-state model, and it has developed and endured to this day.[46]

What set this in stone – often literally – was the invention of a **writing system**. Pyramids and tombs for successive kings required enormous social cooperation and mobilisation of labour, as visible symbols of royal state ideology;[47] but this came centuries after the invention of writing, which suggests that writing was a successful tool for **state construction**, a vital part of a process of smoothing out local differences, creating public space and controlling the people's thinking.[48] Writing seems to have served as propaganda in Egypt before other means were devised.

Continuous inscriptions, with enough content to analyse the language, begin to appear during the Old Kingdom: in the first dynasties, it was probably more emblematic as assertions of royal authority, like the public inscriptions of the Roman Empire and the first uses of Sumerian cuneiform (5.2). From then on, the writing system took on a life of its own as it did in Iraq, operating with increasing freedom from spoken language.[49] It moulded spoken language as all dominant languages do (think of Roman Latin, English in India and the USA throughout its history, just to make some comparative examples) and spread internationally under the New Kingdom; but as writing it remained the language of a new class, the **court scribes**, whose influence waxed and waned with that of the court: it was not necessarily the language of the people.

The legacy of ancient Egypt is called, by many historians, 'our greatest visible inheritance from antiquity'.[50] The earliest dynasties are characterised by a flair for the visual, which included a great capacity for **converting the invisible** into a **visible form**.[51] In the pyramids, Sphinx, obelisks, temples, palaces, sculpture, and in endless painted records of clothing, make-up, ornaments and everyday activities, which survive back to the earliest dynasties, Egypt has left a visual legacy unmatched by ancient civilisations. This may have been true of others which have not left such a record, as choices of materials and climate may not have cooperated; but another consistent theme of Egyptian products is that they aimed at **permanence**. Whereas Bronze Age Iraq, Pakistan and Israel left us little but mounds and stories, Egypt left us a legacy independent of its written literature.

Great visual flair is first shown in the beautiful system of **hieroglyphics** (Greek: 'sacred carved letters'[52]). As with modern Japanese, hieroglyphs could be used flexibly and read from right to left or (like this text in English) from left to right, top to bottom, or a mixture of these – but it was **to suit the space**: writing was arranged to fit the space available.[53] We tend to separate writing from the surface – to abstract its semantics or meaning as if this was on a separate 'plane' – but to the Egyptian mind, these formed **a single fabric**: the writing remains part of the wider visual texture and interacts with it. Writing may decorate a column, but a statue can form part of a sentence as a 'three-dimensional hieroglyph'.[54] In the Middle Kingdom this close fusion of artwork and language began to separate.[55]

As the Old Kingdom began under the highly creative Third Dynasty (see 6.4) a separate, much faster script was developed for use in business, administration, medicine and literature, confusingly called **hieratic** ('sacred script'). This began in columns read from right to left, moving to rows in the Middle Kingdom, still reading right to left like Arabic, Hebrew and most hieroglyphics; it was written on a flat surface made from *cyperus papyrus* reeds found in the delta marshes.[56]

What is more remarkable than the development of this 'double script' is that hieratic did not simply replace hieroglyphic script but continued in use **alongside** it. There was not a simple development to a 'more practical' written language, at least for the next two millennia. The centrality of royal ideology was buttressed by myths in a visual language. (See 6.12 for a response to this 'double script' phenomenon from Theory Two.)

In 2.6 we introduced Derrida's project of **grammatology**: this has been applied to Sumerian cuneiform and to Chinese as non-phonetic scripts, like Egyptian.[57] Before we ask the question, 'Can (how can) psychology be written in Egyptian hieroglyphs?' we need to take account of Derrida's reflection on the borders of phonetic writing. Our reading and writing in such media have accustomed us to **linear thought**, which breaks up the unity of the real world, whereas Egyptian script presents a '**mythogram**' effortlessly holding several elements together in their original unity; to read this script accurately, 'we must de-sediment "four thousand years of linear writing."'[58] One Egyptologist, making exactly the same point, argues that there is more than one kind of communication, and Egyptian scripts have capabilities which alphabetic systems lack, as well as vice versa.[59]

On the other hand, both he and Derrida warn that we must also beware of any mystification in the other direction; that the flip side of 'ethnocentric scorn' is 'hyperbolic admiration': Egyptians had their own ingrained prejudices. For the Egyptian scribe, hieroglyphs had magical properties as gifts of Thoth, the god of scribes and writing, and were not to be analysed: unlike the Sumerians, Egyptians showed no interest in the analysis of their own language, and their 'ethnocentric scorn' was even greater than that of their European critics.[60] Derrida's argument is that there is always **political violence** implied in any form of ethnocentrism, including logocentrism of this kind (mistaking one's language for reality).[61] In Egypt, the state model certainly involved violence, for its internal stability and its external conquests. The central symbols of the state were commemorations of sacred violence, and the human sacrifices necessary to achieve **order**.[62] Almost every Egyptian king had to renew this sacred violence with a display of force at his borders at the start of his reign.[63] His role thereafter required a balance of lethal force and tender care for his people[64] who were often compared to cattle with the king as herdsman.[65]

Every Egyptian had a fixed social role in the preservation of order, in a rigid **hierarchy** – including the king, who was necessarily a lonely figure.[66] It was in fact people at the very bottom of Egypt's social ladder, mine workers in the turquoise mines of Sinai, soldiers or migrant labourers on the receiving end of state 'violence', who made the first recorded **alphabetic inscriptions**, 'a low-budget multimedia writing technology' improvised on the fringes of society.[67] In Chapter 7 (7.2) we will study this story in detail for what it reveals.

When we turn to the Egyptian psychological lexicon (the word list) in the next section, we must bear in mind that, given the medium, it is first and foremost a **psychology of the Pharoah**, tied up with a court culture of deference – and real anxiety for the welfare of the king and his family, identified with the welfare of the state. It is the **psychology of the nation**, a collective personality because all of *Kemet* was embodied in his royal office; the *psyche* of the Pharaoh bound up with their collective identity – the only *psyche* that mattered. Finally, it is the **psychology of a god** because this person was an object of worship: the welfare of the cosmos was also at stake. In Neolithic societies we saw the cooperation of shaman and chief as the embodiment of the collective *psyche*: in Egypt these are fused, and on a much larger scale. A composite model of the *psyche* was applied mainly to – recorded mainly for – the

Pharaohs, and mainly concerning their afterlife. Most Egyptians were buried in the sand, or thrown into the river.[68]

Besides all of this, Egyptian adaptability and creativity can be seen in the early development of their written language: as the shorter hieratic script helped to make writing more efficient, words in the African tongues from further up the Nile were adopted and given hieroglyphs to capture a wider range of ideas.[69] As well as signs that marked things as word-pictures (pictograms or **logograms**) other signs were used for sounds (**phonograms**), and a third category called **determinatives** was developed to help the reader to know which was which.[70] One of these determinatives was a picture of a papyrus roll, tied up and sealed, indicating that a word's meaning could not be expressed in pictures or sounds but only in writing. This made it possible to refer to **abstract ideas** (remember 'abstract' is Latin for 'pulled away' from concrete experience) which cannot be captured in any other way.[71] In English, when we read any abstract term, we often make a subconscious determinative, marking it off as 'academic talk', to lower our expectations of understanding it, in any way other than its context.

6.3 Introducing the Egyptian lexicon of psychological terms

Much of this chapter will be taken up with the examination of these words:

- *åb* = the heart, also the living mind, the seat of intellect and emotion[72]
- *ba* = the soul, the version of the mind which is active after death
- *ka* = the twin or double, to be explained and discussed further below
- *khu* or *aakhu* = the spirit, the final form of a person in an eternal state
- *khaibit* = the shadow which follows a person, tied to their identity
- *ren* = the name, as written down and read in hieroglyphic or hieratic[73]

The *khaibit* or 'shadow' has little commentary: there is less evidence, with the implication that it was less important. A plausible suggestion is that it is self-explanatory: in that subtropical climate, with very little cloud cover, a shadow follows every person, imitating every movement; for those writing hieroglyphs and thinking in images, it becomes a moving hieroglyph of personal identity.[74]

The 'Name' (*ren*) is related to the magical properties of the written language. As an Egyptologist explains, 'the name of a person, inscribed in hieroglyphs, was believed to embody that person's unique identity'.[75] Once anything was carved as a hieroglyph it was in some sense sacred almost by definition, as 'the divine words';[76] but a proper name designating a person was an image, having something closer to the value of a statue: much as our word 'icon' now segues into 'idol'. There was far less of a distinction between two-dimensional or even three-dimensional representations in writing, art or sculpture, simply due to the nature of the writing system.[77] A person's name was their effigy and their signature, giving them a permanent identity in society and even the cosmos. A Pharoah's name was written inside a ring, the *šnw* or 'shenu' (cartouche), the Egyptian version of capital letters, containing his divine titles as a collection.[78]

To erase the image or the inscription – as quite often happened with a change of dynasty – was to destroy that identity.[79] (Recall Heidegger: 'for primitive man, the sign coincides with that which is indicated ... the sign has not yet become free from that of which it is a sign'.[80]) Erasure was seen as a kind of murder.

This identity of word and object, sign and signified, is part of the mystification of a particular language which Derrida calls 'logocentrism': Egyptians did not analyse their own language as if it were only a human creation, but treated it as seamless with the cosmos itself.[81] Sumerians did much the same. Phonetic scripts cast spells; in non-phonetics, 'the written word was magical power'.[82]

This takes us to the first four words in the list: *åb*, *ba*, *aakhu*, and *ka*. Noticing that all are words of one syllable – *aakhu* is often reduced to *khu* – one leading Egyptologist concludes that they were borrowed from **African tongues** further up the Nile or further west, from the many peoples who had joined Egypt in its early stages.[83] These seem to be phonetic additions to the Egyptian language, incorporated into the hieroglyphic system using the *rebus* (Latin: a thing can represent a sound) principle, although images are matched to the sounds. A traditional reading of the list is that they each came from different **tribes** who had entered Egypt, as their specific tribal psychological terms, taken up and absorbed into a synthesis, perhaps given new emphases in the process.[84] If so then the Egyptian 'package' was manufactured there and exported elsewhere.

It is also possible, however, that they **arrived as a package**. We saw from the evidence of archaeology, genetics and linguistics (6.1) that Egyptians included some Nilo-Saharan elements, from the earlier Neolithic in Sudan and its many offshoots across the Sahel to the west.[85] At least some of these elements of a psychological vocabulary could have entered Egypt together. Even so, their meaning would have been transformed in dialogue with the **writing** of Egypt which was a novel technology with very definite magical associations. Even if they all arrived together, they would have been exported rather differently.

Either way, they form part of **African psychology**; only dating is uncertain.

One Senegalese commentator traces this lexicon to his own language, Wolof, as well as Yoruba, Fula and closer relatives.[86] A writer based in Ghana notes connections between some of the elements and Ashanti (modern Akan) psychology.[87] As these are all from the more remote Niger-Congo language family of West Africa, it implies a widespread basis for this vocabulary, either before or after synthesis in Egypt. As it was tied in closely to the ideology of divine kingship, this implies that it travelled further through Africa *after* synthesis in Egypt.

All the terms – individually as well as together – are attempts to capture the invisible, intangible nature of the *psyche*. In no particular order but simply to capture their variety, we have 'body, double, heart, spiritual intelligence or spirit, power, shadow and name'[88] (*khat, ka, åb, aakhu, ba, khaibit and ren*) if we add the word for the physical body – accurately translated 'mortal flesh' – to this list.[89] Each was both sound and image, within the hieroglyphic writing system, with a symbolic meaning. Many bookshops today contain shelves of popular psychology labelled '**mind, body and spirit**' to capture a holistic view of what we are – the older, philosophical meaning of **anthropology**. Egypt had this long list of elements as their standard vocabulary to do the same thing.

Why such a variety? Why such a long list in Egyptian? Henri Frankfort argues that it was 'not due to any inability to think clearly, but to their habit of using **several** separate avenues of approach to subjects of a problematical nature … They did justice to the **complexity** of a problem by allowing a variety of partial solutions, each of which was valid for a given approach to the central problem'.[90] Another illustration of such logic is that every Pharaoh had at least five names, each for a different purpose, to the great confusion of historians.[91]

Bourdieu called this way of thinking '**polythetic** rationality' or 'polythetic logic' from the word polytheism (Greek: many gods), but here we are applying it only to the problem of human beings, not to the wider problem of explaining the existence of the whole cosmos.[92] Derrida diagnosed our difficulties with such a way of thinking: to understand it as people trained in Greek logic, 'we must de-sediment 'four thousand years of linear writing'.[93] Henri Frankfort agrees: 'The ancients did not attempt to solve the ultimate problems confronting man by a **single and coherent theory**; that has been the method of approach since the time of the Greeks. Ancient thought – mythopoeic, "myth-making" thought – admitted **side by side** certain *limited* insights, which were held to be *simultaneously* valid, each in its own proper context, each corresponding to a definite **avenue of approach**'.[94] As Derrida suggests, however, what Frankfort calls 'ancients' has to include China as the surviving 'ancient' (Chapter 8).

Perceptive readers will notice that it is similar, if not identical, to our analysis of modern psychology in terms of a **spectrum** in Chapter 2 (2.1): diverse levels of function, existing simultaneously, each a partial but incomplete solution to the problem of *psyche*. What was different there to the Egyptian approach, and in fact reflected the Greek approach was our attempt to suggest a **synthesis**, to bring this diversity into **a single model** – using the historical narrative of the 'extended past', that of the 'extended present' (the historical development of psychology, told through a mild version of **dialectic**) – and especially, using a framework with philosophical **headings**. We sketched 'a single and coherent theory', proposing levels of function which cannot be reduced to each other.

Already, then, upon meeting Egyptian anthropology we are at the heart of this book's investigation. Passing the traditional barrier of alphabetic and phonetic languages (like English) as a medium of thought, we have reached at least the elements of a 'psychology' in an alien language and context. We read one into Neolithic structures in Chapter 4 but this was an *etic*, constructed reading; here it is *emic*, explicit, constructed for us, on the other side of a translation.

This lexicon first begins to appear in the extended writings of the Old Kingdom about five centuries after the first monumental hieroglyphics appeared.[95] Their arrival is therefore tied in with the Third Dynasty kings, who founded the Old Kingdom, and with the construction of **state ideology** under that dynasty. Any synthesis of the psychological lexicon into a coherent 'package' was achieved under the Old Kingdom dynasties, as part of a **deliberate** political ideology. If we are going to understand Egyptian psychology, this is where we must start.

6.4 Children of Imhotep: The Egyptian renaissance

Egyptian building alone can show us that mathematics, astronomy, stonework, transport and organisation developed rapidly from previous models[96]; and this already tells us something about the Egyptian mind. Practicality and tenacity in problem-solving, as well as tremendous social cooperation, are clearly required; as in Africa today, those who benefited the community were seen as wisest.[97]

The wisest of the wise – a true *homo sapiens* – was **Imhotep**, minister *(tjati)* to Pharaoh **Djoser**, founder of the Third Dynasty and therefore the Old Kingdom, c.2700 BCE. Imhotep is the first scientist, the first architect and the first doctor named in recorded history. It could be argued that he is **the first psychologist** when we take into account what science, architecture and medicine involved.

All historians notice the 'step change' at this point in Egyptian history. Writing takes off as a medium for study. The great pyramids are all built in a century as great projects of planning, improvisation and problem solving, but can also be seen as brilliant exercises in group psychology, as Kurt Mendelssohn explains:

> The pyramid project was creating a type of community which had never existed before. Tribal villagers were **welded by common work** into a people with the **consciousness of nationhood**. It was probably for the first time that they thought of themselves as Egyptians … [It was] a work programme leading to **a new social order** … The pharaoh himself had become the spiritual figurehead of a large and highly efficient administrative machine whose directives came from the priesthood of Ra, who were the real government … These huge heaps of stone mark **the place where man invented the state**.[98]

Imhotep was the figure associated with this in national tradition. As designer of the Step Pyramid, which built on the Sumerian idea of the ziggurat in stone, he is credited with solving the engineering problems involved, by trial and error. It launched an extraordinary century in which the great pyramids were built, the **template** of national history set in place, and the royal **ideology** constructed.[99]

As the synthesis of elements in Egypt's psychological lexicon was closely tied in with **royal ideology** – as we shall see in the following sections – it was not only difficult to separate psychology from politics, but also to separate either from this visible **public legacy**. Among the people (on the above interpretation) the pyramids functioned as symbols of royal authority and national unity in the Old Kingdom; as any politician knows, 'a picture is worth a thousand words'.

The symbolic language was that of the creation around the **cult of Ra**, based at On or Heliopolis (Greek: sun city) in the Nile Delta. Imhotep was himself a high priest of Ra, whose eye was the sun,[100] and the shape of the pyramid conveyed the effect of the **sun's rays** illuminating the land, having risen faithfully; in the eyes of a viewer, this would be associated with the benevolence of the king.[101]

Another symbolic association built into the shape was that of the **primeval hill** rising out of the water in the First Place: a 'universal myth' with clear parallels at Eridu in Iraq, Teotihuacan in Mexico, Cuzco in Peru, the meeting of Ganges and Jumna in India, and in many written myths.[102] In the Ra creation myth, his soul had flown over the primeval waters, called all creation into being and set **time** in motion.[103] Heliopolis was a centre for measuring time with calendars, astronomy and mathematics, so this was a favourite myth of its priesthood; Imhotep would have been highly trained in these arts.[104] His first pyramid at Saqqara (for Djoser) associated this myth with an exaggerated grave mound for the Pharoah and probably – like Sumer's ziggurats – a **stairway for the gods**.[105]

Finally (and equally important in terms of implications for cultural psychology) this rich 'polythetic' symbolism was achieved with mathematical **precision** and careful engineering. In the placement of the square bases by the points of the compass, in the lengths of the sides, in the angles of elevation, and in the ratios of sides to heights, extraordinary care was taken using ordinary measurement.[106]

The dramatic landscape created by these structures was only one example of a global pattern discussed in Chapter 3. Contemporary with the famous Nile landscape were – for example – equivalent 'curated' landscapes on the Atlantic coast: the Isle of the Dead on the Boyne in **Ireland**, the Ring of Brodgar and the Stones of Stenness on the island of **Orkney** and the **Wiltshire** landscape, which includes Stonehenge, Avebury and 'the Empire State Building of the Neolithic' at Silbury, an artificial hill, estimated to have cost eighteen million man-hours of labour.[107] Each one is proof of a formidable mobilisation of labour, around a collective belief system. As in the megaliths, the two elements of **shared belief** and **political unity** are involved: shamans became priests; chiefs became kings.

In the relationship of **Imhotep** and **Djoser**, which seems to be a historical one, we have the consummation of **the Neolithic relationship of shaman to chief**, a division of labour of visionary, designer and adviser to an executive leader. We noted that shamans evolved into priests as chiefs evolved into kings. Imhotep and Djoser fit this model well: they represent the climax of that relationship in the Bronze Age, dominated by its vertical model of society and government.[108]

A division of labour is still evident but the shaman-figure has an **instrument** in his scientific and mathematical training, rather than using himself as a medium through which he grants knowledge. He is the source of policy, if not yet the source of law.

Another difference is in terms of the **brain laterality** involved. Anticipating T2 as our theory of laterality, the rigorous mathematics and clear concepts of the pyramid project embody a **left-hemispheric** advance, just as the public policy and myth-making side of the project resembles **right-hemispheric** subtlety. Yet both emerge from the legislating figure, and equally inform the executive. It is as if Imhotep is now doing the work – as *homo sapiens* and *homo faber* – of both sides, and the executive figure is implementing both: the relationship is brain to brain, rather than hemisphere to hemisphere or 'sharing a brain'. We will return to these issues in the reviews (6.11,6.12) at the end of this chapter.

Another sign of this bilateral advance at the time of Imhotep and Djoser is the extraordinary medical treatise now named after Edwin Smith (see below 6.5). If it is not in fact connected to Imhotep, it is certainly a match for his work as an architect in its mental landscape and reflects the same push forwards over the same period.[109] It may at least reflect Imhotep's 'school' and his sponsorship.

Once the work of **visible** and **invisible construction** was achieved, both lasted and were built upon further. Within a century Khufu (Cheops) was building his own pyramid the 'Horizon', with the help of his own Chief Minister Hemiunu; his son Khafre, styled 'son of Ra', added another Pyramid and the Sphinx.[110]

The work of nation-building having been achieved and the landscape altered permanently, kings and ministers turned to the **obelisk** as a replacement for the pyramid, preserving the symbolism of the sun-god in a sustainable form, which remained popular throughout the New Kingdom.[111] The ideology of the pyramids, conceived by Imhotep and Djoser, endured for **two millennia** as the **template** for ancient Egyptian civilisation, re-asserted after the collapse of the Old Kingdom social order – when pyramids were pillaged and vandalised – and once this was finally abandoned, Egyptian civilisation began its long decline.[112]

6.5 Egyptian medicine and the *åb*

Now we have enough context to interpret the Egyptian lexicon. Mirroring our procedure in Chapter 2, let us work through that lexicon, to see if we can reproduce something like our spectrum of *psyche*. As we did then, we start in the natural sciences with human biology and medicine. Taking each term, we must bear in mind its media (6.2), its origin (6.3) and its political context (6.4).

After the Sumerian period, the Babylonians achieved respectable results in observational **astronomy**, comparable to their modern counterparts. The comparable Egyptian scientific achievement is in medicine – in **anatomy** and **surgery** – providing an essential springboard for Greek medical theory later on. The same limitation notable in Mesopotamian astronomy is also evident: they lacked a **theory** which could take them **beyond appearances**, penetrating to an explanation in terms of processes and causes in our modern (scientific) sense.

What is interesting in this comparison is the characteristic achievement of each civilisation, and what it can tell us about the two respective **worldviews**. If the Mesopotamians excelled in astronomy in order to participate in the decisions of the heavenly court, to catch up with the divine councils,[113] it is equally true to say that the Egyptians excelled in medicine because they had a very different worldview: one in which **human beings** were significantly more important. As one of their wisdom texts from the late Middle Kingdom expresses this creed:

'Mankind is cared for – the flock of God.

For their sakes [literally 'for their *åb* = hearts'] he made heaven and earth,

And drove away the rapacity of the waters;

So that their nostrils should live he made the winds.

They are images of him, come forth from his flesh.'[114]

In a similar text from the New Kingdom, the Pharaoh calls to his people, saying, 'O my living images, my **partners** among men'.[115] His subjects are the images of his divinity and partners of his humanity. This implies a much greater value set on human beings, at least if they are Egyptian: relative to Mesopotamia, this is warm humanism. Instead of peering up into a cosmos of conflicting divine wills like the Mesopotamian, the Egyptian inhabits a world of reassuring familiarity, in which the divine is accessible and, to a greater extent, human life matters.[116] (In 7.3 we will see an expression of this 'image' notion in Hebrew.)

Life expectancy in ancient Egypt was never good by our standards: studies find that death between 30 and 40 years old was the average, even for the social elite.[117] The pyramids are obviously elaborate tombs, but the literature confirms that a great horror and **terror of death** preoccupied the Egyptians.[118]. Unlike the pessimistic Sumerians, the ancient Egyptian response to death was to resist it.

In early hieratic texts of the Old Kingdom (c.2700–2200) there is already a rich vocabulary for external parts of the human body. Egypt had a growing medical reputation[119] which is justified by **advanced anatomy** in the Middle (c.2100–1600) and New (c.1550–1050) Kingdoms[120]. Many of these breakthroughs first appear in the medical literature of the Middle Kingdom, the Classical Age, but are often thought to go much further back, to the time of Imhotep.[121] One famous anatomical text follows the same order – from head to toe – as *Gray's Anatomy*, still a standard reference today, first produced in Victorian times.[122]

As well as the healthy human form these medical texts reveal detailed interest in describing physical injuries and treatments.[123] A qualified UK doctor can even write that Egyptian medicine 'contains much that relates to current surgical practice and it is not difficult to see the workings of the pharaonic doctor'.[124] He goes on to note that the treatments prescribed by ancient Egyptian doctors are often so close to '**thoroughly sound practice**' – in contemporary terms – that the meanings of words in the text can often be worked out from their context, as doctors today are familiar with the same or similar procedures.[125] This quite extraordinary advance, so early in the story of civilisation, enduring over five thousand years to today, was genuinely original to Egypt, not anticipated by Sumer;[126] but (as is often noted) the Egyptians, in their massive conservatism, did not build on their extraordinary initial advances during the Old Kingdom.[127]

It may be that this conservatism was not simply connected to maintaining the ideology of the Old Kingdom. First, if we are correct about the shamanistic roots of the role of scientist and doctor, the initial breakthroughs would be treated as once-for-all **revelations** and permanent insights. Second, given that medicine was led and administrated by **priests**, there was no independence for science. Third, given the magical properties of **texts**, transmission was the central aim.

A final, possible reason for conservatism was the long African experience with medicine. The medical papyri almost certainly reflect a longer **oral tradition** of **African medicine**, expressed for the first time in a permanent written form. The evidence of modern African encounters with Western medicine is suggestive of comparable quality of unexpected wisdom to that in meeting ancient texts.[128]

Despite their remarkably advanced anatomy, the Egyptians had a very primitive understanding of physiology (the processes and functioning of the living body); the one exception to this rule is the heart and **the cardiovascular system**. Their grasp of this is, according to one doctor, 'remarkably close to the truth' as we understand it today, missing only the oxygen.[129] They were aware of abnormal functioning of the heart and had a specific diagnostic term for this: *debdeb*.[130]

The internal organ of greatest interest was **the heart (*åb*)** which was treated as both a **physical and psychological centre**, in much the same way that the brain is treated today. The same word *åb* was used not only for the living organ but also for its wisdom, understanding and intelligence, as well as disposition, will, wish and desire: the best equivalent in our contemporary terms, capturing all of these, is 'mind' as discussed in contemporary neuroscience, psychology and philosophy.[131] The *åb* was considered as the **seat of intellect and emotion**: it was the one organ not removed during the mummification of a dead body because it was needed for weighing on the divine balance, and also arguing its case for salvation after death.[132] The *åb* has been compared to the use of *phrenes* and *kradie* in the poetry of Homer for midriff and heart (coming up in Book Two) in this dual function, which in today's terms, is both physical and psychological.[133]

Western culture over the last four hundred years has seen **the brain** as the seat of perception, thought, emotion and mental life within the human body. This is by no means the consensus view, globally and across cultures, even today – but in the ancient world, there was a lively debate on this issue between the Greek philosophers **Plato (head)** and **Aristotle (heart)** as we shall see further along in Book Two. Plato's intervention on the 'brain' side of the debate, in *Timaeus* for example, is not scientific in character, involving myth-making rather than logic.

This debate goes back to a definite commitment in Egyptian medicine to the side of the heart, which – in turn – had an enormous influence on Greek and Roman medicine.[134] Aristotle's father had been a court physician, at the time of greatest influence from Egypt to Greece; and numerous scholars have seen the influence of this throughout his philosophy, including his view of the seat of the *psyche*.[135] Aristotle defines his treatise *Peri Psyches* (more famous in Latin as *de anima*) as the climax of **Greek psychology** but throughout this text assumes the Egyptian tradition in assigning the functions of this human 'mind', not to the brain, but to the heart. Aristotle's and the Egyptian view were far from unusual.

Despite according it far less importance to our psychology than modern science, Egyptian medical manuals contain 'the earliest known description of the brain', each skull cavity and connective part labelled in hieratic using their specialist vocabulary for skull (*djennet*), vertebra (*tjes*), membrane (*netnet*), viscera (*ais*) and brain (*amem*).[136] Although the brain was connected to sight, hearing, smell and taste, the Egyptians did not associate the brain with **thought** or **control** of the body: these were located in the heart, along with all emotions[137] Dementia was (logically) attributed to deterioration of the heart, not the brain.[138] Head trauma was recognised and treated, but its significance mostly downplayed.[139]

Given their view of the heart as an entity at once physical and mental, it seems that the Egyptian physiology of the *åb* functions at the same time as a form of **psychological theory**. The physical organ felt pumping within us when alive was understood to have an inner aspect, as the seat of thought and feeling. Just as **neurology** and **brain science** are now seen as part of psychology, with more or less emphasis in different schools of thought, so **cardiology** (study of the heart) and **cardiovascular physiology** were then part of psychology; presumably also with different emphases. The limited physiology in Egyptian texts is therefore compensated by extensive use of *åb* in other literature (6.6), where it always refers to the mind and mental activity, *as well as* retaining its reference to the physical organ. One word means both **physical organ** and **mental experience**.

We should not lose sight of the fact that the ancient Egyptians, as early as the Old Kingdom, first made the link between **body and mind** we still make today, even if they nominated a different organ as the bridge between the two. This entire discussion begins in Egypt; so Egypt deserves credit for this innovation.

The irony here is that those psychologists who are most tempted to dismiss an ancient, proto-scientific theory such as the *åb* as worthless and contemptible, are likely to be those most committed to the **identification** of mind and brain today. Yet their whole project of treating anatomy, physiology and neurology as foundational for psychology has its ultimate origins in the primitive science of the Egyptians, involving anatomy, physiology and cardiology, before whom nobody on the planet had taken a comparable, recorded interest in the topic.

6.6 The living *åb*: Cognition, phenomenology and conscience

The fact that *åb* meant 'mind' as well as 'heart' gives it considerable scope for exploration of what we would call **psychology** while staying anchored in its physical and medical meaning. If we substitute 'brain' this can become easier. We will start with its use in a religious text, and then turn to other literature.

The cult of Ra at On (Heliopolis) had to compete with that of Ptah at Memphis (Menfe) which may have gone back to the very beginning of the First Dynasty.[140] In an Old Kingdom text Ptah was called 'the *åb* in every breast and the tongue in every mouth of gods as well as of men, of cattle and of all living things'.[141] Ptah is thus a way of describing the mystery of human creativity in mythical terms, much as we have seen with the uses of Sumerian myth (5.7):

> Every divine word came into being through that which the *åb* of Ptah thought and the tongue of Ptah commanded. Thus every kind of work and every handicraft, and everything done with the arms, and every motion of the legs and every action of all the limbs takes place through his command, which is conceived in the *åb* and brought about by the tongue.[142]

Note that this was written in non-phonetic, pictorial language. More literally the final phrase can be translated: 'became, in the heart, and became, on the tongue'.[143] Ptah can be translated '**conceptualisation**' and 'executive function' in the jargon of **cognitive psychology** and cognitive archaeology (4.6); he is also the **relation** between these, a 'conceptual operative schema' consisting of both '**thinking mind**' and 'doing mind', '**theoretical reason**' and 'practical reason'.[144] Note that here is a direct reference to human beings in general as *homo sapiens* and *homo faber*, not to the Pharoah; and *åb*, identified with Ptah, can be substituted for the first term in each pair as the leading or intellectual function.

This example demonstrates two things: first, across the language barrier which separates a non-linear or non-phonetic script from a linear or phonetic script, *åb* was used in a similar way to our Latin-based 'psychological' vocabulary; and second, that both media are attempts to capture something basically mysterious. Mastering the jargon in our 'tongue' is not the same as getting a secure grasp on concepts, 'what we are on about'. Seen from the other side, both seem arbitrary.

We have seen plenty of evidence of human creativity in ancient Egypt. Ptah is a way to describe the craft of the builder, the surgeon, the scribe, or the farmer. But the power of Ptah in the *åb* guides the architect, the adviser, and the minister; and the emphasis of the Memphis text is on action through utterance. First the thought is **conceived** in the *åb*, and then it is **commanded** into existence, from the abstract to the concrete; in Greek the word made flesh, *logos* incarnated.[145]

Going back a step in cognitive terms, the text goes on to explain how the sight of the eyes, the hearing of the ears and the smelling of the nose are reported to the *åb*, which goes on to the cognitive and executive processes described. The living *åb* is like **a royal court**, receiving information, exercising its cognitive functions and executive function through organs of government. The tongue is one kind of minister, the hand is another. Once again in Egyptian literature, we find a premonition of an idea to be found in Plato: the **analogy** of the state and the soul in *Republic*.[146] As the king is both man and god, and 'we' (imagining ourselves as ordinary Egyptians) are like him, we are also like a god: this is why Ptah makes sense as a description of human faculties in general. Any analogy of divine and human cognition has this solid basis in ancient Egyptian society.

Our treatment of this text has restricted it to the waking state of consciousness. The Egyptians were also interested in, even obsessed with **dreams** as a clue to the invisible realm[147]: and they developed a tradition of interpretation which is mentioned in other ancient literature as characteristically Egyptian.[148] It could be considered an embryonic 'science', although Egyptian conservatism was a barrier even to the *concept* of progress, let alone significant development. A programme of dream interpretation has been brought back into psychology in the twentieth century through the analyses of **Freud, Jung** and their schools.[149]

Although this programme has also been called unscientific,[150] the exploration of different **states of consciousness,** including the dream state, was very much an interest in ancient Egypt. It continues Neolithic interest in alternative states of consciousness led by the shamans (4.3,4.6) but now beginning to reflect upon it as a phenomenon with more detachment, using the new technology of writing. Like some forms of shamanism[151] this is a democratic dream psychology: these alternative states are understood as common human experience, revealing things about people and about their personal destinies rather than group imperatives or cosmographies. All of this is still the experience of the living *åb*, which beats whether dreaming or awake. It is all part of the **phenomenology of the *åb*.**

As well as the medical and religious texts, ancient Egypt produced a wealth of literature. This is particularly true for the 'classical age' of the Middle Kingdom (c.2100–1600). It is worth visiting this rich literature to glean insights into their views of the human mind: its perceptions, emotions and motivations. In fiction and wisdom books, the Egyptians began a tradition of reflection on the human condition, its limits and norms, which continues into Greek *philosophia.* The terms in our lexicon begin to move and interact, to become part of a dramatic script. We move across from cognitive psychology and **moral** and **social psychology**.

One of the first poems from the Middle Kingdom is a dialogue between a man and his heart (*åb*). Nerferti – 'a scribe with clever fingers' – calls his heart to speak out in lament at the hardness of his generations' hearts and the decline of public morality: 'Stir, my heart, and beweep this land'.[152] He expresses the **psychological pain** of speaking out, which makes him reluctant to speak: 'To the heart (*åb*), spoken words seem like fire; What comes from the mouth cannot be endured'.[153] Yet his heart (*åb*) must be stirred to overcome this pain, because weariness of heart signifies dementia and death, and silence would be worse than speaking.[154] We are taken into the **anguish** of the human mind at moral failure and injustice, a major theme of Egyptian literature.[155] More than a millennium before the Jewish prophet Jeremiah would lament the darkness of **the human heart**, the land and its decline, we have it lamented of Egypt in the reign of Amenemhat I (1938–1908 BCE), founder of the Middle Kingdom.[156]

Another dialogue of a man with his own *åb* is *The Words of Khakheperreseneb*, which engages directly with the problem of how such an **internal dialogue** can occur: in modern terms, with fundamental questions of **self-consciousness**. It is even more anguished than *Words of Neferti*. The sage is the lord, his heart his servant, but he laments his lack of control over this wayward servant in a manner redolent of St Paul, Shakespeare or other soliloquies in our literature:

'The seeking of utterances with heart-searching,
made by the priest of Heliopolis …
If only I knew what was unknown to others,
What is still unrepeated!
I would speak this and then my *åb* would answer me;
And I would enlighten it about my anguish …
I am in distress because of my *åb*.
It is a cause of suffering, yet I keep quiet about it!
Another *åb* would show respect.
A brave *åb* amid pain is a companion for its lord …

O come, my *åb*, that I may speak to you …

I speak to you, my *åb*, so that you will answer me.

An *åb* that is touched cannot be silent.

Look, the servant's lot is like the lord's!'[157]

The lament is both about perception – how can I know my own **motives**? – and about control – how can I control my **passions**? We will see later authors return to these themes repeatedly in India, China, Greece and Rome. Here, it appears for the first time more than a millennium – even two millennia – before them.

One of the most famous stories from the Middle Kingdom is a tale in which a servant of the king suffers a 'panic attack' and leaves Egypt suddenly; amid his adventures, he spends much of the poem trying to understand his own actions. He asks himself whether they are his **responsibility** or the responsibility of the gods; and whether there are **unconscious** sources of human moral motivation.

The final resolution is an extended dialogue about this question with Pharaoh:

'The flight which your humble servant made –

I had not planned it. It was not in my heart (*åb*; alternatively, 'mind').

I had not thought of it. I know not what parted me from my place.

It was like the nature of a dream …

I had no cause to be afraid …

Only – that shuddering of my limbs,

My feet hastening, **my *åb* overmastering me**,

The God who fated this flight dragging me away!'[158]

The king's reply to his profession of ignorance is blunt: '… your roving through countries … was at the counsel of your own heart (*åb*) … it was not in my heart (*åb*) against you'.[159] The king thus contrasts his own steady heart with Sinuhe's fallibility and unsteadiness. As he lies prostrate before the new king, Sinuhe confides, 'My heart (*åb*) was not in my body. I did not know life from death'; he compares his fear to his initial panic attack.[160] The princesses offer a resolution of the central psychological question, why Sinuhe fled: simply a traditional fear of the king, who strikes fear into his subjects.[161] This device resolves the plot, but it does not answer Sinuhe's overriding questions, neither the psychological nor the philosophical. It appears to be an aim of the writer of *The Tale* to raise questions for the reader and her *åb*, rather than to answer them fully.

The poem is presented in the frame of a traditional tomb inscription, with the dead man telling us about his life.[162] The living heart (*åb*) of an unusual man is **the central character** in the tale, the essential background to his judgement beyond death and his present state, inhabiting his eternal home, a pyramid.[163] His name means 'son of the sycamore', an emblematic tree (like 'English oak') and symbol of home, and a major theme of the poem is the very conservative message that Egypt is the best land in the world, ruled by the best kings.[164] It may well be a 'set piece' of political propaganda, intended to justify a usurping regime.[165] Nevertheless, as mentioned above, court politics is only the 'frame' for the tale, and what is more interesting is the clearly **psychological content**.

After *Sinuhe*, perhaps the most famous Middle Kingdom poem is *The Tale of the Eloquent Peasant*. Again, it involves a single incident followed by an extended discussion of the issues at stake. A peasant is wronged by a noble, and then argues his case so brilliantly that the king judges that the noble will become his slave.

The secret matters of the living heart (*åb*) are again a central theme. The noble finds his heart **tempted** by the peasant's property, deliberately plots theft, and lies about it afterwards.[166] In his sequence of eloquent speeches, pleading for justice before an official, the peasant confesses that 'what is in the heart (*åb*) is **unknowable**': that moral motivation and the perversity of the human heart are **hidden** from view.[167] There is a limit to cognition: we know what is outside us better than we know ourselves. As so often 'the heart cannot accept truth'.[168]

The mind's **capacity** for truth (*Maat*) is a more positive theme: the whole story depends on this capacity for *Maat*, in the peasant and his judges.[169] The *Tale* bears some resemblance to the biblical book of Job, in its format of speeches of protest before a divine judge and in its theme of cosmic justice – as also to Plato's *Republic*, in its exploration of human participation in political justice.

Lament over the **deterioration** of the human mind (*åb*) is a common theme in Middle Kingdom literature. As well as those already cited, *The Teaching of the Vizier Ptahhotep* from the mid-Twelfth Dynasty (c.1800 BCE) bewails the fact that however hungrily the heart may desire *Maat*, it will eventually wear out:

> 'the heart [*åb* or mind] passes the night in pain, every day;
>
> The eyes are shrunk, the ears made deaf;
>
> Strength now perishes because of the mind's weariness;
>
> The mouth is silent and cannot speak;
>
> the heart [*åb* or mind] has stopped and cannot recall yesterday …
>
> What age does to people
>
> Is evil in every respect.'[170]

We have seen that the adventures of the *åb* – the living heart, or mind – are well explored in the surviving literature. The next step beyond old age and the limits of the living mind is the *ba*, the soul, most clearly equivalent to *psyche* in Greek, i.e. the moral residue left over at the end of life, represented by a bird.

6.7 The *ka* and social psychology

A term which initially seems most alien but is a favourite among Egyptologists is the *ka* (double). The *ka* was 'born with the individual as an **identical twin**, accompanied him throughout life as the **sustaining constructing force**, and preceded him in death to effect his **successful existence** in the next world'.[171]

The ka is represented in two different hieroglyphs. One is a smaller twin image of the person: 'the ghostly double of a man ... a spirit companion and **guardian from birth** to death and in the other life'.[172] The other is a human bust and two upraised arms – originally those of the Pharoah – bearing his royal name and totem.[173] Later it is attributed to all Egyptians; occasionally universalised to all humans.[174]

The *ka* is the **energy or life force** of gods and humans, which can survive bodily death: it is depicted wearing the same clothes worn in life, but eating heavenly food, and the word could mean 'food' as well as (in feminine form) 'labour'.[175] In many ways it resembles the Greek *daimon*, which later became *genius* among the Romans: a personal mission or individual gift, separated from the person, but tied intimately to their personality. The Latin term *genius* has become a psychological term in the West, moving from an outside force to a personal attribute of a person, or the person themselves viewed in a creative sense: but like *ka* it once meant 'animating spirit'.[176] We return to this in 6.11.

ka could even be compared to the Christian Greek *chrism* or *charism*, meaning special **anointing for service** (hence 'labour' above) from which came 'Christ'; and before that the Hebrew *meshe*, anointing, from which comes 'Messiah'. It is *meshe* that is used for the anointing of kings in ancient Israel, and in close parallel, the *ka* is intimately linked to the authority of Egyptian kings.[177] If the *åb* was a court, then the *ka* was the **throne**, or perhaps a hidden **shrine** behind or above the throne. One Egyptologist describes *ka* as 'that detached part of the personality which **planned** and acted for the rest of the person', and again as 'a semi-detached part of personality which had affected a man's **career**'.[178]

The *ka* appears as a personal **mission**, **gift**, **vocation**; a potential to be fulfilled, initially applied to kingship, but gradually generalised within and beyond Egypt to cover a wider range of vocations. It can even be translated **'social function'**. It is taken to live in the heavens, or at least in the invisible realm, which for all ancient cultures is a repository of intangible social roles and dynamics. The two raised arms are often taken to be pointing towards the *ka* in this realm above.[179]

The reason why it appears so often and is treated so much by commentators is that the overwhelmingly important vocation in Egypt – the most important *ka* – was that of the Pharaoh. This was not simply a matter of social elitism, that this person mattered more than other people, but was a matter of national wellbeing because this person was identified with the state. The *ka* of the Pharaoh was in a sense **the *ka* of Egypt**. We saw that Neolithic people routinely projected their own *psyche* onto individuals who could embody and represent its powers (4.5) and this is of course the fundamental claim of Theory One (reviewed in 6.11).

An illustration comes from the Pyramid Texts with the priest's words to King Merenre (Sixth Dynasty) about his children: 'You have put your arms behind them as a *ka*-arm, that your *ka* might be in them'.[180] The '*ka*-arm' refers to the hieroglyph denoting *ka* with a head and two upraised arms: but the last phrase shows that at least this *ka* could be **transmitted**. It was identical with the royal office and its responsibilities, the moral authority (*Maat*) to lead the nation.

The kingship in Egypt was passed through the **mother**, and there is a possible gender relationship in the *ka*.[181] In Egyptian texts the *ka* is born with the man – and it is almost always a man – and associated with vital force, nourishment, a separate yet intimately related 'second self': this could easily be interpreted as a male view of the maternal role.[182] In the Book of the Dead, a late text based on earlier beliefs, the dead man cries out to his *ba*: 'My heart, my mother!... whereby I came into being!... you are my *ka*'.[183] The equation of *ka* with *ba* is unusual but the association of *ka* with motherhood is the key point (6.12). In a later African culture (the Ashanti) had the *abusua* or 'blood soul' imparted at birth by the mother.[184]

Egyptian religion closely reflected the social structure. There were family gods, village gods, regional gods and national gods, arranged in an invisible hierarchy which closely reflected the different social units visible in the landscape.[185] The success of a village was the success of its god; the humiliation of a village, town or region was the humiliation of its appropriate god. In the ancient worldview, local religion is simply an expression of **social identity**, a personification of the shared sense of 'we' as a god with a name: some scholars go further and claim that (at least some) ancient people were well aware of this, drawing fairly clear distinctions between 'gods' in this social sense and 'gods' as separate beings.[186] We have seen that the *ka* can be interpreted as an expression of the social role of an individual; similarly a god was the *ka* of that community in a wider world.

The 'little man' *ka* sign suggests that it means 'self', as a way of making each centre of consciousness into an abstract **object**, as we use the Latin ***ego*** (I am) as a noun: 'the ego', 'an ego' – and more popularly 'your ego', 'his ego', 'my ego' and so on. Egyptians did have another word for 'the self', *tches*,[187] but it functioned like a pronoun to show what belonged to whom in ordinary human interaction, whereas the *ka* is transcendent; more like 'The Self' in modernity.

In ancient Egypt, the main way of encountering oneself was as a **mirror image**: in the Nile, in an irrigation channel off the Nile or in an artificial pool, even (on rare occasions) in a puddle. This image of oneself is normally smaller, and in a script entirely bound to images the natural choice to draw such a 'mirror image' would be as a smaller double of the original 'self'. This could explain the *ka*.

If we combine the two ways of writing *ka* we have a suggestive hypothesis. If the upraised hands symbol is interpreted as meaning 'social function', and the miniature person symbol is interpreted as meaning 'personal identity', then we have a summary of this ancient **social psychology**, summarised in a formula:

personal identity (*ka* as small twin) = **social function** (*ka* as upraised hands)

In any modern culture, there is a lively debate about the extent to which each 'self' is independent or is socially constituted, with the latter normally winning in social psychology. We saw this for instance with Marx (2.3) and Sartre (2.5). What is interesting is the compromise: only 'part of self' is defined by society.

Given what has been said about *Kmt* coming into self-consciousness through the shared pyramid project (6.4), and built around the office of Pharaoh as an act of collective projection – and similar points in Chapters 4 and 5 – as 'the *ka* of Egypt' as a nation, then it seems entirely valid for us to use *ka* for **collective identity** and purpose. Given the equation above, the identity of each **tribe** can be found in its self-identified 'mission' among other tribes: and so we see the competition of **totems** (animals) from tribe to tribe, priesthood to priesthood, which dominates the political history of Egypt. In this sense, Egyptians could articulate their own social psychology using the *ka*. It was social psychology.

If we extend this to the level of nations, our equation means that the **national identity** is found in its particular 'mission' among other nations. Egypt, like all other ancient nations, struggled to maintain its **national unity** around a state ideology, and rarely had the luxury of thinking beyond national survival; but this was more secure in Egypt than most – it was after all 'the first state' – and in the New Kingdom, a sense of **international mission** was indeed evolved, ahead of the same consciousness in its neighbours. Whatever the king wanted was officially what Egypt wanted; his *ka* was at the same time the *ka* of Egypt; there was also a basic vocabulary to articulate a **national mission** and purpose.

The swelling of the national *ka* was at the expense of the individuals within it. In the New Kingdom the citizen's *ka* became **detached** and **externalised**, as if expressing the *psyche* of individuals, symbolising a loss of a sense of freedom, control or creativity, as Egypt became an Empire.[188] This political and social change affected public psychological discourse in literature. The concern with living well – and therefore with the **balance of *åb* and *ba*** – in Middle Kingdom literature is lost in the New Kingdom, which displays an increasing fatalism and obsession with death. Interest moves exclusively to the afterlife; even the role of *ka* is reduced and **postponed**. Egyptian psychology becomes impoverished; and this is the low, late state in which it was encountered by its Greek observers.[189]

The word *ka* gave us the name we still use internationally for the nation: Egypt. At Memphis the Temple of Ptah was entitled 'Mansion of the *ka* of Ptah': *hwt-ka-pth* pronounced 'Hi-Ku-Ptah', which Greek visitors transliterated into their language as *Ai-gyp-tos*. This became a version of 'Egypt' in other languages.[190]

6.8 The *ba* and the art of dying well

We have seen that the *åb* was at the same time both a physical object, felt in the living body and visible in a dead body, and an invisible entity not dissimilar to our concept of 'mind' anchored in the brain. We called it 'the living *åb*' to emphasise its role before death. The *ka* was a bridge between life and death, born with the *åb* and interacting with it in one's lifetime, but also outliving it.

The remaining lexicon has been called 'the earliest chapter in **folk psychology** which has anywhere descended to us … **a psychology of the dead**'.[191] Its last representatives in Alexandria had a deep impact on Western culture, as its last representative from north-west Africa had perhaps the deepest impact of all.[192]

The *ba* is the internal life which endures beyond death, symbolised as a bird.[193] It always had the same connotations of power, strength, courage and **virtue**, enduring beyond death into the afterlife. It represents the **moral core** of the person, the residue from the complex inner life of a living *åb* left over when the body dies.[194] As such it is like the Greek word *psyche* we later find in Homer and Plato; like the Hebrew *lev or nephesh*; and – perhaps – our word 'soul'.[195]

In several **African languages** *ba* means 'ostrich' or another large bird: it could have been coined in the 'Aqualithic' culture of the early Holocene, probably in a Nilo-Saharan tongue, that is, in the region west of the Sudan.[196] In Egyptian it meant '**manifestation**', 'animation': the Phoenix is the manifestation (the *ba*) of Ra the sun-god, who flew over the primeval waters, came to rest on the first piece of land and cried out, calling the world into being, setting time in motion.

The word 'Phoenix' is from Greek retelling of this creation myth; in Egypt it was called the *Benu* bird – now identified as an extinct species of heron, the largest ever, who inhabited the Arabian coast and rarely visited Egypt itself. The tip of every pyramid represented its original landing place in the creation myth.[197] It was the *ba* of Ra; his soul, as the sun was his eye. It seems that the *ba* of every person contained a reference to this myth: an implied **promise** of the return of every human personality to that timeless eternity at the creation.[198]

This myth and this meaning of *ba* have deep roots in Old Kingdom sun worship but over a millennium later, in the New Kingdom, the tomb of Seti I has a spell:

> You shall change into a living *ba* and surely he will have **power** to obtain bread and water and air; and you shall **take shape** as a heron or swallow, as a falcon or a bittern, **choosing** whichever one of these you like.[199]

Although the *ba* of the sun god was definite, the *ba* of a Pharaoh was chosen freely; this is why the *ba* takes a variety of different forms in the hieroglyphs.

An older poem from the Old Kingdom Pyramid Texts – written on the walls of the tombs under the main pyramids during their Old Kingdom heyday – says:

'He is no longer upon earth; he is in the sky!
He rushes into the sky like a heron;
He has kissed the sky like a falcon;
He has leapt into the sky like a grasshopper.'[200]

If there is such a thing as **Egyptian psychology**, therefore, it falls between the two terms *åb* (living mind functions, including cognition, pictured as a heart) and *ba* (soul or moral conscience, pictured as a bird). These capture the range from bodily anchorage to phenomenology of internal experience, which might concern modern psychology, from more materialistic to humanistic schools.

åb (mind before death) + ***ba*** (mind after death) = **Egyptian *psyche***

As there are several dialogues with the *åb*, there is a dialogue between a man and his *ba* from the Middle Kingdom.[201] It is a meditation on what we would now call **existential anxiety**, in the form of a psychological debate in verse, apparently written to perform for an audience. The soul (*ba*), as a key protagonist in this dialogue is, surprisingly, arguing for the benefits of continued living, while the living man, more conservatively, advocates the benefits of a good death:[202]

'This is all too much for me today! My soul [***ba***] has disagreed with me!
Now this is beyond all exaggeration; this is like leaving me alone!
My soul should not depart! He should stand up for me about this!
If my soul [***ba***] listens to me, without wrongdoing,
With his heart [***åb***] in accord with mine [***åb***], he will prosper.
I will make him reach the West, like someone in a pyramid …
Be patient, my soul [***ba***], my brother …'[203]

It is a significant feature of the dialogue that the man and his *ba* are both given 'hearts' – in accord with one another or otherwise – for the dramatic setting as characters. We have a personality within a personality: a persistent problem in the philosophy of mind. In a sense, the dialogue is between the *åb* and the *ba*, between two components of the psychological lexicon on either side of death. We can express this in English as 'A Dialogue between the dead and the living'.

The *åb* desires investment in the quality of the afterlife, through deference and ritual, but the *ba* desires a better quality of life before death. In effect, the two are working in **one another's interest**, and against their own interest – a point that would not be lost on the original audience. It would hold their attention.

Eventually, after a lively debate, laced with many apparent comic touches, the two reach a final resolution and agree on a policy. The compromise is that life should be lived with a view to the quality of the afterlife, but death should not be allowed to shape every living experience. The soul (*ba*) has the final word:

'Throw complaint over the fence,

O my partner, my brother!

Yet love me here, having put aside the West, your body making landfall!

I shall alight when you are weary;

So shall we make harbour together!'[204]

The metaphor of a journey by sea towards the harbour of death is often found in this literature. A balance is sought between enjoying the journey and staying focused on the destination. The Middle Kingdom literature seeks this balance: these writers are concerned with **living well** (*åb*) as well as **dying well** (*ba*).[205] It shows the sense that **balance** that brought this to be called 'the Classical Age'.

Their concern with living according to *Maat*, variously translated 'truth, justice, balance'[206] is an extension of the previous concern with kings exercising their freedom and their power for the good of everyone: this kingship is internalised to an ideal of self-government, every citizen guiding actions according to *Maat*.

Today we would call this normative behaviour, and debate the origin of norms: the Egyptians were clearer about the origin of norms, but were concerned with the human capacity to perceive them, acknowledge them, or implement them. Once again, the themes of Plato's *Republic* and other dialogues are anticipated.

6.9 Views of a future state: *akh* and eternal destiny

Beyond the *ba* and the *ka* is the *akh*, *khu*, *aakhu* or *yakhu* (spirit)[207] pictured as an **ibis** or wading bird. It is more specific in species than a *ba*; and unlike the *ba* (which essentially replaces the *åb*) it can inhabit a living person, and it is more **detachable** from the individual: less personal, and not even tied specifically to human beings. It was strongly associated with **stars**, **light**, **fire,** goodness and virtue – with many literary references to *aakhu*t 'serving the gods' – but it can also have the connotation of a debt or transgression, either to God or another person, in some other African languages.[208] Like our word 'spirit', it can also be translated as '**angel**' and it was associated, like our angels, with the heavenly bodies.[209] From the first dynasty Egyptians built their tombs with shafts on the north side so that the *aakhu* could rise to meet the group of stars circling around the north pole. These stars were 'immortal' because they never set: they were called 'those that know no destruction' or 'no weariness'. To join these was to become immortal and eternal, at one with the ever-circling **cosmos.**[210]

This notion comes very close to the heart of the ancient Egyptian worldview: it captures the powerful drive towards a **static**, **timeless** permanence which most experts have identified as a pervasive theme of the culture. The *akh* is a bridge into that state of permanence; it has echoes in the later Indian psychologies of *atman* and *Brahman*, and the state of *moksha*, which will appear in Book Two.

Old Kingdom priests had to incorporate this element into the new Ra ideology. The flight of the *ba* is not explicitly connected to the circling of the *aakhu* in the night sky, and the *ba* is more closely connected to the individual personality as conscience, but the two notions are connected by their common anchor in the myth of **creation.**[211] As all pyramids were connected with the *ba* through their apex (the Benu-bird landing on the mound in the First Place) and association with the morning, they also stood for all time under the ever-circling *aakhu* at night. The royal cult of Ra inevitably focussed on the day but the *aakhu* gave it a bridge through the night. Ra was given a barge to sail through the night, and another to sail across the sky by day, in a daily cycle of death and rebirth.[212]

The reason for the elaborate mummification rituals of their kings is that Egyptians believed the survival of the body was essential if the soul would be immortal.[213] Life after death needed a body of some kind: and the mummy was to prepare a king for his **immortal body** or *sāhu* to germinate like a seed from his mortal remains.[214] A king of the fifth dynasty was called Sāhu-Ra: an incarnation of the sun god Ra.[215] In the Book of the Dead, the dead man's *ba* says: 'I exist, I exist; I live, I live; I germinate like the plants'. He is reborn, but this is not so much resurrection as **reincarnation**. The same soul is inhabiting a different vessel.[216]

Just after 2000 BCE, in the Middle Kingdom, Amonhemhat I has the *ka*-name (roughly, job title) '**he who repeats births**' and Senusert I has 'he whose births live'. Five hundred years later, the New Kingdom *Book of the Dead* gives spells for controlling future incarnations, in special 'chapters for **making existences**' addressed to ordinary Egyptians. The king of the next dynasty, Seti I, is called *whm mswt*, '**repeating of births**'.[217] This is in the New Kingdom but clearly has deeper roots, going back at least as far as the opening of the Middle Kingdom.

Global shamanism had long suggested that the human *psyche* was capable of alternative accommodation during life, based on the visions of the shaman;[218] Neolithic and Bronze Age politics was often based on leaders' claims to be the incarnation of an ancestor or a god. It does not seem a huge step from this the thought that this process might be **repeated**. Like their medical innovations, it may well be that the Egyptians were simply the first to **record** a much longer oral tradition. Whatever its origins, another reminder to us of how alien and remote Egypt's civilisation is from our own is their adoption of **reincarnation**.

When the Greek historian Herodotus observed Egyptian culture in its last days he insisted that '**the Egyptians were the first** to assert that the soul of man is immortal, and that when the body perishes it **enters into some other** animal, constantly springing into existence ... when it has passed through the different kinds of terrestrial, marine, and aerial beings, it again enters into the body of a man that is born; and that this revolution is made in three thousand years. Some of the **Greeks have adopted** this opinion, some earlier, others later, as if it were their own'.[219] In 6.7 we saw the funeral spell for Seti I: 'You shall change into a living *ba* / You shall **take shape** as a heron or swallow, as a falcon or a bittern, **choosing** whichever one of these you like'.[220] This is royal shamanism, but it presents the important possibility of the *ba* (in this case) **selecting a new body**.

We associate reincarnation with the ancient religion of **India** as it first appears in the first millennium BCE (see Book Two); although this looks ancient from our perspective it comes after the New Kingdom of Egypt. Transmission from India to Egypt is still a possibility, as both were in three-way trade with Iraq;[221] but the first **evidence** is from Egypt. It was much discussed in the Greek world which (as in Herodutus) gave **Egypt** full credit for the idea.[222] Pythagoras, Plato and Plotinus (himself Egyptian) brought it firmly into the Western mainstream.

The reason why it became so strongly associated with India was that it became deeply rooted there in later millennia, formative of the entire culture; but only a marginal belief in the West, largely due to the impact of Semitic religions (7.8). The earliest evidence we possess is in these **inscriptions and titles** for Egypt's Pharaohs c.2000 BCE; given all the above (6.3) its probable origin is **African**.

6.10 Concluding reflections

This survey has **confirmed** that, in ancient Egypt, the lexicon of psychological terms covers a similar range to that of modern psychology, without reduction to one specialised category, nor yet in a comprehensive synthesis. A person could be referred to by their physical body as an object with parts (*ha, hat*)[223]; or their specific organ (only it was a different organ) of thought and feeling (the *åb*); their enduring character or soul (*ba*), by their spirit (*aakhu*); or by their self and social function (*ka*).[224] These categories – once translated and interpreted – can give sufficient **resources** for the practice of psychology: a **psychological 'map'** of the personality, alongside their anatomical 'maps' of the body in medicine.

The fact that this vocabulary was an attempt to capture **shared intuitions** and to describe the human experience accurately, but that this did not necessarily lead to an investigation of relations **between** these intuitions, is more suggestive of what we now call **phenomenology** (see 2.3) than a theory of **psychology** proper. As phenomenology is intended as a **foundation**, supplying data toward systematic reflection – like observation, experiment, fieldwork or **ethnography** – so the Egyptian vocabulary for *psyche* forms a foundation for reflection. We saw that Egyptian **anatomy** described the human body with extraordinary accuracy but that little was built upon this foundation. Egyptian 'psychology' is comparable.

Did the Egyptians build anything on this foundation? Did they create **theory**?

We have seen that, in medicine, the Egyptians provided a huge store of useful **data** to be explained by later theories. There is some parallel with psychology.

When the Greeks began to develop theories of everything, including *psyche*, they had a large, conscious debt to Egypt as the older, **resourcing** civilisation: for example, Plato's profoundly influential psychology shows a conscious debt to Egypt, as Aristotle's biology owes a debt to Egyptian medicine.[225] Together with the Greeks, then: *theoria* is only a **component** of science, and when the Greeks brought in this component, they typically exaggerated its importance. A long process of **re-balancing** theory and experiment, involving debate between schools prioritising each of these, occurred in Greek and Roman medicine.[226] A fair response is to say that *theoria* is a later, Greek idea, and the Egyptians can hardly be expected to conform to this category, invented by a later civilisation.

Derrida's grammatology divides the phonetic languages (as a family) and non-phonetic languages (as a family). Is it possible that *theoria* as conceived by the ancient Greeks inhabits a phonetic thought space and is not meaningful within a non-phonetic thought space, almost by definition? The ancient evidence is not able to answer this question, because we have *two* variables: writing medium and time. It is possible that the division of labour we have proposed between Egypt and Greece is a function of their order in time and not their languages.

Brain laterality (under T2) would suggest that the receptive **right hemisphere** must collect information before the constructive left hemisphere can get to work creating abstractions and theories. Egypt and Greece embody these functions in the correct sequence, suggesting that time rather than medium is the key cause.

Theory involves intuition and deduction, inspiration and calculation, with both sides of brain functioning. In principle, intuition or deduction can occur in phonetic or in non-phonetic media. Once again an implication is that the medium is not the key.

We have found substantial evidence of reflection which approaches **cognitive** psychology (once translated), **phenomenology**, **psychoanalysis** and **existential self-dialogue** (6.6) as well as **social** psychology, **moral** psychology and forms of **transpersonal** psychology, using the categories recognisable in our culture. Placed together with the precise medical reflection on the *åb* as a human organ – always with the caveat that it is a different organ – this could yield something approaching the range of contemporary psychology with *åb* equating to mind.

Like 'heart' in English, *åb* always has two senses: it is always both the **heart** as a physical organ and the **heart** as an internal experience, because 'the Egyptian never wholly dissociated a person from the body as an instrument or vehicle of sensation'.[227] The hard part for us is to stretch this ambiguity to 'mind' as well, because we tend to use 'heart' for emotions, and 'mind' for cognitions; roughly approximating brain laterality (right and left respectively) with our vocabulary.

Egyptian cardiovascular theory is thus a close equivalent to our neuroscience, as the fundamental theory in human biology informs every other area. Just as we read (and write) many books attempting to understand the relationships between 'mind and brain', the Egyptians used a single symbol for both levels.

In effect, **reincarnation** is Egypt's major contribution to psychological **theory** on the other side of death. **Plato** toyed with this idea, as he did with many ideas, presenting philosophical arguments for and against it as if it were a theory. It appears remote and exotic from a modern point of view, but it is unavoidable as an element in the study of ancient psychologies. (See Books Two and Three). Today we would call this a theory in **transpersonal psychology**, but in Egypt in the Bronze Age – as in all previous and contemporary cultures – distinctions of religion, science and psychology, familiar to us, would have been meaningless.

With this and the approach towards cardiovascular theory with the *åb*, we have tentatively identified at least **two theories**: one about the *åb* and one of the *ba*, *aakhu* and *ka* together. These are the building blocks for Egyptian psychology:

Egyptian psychology = psychology of the living
+ psychology of the dead

The use of such a mathematical expression is alien to Egyptian sensibilities, as it is too left-brained and abstract: the terms in the Egyptian lexicon were **symbols** and **metaphors**, not building blocks, and 'the Egyptians could not abstract the survival of man's immortal parts from the continued existence of his body … they could not imagine such a survival without a physical substratum [bottom layer] … the Egyptian mind always tends towards the **concrete**'.[228] The lexicon was understood not as **a list of parts** to be abstracted and separated, not as an exhaustive analysis, but as a cluster of **complementary descriptions** of *psyche* – which illustrates the contrasting approaches of hemispheres and languages.

We have found a **correspondence** between the spectrum of modern psychology in Chapter 2 and the spectrum of Egyptian psychology in this chapter, and identified two candidates for the label 'psychological theory'. What about the further question: is there an overall **synthesis**? In 6.3 we distinguished a set of '*limited* insights, which were held to be *simultaneously* valid, each in its own proper context, each corresponding to a definite avenue of approach' (as the characteristic mode of 'polythetic logic') from a 'single and coherent theory'.

We have managed to approximate the 'spectrum' from Chapter 2 using the Egyptian lexicon, but this was an interpretation imposed on the data from our side. Did the Egyptians themselves have a reading which held this all together?

The answer seems to be a cautious yes: but '**ideology**' is better than 'theory' as an appropriate label for this synthesis. As predicted in 6.2 and 6.4 every part of the lexicon was originally applied to the Pharaohs of the Old Kingdom, and the purpose of these terms was to focus on **the king** as the centre of Egyptian life. We have traced this, term by term, with the various associations of the *ba*, *ka* and *aakhu* to creation myths, and public symbols, in the intervening sections.

It seems that, when Egyptians began to apply these terms to themselves and their after-lives in the later Old Kingdom onwards, this was in the container of national ideology, so their personal psychology was derivative and dependent on the stability and welfare of the kingdom. There was a **national community** and ideology (as well as the project of building pyramids) that had done its work.

This brings us back to a quotation from archaeologist Michael Wood (6.1) that 'centralised power, royal rituals and the cult of the dead intertwined to form the ideology of the world's first state'.[229] We now know that Egyptian psychology was welded into that ideology to form a comprehensive, **persuasive** synthesis.

We saw at the start that the lexicon within this synthesis was one of the most **African** elements of ancient Egyptian civilisation: from the south and not from the north. We also saw that the synthesis itself was led, at its crucial points, by creative people from the **southern** tribes, within the cosmopolitan melting pot of the Nile valley in those centuries. It was at once psychological and political: and the psychological content seems to have **travelled with the total package** down the Nile, south and west, whereas only components went north and east.

The reason why the synthesis resonated with the rest of Africa, and succeeded for so long, was that it was **African in origin**. It was transmitted down through the African kingdoms over the coming millennia, cropping up in language after language, and culture after culture to this day, while other stories played out on the other continents. Just as there were several African 'Neolithics', there was a synthesis forged in the laboratory of the Nile Valley in the African Bronze Age.

6.11 Review of Theory One

Jaynes recognised that Egypt was an excellent case study for his theory.[230] He presents it as a classic example – perhaps *the* classic example – of a bicameral civilisation: collective mobilisation on an unprecedented scale; extraordinary submissiveness to state ideology; a certain simplicity of outlook; complacency, optimism with underlying anxiety: these all suggest a bicameral mind.[231] A difference from Sumer, a god-king rather than a steward-king, was actually an improvement on Sumer purely on the terms of bicameral forms of government, by building the bicameral relationship directly into the hierarchy of the state.[232]

Egypt is a good test case for Jayne's model, as it was relatively undisturbed for much of its early history – certainly for the fourth and third millennia, covering the emergence and the Old Kingdom. Whereas Iraq was constantly disturbed, a global marketplace of peoples, languages, ideas, technologies and influences, a different set of circumstances left pharaonic Egypt 'essentially undisturbed by outside forces, for a period far surpassing in length any such development'.[233] It suits the (otherwise fragile) bicameral model, and Jaynes was aware of this.[234]

This allowed the delicate bicameral social contract to operate almost alone, as the main prop of a Bronze Age civilisation. The ideological stability we see in Egypt, bridging through its political disturbances, is suggestive of the shared hallucination required by T1. The experts all note that the ideology of kingship itself was *never questioned*: all Egyptians seem to have been content to project their executive function onto Pharaoh as their representative, in true bicameral fashion, and to take their lead from the royal court. The Egyptian emphasis on contentment, on cyclical rhythms within a static container, is the one we would expect of a bicameral civilisation (6.9). The total disorientation of the Egyptians in the face of political turmoil equally reflects this model.[235] When we read of the distress of Sinuhe and his inability to explain his own motives, it is possible to read this story on Jaynes's terms as a fictional portrait of a bicameral mind.

Jaynes claims that both the fragility of the Old Kingdom, with its collapse into anarchy and disorientation c.2200 BCE, and the strength of the restoration in the Middle Kingdom less than a century later, illustrate his thesis well.[236] Without a bicameral social contract people became completely lost, and sought one again.

Jaynes interprets the dialogue of a man with his *ba* (6.7) as a clear example of an auditory hallucination: the man is hearing voices, and is reporting on this;[237] although he misses the obviously composed, literary and dramatic quality of the text, taking it rather literally, as though it were a clinical report. He could make the same point more subtly by appealing to cultural context: people were *used* to this kind of experience and could explore it in fiction and comedy. Overall, this is a rather point-missing (and humourless) reading of quite a self-conscious text, probably better read – in its original context – as playing with and exploring the possibilities of **psychological language**; and valuable to us for that reason. The fact that the *ba* and the man are both given an *åb*, and the obvious comedy, do not suggest the sober, childlike, unselfconscious quality required under T1.

Jaynes offers an interesting interpretation of the *ka*: according to his theory, it simply denotes the directive **right hemisphere** from the perspective of the left. The *ka* is 'the will of the gods', a bicameral person hearing his own decisions as those of an independent agent.[238] This interpretation matches all of our data in 6.7 remarkably well, including the idea of the *ka* as an 'identical twin' sibling.[239] It could even be improved on, using independent data about the connections between adequate parental nurturing and adequate right brain development; the gender roles in the Egyptian court could imply this view of the *ka* (see 6.12).[240]

Henri Frankfort notes that 'the Egyptian gods remained aloof ... The actions of individuals lacked divine guidance altogether'.[241] But this can be interpreted as the genius of the system: by embodying the potentially conflicting wills of the gods, by providing a concrete political embodiment of a psychological model, the Pharaoh made the bicameral system much more **sustainable**. An absolute monarchy buttressed by religious ideology meant that *one office* could receive the projection: 'the whole apparatus of government was but an implement for the execution of the royal command'; yet 'his individuality escapes us entirely and in every instance. Even in his lifetime, he appears to belong to the sphere of myth ... The rulers in whose name **every act** of government was undertaken, who erected vast monuments and prided themselves on great deeds, remain totally **impersonal** to us'.[242] The permanency of the office was woven into the ideology: 'a fundamental feature of Egyptian kingship, a feature rooted deeply in the Egyptian mentality' that 'the touchstone for all that was really significant was its **permanence**'.[243] It is a fixed, timeless model, impermeable to evidence.

Finally, the theory predicts that as the bicameral **crisis** occurs, as a **breakdown** of the bicameral mind is experienced, and subjectivity and consciousness begin to break through, then these things should be registered in the cultural record. The unusual continuity of the Egyptian record should offer a prime illustration, spanning the whole crisis. What we have noted in 6.7 about the **New Kingdom** heartache and discontent is a good fit to Jaynes's predictions about that crisis. Jaynes has built in considerable flexibility in terms of timeline: the crisis could begin in the second millennium, even in the Middle Kingdom, and accelerate through the New Kingdom period. Yet his theory at least requires innocence of all parties in the **Old Kingdom**; whereas the history suggests political genius.

From this brief sketch, T1 seems to reach its 'high point' with Egypt. An inbuilt weakness to this test of the theory is that Jaynes had access to most of the data reported in this chapter: Egyptology was advanced at the time of publication. Its literature was basic to his research into antiquity, so his theory was built on this data: and indeed, one possibility is that it reflects this data well, but cannot stretch so well into other data – especially that which has appeared since then.

Once again, as with Sumer (5.8), Jaynes does not engage sufficiently with **language** and misses an opportunity to explore his ideas about mind-space, interiorisation and psychological **metaphor**. We have done so in some detail here (6.5 to 6.10) and it could have been an interesting study to compare this data with his theory.

6.12 Review of Theory Two

McGilchrist mentions Egypt several times: paired with Sumer as the origin of writing; initiating with Sumer the 'empire of writing' through political control; and sharing a similar pattern of development in terms of lateral functions in the script, from pictograms (right hemisphere) to more phonetic elements (left). He compares Thoth, the Egyptian god of writing and science, to Hermes his Greek counterpart, implying that Thoth fathered a different line from Hermes: non-phonetic and phonetic scripts (2.6), which he calls 'syllabic' and 'phonemic'.[244]

Psycholinguistics dominates his reading of Egypt: we can take it a little further in the light of our examination of the Sumerian writing system and what we found. The Egyptian scripts of the Old Kingdom suggest a lateral **division of labour**, with **hieroglyphic** script taking up the – shamanic and mythic – functions of the right hemisphere, as **hieratic** takes the more instrumental functions of the left.

The division of labour between the two scripts reflects the brain's own division of labour, each script providing a suitable container to articulate the activity of one hemisphere. This proposal extends to the **mutual intelligibility** of the two scripts: their mutual translatability resembles the brain's own *corpus callosum* connecting the hemispheres. Their **co-endurance** over two millennia suggests a stable **lateral balance**, a writing technology and intellectual culture unusually well designed around the functioning of the human brain; as the development of hieratic into an increasingly cursive form, ending in demotic, and the marginal appearance of Semitic alphabets, suggests further specialisation from the left.[245]

Using this assumption, we can see that the *users* of hieratic such as architects, doctors and accountants were stretching the envelope of the **left hemisphere** while operating in a **subservient** role towards the priests and the royal patrons who were the users of hieroglyphics. The normative relationship according to T2, with the left hemisphere serving the right, was marked by the social roles of the users. The dual script system protected 'the Egyptian mind' from abnormal functioning provided that these worked harmoniously in their respective roles.

As with the proposed synthesis of Egyptian **psychology**, the Egyptian mind in general depended on the stability and endurance of the civilisation, built as it was with extraordinary wisdom around the needs of human beings in society. The model is so well matched to normal brain functioning, as it is portrayed in McGilchrist's theory, that had it endured it seems that it could have achieved even more. This serves to confirm the portrait of Egypt left by so many Greeks, summarised by Margaret Murray in her classic study:

> Egypt was to the Greek the embodiment of wisdom and knowledge ... the Home-Land of Science as we know it; it was passed on to the Greeks who recorded in [their / our / alphabetic] writing and so gave it to the world.[246]

All of the above implies that Old Kingdom Egypt was an example of a balanced 'bihemispheric advance' much like that McGilchrist portrays in fifth-century Athens two millennia later and the Italian Renaissance: another two millennia away;[247] **more balanced** than the advance in late fourth-millennium Sumer.[248]

The Egyptian writing system, its architecture, its statuary, its state ideology, its literary forms, its medicine and – if we can use the term – its psychology are all innovations on a global scale. Each of the great phases in Egyptian history, but especially the Old Kingdom, represents an **expansion** of a neurological function, with shifts forward in left hemispheric activity balanced by those on the right. (Its stability means that we can observe this dialectic more clearly than usual.)

Other inferences can be made in evaluating Egyptian data using McGilchrist.

His portraits of Homer's poems, Aeschylus's tragedies and most philosophers before Plato suggest an initial right-hemisphere bias in Greek culture like that of Egyptian: as though Greek literature begins where Egyptian literature ends in terms of lateral balance.[249] His negative reading of Greek development clearly implies a positive reading of what they inherited, not dissimilar to Derrida's.[250]

He notes that the Greek prejudice against *muthos* (symbolic communication) – resisted by Lévi-Strauss, Bourdieu, Derrida, Davies and many others – begins with the rejection of their own earlier tradition, as a symptom of the decisive shift to the left hemisphere he identifies in the first half of the first millennium BCE.[251] His bilateral interpretation of Aeschylus's tragedies as the hemispheric mind 'cognising itself' resembles our readings of Egyptian wisdom literature in 6.6 (*åb*) and 6.8 (*ba*) as well as our – and Jaynes's – reading of the *ka* (6.7, 6.11) as exercises in what is now called **phenomenology** or **existential** reflection.[252]

Frankfort gives a good example of the hemispheric difference in Egypt's literature:

> … in Egypt the ingeniousness of the form of any piece of writing stands in **inverse proportion** to the factual information which it conveys … it would seem that either **facts or poetry** prevailed, and that these states of mind were experienced as **mutually exclusive** by the Egyptians.[253]

This can easily be interpreted as a portrait of **separated** hemispheric function. Either the left or the right can process the information, but not both together.

This insight from a respected scholar immediately modifies our interpretation: the lack of integration Frankfort observes is more redolent of the Sumerians in their division of rational analysis and playful myth. Perhaps our interpretation so far is based only on the *potential* of the hieratic-hieroglyphic labour division to reflect hemispheric balance; an over-estimation of the interaction in practice.

Psychological studies have noted that strong lateralisation among the highly intelligent, while liberating each hemisphere to 'do what it does best', can also lead to a developmental delay and certain kinds of dysfunction.[254] The Egyptian mind show some signs of **non-integrated** lateralisation, at the cultural level: in the writing system, the mathematics of surveying and architecture, medical investigations, literary genres and even psychological vocabulary there is a slight abstraction – the activity of the left – but this is not taken as far as it might be in each case because the right hemisphere continues to pull in a different direction.

It is noticeable that this shows a clear **chronological** pattern: the Old Kingdom is the source of almost all left-hemispheric or bihemispheric advances listed.[255] The geometry of the pyramids; the efficiency of separating hieroglyphic from hieratic scripts; the ingenuity of integration of their phonetic and non-phonetic elements; the clarity of the anatomy; all of those things routinely described as 'surprisingly' or 'astonishingly' modern – that is, recognisable from our own, left-dominated culture. Yet (as routinely) Western commentators lament that, following their initial innovations, the Egyptians 'stopped': their conservatism is blamed and treated as the source of their eventual downfall. Yet perhaps it is a **strength** of their model that their lateral **balance** was retained and protected.

Finally, let us consider and evaluate a synthesis of both theories (T1 and T2):

Given the note about matrilineal descent and **maternal nurture** in 6.7, as well as Jaynes's attempt to lateralise the *ka* (as the right hemisphere, 6.11) it is worth considering the light that may be shed on **gender** from the Egyptian ideology.

The *ka* of the king – in terms of his office and fitness for office – was inherited from the Queen Mother; his fitness for office (ideally) was shaped by her actions. If the *ka* is his **right hemisphere** represented in a symbolic form, then we are on the same territory as Narvaez and Tarsha (4.9, 5.10). In their portrait of the relationships between maternal nurture and laterality in Palaeolithic societies and today's USA, they insist that a healthy development of right hemisphere function depends strongly on the quality of maternal nurture, especially in boys.[256]

On one interpretation, this is exactly what was prioritised in Egyptian royalty; and this in the context of an ideology of government and culture found to be a remarkably thoughtful response to Bronze Age developments in other respects. It looks as though the architects of Old Kingdom Egypt had read Narvaez and Tarsha – or rather, had not forgotten lessons from the same ancestral sources.

McGilchrist is dismissive of popular attempts to line up the gender binary with brain laterality so that the left hemisphere is 'somehow male' and the right is 'somehow female'.[257] This does indeed seem too neat and too tight a relationship.

If, however, we take a hint from Narvaez and Tarsha to connect hemispheric development to parental nurture, and connect this insight to Egyptian custom, we could consider moving the relationship **up a generation**. We can have the right hemisphere characterised as the **'mothered hemisphere'** and the left as the **'fathered hemisphere'**. It ties them to biological sex rather than gender.

This adjustment to T2 retains the sense of **resonance** between the two binaries – laterality and sex – without making the same connection inappropriately tight. It could also then be connected with McGilchrist's account of evolutionary origin for the division of hemispheres (4.9): the vigilant (mothering) brain, protective of the young from predators, and predatorial (fathering) brain, protective of the young from starvation and exposure. Although this conservative family model appears to echo the notorious 'Man the Hunter' publications in archaeology,[258] it is also worth noting that – by tying brain laterality to biological sex through parenting in this way – we leave the determination of gender free of either binary.

These observations are once again to serve as a model of handling theories, in the manner of traditional dialectic, by testing and then developing in response. The conclusions, while interesting, are in fact less important than the method.

Discussion questions:

1 Can you sketch a diagram or a map to capture the content of 6.1?
2 Can you imagine reading hieroglyphs? Try it if you have the resources.
3 Which Egyptian 'soul-words' do you find most relatable personally?
4 How did pyramid-building projects help to build Egyptian identity?
5 What would it mean for psychology if intelligence is based in the heart?
6 In what ways can your dreaming self be different from your waking self?
7 If *ka* is a vocation, how would you picture your *ka*? Or that of your family?

8 Does the relationship between living *åb* and *ba* make sense to you?
9 Do you believe in reincarnation? How could you prove it or disprove it?
10 In what ways has this study of ancient Egypt surprised or intrigued you?
11 Do you think Jaynes's interpretation of the *ka* makes any sense?
12 Have you become more aware of the different 'sides' of your thinking?

Recommended Reading

- Henri Frankfort *Before Philosophy* 1946
- Henri Frankfort *Ancient Egyptian Religion* 1948
- Kurt Mendelssohn *The Riddle of the Pyramids* Cardinal 1976
- Margaret Murray *The Splendour that was Egypt* 1949
- Adam Muksawa *Ancient Africa Fully Explained* 2021
- Parkinson (trans) *The Tale of Sinuhe* OUP 1997
- Barbara Watterson *Gods of Ancient Egypt* Sutton 1996
- Barbara Watterson *Ancient Egypt* Sutton 1998

Notes

1 Moore p.146; Putnam p.86; Roberts p.64; Renfrew 1973 defines 'civilisation' as the artificial creation of a new living environment, involving a high population density, increased social stratification, and 'at least two' features out of a list of three: urbanisation, monumental buildings and writing. Early Egypt qualifies as a civilisation although it lacked large cities, because it had all the other features.
2 Diop p.7; Murray p.283 n.3; Wood p.120: Diop is a controversial name in Egyptian scholarship; a Wolof aristocrat from Senegal with some blatantly racist views about other Africans, in his native Senegal, in North Africa and arguably also in Egypt. In spite of these issues, however, his work is no more and no less in need of sifting and sorting than other authors in the Bibliography – Hegel is one example already discussed for both negative and positive contributions. (See Howe p.11 and Ch.14 pp.163–192 for a fair and balanced assessment). The original meaning of *kmt* is controversial for related reasons; typically, Mojsov p.1 relates it to the dark alluvial soil, while Diop p.7 above relates it black skin-colour.
3 Bellwood pp.9–10, 15–16, 26–31,38–9,115–6,148,153; Diamond pp.36, 50–51; Diop p.67; Harari pp.6,15; Roberts pp.10,20.
4 Bellwood pp.126–8,134,136–8; Diamond pp.386–7; Muksawa pp.33–4.
5 Bellwood 101–3,109,135; Diamond p.390; Howe p.148; Muksawa pp.xxv,64,169–171; one of several new competitors with the increasingly outdated 'Neolithic' label that have emerged recently, as mentioned 4.1.
6 Bellwood pp.79–80,93,115; Diamond pp.386,388–9,398–99; Howe p.148; Muksawa pp.40–2; Cavalli-Sforza pp.135–7 notes that this classification of African languages by Joseph Greenberg, once much-criticised and controversial, had become the academic consensus among linguists by the end of the twentieth century. This chapter's argument will proceed by following that consensus.
7 Bellwood pp.97–8,100–1; Diamond pp.390,393–6; Muksawa p.31–2,76.
8 Bellwood pp.101,103,125,136; Diamond pp.387–8,390–1; Muksawa pp.32–3; this contribution from the ancestors of the Nilo-Saharan languages is taken to be significant for psychology (from 6.3).
9 Bellwood pp.103–4,126–7; Diamond pp.388,390; Muksawa pp.40,183; Oliver and Fage pp.50–1.

10 Bellwood pp.126–8,134,136–8; Diamond pp.386–7; Muksawa pp.33–4.
11 Hence the remarks already given above, n.2: the battle lines are drawn, in terms of our Bibliography, with Diop, James and Van Sertima in the 'Afrocentric' camp; Lefkowitz and some of her allies in the conservative and defensive mode of academic orthodoxy; Stephen Howe and John Baines as more balanced representatives of the latter; and perhaps Olofemi Taiwo as the most judicious and reasonable commentator of all - hence the choice of his leadership on this issue from Chapter 1 onwards. Much of the current ideological battle is not in Africa or among Africans, but within the USA and tied into its particular history of racial politics. This chapter attempts to steer a middle course between either form of ethnocentric prejudice.
12 Diop p.22; Mendelssohn p.23.
13 Diop pp.83,125–6.158; Watterson pp.xviii–xix,1.
14 As noted (for example) in Mithen 1996 p.226.
15 Bellwood p.137; Mendelssohn pp.23–7.
16 Putnam p.7; it is worth noting, for example with Mojsov p.xi, that the division into the Old, Middle and New Kingdoms was a nineteenth-century classification, like the three-age theory in 1.4.
17 Nunn p.11, with some extrapolation, working against other estimates.
18 Renfrew 1976 pp.136, 161.
19 Frankfort pp.20,50,131–2; Wood p.125ff.
20 Wood p.125–6; see also Howe p.126 and an excellent account of the political ideology of the first dynasties in Mojsov Ch.2 pp.10–14.
21 Van De Mieroop 2007 pp.35–9.
22 Diop p.150; Howe pp.140,142.
23 Davies p.112; Renfrew 1994 pp.122–3.
24 Hooker p.7; Robinson 2009 p.23.
25 Robinson 2009 pp.34–5.
26 Diop pp.39,62,97; Watterson 1996 p.7; Mojsov pp.40–2,55–6,59,61,71–2,74,77–9 shows how Nubia represented a traditional national enemy and rival from the Middle Kingdom period onwards.
27 As n.16 above.
28 Mendelssohn pp.27,45–6; Murray p.14; Watterson p.20.
29 Davies p.78.
30 Heine pp.3,13ff.; all of this is to come in Book Three, where Alexandria will play a central role in the story.
31 Murray p.98.
32 Murray p.23; Murray, O. p.215; Van de Mieroop 2007 pp.132,140,142,145,192; Van de Mieroop 2017 p.213.
33 Renfrew 59,62 writing Davies 142 129 178–189 Robinson 21,29.
34 Murray, O. p.222.
35 Murray p.xvii.
36 This is not to neglect other significant influences on Greek culture, such as those from further east derived from the Sumerian legacy, and the indigenous Greek capacity for transforming its imports or creating its own culture; it is simply to state the initial case for Egyptian influence on the Greeks. The debates cited in n.2 and n.11 are not only over ancient Egypt but over its relationship to Greece.
37 Howe pp.140–4; Muksawa p.82; Oliver and Fage pp.34–40.
38 Diop pp.156,163,179–201; Howe pp.141, 146–8; Muksawa pp.102–112; Oliver and Fage pp.39–40,44–52.
39 Davies pp.133–4; Diop pp.138–148,179–186; Howe pp.147–8.
40 Putnam p.6.

41 Davies pp.78,102; the word is related to 'black'; see n.2, n.11 for a background to semantic issues raised by this word, but here the point is purely grammatical.
42 Bellwood pp.116,118.
43 Budge lxviii, pp. 68, 197; Budge 1959 pp.191,218.
44 Roberts p.77.
45 Wood pp.122ff.
46 Diop pp.1–2,6,12–21,49,57,71,91–2,134–6,149–150; Howe pp.32,138,142,173; Wood pp.129–130,144.
47 Murray p.255; Roberts pp.67–69.
48 Bellwood pp.129,137.
49 Davies p.81.
50 Roberts p.65.
51 Wood p.128.
52 Davies p.82; Putnam p.90.
53 Putnam p.86.
54 Davies pp.84–9.
55 *Ibid* p.89.
56 Davies pp.84,95–6, Murray p.290; Robinson 2009 pp.25–6; Watterson p.xviii.
57 Derrida 1967 pp.74–81–87–93; Hung pp.vii,2–8,19,23,144; Van de Mieroop 2017 pp.78,235 n.61.
58 Derrida 1967 pp.85–6.
59 Davies p.107; Ruyu Hung makes the same point throughout his extended argument about Chinese and Western alphabetic languages.
60 Davies p.78; Derrida p.80.
61 Derrida 1967 pp.37,130.
62 Wood p.123.
63 Murray p.58.
64 Wilson pp.80, 93, 101.
65 *ibid* pp.88–89; the leading metaphor for the ruler in Sumer was the shepherd. Cavalli-Sforza pp.122–3,170 argues that the cow was first domesticated in West Africa, well before the shrinking of the habitable space through the growth of the Sahara. The choice of the cow metaphor is therefore suggestive for the origins of Egyptian royal ideology: it could have come from Nilo-Saharan tribes to the west or the south of Egypt, like most of the psychological terms listed in the next section.
66 Wilson pp.87, 91, 106ff., 120; Watterson pp.5,34.
67 Davies pp.133–4; McGilchrist 2009 p.274; Sanders pp.41,49–50,91.
68 Murray p.185, Putnam p.61; Watterson pp.32–4.
69 Budge p. lxviii.
70 Davies p.102; Robinson 2009 pp.88–9: this was the standard trajectory in Sumer and China as well as in Egypt
71 Murray p.292.
72 Budge p.37; Murray p.189.
73 Budge 1959 pp.189–192; Murray p.189.
74 Mendelssohn p.44.
75 Davies p.89.
76 Davies p.86; Murray p.290.
77 Davies pp.84–6,89; Derrida p.303.
78 Davies pp.116–7; Robinson 2009 pp.62,69,73,89–91.
79 *ibid.*
80 Heidegger *Being and Time* I.3.17 p.113.
81 Davies p.78; Derrida 1967 pp.3,80.
82 Derrida 1967 p.3; Hung p.xii,100–104; Van de Mieroop 2017 p.91.

83 Budge lxviii, pp. 68, 197; Budge 1959 pp.191,218.
84 Breasted p.51; Murray p.189.
85 Bellwood pp.101,103,125,136; Diamond pp.387–8,390–1; Muksawa pp.32–3.
86 Diop pp.186,190–1.
87 Mendelsohn pp.42–3.
88 Budge 1959 pp.192–3.
89 *ibid* p.189.
90 Frankfort pp.91–2.
91 Mendelssohn pp.24,28.
92 Fowler pp.16–19.
93 Derrida 1967 p.86.
94 Frankfort p.4; Watterson 1996 pp.14,19 makes the same point.
95 Davies p.81.
96 Nunn p.11.
97 Sternberg pp.366–376.
98 Mendelssohn pp.16,46,68,128,134–7,140,146.
99 Breasted pp.182 n.4,184; Mendelssohn p.44ff.; Murray p.14; Spencer p.233; Wood p.127.
100 Mendelssohn p.45; Putnam p.46; Watterson 1996 pp.43–8.
101 Mendelssohn p.57.
102 Frankfort p.156; Mendelssohn p.74; Wood p.124.
103 Breasted pp.11,71–2,76–7,330; Budge 1959 p.224; Watterson 1996 pp.25–9 (for the myth itself).
104 Childe 1981 pp.115,166–9; Mendelssohn p.121.
105 Mendelssohn pp.36–7.
106 Childe 1981 pp.134,168; Mendelssohn pp.62,76–9; Watterson 1996 p.46.
107 Lewis-Williams and Pearce p.243; Renfrew 1976 pp.240,256,262.
108 Lewis-Williams and Pearce pp.85–6; Thomas and Humphrey pp.7,33,37.
109 Nunn p.27.
110 Watterson 1998 pp.17–24.
111 Mendelssohn p.143; Watterson 1996 pp.48–50.
112 Diop pp.205–7; Mendelssohn p.79; Watterson 1996 pp.47,136–147.
113 Toulmin and Goodfield pp.41–45.
114 From *The Teaching for King Merikare*; Parkinson p.226, 233 n.50.
115 From *The Teaching of King Amenemhat*; Parkinson pp.206,209 n.7.
116 Jacobson pp.138–9; Roberts p.73; Wood p.121.
117 Nunn p.22.
118 Murray p.211.
119 Roberts p.77.
120 *ibid* pp.42, 52.
121 Nunn p.11; Watterson pp.34,48.
122 Gray ii, ix, xii; Nunn.
123 Nunn p.57.
124 *ibid* p.29.
125 *ibid* pp.176–8.
126 Roberts pp.67,77.
127 Nunn p.206.
128 Muksawa p.42; Van Sertima pp.140–155.
129 Nunn pp.54–5, Murray p.288.
130 Nunn p.218.
131 Budge p.37; Murray p.189.
132 Murray p.177; Putnam p.55.
133 Moore p.160.

134 Nunn pp.12, 207–9.
135 Anagnostopoulos pp.4–5.
136 Nunn 50–51, 217–226.
137 *ibid* p.54.
138 *ibid* p.95.
139 Nunn pp.46,58–9,174–5.
140 Watterson 1996 p.163.
141 *ibid* p.164.
142 *ibid* p.165.
143 Wilson p.67.
144 Renfrew and Zubrow 1994 p.140,144,154.
145 Wilson pp.64–68; 93.
146 Annas Ch.5 pp.109–152; Plato *Republic* Book 4 to be examined below.
147 Murray p.217.
148 Genesis 37,40,41.
149 For example, in Jung pp.115–6, 176, 194.
150 For example by Wittgenstein 1946 pp.70–71; Sartre 1953 pp.91–96; Popper 1963 pp.37–38.
151 Thomas and Humphrey p.33.
152 In Parkinson pp.134–5.
153 *ibid* p.137.
154 *ibid* p.140 n.10, n. 11.
155 *ibid* pp. 57,59,70–71, 131–2.
156 *ibid* pp.132, xxxi; also see Yirmeyahu/Jeremiah 4:14–19, 17:9–10, 20:9, 23:9.
157 *ibid* pp.146–148.
158 *ibid* p.38.
159 *ibid* pp.35–6.
160 *ibid* p.40.
161 *ibid* pp.41, 52 n.78.
162 *ibid* pp.21,27,42–3,53 n.83, n.84.
163 *ibid* pp.43 n.2, 53 n.83.
164 *ibid* pp..22–6, .43 n.1.
165 Watterson 42–3; Parkinson pp.44 n.7, 45 n.17.
166 Parkinson pp.59–60.
167 *ibid* pp.70–71; p.84 n.77.
168 *ibid* p.148 from *The Words of Khakheperreseneb.*
169 *ibid* pp.13, 68, 86 n.9, 86 n.97, 298.
170 *ibid* p.250.
171 Wilson pp.63, 95.
172 Moore p.160.
173 Budge lxviii; Murray pp.189–190.
174 Murray pp.209–211.
175 *ibid* pp.189,192.
176 Lewis 1963 pp.42,215.
177 Murray pp.190, 211; Shemuel Aleph Ch.16.
178 Wilson pp. 107,127.
179 Childe 1981 pp.88,91; Diop p.189–191,207; Wink pp.3–10.
180 Breasted p.72, translation modernised.
181 Mendelssohn pp.40–43.
182 Breasted p.52; Frankfort p.93.
183 Budge 1959 p.168.
184 Mendelssohn pp.42–3.
185 Budge pp.23,109.

186 Budge p.108ff., Wink pp.6–8.
187 Budge lxviii.
188 Wilson pp.104, 127–129.
189 *ibid* pp.91–2.
190 Watterson 1996 p.167.
191 Breasted pp.52,61.
192 This refers to Plotinus and his school, as well as medieval, Renaissance and modern reception of their work; to Origen ('son of Horus') and Augustine, the deepest shapers of Orthodox and Catholic theology respectively.
193 Budge pp.197–8; Moore p.160; Murray p.210f.; Putnam p.62.
194 Budge 1959 pp.190–1.
195 Moore p.160.
196 Diop p.191.
197 Breasted pp.11,71–2,76–7,330; Budge 1959 p.224; Watterson 1996 pp.25–9 (for the myth itself).
198 Breasted pp.15,55,61.
199 Frankfort pp.98–9, translation modernised.
200 Frankfort p.135.
201 See 6.11 for Jaynes's interpretation of this text and a critical discussion of his interpretation.
202 Parkinson pp.152–4.
203 *ibid* pp.155–6.
204 *ibid* p.160.
205 Wilson pp.104,115, 129.
206 *ibid* pp.94,98,116,119.
207 Wilson pp.63, 95 Wilson pp.63, 95, 107, 118.
208 Diop p.190.
209 Budge pp.22–25.
210 Frankfort pp.100–107; Wilson pp.56–7.
211 Frankfort pp.59–54,64,107,122,136,138,156; Wood pp.124–6.
212 Wilson pp.57–8.
213 Putnam p.54.
214 Budge 1959 pp.196–9.
215 Murray p.17.
216 Budge 1959 pp.196–9; Wright pp.46–7.
217 Murray p.211.
218 Lewis-Williams and Pearce pp.124,128–9,195,244,266–7.
219 Murray p.210; Herodotus 2.123.
220 Frankfort pp.98–9, translation modernised.
221 Childe 1981 pp.124,137–8; Robinson pp.36,173–5.
222 Smart 1989 pp.47–8; Wright pp.45–55,77–9.
223 Budge p.466.
224 Wilson p.76.
225 Wilson p.131; *see also* Plato *Collected Works* p.1763; this will be expanded considerably in Book Two.
226 Conrad et al. Pp.15,36; Lloyd pp.222–3; Nunn p.208; Nutton pp.31–21, 36, 39.
227 Breasted p.156.
228 Frankfort pp.92–3,114.
229 Howe p.126; Wood p.125–6.
230 Jaynes pp.143,159.
231 *ibid* p.159.
232 *ibid* p.178.
233 Breasted p.3.

234 Jaynes p.185.
235 Frankfort p.86.
236 Jaynes pp.196–7.
237 *ibid* pp.193–4.
238 *ibid* pp.184n.8,189–193.
239 Wilson pp.63, 95.
240 Henley and Rossano p.64.
241 *ibid* p.81.
242 *ibid* pp.32–3,46.
243 *ibid* p.49.
244 Davies p.103; Hooker p.8; McGilchrist 2009 p.273,275,278.
245 Davies pp.82, 84–5,93–5; Derrida 1967 p.303; Healey Ch.2 (pp.210–220) for which see 7.2.
246 Murray pp.xvii,xxiii; see note n.36 on the same quotation.
247 McGilchrist 2009 pp.259,299.
248 McGilchrist 2009 296,309ff.
249 *ibid* pp. 263,267–8,272,283,288.
250 Heidegger, Derrida and McGilchrist are all ultimately indebted to Nietzsche for this analysis of Greece.
251 *ibid* pp.283,288.
252 *ibid* pp.273–4.
253 Frankfort pp.139–140.
254 Blakeslee pp.45–6,100–101,107–8.
255 McGilchrist 2009 pp.259,299.
256 Narvaez and Tarsha in Henley and Rossano p.64.
257 McGilchrist 2009 p.2.
258 Henley and Rossano pp.84–6; Whitley pp.219,255.

7 Ancient Israel

7.1 Orientation: Voices from the margins

At some point, according to their own records, an ancient people were ejected from Egypt, or rather escaped to tell the tale.[1] Their ancestors had come from the then-leading Sumerian city of Ur near the start of the second millennium, just as Sumerian culture was coming to an end and handing over to Babylonian leadership;[2] they had travelled right around the Fertile Crescent, into what we now call Israel;[3] settled in Egypt amicably during the Middle Kingdom;[4] but left under very different circumstances some centuries later, at some point during the New Kingdom.[5] Their story is therefore closely bound up with those of the two great civilisations, but at the 'other end' from our coverage in Chapters 5 and 6, which emphasised their beginnings. We are travelling forward in time: this chapter and the next will take us forward towards the 1000 BCE boundary.

In 6.1 we noted genetic evidence for a Neolithic flow of people from Arabia to the Horn of Africa across the Gulf of Aden, speaking Cushitic languages;[6] in Egypt these met others with related languages in the **Afro-Asiatic** family.[7] This explained the fact that Egyptian is in this language family, despite the African sources of its civilisation. A group within this family is called **Semitic** from the widespread flood myth, in which one of the hero's sons was named Shem, an ancestor to these tribes.[8] Linguistic evidence points to a Semitic **homeland** in Lebanon or Syria, near the general Neolithic heartland at the top of the Fertile Crescent (4.2).[9] All these tribes seem to have spread **southwards**: some down the Mediterranean coast to Egypt; some down through the Arabian peninsula; and some entering Iraq under the name of **Amorites**: Akkadian, Babylonian and Assyrian were Semitic languages, which each absorbed Sumerian culture (5.2).[10]

There were plenty of Semitic tribes, however, who did not enter 'civilisation' in this way but stayed on the margins. Many settled in **Arabia**: the word 'Arab' is originally used for nomadic herdsmen, between Egypt and Turkey, but mainly in **Syria**, most moving slowly south through Jordan into the 'Arabia' of today.[11]

DOI: 10.4324/9781003396147-10

These tribes were driven southward by their desire to remain marginal and to avoid the world of the Bronze Age with its hierarchies and empires.[12] This gives us a clue to the Semitic *habitus*. As Iraq and Egypt became increasingly warlike and imperial, in the literature of their elites there is a persistent anxiety about the people on the borders and margins who resist civilisation. Egypt used the word *'apiru* (or *hapiru* or *haberu*) negatively to denote these outlaws or 'bandits', or more neutrally 'displaced persons', refugees, and sometimes simply 'the poor'. It seems that this included both '**Arabs**' and those calling themselves **Hebrews**.[13]

This group of tribes wrote their own orientation: a history, called ***Bereshith***. We saw in Sumerian libraries that the books were named and catalogued under their first lines; the books of the Hebrews, similarly, are named after their first significant words: in translation, *bereshith* means 'in the beginning'. (Its Greek title became **Genesis**.)[14]

It gives a terse but comprehensive account of the 'context for everything', in a text neatly structured in a nested series of circles: of the creation of 'the heavens and the earth' – *ha-shamayim wayyet ha-eretz* – and the **parents of humanity**, *ha-adama* and *hawwa*, of their children; of the great flood (as in the Sumerian legends) and of the **peopling of the earth** afterwards by their 'clans, languages, territories and nations'.[15] Locating his audience on this cosmic map, the writer tells us that 'Shem was the ancestor of the all the sons of **Eber**'[16]: this Semitic branch is the **Hebrews**. A descendant of Eber is Avram, the 'great father' who made the long journey from Ur to the new land in obedience to a vision.[17] This ancestor and his family live exactly like ancient descriptions of the **Arabs**.[18] His grandson Jakov is renamed *Yisrael*, 'wrestles with God', thus yielding **Israel**.[19]

This text certainly fits the profile of *'apiru* who worried the elites. The story of the Tower of Babel seems to be a satire on imperial Babylon, as it appeared to those on its margins in the early second millennium;[20] it is a typically Semitic rejection of 'civilisation' by a nomadic people.[21] There is also a frank admission of the uses of civilisation, as these nomads are at the gates of Egypt – *'apiru* as 'refugees' and 'the poor' – every time there is a drought.[22] This drives the plot of *Bereshith*, which sets up the epic sequel: the book called ***Shemot*** (Exodus).[23]

Nothing is more typical of this people, and their future trajectory, than the fact that their written records do not agree with those of the Egyptians: they were born in controversy, and archaeologists today still debate the two positions.[24] The linguistic evidence does support a mass migration, and its slow reversal,[25] but the archaeological evidence does not support the claims made: 'Whatever the reality, it is clothed in a thick layer of mythical interpretation'.[26] *Bereshith* and *Shemot* introduce a collection of five Hebrew texts, that would be known as **Torah** in later tradition, which itself is the frontage to the larger **Tanakh** (to be called the **Old Testament** in a different arrangement). In this, the narrative of the early Israelite kingdom is a good match to the Neolithic developments[27] traced elsewhere (4.5) with shaman and tribal leader evolving together into a priesthood and chiefdom: between Shaul and **David** an 'ethnic state' is born.[28]

Where other cultures were called into being around building projects – temples (4.2), cities (5.1) and pyramids (6.4) – the Hebrew culture (and later the Arab) was called into being around texts, to a unique extent.[29] Our exposition of this worldview is therefore less archaeological and much more literary than others.

7.2 The voice of the prophet

The presence and importance of Arabic, and to a lesser extent Hebrew, on the world stage today, means that most of us have heard at least one of these two languages spoken at some point. Their scripts look very different on a page but are close relatives: the underlying structure and vocabulary are actually similar. These began very much as the 'outdoor languages' of herders and farmers, the *'apiru* at the edges of empires, while other Semitic languages became imperial.

A feature of both languages which stands out for those learning them today is that they read *from right to left*. This was quite normal in the ancient world: it seems, from current neurology, that this is the right hemisphere's preference.[30] We have seen it in hieroglyphics and hieratic for a related language in Egypt.[31]

What is unremarkable to us, but hides a revolutionary[32] innovation in its time is that these languages are **alphabetic**. Like the Sumerian invention of the city, it was such a successful innovation that it is easily forgotten that it *had* an origin.

The back story matches our portrait of Hebrew and Arab origins in 7.1. As one scholar observes: 'The earliest known alphabet was not the creation of erudite scholars but a hybrid **improvised** in a contact situation **in the desert fringe**'.[33] A perfect symbol of Hebrew is its first appearance in the archaeological record.

While conceptions of the Neolithic were being overturned at Göbekli Tepe, in southern Egypt at Luxor an inscription was found at the Wadi el-Ḥọl (Valley of Horrors). It was dated to the Middle Kingdom, c.1900–1800 BCE, yet obviously alphabetic. It seems to have been written by foreign soldiers or labourers as graffiti, alongside 'the **informal** personal rock inscriptions left by hundreds of ordinary Egyptians during this period … these inscriptions suggest the quick and dirty tool of foreign workers, scratched **in desolate places**'.[34] Further north, on the Sinai peninsula, at the turquoise mines – a perfect symbol of Bronze Age civilisation and its obsession with tradeable, exotic goods – a sphinx was found with graffiti in both hieroglyphic and the Hebrew alphabet, dated c.1900 BCE. When Sumerian scribes were writing *nisaba zami*, 'O **Nisaba** praise' at the end of official documents,[35] to invoke their patron, the graffiti writer was writing an invocation to **Hathor**, the Egyptian goddess who protected mines and miners.[36]

We are clearly at the bottom of the social ladder; and in a situation poetically appropriate for the portrait of the Hebrews in Egypt, painted in

Shemot: 'the Israelites groaned in their slavery and cried out, and their cry for help went up to God'.[37] Yet it is clearly much earlier – indicating that '**the alphabet**'s rise was **not inevitable**' – as Western scholars had assumed, treating it as 'the natural end point of historical development'.[38] The alphabet and written Hebrew remained on the fringe of the two great civilisations for the rest of the second millennium.

Another clue to this social reality was discovered in 2022 in Israel. Inscribed on a comb dated to 1700–1550 BCE is the earliest alphabetic **sentence** yet found: 'May this tusk root out the lice of the hair and the beard'.[39] Clearly, alphabets were in everyday use, at least in this southern city (Lachish), representing 'the emergence of **a new mode of communication**'[40] among fiercely independent Semitic speakers, even beyond a Neolithic way of life. Within a millennium of the first full sentences in cuneiform or hieroglyphic, these appear in alphabets.

Just as Sumerian cuneiform and the two Egyptian writing systems were born in step with one another, around 3000 BCE, and developed into a full language in step with one another around 2500 BCE, they also both took their next big step forward in tandem early in the second millennium. Just as cuneiform was being transformed by its encounter with a Semitic language (**Akkadian**), pulling free from its mooring in spoken Sumerian around 1700 BCE, [41] (5.2), the Egyptian system inspired another bid for freedom on its own borders, which was much more distinct from its parent but was also rooted in Egyptian soil. It was always a possibility for Egyptians to develop an alphabet, as they had long substituted whole-word signs for **initial sounds**; but Semitic speakers familiar with this Egyptian system, probably in Israel, took the crucial step, borrowing a few Egyptian signs but using the sound of Hebrew words, putting them in order.[42] *'alpu*, 'ox', became a picture for the sound 'a'; *beth*, 'house', represented 'b', and so on. There was more than one alphabetic order, but this one prevailed, so in later languages which borrowed this principle the Hebrew letter names were kept.[43] In Greek *alpha* and *beta* are meaningless, except as the names of letters: the alphabet became an artefact in the 'archaeology' of languages.[44]

This will be an important point going forward into Book Two. We have these three stages:

1 That 'there is clearly an Egyptian inspiration behind the invention'.[45]
2 That the letter names are taken from Hebrew words used as pictographs.
3 That the alphabet created in Hebrew then became the global standard.

This, then, is the ultimate origin of the English 'alphabet' you are now reading. It came from the *'apiru*, western Semitic speakers on the edges of the empires, who 'had inherited other political traditions … ideologies of **collective tribal** power and prophecy in which divine authority spoke to peoples, not just kings. Alphabetic writing, low-budget and easier to learn and produce, circulated **outside the court** ... to inscribe things they had not learnt from empires'.[46] This helped to create what have been called 'alphabetic societies' such as Israel and Greece in the first millennium BCE, or India in the first millennium CE.[47] As the principle was revived in early modern Europe it transformed that continent, so that we take the idea of **vernacular literature** (written in the national language) for granted, as we do mass literacy; but, like the alphabet, these are products of a radical approach to writing, in some ways the **reinvention of writing** itself.[48]

We have seen that the natural interface between a culture and an individual is a local group, a team, or in a larger culture a tribe (3.2,4.5). We saw that schools formed the interface between cities and the scribal students in Sumer (5.3,5.4). We conjectured that a certain tribe (6.1,6.2) or a particular team (6.3,6.4) was responsible for a synthesis of political ideology and 'phenomenology' in Egypt.

With Hebrew also, there are signs of a scribal culture with deliberate **intent** to create a new kind of literature appearing in Israel. What is most remarkable is the existence of the written sources themselves: 'The **Hebrew Bible** is the still-functioning artefact of a vernacular revolution'.[49] Even if there were nothing to verify the claims of the Hebrew scriptures in the archaeological record, there is the artefact of **the text** itself, as its **form** alone represents a radical departure.

The central confession of Judaism – closely related to the central confession of Islam, the *Basmala*, or many others in the Qu'ran such as the sixth *Sura*[50] – is:

> 'Hear, O Israel: Yahweh is our God, and Yahweh alone:
>
> you shall love Yahweh your God with all your heart (***lev***),
>
> with all your soul (***nephesh***) and with all your strength (***meod***).[51]

We will return to this in 7.5 to examine the vocabulary used here for *psyche*. At this point our focus is more basic: what is this text **doing**, or trying to achieve?

Seth Sandars proposes that it is calling a people into being: putting into writing 'a traditional discursive task of **summoning** and addressing a people'.[52] It is the voice of a character we have met before, but not for some time: the **shaman**, or in Hebrew terms, the **prophet** (*navi*): 'Rather than assume that a king had the right to speak for a people, we see a very different expectation: that the ideal interlocutor for a people is a prophet'.[53] Before this, Sandars argues, 'literary prophecy, a message circulated to a public **in writing**, did not exist'.[54] In the global Neolithic (4.5) we traced the emergence of 'horizontal shamanism' in early Neolithic tribes, which was more personal, private and **democratic**, potentially practised by everyone, and then from it a 'vertical shamanism', the role of the priest, evolving opposite and in tandem with that of the tribal chief.[55]

Writing, to this point, had been the invention and the servant of the **priests** (in Egypt) and the **scribes** (in Sumer), both of whom served the political leaders. It had not occurred to anyone that the older **shamans** might have a place at this table: they were outside civilisation, among the illiterate barbarians, or at best among the Arabs, the Hebrews, the *'apiru* who would not come to the centre. Building on Sandars's proposal it seems that the new vernacular alphabets were hitched to this wagon, put to work and mobilised as **the voice of the prophets**.

This is a helpful clue to the medium of written Hebrew and, when it happens, written Arabic: the Semitic languages are **prophetic languages**. Boats carried on this stream all become vehicles of prophecy. Sandars notes that the genres of **history** and **law**, in particular, were transformed from their 'imperial' models: 'Biblical law is handed down by a prophet, and biblical history is framed as the working-out of prophecy'.[56] The invention of Hebrew saw 'the inauguration of new ways of writing history, law, and prophecy ... Narrative prophecy serves as a kind of meta-genre, **framing** biblical history and law ... a narrative framework making the prophet himself a character and a protagonist of events ... history and law themselves become **genres of prophecy**: speaking to and binding an audience in the present'.[57] When we turn to the 'psycho-lexicon' of Hebrew, we find it contained within history and law, which are both contained by prophecy.

7.3 Foundations of Hebrew anthropology

The Hebrew arrangement of the *Tanakh* emphasises its prophetic medium as it moves from Torah, meaning 'law' or 'legal teaching', traditionally attributed to the prophet Mosshe (Moses)[58] on to histories by other *navim* (Prophets) such as Schmuel ('Former Prophets') and written prophecies, 'Latter Prophets'. Last is the *Ketuvim* (writings), which include the *Tehillim* (the Psalms), of which more below. Torah consists of five books: *Bereshith*, *Shemot*, *Wayyiqrah*, *Bemidbar* and *Debarim*. As catalogues in Sumer were listed by the opening words of each book (5.2) they are named from their opening lines as noted for *Bereshith* (5.1).

Our central source is the **myth of creation** which forms a preface to *Bereshith* and gives it its title. The God-figure called *Elohim* (related to the Arabic *Allah*) speaks each part of the cosmos into being, in a sequence over **six days**, clearly intended to appear logical and orderly, with human beings coming just before the climax on the seventh day. The key first passage of human creation reads:

> 'And Elohim said, 'Let us make mankind (*adam*) in our image (*tselem*), in our likeness (*demuth*), and them rule over (*rada*) the creatures of the sea, the air, and the land, and over all the earth, and everything that moves upon it.

So Elohim created the man (*ha-adam*) in his own image (*tselem*),

In the image (*tselem*) of Elohim he created him;

In male (*zakar*) and female (*neqeba*) forms, he created them.

Elohim blessed them and Elohim said to them, 'Be fruitful and increase in number; fill the earth and subdue (*kabash*) it. Rule over (*rada*) the creatures of the sea, air and land - all the earth, and everything that moves upon it'.[59]

One scholar observes that this text has functioned, in Western cultural history, like an empty **mould** into which various – often quite alien – ideas have been poured over the centuries; so much so that we could write most of the Western story (at least that concerning humanity and including psychology) using this text alone as a starting point.[60] In Latin the ***imago dei*** ('image of God') is a favourite theme of medieval and Renaissance philosophy and is often hidden in supposedly secular modern thought, rather like Smail's '"ghost theories": older ideas which continue to structure our thinking, without our being fully aware of their controlling presence'.[61] We will argue that this text was **not intended** to be psychological in its original context; and yet it has played host to psychological speculations about the human 'essence' – body versus soul, intellect versus will, reason versus passion – throughout Western history. What matters is that it has **in fact** been this influential, whether or not this was due to **misinterpretation**.

Due to its subsequent significance, in a story which will begin in Roman times (Book Three) with a few hints among the Greeks (Book Two), it is important to **secure** an interpretation of this foundational passage in *Bereshith* at this stage. It is, like everything else in this book, a downpayment or an investment ready for elaboration further down the narrative line. We will **circle outwards** from the core text, from an exposition of the passage itself, to secure our interpretation:

1 The passage in detail: an examination of its vocabulary in Hebrew (7.3)
2 Its immediate context: the first creation myth which is its frame (7.3)
3 Its close context: a second creation myth, beginning the history (7.4)
4 Its wider context: the lexicon of *psyche* in *Torah* and *Tanakh* (7.5)
5 Its practical use: the later temple cult as seen in the *Tehillim* (7.6)
6 Its cultural context: the Hebrew worldview of cosmic *Torah* (7.7)
7 Its impact: this tradition in the story of Western psychology (7.8)

We can assume that *ha-adam* ('the earth-creature') refers to us, *homo sapiens*, as well as to the original readers and hearers. We can assume this partly because modern psychology has evolved in a culture taught by this text: at every level of the functions of *psyche* in Chapter 2, we met this insistence that 'we are all the same' geographically and historically. We owe this imaginary 'participation in a polity that spans time and space' to centuries of saturation in the Bible: not that it was the only source, but it was *our* source, woven into Western culture.[62]

Part of this heritage is the teaching that humans – **male and female** together – are both created as 'image' (*tselem*) and 'likeness' (*demuth*) of the creator. By no means do all ancient creation myths bother to make this clear. *Bereshith* goes on to claim that all humanity is biologically descended from this original couple: we seem to have a revival of the early Sumerian idea of *namlulu* as 'mankind', 'humanity'[63]. There will also be a reset or 'reboot', in a version of the Sumerian legend of the great Flood, in which a new couple become the global parents.[64]

If the *adam* are 'like Elohim', the first question to ask is, 'What is Elohim like?'

Reading the text in its immediate context, the central characteristic of Elohim in the preceding narrative is **authority**. Much like a tribal chief, or a Bronze Age king, this creator speaks and his will is done. The verb *bara* used in the creation of humanity has already been used twice. First the title 'summary statement' is *Bereshith bara Elohim ha-shamayim wayyet ha-eretz*, which translates 'In the beginning **created** Elohim the heavens and the earth': nothing can elude God's authority, as everything is from him. This undistracted focus on one creator is unusual; it forms the basic creed of all **monotheism** (Greek: belief in one god) familiar to us today from the three world religions which begin with this text: Judaism, Christianity and Islam. When this text appears there are only *'apiru,* who are in a social category (7.1) known interchangeably as Hebrews or Arabs.

The other use of *bara* is an equally spectacular assertion of cosmic authority: Elohim *created* the great sea creatures, usually symbolic of wild and untamed monsters, thus proving his strength and his total sovereignty.[65] We thus have **complete** authority, one of spread or dominion, and a **dynamic** authority, one of confrontation In Sumerian terms, the one echoes Anu, the other Enlil. Almost unique among ancient creation myths, which normally display some residue of powerful beings beyond the god's strength, there is no sense of **conflict**. There is no refuge from the word of Elohim, nor is there a possibility of resistance.[66]

We therefore have male and female created to resemble this sovereign maker with total authority. There is an implicit **paradox**: to be like the unparalleled, to be like the one who is like no other. This can only be resolved if it is a **vocation**, a **verb** – 'to attempt to resemble' – a **calling** towards approximation to a model.

What this might mean is clarified by the repetition of the same ideas, even the same verbs, in a more familiar context. The next use of *tselem* and *demuth* is for Seth, the son of Adam – after *ha-adam* becomes separate male and female – who is born 'in his own likeness (*demuth*), in his own image (*tselem*)': these verses appear to draw an implicit parallel between divine creation and human parenthood: Elohim is compared to a father.[67] As a son might aspire to imitate his father, so creatures of Elohim (here under the name Yahweh) imitate God. The *first* use anchors this in a created equality of sexes: it is for daughters too, but this is not spelt out, any more than the analogy with parents is spelt out.

We can make progress in interpretation because the Hebrew in this text, while alphabetic, is related to the Akkadian, Babylonian and Assyrian vocabularies in cuneiform: all are **Semitic**. We can use this to interpret it in its cultural setting, using a wider literature to inform interpretation, with due caution to variations.

The key words *tselem* ('image') and *demuth* ('likeness') were normally used for public representations: *tselem* is normally used for three-dimensional **statues**, reliefs and carvings – very common indeed in Sumer, Egypt and throughout the Bronze Age world – and *demuth* is normally used for two-dimensional **icons**, characters designed to evoke something, mental images: today we might even say 'memes'. Elohim is commissioning his creature to represent him as an active, living embodiment of his character, like a moving statue, like a personal signature; and very much like a king sending an **ambassador**. When Elohim says, 'Let us make *adam*', this is a divine king addressing his heavenly court, announcing the selection and **appointment** of a suitable representative.[68]

Like its monotheism this template for *namlulu*, 'humanity', has consequences. It was possible in Sumer (5.7) to trace mythical explorations of human psychology in the personalities of Anu (human dignity and authority), Enlil (human freedom and decisiveness), Enki (human wisdom and understanding) or Inanna (freedom and creativity) but this was always **subconscious**, implicit, broken into separate elements. It continued the fairly random projections of the Neolithic (4.5). What is new in this Hebrew conception is that everything becomes **conscious**, explicit and brought into focus. This is the foundation for moral psychology: the voice of the prophet not only directed outward but inward as the human **conscience**.

Elohim is not only a king but also an artist: not only Djoser, but also Imhotep. A cosmos initially 'formless' (*tohu*) and 'empty' (*bohu*) is formed and filled, with three days of forming and three days of filling; these days are aligned in three sets:

- **Time** is set in motion on the first day, 'the first day' followed by the first night; the bodies to govern time are created on the matching fourth day.
- The great **spaces** of sky and sea are separated on the second day, only to be filled like the heavens, with birds and fish on the matching fifth day.
- The **home** of land and plants is formed on the third day, to be inhabited by animals and humans to eat their produce on the matching sixth day.

This is made clearer in the form of a table, showing both sequence and pattern:

Day One	**Day Four**
heavens	heavenly bodies
daily time order	annual time order
Day Two	**Day Five**
sea	sea creatures
sky	sky creatures
Day Three	**Day Six**
land	land creatures
plants	humanity

This conveys a sense of planning and design: Elohim is supremely creative. The days are punctuated by **legislative** acts ('let there be'), **executive** acts ('… and it was so') and **evaluative** acts ('and Elohim saw that it was good'), ending with a total evaluation of the end of the sixth day: 'and it was very good' (*tov meod*).[69]

We seem to have the Sumerian triad Anu, Enlil and Enki united in one person; indeed, with Sumerian roots, this could have been precisely its author's intent. The cosmos was designed, executed and appraised like Neolithic architecture (4.4) in the original division of labour between the shaman, the carver and the leader (4.5); the difference is that **prophecy**, not shamanic trance, is the source.

As context for interpreting *tselem* and *demuth* this clearly implies a **vocation** to creativity as part of the image. Earthly representatives of Elohim, it is implied, are called to emulate their rational creator, to develop all the inbuilt potential of their surroundings with **ingenuity**, able to **plan** and execute an orderly design: as ***homo sapiens*** to understand, to plan and design, and as ***homo faber*** to master their materials brilliantly towards the achievement of a satisfying end result. An echo of the myth of Ptah, which has been interpreted along the same lines (6.6); but to use Bourdieu's language, without the 'polythetic logic' normal to mythic thought, because this is not polytheism. Each of us can unite it all, like Elohim. Instead of a community of gods representing different facets, there is one face.

The presentation of creation as a work of art, of Elohim building a satisfying theatre for his pleasure, anticipates the building of a **model** on the human level which **mirrors** the whole creation. In *Shemot* God commands the building of a **tabernacle** (*mishkan*) as a place of worship, just after the people have escaped from Egypt; when they enter the promised land (now Israel) this is rebuilt as a stone **temple**. Jewish rabbis (teachers, scribes, experts) and mystics of later ages have interpreted the shape and building process of this place of worship as a model and mirror of the creation, with each part corresponding to one of the days listed above.[70] The temple becomes a model of the cosmos, or the myth an allegory of the temple, exploiting the idea of **correspondence** (3.4; see 7.6).[71]

One key difference from other Neolithic and other Bronze Age models is how precise, prescribed, specific and 'tidy' it appears within the national legal code of the Hebrews – as though regulating what was universally recognised from previous ages. In this sense, it affirms our findings from the Neolithic (4.4, 4.5, 4.6). In the third book of Torah, *Wayyiqrah*, the sacrifices made at the place of worship are also regulated and prescribed in great detail. There is a priesthood, but in *Shemot* Israel's God shares his desire to expand that office universally:

> 'Although the whole earth is mine, you will be for me
>
> **a kingdom of priests** and a holy nation'.[72]

The priestly vocation, like the 'kingly' vocation, while expressed in specialised roles is ultimately collective. Every member of Israel is God's representative. In *Bemidbar*, the prophet Mosshe (Moses) expresses the desire 'that all the people of Yahweh would be **prophets** (*navim*) and that he would put his Spirit (*ruach*) in them all.[73] In Neolithic terms (4.5) the collective *psyche* and every individual *psyche* within it is called to reflect the ancient specialisations of the shaman, the priest and the leader: to lead in terms of **inspiration**, **tradition** and **initiative**.

We are left to infer that *ha-adam*, made in the image and likeness of Elohim, will also exercise authority; but in the nature of Elohim's total authority, this cannot be shared completely. The likeness is not perfect.[74] Humans will create as Elohim creates, both artistically and biologically, but as his creatures, within his creation: this is presented only as **analogous** to the imitation of a parent by a child.

Let us turn to the meaning of the verbs: 'And let them **rule** ... over all the earth'; 'Fill the earth and **subdue** it'. The first verb is *rada*, a normal 'ruling' word for kings but here extended from rule over people to that over non-human creatures: in the ancient Near East kings were often compared to shepherds, but here this means living as shepherds.[75] Like a good **farmer** (or a pet owner) Elohim has provided for his creatures: the sea for the fish, the sky for the birds, and most centrally the dry land and its fruit-bearing plants for wild animals and humans.

In effect, with *rada* the divine king is **delegating** a measure of authority: giving *ha-adam* responsibility for a selection of creatures on the list, those that move on the land like himself. While filling the earth alongside them, humans are called to protect and provide. It is a mythic rationale for Neolithic pastoralism.

The second word *kabash* means 'to **tame**, to take ownership, to possess and to control'. As *rada* seems to apply to direct care for the animals, the creatures of days five and six, *kabash* seems to apply to the **land** and the **plants**, creatures of day three.[76] Humans cannot 'fill the earth' unless they tame it in this way: it is part of the invitation. Reflecting Elohim's royalty, this means: 'take authority'.

The *Bereshith* divine commission then appears as a redescription of **Neolithic** breakthroughs in the Holocene. We have been working with *rada* and *kabash* all along. This text, like its language, is the ideology of nomads, *'apiru*, Arabs.

This meaning is clarified and confirmed by what follows immediately after it. Elohim rests on **the seventh day**, blesses it and sets it apart as a special day of rest for his creatures also. Thus, the story is that of the primeval week, setting the pattern called **Shabbat**: and later Torah texts refer to it for this purpose.[77]

Humans are instructed to rest themselves, their livestock and their servants for one day a week, as a matter of health and justice; and this is elaborated into a whole system with **years of rest** for the land, which is allowed to lie fallow and unploughed every seven years, a 'year of Shabbat' both to rest the land and to give help to the poor.[78] Moreover, every seven years of Shabbat, that is, every forty-nine years is a special Shabbat year called **the Jubilee** for the cancelling of all debts throughout the nation, restoring the inheritance of each tribe and 'levelling the playing field', to offset any growing injustices in the nation.[79]

All of this leads out directly from the immediate context of the creation myth, anchoring the interpretation of *rada* and *kabash* as well as *tselem* and *demuth*. The teaching about 'image' and 'likeness' is embedded in a national law code, which is **designed to protect** the health and welfare of every human being, rich and poor, as well as their domesticated **animals**, and **the land** they inhabit. The creation myth has a clear moral, social, economic and environmental **purpose**: to teach those who will hear it how to behave within the world they inhabit. It teaches that humans are **responsible**: for themselves, for each other, for all the non-human creatures in their care, and for the land they farm. They can succeed or fail in this task: obedience will bring blessing and disobedience punishment.[80]

We now have a secure interpretation of the 'image of God' from *Bereshith*. If it seems thin on **psychological** content, that is the whole point. From the start we were seeking to anchor it against **future** interpretations in Western psychology where it will be interpreted differently: wrenched out of context, ignoring the original language and setting, to justify theories from quite different sources.

We are going to draw out a psycho-lexicon from the Hebrew language parallel to that for Egyptian (6.3, 6.10) which is indeed rooted in this creation myth. It is not simply that there is no psychological content, only that it must be extracted by careful exposition, open to the 'deconstruction' of Western ways of thinking shaped by Western language and tradition, in the same way as we have done for the Neolithic, for Sumer and for Egypt. These others are helpful for challenging Eurocentrism, as exercises (see Introduction 1, 2 and 3) with some relevance for Western psychology; but the Hebrew tradition has been directly formative. This first needs to be acknowledged (7.8), and then its distinctive character rediscovered.

This anchored interpretation seems to be overwhelmingly **ethical**: it introduces the books of Torah or '**legal teaching**'.[81] Its purpose seems to be to anchor law, to justify a system of norms for the relationships between people within society, between their society and other societies, between humanity and other species, domesticated and wild; and last between these and the land supporting them.[82]

Note, finally, that the argument of 7.2 concerning the **form** and **genre** of Torah perfectly matches and dovetails with its explicit **content**. The storytelling from *Bereshith* tells us through myth exactly what the literary form tells us through its means of communication: its implicit politics. 7.3 essentially repeats 7.2 but in terms of content rather than genre. This correspondence is encouraging for each of the two interpretations, as they appear to confirm one another, despite coming from independent sources: two different Hebraic scholars with different agendas.[83] At the risk of repetition from 7.2, the **genre** assumes radical equality in the community of writer and audience, a novel form of writing for its period.

The content at the beginning of the same text, we now discover, teaches exactly the same lesson through **myth**, as a preamble to the system of law. In Sumer we found that the cuneiform writing medium struggled to keep up with the mythic genre with its nuanced story-telling (5.4–5.7), but the invention of Hebrew has provided a medium better suited to this task. A *navi* is a shaman with a script.

7.4 Commentary in *Bereshith*: first shoots of a Hebrew *psyche*

On the other side of the Shabbat teaching is the famous story of Adam and Eve in the garden of Eden. Elohim is expanded to *Yahweh Elohim*, 'the God who is', and is more like a character in the story.[84] This does contain some 'component words' of a kind comparable to the Egyptian psycho-lexicon (6.3); we can start to formulate a **Hebrew phenomenology**, if not psychology, which could serve – like Hebrew itself – as a reply to the Egyptian phenomenology (coming in 7.5).

In Hebrew *ha-adam*, 'the earth creature', is so called because he (or it) is made from *ha-adama*, 'the dust of the earth': it is simply a pun, a label based on this origin. Yahweh Elohim takes this dust and breathes into it 'the breath of life' (*nishmach hayyim*) so it becomes a 'living soul' (*nephesh hayyah*).[85] Here is the Hebrew equivalent for *psyche*: the noun ***nephesh***. We will see the importance of this for Torah and Tanakh in the following sections, but it first appears here.

As in the first creation myth, this is really an androgynous creature who is then split into **two halves**: *ha-adam* is sent to sleep, and a woman is made from his ***basar***, his flesh. Already, here at the start, we meet approximations of body and soul, as *basar* and *nephesh*: but we must not jump to any (logocentric) conclusions.

Now the waking half of *ha-adam* labels himself *ish* ('man' in terms of gender) and his companion *isshah* (woman in the same sense).[86] Distinction of genders results from **two acts** of creation, first the breathing to make *nephesh* and then the splitting into two. The woman is, in other words, as 'human' as the man; as *zakar* and *neqeba*, male and female, **together** carried the image and likeness of Elohim during the creation week. This is not true of all ancient creation myths.

Creativity in 7.3 was matched by biological fertility: 'the *adam*' divided into the male (*zakar*) and female (*neqeba*), blessed with fertility and sent to reproduce, filling the earth. Interestingly, in Hebrew biological **sex** is distinguished from social **gender**: these appear separately, in the first and second creation myths respectively. Man (*ish*) and woman (*isshah*) are **social** categories.[87] The 'image and likeness' of Elohim are seen in sexual fertility, but this is not equated with gender: as **biological** men and women are equally made in Elohim's likeness.

Only after they are disobedient to Yahweh Elohim, judged and changed in their relationship to one of dominance and submission, does *Ha-adam* name *Hawwa* ('source of life', that is, mother) as he has named the other creatures.[88] Now it is a less equal relationship, but there was an original **equality** – just as in the first myth. **Inequality** appears as a result of disobedience (both *Adam* and *Hawwa*): *his* punishment is the difficulty of making a living, *hers* of painful childbirth.

As gender is distinguished from biological sex, their social roles after Yahweh's judgement – both under his punishment – are not allowed to obscure equality before it; future inequalities had to be 'read back' into creation retrospectively, because the text itself is careful to subvert such a conservative state of affairs. The text functions as a prophetic intervention insisting on the rights of women.

The two creation accounts appear to fit together, as a single account from two different perspectives: a large-scale version which serves as a 'map', followed by a small-scale version with dialogue, drama and interactions of characters. In one, humans are placed in context, in a larger frame ('What kind of creature?') whereas in the other we begin following history from inside the human world.

The English writer Francis Bacon said of the study of ourselves, 'as it is the end and term of natural philosophy in **the intention of man**, so notwithstanding it is but a portion of natural philosophy in **the continent of nature**'.[89] Psychology and the human sciences appear central from where we are standing, but in the larger scheme of things, humans are only a component. From a writer soaked in the Bible's worldview,[90] this captures the distinction between the accounts well.

Another interpretation is that these two accounts of human origins came from two different authors: the first from a priest, the second a more prophetic writer with a different vocabulary and agenda.[91] Co-authorship is plausible on the text's own terms (two brothers, one a prophet, the other a priest)[92] but this view is now largely abandoned, with *Bereshith* viewed instead as a carefully edited unity.[93]

Even if these were independent accounts, this would still be an unusual myth, because the norm in the ancient world is multiple accounts offered as *possible* solutions to the question of origins; the myth as a **hypothesis**. Here, there are only two offered as definite, final and authoritative – and also compatible. The Egyptian mind, for example, was content to entertain multiple versions, using the 'polythetic logic' described by Bourdieu; the Hebrew mind, it seems, had a much more definite, concrete and realistic tenor.[94] From the second account at least, *Bereshith* continues the national narrative seamlessly through the books of Torah into the rest of the Tanakh. The account of *nishmach hayyim* ('breath of life') and *nephesh hayyah* ('living soul'),[95] *ish* and *isshah*, *Adam* and *Hawwa* is not self-located in a world of timeless myth, but on a visible horizon of history.

In worldview terms Torah and Tanakh give the **story** element of the Hebrew worldview, but they also have a **symbolic** role in later Judaism. Their literally-minded soberness also invites possible elaboration (7.10) in some sophisticated **reflection**, and they contain **songs**. It is a complete ideological package. Let us turn to the poetry of Israel, for some insight into the Hebrew phenomenology.

7.5 Commentary in Tanakh: First fruits of Hebrew *psyche*

The best commentary on *Bereshith*, to anchor and confirm its meaning, is the rest of Torah and the collection of Hebrew lyric poetry (songs) near the end of the Tanakh, called *Tehillim*. They are placed in the centre of Christian Bibles as the Psalms. The *Tehillim* is built around the vivid personality of King David, organised into five books with David given as the author of the early poems.[96]

The great confession of *Debarim*, called the *Shema* (Hebrew: Hear! Listen up!) calls a nation into being (as explained in 7.2) using three definite **components** of the collective personality, which are also the components of every individual personality, in a magisterial movement from the innermost to the outermost:

> 'Hear, O Israel: Yahweh is our God, and Yahweh alone:
>
> you shall love Yahweh your God with all your heart (***lev***),
>
> with all your soul (***nephesh***) and with all your strength (***meod***).[97]

These terms are used very **consistently**. *lev* is the deepest reserve of humanity, the place we would translate as 'heart' (its primary meaning) or perhaps '**spirit**' – the place of response to God, barely known to the person, but known to God.

The *nephesh* is the conscious self, most easily translated 'soul', but '**mind**' and '**emotions**', '**character**' and '**personality**' are each within its range of meaning.

The last, *meod*, is not identical to 'body' but means 'capacity for action', hence 'strength' as translation. This is controlled by *nephesh*, which is directed by *lev*.

The Psalmist may be alluding specifically to this command when he cries out:

> How gorgeous is your sanctuary, Yahweh, leader of many!
>
> My soul (***nephesh***) yearns – yes, even lusts – for your courts:
>
> My heart (***lev***) and my flesh (***basar***) cry out for the Ever-Living![98]

Just as in the *Shema* he starts with his *nephesh*, which is the seat of emotion, thought and decision, the main voice writing the psalm: the writer is primarily expressing his **feelings**. We have seen this term used in *Bereshith* (7.4). Yet like any good poet, he adjusts the expected order: he goes deeper **inward** (to his *lev*, his heart or innermost being) and then **outward** (his *basar*) for emphasis. He also changes the wording: we have *basar* instead of *meod*, 'flesh' rather than 'strength'. The implication is that *basar* is the body when feeling a palpable hunger or thirst – the body in a more **passive** mode – whereas *meod* is **active**.

The point, just as it is in the Shema, is a devotion of **the whole** of one's being, and a threefold list of three aspects, levels or components **approximates** this.

A word we missed out in 7.3 was ***ruach***, the closest Hebrew word to 'spirit'. It is shared with Elohim and (if this means the same) with Yahweh: in *Bereshith*, in the preamble to the creation week when the cosmos is still *tohu* and *bohu*, 'formless' and 'empty', we are told that *ruach Elohim*, 'the spirit of God', was moving over the face of the dark waters.[99] Just before he decides to send the Great Flood, Yahweh speaks of his dealings with humans grating in his *ruach*; and we are told of the pain in his heart (*lev*) that his creature is disobedient.[100]

We have seen, in Sumer (5.7) how descriptions of the inner experiences of gods can be a guide to Bronze Age psychology. For Israel's God *ruach* is used here as a synonym for *lev*: God's heart is his spirit, possibly seen in a different aspect or nuance. For humans, however, the relationship of *lev* to *ruach* appears almost parallel to that between *basar* and *meod*: as the flesh is filled with strength to express itself, the *lev* needs *ruach* to fill it; and that *ruach* will come from God.

Not forgetting that in the second, garden-based creation story, the *nishmach hayyim* ('breath of life') of Yahweh turned the dust of the earth (*ha-adamah*) into a living soul (*nephesh hayyah*), we also have *nephesh* as something that can be imparted.[101] *Ruach* can enter *lev*, *nephesh* can enter *adama* and *meod* can energise *basar*. In each case, the source of imparted vitality is the same: God.

In summary: ***nephesh*** is the closest Hebrew equivalent to ***psyche***; as *lev* is the place of reflection and moral centre, deeper than *nephesh* which clothes it like a **sheath**, and also actions its commands; as *ruach* is an alternative to *lev*, shared with Yahweh and received like an inspiration, with *lev* as its natural container.

Basar means our physical selves considered as receptive, in common with all the other creatures of the fifth and sixth days – the part which feeds, clothes, and reproduces; and *meod*, 'strength', seems to be the overall capacity for *basar* to express the desires of *nephesh*, rooted in the ultimate decisions of the inner *lev*.

Thus, as we did for the Egyptian lexicon, we can draw a provisional spectrum:

- Biological *psyche* is (roughly) *basar*
- Behavioural *psyche* is (roughly) *meod*
- Conscious, cognitive, affective and conative *psyche* are all *nephesh*
- Existential, moral and at least a more reflective social *psyche* are all *lev*
- Transpersonal *psyche* is *ruach*

The spectrum of *psyche* toured in Chapter 2 is at least as clear here as it was in Egypt. Although Egyptian phenomenology is more **complete**, reaching an 'anatomy of the invisible', the Hebrew categories are much more **definite**. Consistency of usage follows from the clear intellectual leadership of prophetic sources of knowledge. A certain **unity** and tightly-knit **coherence** follow from the single object of worship, identified as a single coherent personality.

These are also coupled with a much more concrete theology and cosmogony. The relationship with God and the cosmos is more **precise** than other worldviews, tied to a single history, a single system of law, and a consistent political ideology.

What is remarkable is that where Egyptian phenomenology was rooted in the future state, in the afterlife, with only the *åb* entirely this side of the grave and the *ka* crossing the border, Hebrew phenomenology has no interest in the afterlife whatsoever, and every category concerns their **present existence**. In this sense, Hebrew phenomenology is much more like modern psychology.

Comparing the two systems, the *åb* seems to cover all of *basar*, *meod*, *nephesh* and *lev*: it is biological, behavioural, conscious and intentional – and both mean 'heart' in a double sense, as the physical organ and the moral centre. In Egypt, *ba* took some of the function of *lev*, but it was explicitly beyond death, whereas *lev* never hints at such a state. Therefore, effectively, Hebrew psychology is much more detailed, concrete, and potentially more **scientific** in character: it offers a phenomenology for experience as it is lived, not as it aspires to exist in a future life. Its very concreteness exposes how **ideological** and how deliberately fictional Egypt's system was. Where Egypt dreamed, Israel seems fully awake.

The one interesting point of contact is Egypt's *ka* with Israel's *ruach*: both have the connotation of a special anointing, a **divine mission**. As the *ka* supervenes on the *åb* and the *ba*, acting as the bridge between this life and the next, born with the *åb* and living alongside it, and then becoming a companion to the *ba*, *ruach* is distinct from *lev*, and in a sense also outlives it as it comes from God. If *ka* is a vocation, it is reserved for the gods, as *ruach* is reserved for Yahweh.

Finally, there is no Hebrew equivalent to *aakh*, *khu* or *aakhu*, the eternal spirit in the ever-revolving heavens; and no equivalent to *ba* except as a metaphor. As the single Egyptian concession to everyday existence and experience, the *åb*, is made to do service for multiple everyday functions, which fan out into a whole phenomenology in Hebrew, so there appears a certain symmetry to the fact that neither of the Egyptian words which are entirely restricted to the after-life has any translation or equivalent in Hebrew. The contrast of emphasis between this life and the next is complete. Hebrew focuses on this life, Egyptian on the next.

This practical focus seems indebted to Avram's Sumerian family background as the tribal pioneer, who 'set the switches' and formed the culture before it grew. Much of the Hebrew phenomenology seems like a revival of what was lost in Sumerian culture when it was submerged in another branch of Semitic culture. Avram's family seem to have left Sumer at precisely that moment, perhaps in protest; and as they brought with them a cosmopolitan vision and a satire of Babylonian *hubris* (the Tower of Babel story) there are hints in this direction

The contrast between the two psychologies – or, more modestly, phenomenologies – is illustrative of many things already observed in this book. The writing system is closely related to the possibilities of psychological description: as Snell says, 'the concept of the 'soul' ... is tied up with the whole character and orientation of a language'.[102] The **psychology** depends on the **medium**. The writing system, in turn, is also closely bound up with its **society**: it contains implicit politics. All three of these things – society, written medium, psychology – are together expressions of Benedict's collective personality, Kant's worldview, Chomsky's switch network, Derrida's collective mind, or Bourdieu's *habitus* (3.2 and 3.3).

7.6 The principle of correspondence

It was mentioned after the explanation of Neolithic architecture (in 4.4) that Israel would offer a particularly precise and deliberate form of that principle. Let us make good on that promise and bring that theme into this exposition. It helps to explain the remarkable consistency of the Hebrew lexicon for *psyche*.

The longest of the *Tehillim* is built around the Hebrew alphabet as an acrostic poem, working through the alphabet in order, with a verse devoted to each. The ardent young man cries out to Yahweh about his struggle to be faithful:

> 'I have hidden your word in my heart (*lev*) that I might not sin against you'.

This is probably a late entry to the Tehillim; certainly late – c.600 BCE – the prophet Yirmeyahu (Jeremiah) gives God's promise to Israel that in the future:

> 'I will put my law (*Torah*) in their minds and write it on their hearts (*lev*)'.

The implication in both cases is that the *lev* can be the Holy of Holies, *kodesh ha-kodashim*, the very centre of the temple (or the tabernacle, if it is earlier) because it can store the holy law (*Torah*) and commandments of Yahweh. In reverse, it suggests that these were always *intended* as a model of the human heart. At a communal level, this was clear enough: it was the heart of Israel as a nation. What makes this more pointed is the potential - gradually realised within the tradition - for reduction to the level of the faithful individual.

It seems that the Tabernacle and the stone temple which replaced it were built with a rich, multi-level **correspondence**: at least in these later interpretations, and it seems (by their use in passing) that they are only drawing out what was always understood. The ark in the **inner sanctuary**, the *kodesh ha-kodashim* or Holy of Holies, is compared to the **human heart** (*lev*): this contains the core of Torah, the central *mishvot* or judgements of Yahweh, meaning that the heart carries a permanent reverence for Yahweh, for his presence and his character.

By what appears to be a legitimate extension, the **outer sanctuary**, *kodesh* but not *ha-kodashim*, which shields and contains it, corresponds to ***nephesh*** as the shelter, sheath and enclosure for the reverent heart, in a mind ordered by the divine commands of Torah. The stone temple itself with its **outer courts** then corresponds to *basar*, the outward form of *nephesh*. These three levels of anthropology, from innermost to outermost, are modelled in its architecture.

Thus, as well as corresponding to the **cosmos** as depicted in *Bereshith* with its sequence of days (*yamim*), this is an increasingly explicit **psychological model**.

Where the detailed Egyptian anatomy and phenomenology (as we have called it) capture the spectrum of psychological functions or 'levels' we uncovered in Chapter 2, the Hebrew model also contains the microcosmic-macrocosmic systems of correspondence first introduced in 3.4 and explored in the Neolithic worldview (4.4): a visible structure standing mid-way in a **threefold scheme** of correspondence, *psyche*-cosmos-structure, where the structure resonates with the *psyche* as its microcosm and both resonate with the *cosmos* as macrocosm.

There is also a **fourth level**, the community of Israel. This is the central human meaning of the correspondence – more **sociological** than psychological. Storage of the 'testimony', the core of the Torah (the *mishvot*, judgement of Yahweh) in the ark is a symbol of the community's faithfulness to Yahweh; it is, first and foremost – and certainly in its original meaning – a **social symbol**. It is not illegitimate to extend this to the individual believer, as the Psalmist does; but this meaning 'drops down' from the main social meaning as a supplement.

King David writes constantly in the first person, in direct interaction with God, but he writes first and foremost in his capacity as king, as **representative** of a nation, a political form of a **microcosm**. David's sufferings are the sufferings of Israel, as David's frustrations are the frustrations of Israel, and his triumphs are their triumphs. As in Egypt, collective identification with the king was basic.[103]

Compared with global Neolithic findings, we find two differences. The Hebrew correspondence, while it has the same rich appeal to the imagination, giving pleasure of resemblance, pattern and recognition, is much **tidier**, more **precise** and almost **clinical**, less dreamlike and more **grounded**. It is as though Hebrew shamans – now called *navim*, prophets – seek to organise the existing pattern.

A second difference is that the psychological concept is, at the same time, far less **mechanical** than all this third-person description would suggest. It is more second-person, in the style of **love poetry** and song lyrics. Jacobsen has seen a 'Thou'-quality to Sumerian myth-making and its 'psychological insight'[104]; in the *Tehillim*, especially those connected with David, there is personal intensity:

'Yahweh, you have searched me and you know me.
You know when I sit and when I rise;
you perceive all my thoughts from afar …
You hem me in - behind and before;
you have laid your hand upon me...
For you created my inmost being;
you knit me together in my mother's womb …
All the days ordained for me
were written in your book
before one of them came to be.
How precious are your thoughts, O God!
How vast is the sum of them!'[105]

7.7 Hebrew *logos* as law

A final point of comparison is not the various **components** of Hebrew *psyche*, but what holds them all **together**. In this book we have usually allowed written language, as the medium of thought, to take the role of *logos* in 'psychology'. It is worth also noting another sense of *logos*, in patterns of cosmic lawfulness. Modern science, whatever its official explanation, cannot operate without this.

One Sumerian myth had 'a set of rules and regulations … to make the cosmos run smoothly and effectively': the set of culture-shaping patterns called ***Meh***'s.[106] (5.4, 5.5) This concept (1) acted as a potential bridge between the heart of the individual and the wider society and (2) provided a shared law or norms, much like the justice that will form a bridge between *psyche* and *polis* in Plato's *Republic*(3.4).

The Egyptians had a much more culturally embedded equivalent called ***Maat***, based on the visual metaphor of an architectural levelling device, or a balance for matching weights.[107] It was taken as a permanent part of the cosmic order, and as a bridge between this life and the next – 'enduring in potency'[108] because 'Doing *Maat* is the breath of life'.[109] Although our account in Chapter 6 has emphasised the **political** ideology, **cosmic** *Maat* was a bridge between the different elements of the Egyptian lexicon:

> '*Maat* itself is from all eternity …
>
> It is the standard of god's word.
>
> If it is scales, it tilts not;
>
> If a balance, it is not partial …
>
> So speak *Maat*! Do *Maat*!
>
> For it is mighty, great enduring …
>
> Can the scales tilt, when theirs are the pans which weigh things?'[110]

This appeal to an ethical ideal, which transcends all particular circumstances, is intimately connected to the Egyptian psychological model, as every component of the model is related to this **measure** of moral judgement. (See 6.3 and 6.10.)

A similar appeal to an overarching *Torah* underneath all psychological activities and all social activities appears in ancient Israel (7.5,7.6.) Each resonating level of correspondence is unified under *Torah* as unsearchable, benign wisdom (*hakhma*), judgements (*mishvot*) or understanding of Yahweh. Unlike *Meh* and *Maat*, *Torah* is tied directly to the personality of Elohim or Yahweh. In general, the *hakhma* and *mishvot* differ from *meh* in five ways: (1) they are **revealed** by the *navim*, no longer mysterious and unsearchable; (2) they are **reliable**, not subject to divine whims or – like *Meh* in the myth of Inanna and Enki – the vagaries of a divine soap opera; (3) they are **coherent**, because a single divine personality is the source and is sovereign in practice, as Anu was not; (4) they are **knowable**, because people resemble their creator in some ways; (5) they are **pleasant**, because he desires their health. In 7:10 we will point forward to uses of this in rabbinical Judaism.

The Hebrew 'model', therefore, is a response to both Sumerian and Egyptian 'models' and goes beyond them, coming from a people group on the margins of both (7.1, 7.2). It is as practical and this-worldly as the Sumerian model, but as complex and comprehensive as the Egyptian, with a very clear sense of a divine law connecting its elements. Its coherence stems from its relatively small source group: the prophets (*navim*) and priests of Israel, the texts of Torah and Tanakh.

7.8 Summary and legacy

A key to Hebrew anthropology is that it is not **static**: we are not treated to an 'anatomy of the soul' as a **theory** for contemplation, but as a **prescription** to live well in Yahweh's creation. The 'image' of this God, we must remember, is a **verb** more than it is a noun: a basic insight lost in much subsequent reception.

Between *homo sapiens* and *homo faber*, the emphasis is most definitely on the latter. The only kind of **contemplation** in this worldview is keeping 'the eye of the heart' constantly on God's personality and character, or keeping 'the ear of the heart' constantly attuned to his voice. These are expected to occur while engaged in worldly activity, not as separate activities, let alone vocations. The Hebrew worldview is **practical**.

Psychology as we know it is possible because we can assume common nature. This was a major theme in Chapter 2, but it is also a theme in this chapter. Everyone has *basar*; everyone has *nephesh*; everyone has *ruach*. All share this common **human nature** with these three components, however they and their relations may be understood; and we all share a **calling** to direct them to God.

The Egyptians had begun to 'democratise' *psyche* from the king downwards, so at least one Egyptian had *psyche*. It was always democratic with the Sumerians, but in their totally minimalist way: in a sense, no Sumerian has *psyche*. Among the Semitic refugees from two mighty Bronze Age civilisations, we discover a radically democratic, **egalitarian** model, in which all have *psyche*. This makes psychology, and all Western civilisation as we know it, a possibility. This is one valid insight from Hegel's project (1.8): his Europe 'knows that all are free',[111] although (like most philosophers) he neglects the Semitic sources of this idea.

We are not surprised by this basic assumption of the Hebrew worldview and its anthropology precisely because it is now so deeply ingrained in our civilisation and our worldview. As we have seen in previous chapters, it was by no means normal, in the Neolithic or the Bronze Age, for all members of a society to be considered, or even to consider themselves, as possessing *psyche* in an equal measure. It is certainly not the norm among the ancient Greeks (Book Two).

We usually attribute the origin of psychology, like democracy and history, and philosophy and tragedy, to the ancient Greeks. They were certainly **necessary** – none of this could have happened without them – but equally, they were not **sufficient**. A Jew of the first century, brought up speaking and writing Greek, compared the Greeks to the soil,[112] but insisted that the seed in it was from the Jews; he compared the Greeks and Romans to wild olive branches, grafted onto an older Hebrew vine. He meant his community, but it fed into Western culture.

Moreover, not only is there a democracy of *psyche* in that everyone possesses it equally, and nobody is treated like an animal, but all possess humanity. There is also a kind of democracy of the **components** of a human being, so that *psyche* is neither elevated nor reduced in its importance. In direct contrast to the tendency – again since Neolithic times – to turn human nature into a hierarchy with *ruach* superior to *nephesh*, or *nephesh* superior to *basar*, **all are affirmed** as essential components of *homo sapiens*. We are not human without them all. If all humans were created as taught in *Bereshith*, we are each made of both *ruach* and *basar*.

This doctrine meant that Jewish thinkers initially could not contemplate life after death, precisely because they would not detach *ruach* from *basar* even in concept.[113] It took further steps to believe that dead bodies could be raised by Yahweh, because whole *people* could be raised by Yahweh. It all had to happen **together**, or not at all. These steps were made in the first millennium BCE; they reached the Arabs and were inherited by Islam. All continued to believe in the Hebrew **unity of personhood** – first taught in *Bereshith*, affirmed and assumed throughout Torah and Tanakh – as they believed in **equality between persons**.

The Greeks, like some Sumerians – and many Egyptians (6.9) – were content to imagine their invisible *psyche* going to another realm, with no physical body or with a different kind of body, such as a star, inhabited by free-floating *psyche*. The Semitic mind could make no sense of this **abstraction** from human nature and Semitic resistance to it is evident (at least initially) upon every encounter.

Reincarnation – which as we have seen, was originally an Egyptian idea before it was found in India – was meaningless to the Semitic mind because souls are not able to inhabit different bodies: *nephesh* is tied to *basar* as **fused identity**. 'Out of the body experiences' were certainly possible and the Tanakh reports plenty of them among the *navim*; but this was not a rehearsal for death with the soul getting a foretaste of its freedom. It was an experience of **inspiration** by the *Ruach Hadashah*, the holy spirit of Yahweh, into the *ruach* of the *navi*: we have connected this back to the early Neolithic sociology of the **shaman**.

It is worth pointing out that in the recent history of psychology as a discipline it has often been the Jewish thinkers[114] – those of Semitic descent and heritage – who have similarly anchored *nephesh* in *basar*, refusing to detach the two; in fact, sometimes going further and reducing *nephesh* to *basar* in **materialism**.

Freud is the obvious example. As we shall see in the next volume, and indeed throughout this series, there is a tendency of the dominant 'Indo-Europeans' in Western culture (see Book Two) to let *psyche* become detached from physical anchorages, 'floating off' into what theologians call '**spiritualism**' or what philosophers call '**idealism**': just as the Semitic role – even mission – has often been to counter this. The same 'grounded-ness', in a tradition **anchoring** soul in body, *psyche* in *soma*, or *nephesh* in *basar*, has been effective through the *dar al-Islam* and the impact of the Arabic side of Semitic roots (highlighted in 7.1). Transmitting different versions of the stories encountered in *Bereshith*, before Islam in the **Jahili** culture[115] and afterwards in the **Qu'ran**, Arabic culture has for the most part continued the Hebrew pattern of affirming the body, resisting 'spiritualism', and treating the human being as an **indissoluble unit**.[116] We will need to return many times to this issue, but now we have laid the foundations.

7.9 Review of Theory One

Jaynes has plenty to say about the Hebrews, alongside the Egyptians, Mayans, Babylonians and other Bronze Age civilisations, all as examples of his theory of auditory hallucinations during the 'bicameral era', and societies built on these hallucinations. When Yahweh speaks to his *navim* this is much the same as any other shaman, prophet or oracle among Israel's neighbours. Jaynes offers us a **single story** covering all civilisations, without any distinction or qualification. This story proved a strong match to Egypt (6.11) but much less applicable to the Sumerian data (5.8).

In 4.5 we saw the continuous emergence of the roles of the shaman and priest alongside the chief and king; in ancient Israel, there is a distinction between priest and prophet, not only as roles but as social offices. The prophet inherits the mantle of the shaman, hearing the voice of Yahweh and transmitting it to the people; but the content of Hebrew prophecy is much more **detailed**, **political**, **personal** and **defined** than anything we see *outside* this tradition, which by comparison is more like characters interacting in a novel. Jaynes has no acknowledgement of this difference: for him, the gods are all equally unreal and all myths equivalent. The bicameral mind must dream.

His theory does have some room to adapt to this distinction, however, because he explicitly emphasises the emergence of what others have called the vertical or priestly form of shamanism, as a precondition for large settlements.[117] The hallucinations have to be interpreted 'vertically' – in terms of the local political authority – for the bicameral society to work. If the proposal from this chapter (7.2) is correct, that the Hebrew language represents the voice of the prophet in the sense of a 'comeback' of classic or horizontal shamanism in a new form, then this would immediately imply a disruption of the bicameral society, not by moving **forward** through the breakdown into full subjective consciousness, but by going **backward** into a pre-bicameral state. When Mosshe says in *Bemidbar* 'I wish that all the people were prophets',[118] this **subverts** the bicameral model; but Mosshe is looking forwards as well as backwards. We can see this clearly in a parallel with the verse from *Shemot*: 'Although the whole earth is mine, you will be for me a kingdom of priests and a holy nation'.[119] *Bereshith* presents an original design for humanity to be ambassadors of Yahweh Elohim in creation, representing his interests, and this vision for Israel points back to that design.

Jumping ahead into the next millennium, to illustrate this point, a *navi* called Yoel has a vision in which Yahweh promises: 'I will pour out my *ruach* on all people. Your sons and daughters will prophecy, your old men will dream dreams, your young men will see visions. Even on my servants, both men and women. I will pour out my *ruach*'.[120] On Jaynes's terms, this sounds very much like the **breakdown** of the bicameral mind: all are owning the role of shaman. By this point, on Jaynes's theory, they should be having precisely such visions because if **all** are prophets, then in the sense of social role, **none** are prophets and all are simply 'hearing God for themselves'. The words of

Mosshe himself come late in the Bronze Age, when the bicameral crisis *should* be occurring. All that is new here is that the Hebrew mind looks back to the 'pre-bicameral state', to early Neolithic (or Upper Palaeolithic) societies, having never been happy with the change to a bicameral state, and it clearly labels and recognises the change.

Jaynes himself acknowledges that not all of humanity entered into civilisation during the Bronze Age: not all of humanity became bicameral. The Hebrews or Arabs represent those on the edges, on the margins, fiercely independent and ambivalent about Neolithic breakthroughs, **sidestepping** the bicameral phase or diluting its profile. It raises the same problems for Jaynes's theory as Neolithic communities in general which have sidestepped this phase. The problem is that it – uniquely – has a literature; and yet Jaynes treats this literature like all the others.

On balance, then, T1 is on far less comfortable ground accounting for this data. It is a 'blind spot' for this theorist, whose interests were distracted elsewhere in the ancient world and who (once again) neglected the central role of language, and who also (once again) is in too much of a hurry to confirm his own model. A greater openness to the distinct cultural 'personalities' of civilisations would have improved his theory.

Our own sequence of reviews of T1 can help to fill this gap. In the Neolithic we found a fruitful connection of the 'construction hypothesis' concerning the symbolic associations of Neolithic architecture (4.2 to 4.4) and Jaynes's theory of the development of psychological language as a process of interiorisation, using metaphors from the visible world to express the invisible *psyche* (3.8, 4.7). There we found that archaeologists had independently formed a theory which could be made congruent with his own, showing a clear development from Neolithic to Bronze Age. In our accounts of the first writing systems in Sumer (5.2) and Egypt (6.2) we traced these connections more explicitly in each case, while noting Jaynes's own blindness to the potential of such systems for developing his theory (5.8 and 6.11). Now with the narrative of the Hebrew alphabet stemming from Egyptian hieroglyphs (6.2,7.2) we have a single line of development running from Neolithic origins to the early first millennium.

7.10 Review of Theory Two

As already noted (4.9) Iain McGilchrist is very much a living, working author, and this has helped his engagement with the Hebrew tradition. In *The Master and his Emissary* he had nothing to say about Israel or this tradition at all. His focus in the ancient world was on Greece, because he sees this as the primary source of Western civilisation, which is his target. As we saw in Chapter 1 (especially 1.8 to 1.10) this is the traditional, if narrow, view. As he modestly confesses, 'I am no historian'.[121] (This is immediately after his one mention of Arab sources, in the humble role of transmitting the Greek texts to Europe).[122]

More importantly, he was focused on 'the conflict that forms the subject of this book'[123] – his dialectical account of the intertwining of the brain hemispheres as the hidden dynamic behind the development of the civilisation. Here is the main reason why the Semitic contribution is neglected – and it is not dissimilar to the account of T1 for this chapter. As the different hemispheres deal with a **higher level** of functioning – with the most specialised, most highly educated and most **'civilised'** elements of the culture – where brain lateralisation is expressed in a literate form, while the more basic functions remain unified and independent of such complexity, T2 is dealing with the very things which, as we have seen, the ancient (Western) Semitic cultures tended to avoid. As lateralisation was rather tentative in Neolithic cultures, it was also tentative among the **marginal** *'apiru*. To avoid the Bronze Age was precisely to avoid 'bihemispheric advance'.

In his new book, however, the massive **sequel** entitled *The Matter with Things*, he has engaged extensively with religious traditions directly descended from the ancient Hebrew and Arabic sources explained and discussed in this chapter. His last decade of research and dialogue between the two publications has allowed a rich engagement with traditions which were neglected in the first book. His own theory has driven him to respect Judaism, Islam and the various sects within the Semitic religious orbit for their **mystical** orientation, which he now understands as an important expression of the functioning of the **right hemisphere** – another much-needed **ally** against the reductionist tendencies of the left hemisphere.[124]

He quotes one of the *Tehillim* in this respect – his first engagement with the text of *Torah* or *Tanakh*[125] – but his most interesting passage is a quotation from the twentieth-century rabbi Abraham Heschel, illuminating the rabbinic traditions of ***halakhah*** and ***aggadah***. As McGilchrist notes, it corresponds to the distinctions of hemisphere functions in T2: *halakhah*, 'the rationalisation and schematisation of living', literal and legalistic, detailed and definite, directive and quantitative, embodies the functioning of the left hemisphere; whereas *aggadah* is the precise opposite, 'metaphorical and imaginative', concerned with meaning and purpose over technique. It is an instrument for exploring and expressing the indefinite.[126] He portrays Jewish thought as a fruitful dialogue between these twin traditions.

This is an outgrowth of rabbinical **Judaism**, a tradition built over two millennia in the orbit of advanced urban civilisations; it is also well outside our timeline. Nevertheless, it is also a tradition which zealously cleaves to Hebrew sources in *Torah* and *Tanakh*, *Tehillim* and temple: it could not have developed *halakhah* or *aggadah* without finding **justification** and **inspiration** from these sources. It, therefore, demonstrates the same principles we have been building from Sumer and Egypt: that every literate culture, given the time and the opportunity, tends to find a means of expression of lateral brain function on a macrocosmic scale.

There were Semitic civilisations on the eastern flank of the Fertile Crescent: the Akkadians, the Assyrians and the Babylonians. As we have seen (5.2, 5.9)

Akkadian balanced Sumerian eventually in hemispheric terms; and **hieroglyphic** script always had hieratic for this purpose (6.2, 6.12). Heschel's example simply fits the pattern, and confirms our developing hypothesis; albeit by entering the Common Era. It answers the question left by the marginal status of Hebrew in the Bronze Age.

As well as these two different symbolic systems, both using the Hebrew script as their basic medium, we can make an observation about Hebrew script itself. As the first alphabetic script (7.2) it has endured, as Chinese *wen* has endured, (8.3) across more than three millennia. Its development can be compared to its many 'children' in the huge family of alphabetic scripts over this time frame, and this too can be related to brain laterality and its expressions in language.

In his analysis of scripts and brain function, McGilchrist explains that the right hemisphere prefers **columns** to rows; **top to bottom** if in columns; **right to left** if in rows; in terms of textual content, it prefers contextual meanings without vowel marks between the **consonants**; and that written Greek steadily evolved away from all of these over a millennium, from a closer initial resemblance to Egyptian hieratic. It moved from columns to rows by 1100 BCE; from a right-left direction to alternating directions (like ploughing a field) by 600 BCE; and to its current mode, reading from left to right, by 400 BCE. In other words, the left hemisphere 'got its own way' in the evolution of Greek according to T2.[127] Putting this together with the linear narrative in 7.9 above, we seem to have a story of the gradual **encroachment** of the left hemisphere.

As hieroglyphics had resisted reduction to a phonetic script, Hebrew resisted these developments to a certain point. Placing them in order:

*Orthographic choice**	*Hebrew*	*Greek*
Rows or columns?	Left wins: move to rows	Left wins: move to rows
Right to left or left to right?	Right wins: right to left	Left wins: left to right
Insertion of vowels?	Right wins: no vowels	Left wins: vowels added

*Orthography = correct writing style; Greek *orthos* = correct, *graphos* = writing

Therefore, Hebrew as a writing medium only conceded a compromise with left hemispheric functioning on the first point: by moving from columns to rows. It successfully resisted the considerable pressures, from Iron Age and subsequent cultural changes, to move further into the positive feedback loop with Greek.[128] (This is more impressive when we consider that most scripts followed Greek, through its effect on Latin.)

This additional point against the other suggests a possible hypothesis: that the writing medium must preserve normative roles (right hemisphere leadership) in its orthography, in order to carry thought systems which also reflect hemispheric balance. By remaining 'friendly' to the right hemisphere at the visual level, of orthography, Hebrew was also better able to develop the later balance of *halakhah* and *aggadah*.

This meta-review will prepare us for our final visit to a very different cosmos.

Discussion questions:

1. From the Orientation do you feel clear about all the names involved?
2. Can you summarise the overall argument of 7.2 in five or six points?
3. What if any implications does the 'image of God' have for psychology?
4. What was your response to the distinction of sex and gender in 7.4?
5. Did you find that Hebrew 'soul words' connected with you personally?
6. Do you find Hebrew aesthetics of prayer and worship attractive, or not?
7. Which concept of law made the most sense to you? Sumer, Egypt or Israel?
8. Do you find yourself drawn to materialism or spiritualism, or neither?
9. Do you feel that the Review of T1 in 7.9 is a reasonable assessment?
10. What knowledge, if any, do you already have of Islamic civilisations?

Recommended Reading

- The Bible in the New International Version (texts cited)
- Abdullah Al-Udhari *The Arab Creation Myth* Archangel 1997
- Margaret Barker *Temple Mysticism* SPCK 2011
- Kenneth Cragg *Readings in the Qur'an* Collins 1988
- Lester Cragg *Ancient Israel* Continuum Press 2007
- Richard Hoyland *Arabia and the Arabs* Routledge 2001
- J. Richard Middleton *The Liberating Image* Brazos 2005
- Seth Sandars *The Invention of Hebrew* First Illinois 2007

Notes

1 Shemot (Exodus) Chs.1–15, 20:1–2.
2 Bereshith 11:28,11:31,12:4ff.; Van de Mieroop pp.42–3,56–7,70–1; Walker p.27.
3 Shemot 12:6–9.
4 Bereshith 12:10–20, 46:1–27.
5 Bereshith 15:13–14; Shemot 12:40–41; the accepted range of dates falls at some point within this.
6 Bellwood pp.103–4,126–7; Diamond pp.388,390; Muksawa pp.40,183; Oliver and Fage pp.50–1.
7 Bellwood pp.126–8,134,136–8; Diamond pp.386–7; Muksawa pp.33–4.
8 Bereshith 5:32,6:10,13,9:18,10:1,21–32; also Dalley p.7.
9 Bellwood pp.126–8,133–4,136.
10 Bellwood pp.103–4,126–8; Grabbe pp.46–7; Hoyland p.46; Kramer pp.288–9; Van de Mieroop 2007 pp.34,51,55,87; Van de Mieroop 2017 pp.42–3,56–7,98,146–9,198.
11 Hoyland pp.2–8,229–233.
12 Hoyland pp.89–90,96,100,113–4,117–9.
13 Grabbe pp.40–43,48–9,59,64,104–5; Hoyland pp.100,120.
14 The Greek translation was made after the conquest of Egypt by the army of Alexander the Great. We will touch on this in the next volume, as we trace the content of this chapter into that period.
15 Bereshith Chs.1–10; Grabbe pp.19–21,105–6 adds to the tribal vocabulary used here.

16 Bereshith 10:21.
17 *ibid* 11:10–26; this is Abram, who became Abraham in Christian tradition, or Ibrahim in Arab tradition.
18 For example: Bereshith 12:10–16, 13:1–18; 18:16–33; 19:1–29; 20:1–18; 26:25; 47:1–13; and throughout text.
19 *ibid.*
20 Middleton pp.201–4.
21 *ibid* 11:1–9.
22 *ibid* 12:10, 41:54,42:1–2,43:1–2,47:1332:28,46:1,48:21,49:2,28.
23 Bereshith 15:13–14,50:24–26; Shemot Ch.1.
24 For example: Grabbe pp.23,30–34, 85–8 versus Rohl pp.277–289.
25 Bellwood p.128; Grabbe p.85.
26 Grabbe pp.84–8.
27 Childe 1954 pp.53,73; Childe 1981 pp.91,114; Diamond pp.268–272.
28 Grabbe pp.108–9,113–6,120.
29 Seth Sandars in *The Invention of Hebrew* 2009 gives an excellent account of this distinctive orientation.
30 McGilchrist 2009 pp.275–7.
31 Davies pp.84,95–6, Murray p.290; Robinson 2009 pp.25–6; Watterson p.xviii; we also noted in 6.2 that languages in this group characteristically have a stem of 3 consonants in each written word.
32 Using this term advisedly and restrictedly in the light of points made in 1.6.
33 Sandars p.40.
34 *ibid* pp.40,49.
35 Roux p.332; Walker p.43.
36 Sandars pp.49–50,91.
37 Shemot 2:23.
38 Fukuyama pp.xii, 56–69, 143–156; Hegel 1956 pp.103, 108–110, 342, 442, 456–7; Sandars pp.40–43.
39 Vainstub et al. 2022 p.103.
40 Sandars p.2.
41 Bereshith 11:28,11:31,12:4ff.; Van de Mieroop pp.42–3,56–7,70–1; Walker p.27.
42 Healey pp.210ff.
43 *ibid* pp.212–3.
44 *ibid* pp.218–9.
45 *ibid* pp.210–11.
46 Sandars p.6.
47 *ibid* pp.2,43.
48 *ibid* pp. xiv, 2,10–11,33.
49 *ibid* p.170.
50 Sura 6:102–3 quoted in Cragg 1988 p.89.
51 Debarim 6:4–5.
52 Sandars p.165.
53 *ibid* p.164.
54 *ibid* p.165.
55 Lewis-Williams and Pearce pp.86–7; Thomas and Humphrey pp.7,78–85.
56 Sandars pp.164–5.
57 *ibid* pp.159,165.
58 Patrick pp.8–9.
59 Bereshith 1:26–8; author's translation, using published versions to highlight the elements most relevant here.
60 Middleton p.18.
61 Smail pp.2–3,42–3.

62 Sandars p.35 – taking into account the entire argument of Ch.1 (p.13–35).
63 Kramer pp.264,285–6.
64 Kramer pp.33,74,129,262–3; Kriwaczek Ch.4 (pp.66–76).
65 Middleton pp.67,73,264.
66 *ibid*; a theme preserved in the text of the Qu'ran, and Jahili Arabic myths in between: see al-Udhari pp.45ff.
67 Bereshith 5:1–3.
68 Middleton pp.55–60,88–9.
69 *ibid* pp.65–6.
70 Barker 2004 pp.16-32
71 *ibid* 2004 pp.16–21 and 2001 Ch.1 (pp.14–39).
72 Shemot 20:5.
73 Bemidbar 11:29.
74 Middleton pp.45–7.
75 *ibid* p.51.
76 *ibid* p.52.
77 Shemot 20:8–11; Debarim (Deuteronomy) 5:12–15.
78 Shemot 23:10—12; Wayyiqra (Leviticus) 25:1–7,26:1–13,34–35; Patrick pp.91–2,111–2, 181–2.
79 Wayyiqra 25:8–55, Debarim 15:1–11.
80 Wayyiqra 26:14–46, Debarim 28:1–68.
81 Patrick pp.8–9.
82 Challenger 2020 provides an excellent (if unintentional) defence of many of the values enshrined in this law, as well as an excellent (if equally unintentional) defence of McGilchrist's cutural critique.
83 Sandars in 7.2, Middleton in 7.3.
84 Shemot 3:14.
85 Bereshith 2:7.
86 *ibid* 2:21–3.
87 Middleton p.50.
88 Bereshith 3:20.
89 Bacon 1605 II.IX.1 p.105.
90 Harrison pp.7,72.
91 Garrett Ch.1 (pp.11–30).
92 Shemot 4:14–17,7:1.
93 Garrett pp.82–3,244–9; Grabbe pp.44,83; Middleton pp.16n.3,203.
94 Fowler pp.16–19,21.
95 Bereshith 2:7.
96 Wolpe pp.xv,15–27 gives a brilliant summary of the character of David in Tanakh from a Jewish perspective.
97 Debarim 6:4–5.
98 Tehillim 84:1–2 author's translation.
99 Bereshith 1:2.
100 *ibid* 6:3,6:6.
101 Bereshith 2:7.
102 Snell p.15.
103 Martin pp.52,62 in an excellent commentary on *Tehillim* 86.
104 Jacobsen pp.170,172,175.
105 Tehillim 139 vv.1,2,5,13,17.
106 Jacobsen pp.115,125.
107 Budge pp.52 n.1, 134,160–2, 170; Parkinson pp.13,298; Wilson pp.92,116,119.
108 Parkinson p.252.
109 *ibid* p.65.

110 Quoted from *The Tale of the Eloquent Peasant* in Parkinson p.73.
111 Hegel 1956 p.104.
112 Shaul who became Paul the Christian, in Romans 11:13–24; with a different metaphor in Ephesians 2:11–22.
113 See Wright 2003 Ch.3 (pp.85–128).
114 Thinking of the influence of Freud and his followers in the first instance, as well as other modern schools.
115 See al-Udhari pp.14–25 and his Suras 16–22 pp.136–171.
116 See Parrinder Ch.8 (pp.151–177) for a good example.
117 Lewis-Williams and Pearce pp.86–7; Thomas and Humphrey pp.7,78–85.
118 11:29.
119 Shemot (Exodus) 20:5.
120 Joel 2:28–9 (to use the form of Yoel in English Bibles).
121 McGilchrist 2009 p.296.
122 *ibid.*
123 *ibid* p.319.
124 McGilchrist 2021 pp.5–7,45,851–2,1054 (reductionism);1201,1220,1269,1234, 1282–3,1375 (on mysticism).
125 *ibid* p.1258.
126 *ibid* pp.1229–1230.
127 McGilchrist 2009 pp.275–7.
128 Davies pp.93–8; McGilchrist 2009 pp.267,278ff.; but as McGilchrist would point out here, the appearance of any written language already represents the agenda of the left hemisphere.

8 Ancient China

8.1 Orientation

China was the last independent civilisation to emerge outside of the Americas.[1] Some of the waves of *homo sapiens sapiens* coming out of Africa at 50kya did not cross the land bridge at Alaska but stayed within Eurasia on the Pacific coast.[2] Although its Bronze Age came later than others, Chinese civilisation has **outlasted** them all and it survives as a direct link back to Neolithic roots.[3] China has developed so independently and remotely that it is a perfect foil to 'Eurocentrism', giving us clues as to which social and cultural features are universal and which are not.[4]

With the Himalayan plateau to the west, a major difference is that 'the innate mental compass of the Chinese points not north-south, but **east-west**'.[5] China is divided by three rivers, all rising in the Himalayan foothills and draining into the Pacific: listed from north to south, the Hwang-Ho (Yellow River), the Chang Jiang (Long River) or Yangtze, and the Hsi (Pearl). Each characterised as a dragon in Chinese folklore, they connect *shan* (mountain) to *shui* (water), creating the first opposition of the opposite cosmic principles we will discover as a pervasive feature of Chinese culture, and together representing one fundamental **symbol** (one could say **hieroglyph**) in the Chinese *psyche*.[6]

Much like Africa, early in the Holocene China was warmer and wetter than it is today; rhinos and elephants were hunted into the Bronze Age, and near the Hsi river rice cultivation may have begun very early, in the ninth millennium. It led to one Neolithic expansion through Taiwan to Indonesia and the Pacific.[7] In the north between the Hwang-Ho and Chang Jiang, millet and rice took the same roles as wheat and barley in west Asia; and as there, this led to a massive expansion from c.7000–2000 BCE, retaining a very high **density** of population ever since.[8]

Many regions had large villages organised in a clan structure, which became a foundational feature of Chinese civilisation. It became more unequal, a class of aristocrats fighting over territory, trading and building chiefdoms – like other late Neolithic cultures worldwide.[9] One chiefdom called **Shang** created a northern kingdom spanning the Hwang-Ho c.1750 BCE, which developed some unique bronze-making skills, an accurate calendar and a writing system.[10]

DOI: 10.4324/9781003396147-11

This was not the only such kingdom but its **writings** survived in one capital, Anyang. Their discovery in the nineteenth century, near the end of the last empire, gave a rich source of information for this early period confirming what histories had always claimed: that the Shang was a key **source** of Chinese civilisation.[11] This sphere slowly expanded on the back of the Neolithic population movement: from north to south down through China, through SE Asia, and north into Korea, creating the huge **sphere of Chinese influence** consolidated by its empire and its writing.[12]

8.2 Building the Chinese worldview

Much of our knowledge of ancient China has to be disentangled from history between then and now: although the great **continuity** of Chinese history is a strength, it means that there is an accumulated tradition of cultural memory affected by later politics. We do not always know if a belief is only *attributed* to an earlier time by later propaganda, or was a historical fact. Precisely because we are dealing with an unusually coherent 'personality' at the collective level, individual memories can be difficult to establish. This is true to some extent of all civilisations surveyed in this book but China has been particularly selective.

Perhaps the greatest work of creative fiction from ancient Egypt was its social and political ideology, tying the whole culture around the divinity of the king.[13] The Shang kings, their scribes and their successors were also skilful architects of **national ideology**, creating myths but also literal histories to bring a sense of national unity, continuity, and legitimacy.[14] When the Ch'in empire emerged in 221 BCE, from the same area as the Shang, it grafted itself onto this heritage.[15]

As with each story in this book, the methods of archaeology have provided us with an independent witness to the past. Historical Shang culture had a strong current of **shamanism**, with a major role for the *wu* or *shih* as a fortune-teller, dictating to a scribe (*ru*). There was a preoccupation with the spirits of ancestors and (as in Egypt) the after-life of the present king beyond his death.[16] A vassal state of the Shang to the west, called **Zhou**, rebelled and replaced the Shang right at the end of the second millennium BCE. It changed little of what it had inherited, but improved on it and enlarged the territory.[17] The king was styled *T'ien-tzu* ('Son of Heaven') and held office by the favour of *Shang-Ti* ('Lord on High').[18] The Chinese city, unlike the city-states of Sumer, 'began in the Bronze Age not as a centre of population and commerce, but as **a ritual enclosure** where the king and his diviners mediated between earth and heaven, mankind and nature, living and dead, past and future'.[19] Like most features of Bronze Age civilisation, especially in Egypt, it is essentially a Neolithic model with added technologies.

Many attitudes which became normal in imperial China have their roots here: 'The Zhou thought of themselves as surrounded by **barbarian peoples** waiting for the benevolent effects of Zhou tranquilisation'; and these 'barbarian dogs' (*ch'üan-jung*) might need encouragement.[20] The Zhou kingdom came to think of itself as *Zhungwo*, the 'middle land' or '**Middle Kingdom**', its vision of the earth literally centred on Songshan, a mountain in the Himalayan foothills.[21] In centuries to come it was a thriving culture while Europe was still, in Zhou terms, *ch'üan-jung*; endurance, while Western powers rose and fell, justified its sense of privilege. If we consider that these powers which rose and fell include the Persian Empire, the Roman Empire and the Arab empires we can see a fair comparison to pharaonic Egypt.

National ideology was encoded in the **Four Classics:** history (*Shih Jih*), rites (*Li Jih*), poetry (*Chih Jing*) and divination (*Yi Jing*).[22] We will examine the last of these in detail because it is especially formative for Chinese philosophy and psychology (8.4). Together, in the judgement of one South African historian, 'their vast influence resembles that of the Bible in the West, woven into the very fabric of national being'.[23] This body of texts was the oldest core of what would later become the later imperial curriculum for the state examinations.[24]

It is worth noting the distribution of all four, suggesting the deliberate formation of a Chinese worldview. In 3.3 we noted a current analysis of worldviews which breaks them up into four components: group **stories** such as national founding myths and creation myths; **rituals** and practices to embed group beliefs in the actions of the body; a system of group **symbols**; and a cognitive instrument of some kind, a **philosophy** of questions and answers behind collective identity.[25]

National identity was forged by the Zhou court scribes with **all four elements** in the construction of its worldview, encoded precisely in these Four Classics – stories in the **history** (*Shih Jih*), *praxis* in the **rites** (*Li Jih*), symbolic patterns in the **poetry** (*Chih Jing*) and a collective philosophy in the system of **divination** (*Yi Jing*).[26] Ancient China long **anticipated** the construction of such analyses.

This suggests a particular skill in **political psychology**, the understanding and management of human beings in a large society. This was indeed the feature of Chinese civilisation which was noted and celebrated by European thinkers as they turned outwards in the early modern period. In 1697, Leibniz could write:

> I consider it a singular plan of the fates that human cultivation and refinement should today be concentrated as it were in the two extremes of our continent, in Europe and in China ... if we are their equals in the industrial arts ... certainly **they surpass us** ... in **practical philosophy**, that is in the precepts of ethics and politics ... the laws of the Chinese ... are directed towards the achievement of **public tranquillity** and the establishment of **social order**.[27]

Before the establishment of a unified Chinese state finally calling itself Ch'in towards the end of the first millennium, which gives us the word China, the evidence suggests self-conscious formation of a core national identity. The fact that the eventual winners in the competition for national leadership – the Ch'in – were from the same **region** as the Shang and the Zhou clearly helped with the transmission and survival of a royal ideology from centuries earlier; as did the fact that it was so **effective**.[28] There are clear parallels with the achievement of those who shaped ideology in Old Kingdom Egypt (6.4), and like them, the Zhou had the rudiments of a distinctive psychology.

8.3 Chinese *logos* on the right: *wen*

The independent invention of a writing system in China proves – as do the later American scripts – that such a technology can evolve anywhere given the universal neural capacities of our species, and the constraints of the 'patterns of culture'.[29] Moreover, once invented, the scripts of China, Sumer, Egypt, Crete and mainland Greece 'all developed in much the same way, with respect to their internal structure' during the Bronze Age.[30] This in itself has implications (including confirmation) for Chomsky's project of anchoring linguistics in neurology and genetics,[31] and also for Derrida's project of a 'grammatology' and 'cultural graphology' (2.6, 3.2)in creative dialogue with psychology.[32]

In every culture writing was closely connected with **divination**; but in China, it may even have **originated** from pressure to read royal omens and to compile omen lists – which were equally popular in Sumer at the time.[33] The shoulder-bone of a cow or the shell of a tortoise were heated and cooled; the particular shapes of the cracks could be 'read' as the voices of ancestors communicating guidance, advice and warnings, the little marks called *pu-tz'u* or *chia ku wen*.[34]

Just as in Sumer, archives of interpretations were stored, like a stock of legal judgements, to guide future interpretations.[35] These are our main sources for Shang culture; scholars suspect that the script had very long Neolithic roots.[36] Yet the earliest *chia ku wen* are still **readable** by Chinese people today: there is a continuous culture of literacy stretching back to Shang China. The word *wen* came to stand for the whole system and for the 'civilisation' that it creates.[37]

The diviners and the inscribers were not the same people: there was a class of *shih* and of *ru* respectively.[38] Those trained to write the script – and the larger, growing number trained to read it – would have their minds trained through it over the centuries and the millennia, to think in a distinctively Chinese way.[39] This initially meant in a Shang way, then Zhou and eventually the empire. As in Egypt, this was closely connected to the formation of a **state ideology**, not only among individuals but socially, in an ever-growing sphere of state influence.[40]

Like hieroglyphs the script was continuous with painting and flexible, matching the surface; but, equally, emphasising careful posture and correct movement.[41] The scribal discipline of Chinese schooling is a good example of Bourdieu's *habitus*: 'permanent internalisation of the social order ... in the form of **bodily postures**'.[42] Growth of schooling, first among *ru* then more widely, became an instrument of state control.[43] As noted concerning Sumer (5.5), the Taiwanese philosopher Ruyu Hung coined **graphocentrism** as the Chinese equivalent of Western phonocentrism, with both as different expressions of logocentrism: in this case, the '**cult of the written word**'.[44] Hung's perspective is a helpful correction to any 'hyperbolic admiration' for the Chinese system simply because it is unfamiliar and misunderstood;[45] Derrida warns against any kind of mystical prejudice as a sort of Eurocentric tourism. As in Sumer and Egypt it faces logocentrism on both sides.

The script involves thinking of the surface as a grid, filling an imaginary square with a series of strokes, to form **roots** (*bushou*), and then larger **characters**, in which the context – not the single word in isolation – decides the meaning.[46] A mark to the left or bottom of the character indicates the general **word class** (a 'determinative') while another to the right indicates **sound**, but a huge variety of sounds and meanings can be conveyed by exactly the same character.[47] The same character can function as a noun or a verb, depending on the context.[48]

The original form is normally read downwards in columns, clearly following the reading preferences of the **right hemisphere** (7.10).[49] Contextual interpretation is also a right-brain preference.[50] Most clearly of all, the form of thought guided by this script is essentially **poetic**: 'The allusions and connections, the currents of logic, are **subtle** and sometimes unpredictable … they read like poetry'.[51] It can be used logically, as we shall see, but for the reader 'words in Chinese are not just semantic signifiers. They are distillates of Chinese thought, saturated with **association** and **ambiguity**, ready to unfold **layers of meaning** that differ according to context'.[52] The Chinese writing system displays the fluid, subtle characteristics of the right hemisphere even more clearly than the writing systems in Egypt, and as a living tradition.

The right hemisphere delights in resemblance as well as discerning differences. When the principle of **correspondence** was first introduced (3.4) this prepared us for its multiple reappearances and applications in Neolithic societies, Sumer, Egypt, Israel – and now China. A verse from one early layer of the *Yi Jing* reads:

> We make observations of the patterns (*wen*) in the heavens
>   with a view to understanding the seasonal changes;
> We make observation of man's patterns (*wen*)
>   with a view to transforming and completing the society of man.[53]

The same word *wen* is used for what we would call the scientific laws studied in astronomy and for the laws of human behaviour (like the Sumerian *Meh*'s) and it is – by the time this is written – the word for the script, writing or characters. It has been summarised in English as '**forms** in the sky and **norms** on the earth';[54] and the implications of using the same word *wen* for both is that these can be described adequately with the same **medium**: using the Chinese characters.[55]

Chinese philosophers use the principle of correspondence routinely: 'While every man, as an individual, has his place, he can also be **identified** with the universe. This idea … runs through virtually the whole of Chinese philosophy'.[56] Reflection on one level, always and automatically, **resonates** with other levels and *wen* itself encourages this **resonance**. Chinese thought is always seeking 'the deeper sense of reality in which the **outer** and **inner** are to be found'.[57]

8.4 Chinese *logos* on the left: *Yi Jing*

In Shang times – and probably much earlier – two methods of divination led to two different **symbolic systems**, which became intimately intertwined. One is the writing system, begun, as we have seen, around the heating and cooling of **bones** and tortoise **shells**, and used – like Sumerian cuneiform – as a memory aid, a data-processing system to remember past interpretations of the *pu-tz'u* and to build up a library of omen readings. From this inauspicious beginning,[58] it evolved into one of the world's great scripts – often compared to the *algebra* which was developed by the Arab civilisations and given to Europe.[59] The other symbolic system is a binary notation, used to record divination from dropping groups of yarrow (or milfoil) **sticks**, which evolved into the Book of Changes.[60]

The *Yi Jing* or Book of Changes is a unique feature of Chinese civilisation with no obvious parallels elsewhere. Unlike most Bronze Age artefacts, it was never restricted to an elite; and like the writing system, it is still in daily use in China. We could say *wen* taught China to communicate; *Yi Jing* taught China to think.

At the most basic level, it is a **horoscope** (Greek: time observer).[61] Daily reality for millions of people, stretching back beyond the Neolithic into earlier times, was **anxiety**. The role of the shaman in early times, of personal gods in Sumer, community totems in Egypt, prophets in Israel – and rituals in them all – was to manage this basic aspect of the human condition.[62] At the simplest level this is fatalistic, asking the question, 'What will happen?' For most people, however, it is not simply a factual enquiry (about fate) but a practical request: for **advice**.[63]

The question that Chinese people bring to the *Yi Jing* is, 'What should I do?' It is therefore a search for **wisdom**; which brings it closer to one of our original Greek words from the Preface: *philo-sophia*, the love of, desire for, wisdom.

This is what 'philosophy' meant in its original setting in ancient Greece, so it is not extraordinary that the *Yi Jing* eventually became 'the beginning of Chinese **philosophy**'.[64] In the ancient world, anything we are able to think about calling 'psychology' comes on the map of philosophy, so this is a promising beginning. Whenever it began, under the Zhou the *Yi Jing* was 'transformed from a text of divination into a text of philosophical wisdom' shaping all of Chinese culture.[65]

We noted that the writing system has a clear bias to the **right** hemisphere like the Egyptian hieroglyphic system. This second system has the characteristics of the **left**: 'a complete system of symbolic constructions based on strict rules of logic', building 'a way of thinking to be systematised in systemic structures'.[66] (Recall Heschel's *halakhah*: 'the rationalisation and schematisation of living' in 7.10).

The oldest layer of *Yi Jing* was a simple question requiring only '**Yes**' **or** '**No**', at its simplest gained through tossing a coin.[67] These two were represented by a solid or a broken line (*yao*) respectively, so it is a **binary system** at its base (of which more below). The answers could just as well be represented by 1 and 0.

Next, the *yao*s are combined in a pair, yielding **four** possible combinations of solid and broken lines between that pair: $2^2 = 4$ or in binary 00, 01,10 and 11.

A third line of pairs is added, solid or broken; three pairs yield **eight** possible combinations, **trigrams** or *guas*. $2^3 = 8$ or 000,001,010,011,100,101, 110,111.

These eight were **personalised**: each given a name (Creative, Receptive, etc.), a characteristic (such as strong, dangerous, penetrating, joyful) – even sometimes linked together as a **family** of eight people: a father, a mother, three sons and three daughters.[68] The character for 'boat' is a vessel with eight mouths, that is eight passengers; so it could be related to one of the Neolithic flood legends.[69]

These eight 'characters', figures or *guas* were derived from three sets of *yaos*. Finally, every trigram or group of three is paired with another trigram to form a six, a **hexagram** figure or *gua*: six combinations of the original binary. The total number of possible hexagrams is then sixty-four: $2^6 = 64$. At each step we are using **binary numbers**, 'base two', and growing the set of possible outcomes using strict rules of logic.[70]

This complete set of **sixty-four possible outcomes** forms the *Yi Jing* system. As each of the eight trigram *guas* from three *yaos* is given a distinct 'personality' as one unit inside the complete set, each of these sixty-four *guas* is given one; and these are taken to represent the possible settings and outcomes for all **decisions**.

A **place value** is given to the resulting combinations by treating the bottom line as the first place, the next up as the second, and so on, up to the sixth place. At this point it stops being strictly **mathematical** by not simply counting in binary from 000000 to 100000 = 64; it is more like a series of **visual patterns**, moving or flowing up the sequence in a **logical** order, from 'all six yes' to 'all six no'.[71]

The mathematical logic of the binary combinations generates a complete set of hexagrams or *guas*, 'figures', taken to describe every possible **situation** – and therefore functioning as a symbol for a complete description of the cosmos. It is a **model**, that is, a product of the **left hemisphere**, a second-order creation; but it is also a symbol of a cosmos that is generated by the interaction of only two complementary principles, an association helped by the poetic quality of *wen*, a product of the **right hemisphere**, which remains open to primary experience.

The binary number system in itself is not unusual: before China, it can be found in Egyptian mathematics[72] and the exact system of weights and measures used by the Indus civilisation in Pakistan in its extensive trade with early Sumer.[73] It is more significant as a signal of cultural **brain lateralisation** that a binary form of divination was converted into such a logical form. Given our observations of **symbol systems** in Sumer (5.3,5.9) and especially in Egypt (6.2,6.12) about the balance or the lack of balance of hemispheric function – about giving both the hemispheres a voice – it is tempting to read the Chinese systems as having this **complementary** role. Given the natural comparison between Egypt and China as 'introvert civilisations', in the terms set by John Baines and Ruth Benedict,[74] we would expect China's lateral balance to be 'self-contained' in this manner. Hence our section titles: *wen* is '*logos* on the right', and *Yi Jing* 'logos on the left', as each other's *yin* and *yang*.

This intuition, that the *Yi Jing* might have potential as a **rational instrument**, is confirmed by its subsequent development into Chinese philosophy and from it, Chinese medicine, **psychology** and equivalents of all the Western disciplines. It is carried on the medium of *wen*, the writing system, which remains in the lead but facilitates, according to the neurology and normative phenomenology of T2 (3.9).

For all its strangeness at first encounter – especially to the (modern) Western mind – it is a key to understanding **the Chinese *psyche*** and literary culture. *Yi Jing* helped to forge a sense of Chinese cultural identity, before unification in 221 BCE and through the millennia of imperial history. The great books of the Axial Age by Laozi, Kongzi (Confucius) and Mengzi (Mencius) – which appear in Book Two – can be read as extensions to the commentary on *I Ching*. Indeed, a significant proportion of the commentary is traditionally attributed to Kongzi. Conversely, it is possible that his influence in imperial China is responsible for placing the *I Ching* permanently at – or near to – the centre of Chinese culture.

8.5 Origins of a binary logic

Connecting the two faces of Chinese *logos* to the landscape, Philip Ball writes:

> There is a particularly beautiful aspect of the **yin/yang dialectic** that runs through all of Chinese thought and artistic expression, namely the contrasts of mountain and water: *shan* and *shui* … Mountains rise, waters descend. But they are **symbiotic**: rivers begin in mountains, and they are the sculptors of mountains. In this way, *shan* and *shui* can **represent the entire cosmos**.[75]

There are several points to be drawn out here, including 'yin/yang dialectic', to be explained within this section. Let us begin the analysis with the final phrase. There is of course an ethnocentrism implied in the identification of China with the cosmos. Nevertheless, even with this caveat, China can exercise a helpful discipline for Western 'tribalism'. It may be that it can also reconnect us with deeper sources than a Bronze Age script.

In the remote past, people had considered the Chinese landscape in terms of the **balance** of *shan* (mountain) to *shui* (water) printed like a character on the Chinese *psyche* (8.1).[76] This gives a context to the interpretation of the solid or broken line (*yao*) at the foundation of *Yi Jing*.

The broken line is equated with ***yin***, a **feminine** or **receptive** principle behind *shui*, associated with water; the solid line is equated with ***yang***, a **masculine** and **active** principle behind *shan* as one outward manifestation. Considering the poetic quality of Chinese thought expressed in the writing system (8.3), the way of thinking and the interpretation of the *Yi Jing* work together, not unlike the two cosmic principles.[77]

The two principles are the 'pervasive and basic **categories** of identification and description' behind all experience, all phenomena: not just of *shan* and *shui*, but 'light and dark, motion and rest, hard and soft' and including male and female:

> '… the world is composed of **activities** of *yin* and *yang* forces which systematically form world-situations in which we find ourselves … incorporating human beings as part and parcel'.[78]

Coming to *Yi Jing* with the question, 'What should I do?' it turns out that the answer is not simply a particular figure from sixty-four *guas*: it is woven into this larger cosmology by the fundamental equation of *yaos* (solid and broken) with *yin* and *yang*, and by their constant role in 'the rise and development of reality' in what can be called (from the Greek, 3.5) **dialectical** development.[79]

This generalisation to paired cosmic principles was basic to interpreting *Yi Jing* from Zhou times, and probably Shang, or even earlier: 'the fundamental ideas, that the universe is a **dynamic system** of incessant change from the simple to the complex and that the Two Modes [*yin* and *yang*] are the agents of the change must have ante-dated the compilation of the book by centuries'.[80] We cannot be entirely certain which came first: whether the binary divination with yarrow sticks came before the dialectical cosmology which is its interpretation; or the cosmology came first and led to a specific method of binary divination.

Our exploration of the **Neolithic** roots of Bronze Age culture in 2.5 and Chapter 4 is also relevant. Lévi-Strauss called myth the language of the *psyche*[81] and said a key element of the grammar of this language is **binary opposition**: pairs of opposites such as life/death or male/female which reveal 'how the brain works' underneath language, the 'deep grammar' of the human mind.[82] This is a global observation which we used to decode the visions of the shaman (4.3). Structuralist anthropology, 'reverse engineering' mythic phenomena, found a subconscious '**binary logic**' wired into our neurology.[83] In Sumer also 'Binary opposition has been called the first paradigm of divination ... Human thought often expresses itself through **dyadic pairs**; structuralist anthropology sees it as one of the basic features of the ordering of the universe'.[84] Characteristic of this binary logic is that there is no effort to **resolve** the perceived tension, only to place the two opposite principles beside one another, to mark a **difference**.[85]

This is a precise description of the earliest encounters of the *Yi Jing* and *Wen*, where the binary is simply observed, placed and not resolved. In the philosophy of the Zhou in the first millennium, there is a sustained effort to **connect** the two principles under a single fundamental principle, such as the *dao* (the origin of change) or the *tai-ji* (the process of change), and **resolve** the opposition; but this is not how the tradition begins.[86] This is the philosophical equivalent of the other changes to the economy, society and politics in the Bronze Age and after; it marks the direct transformation of a Neolithic heritage into **philosophy**, in a pattern later to be repeated by the early Greek philosophers. (See Book Two)

We can therefore look deeper than Chinese (or Taiwanese) 'graphocentrism', and the usual puzzled explanations of Western observers meeting *Yi Jing*.[87] We can understand the *Yi Jing* as a survival of **Neolithic binary logic** in a Bronze Age setting. One that has, moreover, endured well beyond the Bronze Age, in the unification of China, two millennia of imperial culture, the civil war, and communism. In Western culture, we have noted the survival and penetration of shamanistic culture in Bronze Age settings through Semitic languages (7.2, 7.9) which have kept Western civilisation rooted in previous ways of thinking. Early in Book Two we will consider this aspect of ancient Greek culture as a recently revived theme in understanding Western culture during the twentieth century.

Putting together the two relationships of *Yi Jing,* back to binary structures and forwards as 'the beginning of Chinese philosophy' (8.4), we seem to have an answer to a question which has haunted this investigation from the beginning. Do the **binary oppositions** of structuralism, which are supposed to reveal 'how the brain works', have any connection to the hemispheric division of the brain?

One answer, from the Chinese evidence, seems to be that the inbuilt capacity for structuring human experience into binary oppositions is a premonition of the functioning of the **left hemisphere**. In 6.11 we have traced a single line of development in the symbolic systems observed in this book, from the Neolithic through to the first alphabet; in 7:10 we glanced ahead at hemispheric developments within early alphabetic scripts. If *Yi Jing* is (a) unique, (b) clearly linked to binary structure, (c) clearly linked to philosophical thought, we seem to have found the missing link. The capacity for binary structure seems to be based on the left hemisphere making distinctions, creating categories and lists, in a simple and rigid form. The primary experience before these distinctions, and resolution after them, seem to be the mediating function of the right hemisphere.

The two foundational symbolic systems of China, *Yi Ching* and *wen*, both had roots in methods of divination and they had become **intertwined** by Zhou times, if not before. Together they provide a link back to the Neolithic in the Chinese mind, to the worldwide binary logic revealed in Neolithic *mythos*, which is itself understood (at least by structuralists) as 'the human mind in its fundamental form, regardless of the particular society in which it appears'.[88] We have a hypothesis which integrates structuralism with lateralised functioning of the brain.

8.6 Intimations of Chinese *psyche*

Now that we have introduced the twin symbolic systems used in ancient China, roughly corresponding to later Greek *mythos* and *logos*, or poetry and logic, it is finally possible to look at their applications. Just as in Sumer, Egypt and Israel, we are not expecting full psychologies, but a **framework** for doing psychology: as usual in the ancient world, this means locating something called philosophy. This brief sketch of the origins of Chinese civilisation will serve as background to the substantial contributions to global **psychological thought** by writers of Chinese in the first millennium, which will form a backdrop to Greek thought in Book Two and throughout the series as a parallel development.

Western philosophy is often divided into three parts: natural philosophy, the study of knowledge and practical philosophy.[89] As we saw in 2.1 and throughout that chapter, psychology is informed by all three branches of the philosophical tree and the various sciences related to them.

Let us apply the principles of 8.4 and 8.5 to a brief survey of Chinese thought.

In many ways the binary cosmology (the natural philosophy) has already been sketched (8.4, 8.5) as the principle of correspondence (8.3) which encourages 'deep thinking on the nature of the world and the nature of the human self' as a single unit.[90] The *ying* and *yang* elements have been tentatively identified manifestations of natural symmetry: 'in the **genetic code** and the theory of sub-elementary **particles**', for example.[91] It is certainly not difficult to find polarities in the physical world: indeed Western philosophers became obsessed with such patterns two centuries ago, based on the discoveries of electrostatics, magnetism, and modern chemistry.[92] The key feature of Chinese scientific thought is that 'the individual thing or person is only understood and acting in the **context** of a field and **web** of forces'.[93] The functional levels model sketched in Chapter 2 has some resemblance to this.

Given this dialectical worldview, theories of **knowledge** can be based on it not dissimilar to those we have encountered in Hegel and Heidegger (2.3 and 3.5). A dialectical process begins with meticulous and receptive **observation** (*guan*) as free of preconceptions as possible, followed by an equally careful process of 'digestion', processing what has been found and exploring its **resonance** (*gan*), before – again cautiously and meditatively – finding the appropriate **response** (*ying*), which may be further observation or a 'comprehensive integration'.[94] It implies a view of *psyche* in 'cognitive action' which is **detached** and **cautious**: one fitting closely with the portrait of right-hemisphere leadership in T2 (8.8).

It is in the philosophy of **action** that Chinese thought has been world-leading, as noted for example by Leibniz (8.2). Rather than attempting to construct a view of ethics using natural-scientific principles, Chinese thought begins from within human **agency**; which takes us back to the *Yi Jing*. This was not simply treated as fortune-telling: from Zhou times and building layer on the layer from then, a **commentary** was added explaining how each hexagram (or *gua*) represents the current situation, which ultimately tends towards a particular **future outcome**.

The hexagram is revealing the 'germ' or 'seed', where each situation is heading:

> ... the individual came to share in shaping fate. For his actions intervened as determining **factors** in world events, the more decisively so, the **earlier** he was able with the aid of the Book of Changes to **recognise** situations in their germinal phases. The **germinal phase** is the crux. As long as things are in their **beginnings** they can be controlled, but once they have grown to their full consequences, they acquire a power so overwhelming that man stands impotent before them ... The **hexagrams** and lines in their movements and changes mysteriously reproduced the movements and changes of the **macrocosm**.[95]

We have been equipped with several tools to come to terms with this way of thinking in Chapter 3. The cumulative effects of **choices** in the formation of a culture – the setting of the switches – and the importance of beginnings (3.2) were applied there to the **shaping** of individual and collective personality. The concept of worldview (3.3) prepared us for analysis of the collective outlook of a culture – of which this can be a particularly challenging example. The idea of correspondence between microcosm and macrocosm (3.4) has prepared us for the poetic relationship assumed between the user and the world of her action.

The French psychologist Blandine Brill captures something of what this means:

> ... real life is characterised by the **unfolding** of unpredictable events within a persistently changing environment. Given such variation of the situation, how would the (necessarily huge) repertoire of internal representations not only be acquired, but also be translated into appropriate behaviour? The **process** that "bridges the gap" between idea (representation) and behaviour, seems a "**miracle**" ... and is often taken for granted.[96]

This is a portrait of the analytical 'left brain' baffled by the complexities of life, which are mainly handled by subconscious **intuitions** of the right hemisphere.[97] The *Yi Ching* provides a vehicle for the exploration of human ethical intelligence in some ways analogous to a therapist; a companion, teasing out **motivations**. In his review of this technology, Carl Jung tries to capture 'the psychological phenomenology of the *Yi Jing*' by comparing it to a person in the most intimate conversation with him: in other words, as a subtle instrument of **self-knowledge** and **self-awareness**.[98] Hellmut Wilhelm calls *Yi Jing* 'a unique manifestation of the human mind'.[99]

Finally, if *Yi Jing* has given us a basic analytical framework for something approaching psychology in Chinese, the writing system also has its contribution. Like the Egyptian systems of writing (6.2) the Chinese system included a system of **determinatives** to give the reader clues to the kind of word in use.[100] Equivalent to the Egyptian *åb*, represented by a picture of a human heart as used in medical diagrams (6.5), Chinese had the word *xin*, often translated 'heart-mind', to serve a similar function. (Like the other Bronze Age cultures examined, the Chinese located thoughts and emotions here and not in the brain.) They marked words and compounds concerning the thoughts, feelings and actions of *xin* with this 'heart-signifier' as a deteriminative: as we would know how to place a word if it began with *psycho-* in Greek or perhaps *cogni-* in Latin.[101] It was only the most important of a range of 'psychological' words/signifiers, facilitating this kind of discourse: we will explore these in Book Two.

In conclusion, a summary and appreciation from a great historian of China, to lay down as a marker here in the first volume, and to justify many future visits:

> Chinese civilisation was the guiding spirit of a very large section of humanity, giving it its writing, its technology, its conception of man and the world, its religions and its political institutions. The land of China itself, Korea, Japan and Vietnam all form part of the same cultural community. But China's influence radiated far beyond that... The West, which has borrowed from China right down to our say without realizing it, is far from recognizing its sizable debt to her, but for which we ourselves would not be what we are.[102]
>
> Jacques Gernet, *A History of Chinese Civilisation*

8.7 Review of T1

Jaynes barely mentions China in his main text, and then tends to classify it according to his model, rather than recognise its individuality.[103] We have identified this as a general weakness along with its weak (logocentric) linguistic base, which exposes it to 'missing the point' of ancient languages in many cases. In a recent update, Jaynes's student Brian McVeigh does apply T1 to ancient China and makes a valiant attempt to show that, because it came late to the Bronze Age, by the time China has writing it is already 'post-bicameral', with people already conscious in our sense, which can explain the lack of evidence of a bicameral phase.[104] He then applies statistical measures to the vocabulary of Zhou Chinese texts to show that their vocabulary evolves an interior space in accordance with T1. This is done clumsily, however, without due historical reflection: we noted this in our review of T1 on Sumer (5.8) and the same applies with China.

Let us consider one aspect of our investigation which plays to the strengths of T1.

We have explored the lateralisation of social and especially leadership systems from 4.5 onwards. Provisionally lining up developing categories of **government** with the characterisation of hemispheres in *The Master and his Emissary*, there is *some limited* legitimacy to a division of labour in terms of hemispheric roles:

Economy	*Left hemisphere*	*Right hemisphere*
Upper Palaeolithic	Informal band leader	Classic shaman
Early Neolithic	Tribal leader	Classic shaman
Late Neolithic	Hereditary chief	Hereditary priest
Bronze Age	King or emperor	High priest
Iron Age	Executive role	Legislative role

Only the middle three rows are claimed as bicameral under T1: the Palaeolithic is not bicameral and never defined; the Iron Age is defined as post-bicameral in the wake of a drawn-out crisis, in which consciousness appears.

For the middle three rows, however, this makes perfect sense in terms of T1: the individual and political 'executive' is guided by his *ili* (in Sumer) or his *ka* (in Egypt) or those who can represent it in social terms, and this is the role given on the right. The bicameral mind has such a clear division of labour, with neither side conscious, and the bicameral person reduced (in our terms) to the purely executive role on the left.

Turning to China, however, there is a problem, which we will explore in Book Two. T1 claims that **law** and **legislation** evolve to replace bicameral control in the situation of crisis: conscious individuals need a new form of social control. Sumer – which should be 'classic' bicameral before 2000 BCE – has an enormous **interest** in law to restrain individuals as early as the third millennium. How can this fit the theory? The point of law is to restrain conscious, subjective people. Conversely, China arrives late in the Bronze Age, already undergoing a crisis towards consciousness, in obedience to the single T1 timeline; yet its central tradition (Kongzi, see Book Two) **avoids** law, and seeks different methods of social control. In both cases, the data **does not match** what is predicted by T1.

China – as so often – exposes the local Eurocentric biases in Western theories.

We have not yet given up on T1. It survived and sometimes even helped with the interpretation of data in the Neolithic (4.7), Sumer (5.8), Egypt (6.11) and to some extent, Israel (7.9). Its writing theory made sense of the Neolithic data: in fact, better sense than it did of later writing systems. Its theory of the *ka* was a great help in understanding and expanding upon Egyptian political ideology. It will travel with us into Book Two, where it will make a fresh set of predictions.

In this book, because our timeline is a perfect match to Jaynes's bicameral era, we have had the constant presence of one neural configuration (the bicameral) against which to test historical data. Things will become more interesting and more complex in Book Two as we enter the long 'crisis' – with the breakdown of the bicameral mind and the birth of more modern subjective consciousness.

8.8 Review of T2

We are ending Part 2 where we ended Part 1: with Iain McGilchrist's theory. As first noted in 5.9 he brings a knowledge of Chinese civilisation, particularly the character of *wen* and scribal culture, into his portrait of civilisation, exploiting some of its potential as a counter-example to the West.[105] Japanese is carefully treated as a later – but highly creative – derivative of ancient Chinese culture.[106]

As also noted in 5 9, T2 incorporates much of Derrida's 'grammatology' despite a lack of exposure to ancient alternatives in his shorter historical sweep and also despite no apparent debt to the Algerian. It avoids 'logocentrism' better than T1 through (slightly dated but) sophisticated comparative linguistics:[107] indeed T2 and McGilchrist's entire programme outflanks, includes and updates Derrida's.

Avoiding both 'ethnocentric scorn' and 'hyperbolic admiration' for Chinese culture, T2 uses this example to show how an **advanced** culture can grow in a quite different direction.[108] With the wide and growing awareness that the Western model of civilisation is in trouble and in need of diagnosis and therapy, China is – he implies – a better model to give us 'leverage' on the West than **regressive** movements, such as the funded revival of shamanistic medicine, (4.6)[109] or the advocacy of Palaeolithic mothering practices, ignoring mortality rates (4.9).[110]

There may well, of course, be a middle ground incorporating elements of both approaches if the latter are shorn of 'hyperbolic admiration' for ancient cultures.

In this chapter, we have eroded the discipline from previous chapters of keeping talk of brain lateralisation 'back' until these reviews. That is partly because it is so **obvious** in Chinese culture – as though the whole point of T2 was built into this civilisation three thousand years ago – and because T2 clearly depends on Chinese input. As the more discerning reader will have guessed by now, this book draws on the programme set out in T2 as a central **guiding framework**.

For all these reasons the whole chapter has been leading up toward this review as its foundational argument, working toward a preliminary conclusion, as this is a work of **cultural psychology** as well as opening a **history of psychology**.

We have applied our earlier **hypothesis**, developed in Chapters 5 and 6, that public symbolic systems in a Bronze Age culture tended to express brain laterality by giving each hemisphere a sustainable 'voice' with its own script.

What we have found in the progress towards psychology, for example in our analysis of the *é-dubba* (5.5) is that there was a need for re-integration of left-hemisphere advances with right-hemisphere functioning, just for balance, and a means to maintain normative functioning with the Master leading the Emissary. Early cuneiform was highly lateralised to the left and even 'segregated' into compartments. Myths retained hemispheric balance in an **oral** form, providing an overall 'symmetry' within the culture, showing a capacity for psychological discourse not reflected in the scribal culture until the arrival of Akkadian (5.9).

Looking across from Iraq to Egypt (6.2, 6.12), and in the other direction China (8.3,8.4,8.6) we found dual systems of representation from the start which gave each hemisphere its 'voice' in a sustainable way so that the culture developed a bilateral balance more comfortable for the brain. For those entering the literate elite, this meant a less distorted experience of education and a more expressive form of literacy. It seems that 'the empire of the mind' needed time to adjust to new technology; Bronze Age literacy tells the story of 're-housing the brain'.

	Left hemisphere	*Right hemisphere*
Iraq	Sumerian cuneiform	Akkadian cuneiform
Egypt	hieratic	hieroglyphic
Israel	*halakha*	*aggadah*
China	*Yi Jing* (as genre)	*wen* (as medium)

To any scholar, this table is a massive simplification of multiple complex issues, and we have noted the ambiguity regarding Sumer (5.9); but it is an attempt to capture the basic hypothesis inducted from data in Part Two. It attempts to capture the functions, outcomes and 'fruits' of these systems in their respective cultures: those on the left are more scientific, and those on the right are more poetic, mythical and ideological. The table proposes this division as a common pattern.

The unexpected extension of this model to a later development of Hebrew tradition was prompted by McGilchrist's sequel (7.10). We could add a similar example as an extension of Chinese tradition. In the early Common Era, when rabbinical Jews were evolving *halakha* and *aggadah*, a new people began to adopt the Chinese writing system: the Japanese. They borrowed the Chinese characters and adapted them to a very different spoken language, creating the *kanji* writing system. Yet they have also created a parallel system based only on the sounds of syllables: the *kana* system. Written Japanese is normally a blend of both. Together,*kanji* and*kana* constitute an unsually complicated writing system.[111]

This seems to confirm the theory expressed in the table. Our brain laterality seems to demand expression at public level in symbol systems. Each culture and each civilisation has solved the problem differently, but we can see a pattern emerging which bridges across these differences. Written language organises the collective mind of a culture, and that collective mind stretches language until both hemispheres are expressed.

We noted that the binary logic of *yin* and *yang* can be (and has been) applied to a range of scientific data, and among these are medicine and psychology: in Chinese medicine, this is exactly what is involved as the main underlying principle of physiology, diagnosis and treatment.[112] What we did not explore there is the possibility of its reverse connection to brain laterality: that rather than helping to **explain** our hemisphere function, the hemispheric function was its true **origin**.

It is tempting to read the duality or polar opposition of *yin* and *yang* in terms of brain laterality. Indeed, it seems to fulfil the 'promise' of Neolithic binary logic. We understood that logic itself as a manifestation of the left hemisphere in 8.5, the first in the historical record: in doing so we have succeeded in extending T2 much further back in time, not only through the Neolithic, but past it into the Upper Palaeolithic period. If that is provisionally accepted, is it also true that the Chinese example of binary opposition, *yin* and *yang*, **describes our brain hemispheres**?

Could this have occurred? On McGilchrist's own arguments, very much so. He notes at the start of his essay that 'We can inspect the brain only 'from the outside' … . But we can inspect the mind only '**from within**''.[113] We noted his respect for **Hegel** and **Heidegger**, noting their 'extraordinary' intuitive insights into the interaction of the two hemispheres in their own thought processes,[114] and tells us his title and central metaphor are borrowed from their tradition.[115] He pays the same compliment to **Aeschylus** as revealing similar extraordinary intuitive self-awareness.[116] However we interpret them, all ancient lexicons of *åb*, *ba*, *ka*, *lev*, *nephesh* and so on are sourced from someone's introspection.

If certain particularly gifted people are capable of grasping intuitively the inner complexities of their own lateral functioning and capturing this in words, both in ancient and modern settings, then we have good grounds for believing that the Chinese interpretation of the *yaos* as opposite principles was an **intuition** of the functioning of Chinese **minds**. Given its clear roots in the Neolithic it is probable that this intuition was more like the visions of the shaman or myths of Sumer, **projected** outwards from the self, not 'returned' nor acknowledged as their own (4.5, 5.7). Even Hegel and Heidegger did not identify their intuitions as the exchange and interaction of brain hemispheres; although Heidegger did begin to grasp a connection between his own phenomenology and Chinese philosophy of a recognisably similar kind.[117]

When we compare the portrait of respective hemispheric functions in T2 with Chinese philosophy and '**mutual origination**' of binary principles, '**mutually supporting**, transforming, balancing, enhancing and furthering',[118] it is easy to see the resemblance, and why McGilchrist has such respect for Chinese (and Japanese) culture. Conversely, if Chinese medicine is ultimately based – if only unconsciously based – on brain laterality, then it would apply to psychosomatic illness and psychiatric health at the very least; that is, to anything related to the brain.

As noted in its first review (4.8) this theory travels well because it is scientific. Its portrait of China is an enormous improvement on many previous Western 'takes', because it is not simply comparing opposite poles at the cultural level but applying well-developed neurological theory as an explanation for the underlying dynamics of both 'poles', both Western and Chinese civilisation.

We have found a cultural equivalent of this basis in the global Neolithic phase. McGilchrist compares our consciousness to a tree with the hemispheres as the two major **branches**, 'two vast coherent neurological systems, each capable of sustaining consciousness on their own',[119] but a shared **trunk** below a division of hemispheres in our basic animal functions, in a sense of 'self' that is already one and does not need to be integrated.[120] The **global Neolithic** is analogous, a cultural equivalent for this neurological 'trunk' dividing into higher branches.

This might give us a clue to some wildly speculative conclusions to this review, because one observation McGilchrist does not make, but his whole argument seems to imply, is that what the world needs is more of this Chinese culture – not communism, but the long cultural tradition – and that this is happening already with the (precarious but) tremendous global presence of China today. His portrait of Western culture from the inside is grim, dark and pessimistic:

> '… we have entered a phase of cultural history in which negative feedback between the products of action and the two hemispheres has given way to **positive feedback** in favour of the left hemisphere. Despite the primacy of the right hemisphere, it is the left hemisphere that has all the cards'.[121]

This, you may remember, is based on the biological principle of **homeostasis** in a living organism: a **negative feedback** loop which adjusts back to equilibrium (3.9, 4.9, 5.10).

Note, however, that we have collected some initial evidence of what we might call lateral **homeostasis** at the **cultural** level. First within Neolithic cultures, the growth of different kinds and institutions of authority seemed to keep in step, the role of the shaman evolving alongside the roles of executive leadership; as we have summarised in 8.7 above, this can be given an – admittedly cautious – interpretation in terms of laterality. There seems to be a '**social homeostasis**'.

Within the Bronze Age civilisations, we have built up a slightly more confident hypothesis (above) concerning what might be called '**symbolic homeostasis**' in the largest units of human community, summarised above in a table and the claim 'that public symbolic systems in a Bronze Age culture tended to express brain laterality by giving each hemisphere a sustainable 'voice' with its own script'.

In Egypt, this worked extremely well and was sustainable over several millennia because, as we noted then (6.12), users of hieratic such as architects, doctors and accountants were free to develop the left hemisphere while operating in a subservient role towards the other scribal class, the priests, representing a script (hieroglyphic) better designed for the right hemisphere. Sumer achieved something similar later with the dominance of Semitic (Akkadian) cuneiform in a 'twin-tongued' system, where the new language worked better for the right, but switched to a left to right orientation as if to balance this.

In China, we have a model similar to Egypt's, and lasting over comparable time periods: the twin institution, from the beginning or almost the beginning, of a working symbol system as an effective voice for each hemisphere. The Chinese blend was correctly structured, and more intimately structured than in Egypt, because the left hemisphere's 'voice' operated almost entirely inside the other as a medium. In Egypt their cooperation was dependent on the cooperation of two classes; in China cooperation was simply dependent on the coherence of a single class who formed the harmonious 'brain' of that civilisation for most of its history.

We are slowly 'scaling up' our answer, climbing the stairs of the macrocosm to reach the necessary level. If small Neolithic societies could contain the limited lateral development within them through evolving systems of government; if this pattern continued in their long evolution towards Bronze Age monoliths; and if these monoliths – more rather than less clearly, and faster rather than slower – could add a new form of homeostasis at the new level of complexity; then can we 'scale up' one more step to the interaction of these civilisations?

We first asked this very question in 4.8 when reviewing T2 for Neolithic data. Since then, we have noted several relationships between civilisations such as the contrast of 'extravert' Sumer and 'introvert' Egypt (by extension, China) in 5.8 and 5.9, with unexpected support from otherwise sober scholars of each; and as a corollary with Sumer, observed that its temperament made it more dependent on other cultures and civilisations: it was less self-contained, as Ruth Benedict had observed of several much smaller, simpler Neolithic cultures she reviewed.

Finally, at this point we made the connection to Greece, resembling Sumer in this respect: a provisional judgement to be investigated in the next volume. It would be then a matter of a 'scaling up' from Greece to 'Western civilisation': working out whether this is a legimate move.

We, therefore, have a – highly precarious and provisional – Chinese answer to McGilchrist's anxiety: that there seems to be a self-correcting behaviour, even a **homeostatic mechanism** built not only into our biology but into our cultures. If we observe the precarious state of Western culture in McGilchrist's portrait, we can also observe that a potential **antidote** has risen to meet this very illness, with the rise of China on the world stage. It does not mean there is nothing to do; it does not negate McGilchrist's project; it could be that he is indeed one of the prophets pointing to the promised land. This observation, modest as it is, simply gives some **hope** and encouragement to his project.

To underline the point, I will end with a quotation from a Chinese philosopher, Chung-Yi Chen, who is still a Professor at the Chinese University of Hong Kong:

> ... it is in the process of time that the *yin* and the *yang* are interacting as alternating. Because of this, one could expect that reaching the limit of the worst would mean a return to a better condition.[122]

Discussion questions:

1 Re-read the Orientation: any surprises or new perspectives on China?
2 What preconceptions about Chinese culture did you bring with you?
3 Do you find the poetry of *wen* attractive? What are its limitations?
4 Can you imagine how *Yi Jing* could work intellectually? Or personally?
5 Can you see any other connections back to content in Chapter 4?
6 Which (if any) sketch of Chinese philosophy seemed most intriguing?
7 Do you agree with the Review of T1 concerning its Eurocentric bias?
8 What do you make of the speculative argument built in reviewing T2?

Recommended Reading

- Philip Ball *The Water Kingdom*
- Fritjof Capra *The Tao of Physics*
- Cheng, Chung-ying 'The *Yi-Jing* and *Yin-Yang* way of thinking' in Mou, Bo (ed.) *History of Chinese Philosophy*
- Jaques Gernet *A History of Chinese Civilisation*
- Ruyu Hung *Education Between Speech and Writing: Crossing the Boundaries pf Dao and Deconstruction*
- Charles Moore ed. *The Chinese Mind*
- Oliver Moore *Reading the Past: Chinese*
- Witold Rodzinski *The Walled Kingdom*
- Richard Wilhelm (*trans.*) *I Ching* in Moore, Charles (ed.) *The Chinese Mind*

Notes

1 In Book 2 this statement will be qualified, especially by other examples in India, Africa and Europe.

2 Bellwood p.209; Childe 1954 p.42; Wood p.83; this places the emphasis in the north, where the Shang and Zhou were based; within the space of imperial China the south was also very important.
3 Gernet p.44; Roberts p.129; Rodzinski p.11; see the links made below to Neolithic structures.
4 Gernet p.31; Wood p.84; precisely its role for T2.
5 Ball p.13.
6 Ball pp.12–13,25,19,23,29,52–3,75; Kruger p.1; Roberts p.128.
7 Bellwood pp.205,211,277–8,284–5,289,297; Gernet p.37.
8 Bellwood pp.84,210–214; Kruger p.5; Roberts pp.128,130,133.
9 Gernet pp.27,44; Kruger pp.6–7; Rodzinski pp.13,16,23; Wood p.89.
10 Gernet pp.28,39–41; Kruger pp.8–12,14–15,19; Roberts pp.130–2; Rodzinski pp.15,17,20; Wood p.88–9.
11 Ball pp.50–1,71; Gernet pp.45–6; Kruger pp.12,18;; Rodzinski p.19; Wood pp.83,87.
12 Bellwood pp.232,271–2,284; Gernet pp.3,26; Roberts pp.128,133.
13 Wilson p.81.
14 Ball pp.14,47,55ff.
15 Gernet pp.58–9,78–81; Rodzinski pp.40–1.
16 Ball p.50; Gernet pp.45–6,49; Kruger pp.7–9,17; Thomas and Humphrey pp.196–216.
17 Gernet pp.44,51–2; Kruger pp.25ff.; Roberts p.132; Rodzinski pp.21–5.
18 Gernet p.54.
19 Wood p.84.
20 Gernet p.52; Roberts p.132.
21 Wood pp.85,89.
22 *ibid* p.89.
23 Kruger p.57; note that his Dutch Protestant ancestry biases his view of 'the West'.
24 Gernet pp.158ff.,203ff.,331ff., 345–6,438ff.; Kruger p.243.
25 Wright 1992 p.124.
26 Chan p.16 in Moore, Charles (ed.) *The Chinese Mind*; Wood p.89.
27 Gregory pp.44–5.
28 Gernet pp.58–9,78–81; Rodzinski pp.40–1.
29 Hooker p.7; Robinson 2009 pp.18–23.
30 Hooker p.8; see also p.103 for an elaboration of one common principle.
31 Chomsky pp.43–53,98; Lyons pp.83,86,96; Magee 1982 175—9,184–7.
32 Derrida 1967 pp.74–5,83,93.
33 Gernet p.32; Van de Mieroop 2017 pp.90–91,97,113.
34 Gernet p.45; Moore p.19.
35 Gernet p.45; Van de Mieroop pp.90,97,117.
36 Kruger pp.7–9; Moore pp.18–19; Robinson 2009 p.18; McVeigh p.70 cites one source proposing 6000–5000 BCE, and we have considered symbolic systems even further back in 4.2,5.2, 7.2,7.9.
37 Gernet p.46; Wood p.88; Renfrew's working definition of a civilisation reflects a West Asian mindset where the civitas became central, and writing is explicitly optional: see 1973 p.212. In China the equivalent mindset is centred on written culture, and it is rather the urban condition for 'civilisation' which is optional.
38 Moore p.25.
39 Eriksen p.121; Gernet p.32; Hung Ch.3 (pp.44–83).
40 Hooker p.7; Rodzinski p.20.
41 Hung pp.46,55; Moore pp.33–8.
42 Eriksen pp.159–60.
43 Fowler p.26.

44 Hung p.xiv.
45 Derrida 1967 p.80.
46 Ball pp.3,73; Kruger p.19; Moore pp.11–13.
47 Gernet p.33; Moore pp.7,9,14–15.
48 Moore pp.12–13; Robinson 2009 p.75.
49 McGilchrist 2009 p.276.
50 Blakeslee p.21.
51 Ball p.69.
52 Ball p.3.
53 Hughes p.81.
54 Kant also famously admired 'the starry heavens above me and the moral law within me': 1996 5:162 p.269.
55 Cheng p.77.
56 Chan p.140 in Moore Charles (ed.) *The Chinese Mind.*
57 Cheng p.79.
58 This is an intentional pun in case you spotted it.
59 Gernet p.32; Perkins pp.109,142; Van de Mieroop 2017 pp.91,113.
60 Ball pp.47–9; Gernet p.85; Kruger pp.53,83.
61 Chan p.16 in Moore, Charles (ed.) *The Chinese Mind.*
62 Ehrenreich pp.22,47,120 and Harari pp.11–12 for one explanation in terms of evolutionary psychology.
63 Wilhelm pp.53,57.
64 Cheng pp.71,102.
65 Cheng p.71; Wu p.341 in Moore, Charles (ed.) *The Chinese Mind.*
66 Cheng p.89; Fang p.239 in Moore, Charles (ed.) *The Chinese Mind.*
67 Wilhelm pp.44,723–4.
68 *ibid* p.50.
69 Kang and Nelson pp.xii,95; see Ball pp.62–4; it even resonates with *Bereshith* 7:13,8:18,9:18–19,10:1,10:32. As so often occurs in the study of the ancient world, surprising correspondences and parallels of this kind will crop up, but it is hard to tell whether they are important clues or 'red herrings', especially if they happen to resonate with a particular agenda in the current writing of history.
70 This account is taken from Richard Wilhelm's introduction to his translation pp.49–59.
71 Wilhelm pp.730–1.
72 Murray pp.105–6.
73 Renfrew and Zubrow pp.17–18,26–7.
74 Baines pp.33–4,43–4 in Lefkowitz (ed.)1996; Benedict p.161.
75 Ball p.75.
76 Ball pp.12–13,25,19,23,29,52–3,75; Kruger p.1; Roberts p.128.
77 Chan p.50 in Moore, Charles (ed.) *The Chinese Mind*; Cheng p.72.
78 Cheng pp.72,84.
79 *ibid* pp.85,89.
80 Chan p.51 in Moore, Charles (ed.) *The Chinese Mind.*
81 Lévi-Strauss 1978 p.47.
82 Lewis-Williams and Pearce pp.151,157.
83 Lévi-Strauss 1978 p.5; Lewis-Williams and Pearce pp.160–1.
84 Van de Mieroop 2017 pp.124–5.
85 Lewis-Williams and Pearce p.151; but we have also noted the characterstic search for a 'third thing', a mediating component, as the everyday world mediated between the subterranean and aerial visions of the shaman in 4.3 adn 4.4. In Book Two we will explore the attempts of Chinese philosophy to find a 'third thing' to reconcile the two cosmic principles, and the effects of this on psychology.

86 Cheng pp.75,81,89–93.
87 One classic is Kruger's 'No-one now understands it … it seems merely a cabalistic manual for sorcerers' p.53.
88 Hawkes p.54.
89 Bacon 1605 VII.6–IX.1 p.105; Kant *Critique* A xxi PP.104–5, B viii P.106, B 868–9 P.695–6; Heidegger *Letter on Humanism* 1978 pp.195–6,232; Locke *Essay* IV.XXI p.385.
90 Cheng p.71.
91 *ibid* p.92: see also McManus Ch.6 pp.121–145 (biochemistry) and Ch.15 pp.354–9 (physics, including an interesting testiony by the Nobel prize-winner Chen Ning Yang). The principle was celebrated at some length, but with less rigour, in the bestseller *The Tao of Physics* by Fritjof Capra (1983).
92 Well treated in Richard Holmes's *The Age of Wonder* (Harper Press, London 2009).
93 Cheng p.92.
94 Cheng pp.76–8,80.
95 *ibid* pp.53–4.
96 Quoted in Henley and Rossano p.104.
97 McGilchrist 2009 p.187 – just one example, but this is a theme of Part One of *The Master and his Emissary*.
98 Jung in Wilhelm pp.26,34–5,39.
99 Wilhelm pp.16–17.
100 McVeigh pp.81,177–194.
101 *ibid* p.74.
102 Gernet pp.1–3.
103 McVeigh pp.59,162–3.
104 *ibid* pp.70–2.
105 *ibid* pp.277–9,311,455,457–8,502n.1,516n.95.
106 *ibid* pp.168,258,277,368,452–3,453–6.
107 Davies p.103; Hooker p.8; McGilchrist 2009 p.273,275,278.
108 Derrida 1967 p.80.
109 See Machinga and Marovic for a representative contemporary argument.
110 'The Missing Mind', in Henley and Rossano Chapter 5 pp.55–69.
111 McManus pp.80-2; Oliver Moore pp.73–6.
112 Cheng pp.74–5.
113 McGilchrist 2009 p.7.
114 *ibid* pp.91,203–207,231 (Hegel); pp.149–158,314,449–50 (Heidegger); 527 (references to both).
115 *ibid* pp.14,204,234.
116 *ibid* pp.273–4.
117 Reinhard May's *Heidegger's Hidden Sources* (trans. Parkes, G., Routledge London 1996) traces this story.
118 Cheng p.75.
119 McGilchrist 2009 pp.226.
120 *ibid* pp.185,221, referencing and critiquing the essential message of Damasio pp.xxiii,27,249–252.
121 *ibid* p.232.
122 Cheng p.93.

Bibliography

Althaus, Horst *Hegel: An Intellectual Biography* (Polity Press, Cambridge 2000)
Al-Udhari, Abdullah *The Arab Creation Myth* (Archangel Press, Prague 1997)
Annas, Julia *An Introduction to Plato's Republic* (OUP 1981)
Andrews, Michael *The Birth of Europe: Colliding Continents and the Destiny of Nations* (BBC Books, London 1991)
Aristotle 'Organon' in *Great Books of the Western World* Vol. 8 (ed. Hutchins R.M., Encyclopedia Britannica, London 1952)
Armstrong, Karen *The Great Transformation* (Atlantic, London 2006)
Bacon, B., Khatiri, A., Palmer, J., Freeth, T., Pettitt, P., & Kentridge, R. (2023) An Upper Palaeolithic Proto-writing System and Phenological Calendar. *Cambridge Archaeological Journal*, 1–19. doi:10.1017/S0959774322000415
Bacon, Francis 1605 *The Advancement of Learning* (Everyman, London 1973)
Bacon, Francis 1620 *The New Organon* (ed. Jardine, L. and Silverthorne, M., CUP 2000)
Ball, Philip *The Water Kingdom: A Secret History of China* (Vintage, London 2016)
Barker, Margaret *Temple Theology: An Introduction* (SPCK, London 2004)
Barker, Margaret *Temple Mysticism: An introduction* (SPCK 2011)
Beiser, Frederick *The Cambridge Companion to Hegel and Nineteenth Century Philosophy* (CUP 2008)
Bellwood, Peter (ed.) *The Global History of Human Migrations* (Blackwell, London 2013)
Benedict, Ruth *Patterns of Culture* (Routledge and Kegan Paul, London 1935)
Blakeslee, Thomas R. *The Right Brain: A New Understanding of the Unconscious Mind and Its Creative Powers* (Macmillan, London 1980)
Bowie, Andrew *Introduction to German Philosophy: From Kant to Habermas* (Polity Press, Cambridge 2003)
Breasted, J.H. *Development of Religion and Thought in Ancient Egypt* (Harper and Row, London 1959)
Brett, George Sidney *A History of Psychology I: Ancient and Patristic* (Palala Press 2018)
Brogan, Hugh *The Penguin History of the United States of America* (London 1985)
Brown, Stuart 'The Seventeenth Century Intellectual Background' in *The Cambridge Companion to Leibniz* (ed. Jolley, Nicholas, CUP 1995)
Budge, Sir E.A. Wallis *An Egyptian Hieroglyphic Dictionary Volume 1* (Dover Publishing, London 1978)
Budge, Sir E.A. Wallis *Egyptian Religion* (Carol Publishing, Secaucus, N.J. 1997)

Burrow, John *A History of Histories: Epics, Chronicles, Romances and Inquiries from Herodotus and Thucydides to the Twentieth Century* (Penguin, London 2009)
Caputo, John 'People of God, People of Being: The Theological Presuppositions of Heidegger's Path of Thought' in *Appropriating Heidegger* (eds. Faulconer, James E. and Wrathall, Mark A., CUP 2000)
Cassirer, Ernst *An Essay on Man* (Yale University Press, London 1944)
Cavalli-Sforza, Luigi Luca *Genes, Languages and People* (trans. Seielstad, M., Penguin, London 2001)
Celenza, Christopher S. 'The Revival of Platonic Philosophy' in *The Cambridge Companion to Renaissance Philosophy* (ed. Hankins, J., CUP 2007)
Ceram, C.W. (ed.) *The World of Archaeology: The Pioneers Tell Their Own Story* (Thames and Hudson, London 1966)
Chadwick, John 'Linear B' in *Reading the Past: Ancient Writing from Cuneiform to the Alphabet* (ed. Hooker, J.T., Guild Publishing, London 1990)
Challenger, Melanie *How to Be Animal: A New History of What It Means to Be Human* (Canongate, Edinburgh 2020)
Cheng, Chung-ying 'The *Yi-Jing* and *Yin-Yang* way of thinking' in *History of Chinese Philosophy* (ed. Mou, Bo, Routledge, London 2009)
Childe, V. Gordon *The Aryans: A Study of Indo-European Origins* (Kegan Paul, Trench, Trubner and Co. Ltd., New York NY 1926)
Childe, V. Gordon *What Happened in History* (revised edition, Penguin, London 1954)
Childe, V. Gordon *Man Makes Himself* (illustrated edition, Moonraker Press and Pitman, Bradford-on-Avon, Wiltshire UK 1981)
Chomsky, Noam *Language and Responsibility* (Harvester Press, Sussex 1979)
Clark, Grahame *World Prehistory in New Perspective* (3rd Edition, CUP 1977)
Clarke, Andy *Supersizing the Mind: Embodiment, Action, and Cognitive Extension* (OUP 2011)
Clarke, Desmond *Descartes's Theory of Mind* (OUP 2003)
Cole, Michael *Cultural Psychology: A Once and Future Discipline* (Harvard University Press, Cambridge MA 1998)
Copleston, F.C. *Aquinas* (Penguin, London 1991)
Cragg, Kenneth (trans. ed.) *Readings in the Qur'an* (Collins, London 1988)
Dalley, Stephanie (trans. ed.) *Myths from Mesopotamia* (OUP 1989)
Damasio, Antonio *Descartes' Error: Emotion, Reason and the Human Brain* (Picador Vintage Books, London 2006)
Daniel, Glyn *A Short History of Archaeology* (Thames and Hudson, London 1981)
Darvill, Timothy *Stonehenge: The Biography of a Landscape* (Tempus Publishing, Stroud, Gloucestershire UK 2006)
Davies, Norman *The Isles: A History* (Macmillan, London 1999)
Davies, W.V. 'Egyptian Hieroglyphics' in *Reading the Past: Ancient Writing from Cuneiform to the Alphabet* (ed. Hooker, J.T., Guild Publishing, London 1990)
Derrida, Jacques *Of Grammatology* (trans. Spivak, G.C., Johns Hopkins University Press, London 1967)
Derrida, Jacques *Acts of Religion* (ed. Anidjar, Gil, Routledge, London 2002)
Descartes, Réné *Discourse on Method and the Meditations* (trans. Sutcliffe, F.E., Penguin, London 1968)
Diamond, Jared *Guns, Germs and Steel: A Short History of Everybody for the Last 13,000 Years* (Vintage, London 2005)

Diop, Cheikh Anta *The African Origin of Civilisation: Myth or Reality* (ed. trans. Cook, Mercer, Lawrence Hill Books, Chicago, IL 1974)

Ehrenreich, Barbara *Blood Rites: The Origins and History of the Passions of War* (Granta, London 1997)

Eriksen, Thomas Hylland and Nielson, Finn Sivert *A History of Anthropology: Second Edition* (Pluto Press, London 2013)

Everson, Stephen (ed.) *Companions to Ancient Thought 2: Psychology* (CUP 1991)

Farrell, Martin *Historical and Philosophical Foundations of Psychology* (CUP 2014)

Forman, Werner and Quirke, Stephen *Hieroglyphs and the Afterlife in Egypt* (British Museum Press, London 1996)

Fowler, Bridget *Pierre Bourdieu and Cultural Theory: Critical Investigations* (Sage, London 1997)

Frankfort, H. and H.A. (eds.) *Before Philosophy: The Intellectual Adventure of Ancient Man* (Penguin, New York NY 1949)

Frankfort, H. *Ancient Egyptian Religion: An Interpretation* (Columbia University Press, New York NY 1948)

Friedman, Michael *A Parting of the Ways: Carnap, Cassirer, and Heidegger* (Open Court Publishing, Peru, IL 2000)

Fukuyama, Francis *The End of History and the Last Man* (Penguin, London 1992)

Garrett, Duane *Rethinking Genesis* (Baker Book House, Grand Rapids MI 1991)

Gernet, Jacques *A History of Chinese Civilisation: Second Edition* (trans. Foster, J.R. and Hartman, C., CUP 1996)

Girard, René *Things Hidden Since the Foundation of the World* (Bloomsbury, London 2016)

Girard, René *Violence and the Sacred* (Continuum, London 2005)

Grabbe, Lester L. *Ancient Israel: What Do We Know and How Do We Know It?* (Continuum, London 2007)

Gregory, John S. *The West and China since 1500* (Palgrave Macmillan 2003)

Harari, Yuval Noah *Sapiens: A Brief History of Humankind* (Vintage, London 2011)

Harrison, Peter *The Fall of Man and the Foundations of Science* (CUP 2007)

Hawkes, Terence *Structuralism and Semiotics* (Routledge, London 1997)

Haywood, John *The Great Migrations* (Quercus, London 2008)

Healey, John F. 'The Early Alphabet' in *Reading the Past: Ancient Writing from Cuneiform to the Alphabet* (ed. Hooker, J.T., Guild Publishing, London 1990)

Hegel, G.W.F. *Phenomenology of Spirit* (trans. Miller A.V., OUP 1977)

Hegel, G.W.F. *The Philosophy of History* (Dover, New York, NY 1956)

Heidegger, Martin 1927 *Being and Time* (trans. Macquarrie, J. and Robinson, E., Harper and Row, New York, NY 1962)

Heidegger, Martin 1929 *Kant and the Problem of Metaphysics* (trans. Taft, R., Indiana University Press, Bloomington, IN 1997)

Heidegger, Martin 1947 'Letter on Humanism' in *Basic Writings* (trans. Capuzzi, F.A., ed. Krell, David F., Routledge and Kegan Paul, London 1978)

Healey, John F. 'The Early Alphabet' in *Reading the Past: Ancient Writing from Cuneiform to the Alphabet* (ed. Hooker, J.T., Guild Publishing, London 1990)

Henley, Tracy B. 'On Prehistoric Psychology: Reflections at the Invitation of Göbekli Tepe' in *History of Psychology*, *23* (3), 211–218

Henley, Tracy B. and Rossano, Matt J. *Psychology and Cognitive Archaeology: An Interdisciplinary Approach to the Study of the Human Mind* (Routledge, Oxford 2022)

Hesiod *Works and Days* (trans. Wender, D., Penguin 1973)
Hogg, Michael A. and Graham, M. Vaughan *Social Psychology* (7th Edition: Pearson, London 2014)
Hooker, J.T. (ed.) *Reading the Past: Ancient Writing from Cuneiform to the Alphabet* (Guild Publishing, London 1990)
Howe, Stephen *Afrocentrism: Mythical Pasts and Imagined Homes* (Verso, London 1998)
Hoyland, Robert G. *Arabia and the Arabs from the Bronze Age to the Coming of Islam* (Routledge, Abingdon, Oxfordshire 2001)
Hung, Ruyu *Education Between Speech and Writing: Crossing the Boundaries pf Dao and Deconstruction* (Routledge, London 2018)
Husserl, Edmund *The Crisis of European Sciences and Transcendental Phenomenology* (trans. Carr, D., Northwestern University Press, Evanston, IL 1970)
Husserl, Edmund *Ideas Pertaining to a Pure Phenomenology and to a Phenomenological Philosophy, Third Book: Phenomenology and the Foundations of the Sciences* (trans. Klein, T.E. and Pohl, W.E., Martinus Nijhoff Publishers, London 1980)
Husserl, Edmund *Ideas Pertaining to a Pure Phenomenology and to a Phenomenological Philosophy, First Book: General Introduction to Pure Phenomenology* (trans. Gibson, W.R.B., Routledge, London 2012)
Inglis, Fred *Culture* (Polity Press, Cambridge UK 2004)
Irwin, Terence *Classical Thought: A History of Western Philosophy 1* (OUP 1989)
Jacobsen, Thorkild 'Mesopotamia' in *Before Philosophy: The Intellectual Adventure of Ancient Man* (eds. Frankfort, H. and H.A., Penguin, New York 1949)
James, George G.M. *Stolen Legacy: The Egyptian Origins of Western Philosophy* (Allegro Editions 2017)
Jaspers, Karl *The Origin and Goal of History* (trans. Bullock, M., Routledge, London 2021)
Jaynes, Julian *The Origin of Consciousness in the Breakdown of the Bicameral Mind* (Houghton Mifflin, Boston 1982)
Jefferson, Thomas *Declaration of Independence* (Grafton, John ed., Dover NY 2000)
Johnson, Matthew *Archaeological Theory: An Introduction* (2nd Edition) (Wiley-Blackwell, Chichester, West Sussex 2010)
Kang, C.H. and Nelson, Ethel R. *The Discovery of Genesis* (Concordia, St Louis MO 1979)
Kant, Immanuel *Practical Philosophy* (CUP 1996)
Kant, Immanuel *Critique of Pure Reason* (trans. Guyer, P. and Wood, A., CUP 1998)
Kant, Immanuel *Correspondence* (trans. Zweig, A., CUP 1999)
Kant, Immanuel *Anthropology, History, Education* (trans. Zöller, G. and Louden, R.B., CUP 2011)
Kant, Immanuel *Philosophy of Material Nature* (trans. Ellington, J.W., Hackett Publishing, Indianapolis, Indiana 1985)
Kaufmann, Walter *From Shakespeare to Existentialism* (Princeton University Press, NJ 1980)
Kiev, Ari *Transcultural Psychiatry* (Penguin, Middlesex UK 1972)
King, Russell (ed.) *Origins: An Atlas of Human Migration* (New Burlington Books, London 2007)
Kragh, Helge *An Introduction to the Historiography of Science* (CUP 1989)
Kramer, Samuel Noah *The Sumerians: Their History, Culture, and Character* (University of Chicago Press, London 1971)

Kristiansen, Kristian and Larsson, Thomas B. *The Rise of Bronze Age Society: Travels, Transmissions and Transformations* (CUP 2005)
Kriwaczek, Paul *Babylon: Mesopotamia and the Birth of Civilisation* (Atlantic Books, London 2010)
Kruger, Rayne *All Under Heaven: A Complete History of China* (Wiley, London 2003)
Kuehn, Manfred *Kant: A Biography* (CUP 2001)
Leach, Edmund *Lévi-Strauss* (Fontana, London 1974)
Leahey, Thomas Hardy *A History of Psychology: Eighth Edition* (Routledge, London 2018)
Leakey, Richard E. and Lewis, Roger *Origins: What New discoveries Reveal About the Emergence of Our Species and Its Possible Future* (Macdonald and Janes's, London 1979)
Lefkowitz, Mary R. and Rogers, Guy Maclean *Black Athena Revisited* (University of North Carolina Press, London 1996)
Lévi-Strauss, Claude 1978 *Myth and Meaning* (Routledge, London 2001)
Lévi-Strauss, Claude *Structural Anthropology* (Penguin, London 1963)
Lewis, C.S. *The Discarded Image: An Introduction to Medieval and Renaissance Literature* (CUP 1964)
Lewis-Williams, David and Pearce, David *Inside the Neolithic Mind* (Thames and Hudson 2018)
Lewis-Williams, David *The Mind in the Cave: Consciousness and the Origins of Art* (Thames and Hudson, London 2002)
Liu et al. (2015) 'The Earliest Unequivocally Modern Humans in Southern China' in *Nature* 14.10.15
Lloyd, G.E.R. *Greek Science* (Folio Society, London 2012)
Lloyd, G.E.R. *Disciplines in the Making* (OUP 2011)
Locke, John *An Essay Concerning Human Understanding: An Abridgement* (J.M. Dent and Sons, London 1976)
Lovejoy, Arthur O. *The Great Chain of Being* (Harvard University Press, Cambridge MA 1964)
Lucretius *De Rerum Natura* (trans. Latham, R.E., Penguin, London 1951)
Lyons, John *Chomsky* (Fontana Modern Masters, London 1970)
MacGilchrist, Barbara, Myers, Kate and Reed, Jane *The Intelligent School* (Sage Publications, London 2004)
Machinga, Mazvita Margaret and Marovic, Zana 'African Shamanic Knowledge and Transpersonal Psychology: Spirits and Healing in Dialogue' in *The Journal of Transpersonal Psychology*, Vol. 49, No.1, 2017
Magee, Brian 1982 *Men of Ideas: Some Creators of Contemporary Philosophy* (OUP)
Magee, Brian 1997 *Confessions of a Philosopher* (Phoenix, London)
Mann, Charles C. 'Birth of Religion: Turkey's 11,600-year-old Temple Reflects the Origins of Worship' in *National Geographic* Vol. 219 No.6 June 2011
Martin, Francis 'The Word at Prayer: Epistemology in the Psalms' in *The Bible and Epistemology* (ed. Healey, Mary and Parry, Robin, Paternoster Press 2007)
Martin, Thomas R. *Ancient Greece: From Prehistoric to Hellenistic Times* (2nd edition: Yale University Press, London 2013)
Marx, Karl *Selected Writings* (ed. McLellan, David, OUP 1977)
McGilchrist, Iain *The Master and His Emissary: The Divided Brain and the Making of the Western World* (Yale University Press, London 2009)

McGilchrist, Iain *The Matter with Things: Our Brains, Our Delusions and the Unmaking of the World, Volume One: The Ways to Truth* (Perspectiva Press, London 2021)

McGilchrist, Iain *The Matter with Things: Our Brains, Our Delusions and the Unmaking of the World, Volume Two: What Then Is True?* (Perspectiva Press, London 2021)

McCumber, John *Time and Philosophy: A History of Continental Thought* (Acumen, Durham 2011)

McManus, Chris *Right Hand, Left Hand: The Origins of Asymmetry in Brains, Bodies, Atoms and Cultures* (Weidenfeld and Nicholson, London 2002)

McVeigh, Brian J. *The "Other" Psychology of Julian Jaynes: Ancient Languages, Sacred Visions, and Forgotten Mentalities* (Imprint Academic 2018)

Mead, Margaret *Growing up in New Guinea* (Penguin, London 1942)

Mendelssohn, Kurt *The Riddle of the Pyramids* (Cardinal, London 1976)

Menn, Stephen *Descartes and Augustine* (CUP 1998)

Middleton, J. Richard *The Liberating Image: The imago dei in Genesis 1* (Brazos Press, Grand Rapids, Michigan 2005)

Mitchell, Rosamund and Myles, Florence *Second Language Learning Theories* (2nd ed., Hodder, London 2004)

Mithen, Stephen 'From Domain Specific to Generalised Intelligence: A Cognitive Interpretation of the Middle/Upper Palaeolithic Transition' in *The Ancient Mind: Elements of Cognitive Archaeology* (eds. Renfrew, Colin and Zubrow, Ezra, CUP 1994)

Mithen, Stephen *The Prehistory of the Mind: The Cognitive Origins of Art and Science* (Thames and Hudson, London 1999)

Mithen, Stephen *After the Ice: A Global Human History 20,000–5,000 BC* (Weidenfeld and Nicholson, London 2003)

Mojsov, Bojana *Osiris: Death and Afterlife of a God* (Blackwell, Oxford 2005)

Moore, Charles (ed.) *The Chinese Mind: Essentials of Chinese philosophy and culture* (University Of Hawaii Press, Honolulu 1968)

Moore, George Foot *History of Religions Vol I* (T. and T. Clark, Edinburgh 1914)

Moore, Oliver *Reading the Past: Chinese* (British Museum Press, London 2000)

Muksawa, Adam *Ancient Africa Fully Explained: Geography, Prehistory and the Rise of Its Civilisations* (self-published on Amazon 2021)

Murray, Margaret *The Splendour That Was Egypt* (Sidgwick and Jackson Ltd., London 1949)

Murray, Oswyn *Early Greece* (Harvester Press, Sussex UK 1980)

Nunn, John F. *Ancient Egyptian Medicine* (British Museum Press, London 1996)

Narvaez, Darcia and Tarsha, Mary S. 'The Missing Mind: Contrasting Civilisation with Non-Civilisation Development and Functioning' in Henley, Tracy B. and Rossano, Matt J. *Psychology and Cognitive Archaeology: an Interdisciplinary Approach to the Study of the Human Mind* (Routledge, Oxford 2022)

Oates, John (ed.) *The Foundations of Child Development* (Blackwell, Oxford 1994)

Oliver, Roland and Fage, J.D. *A Short History of Africa* (Penguin, London 1966)

Oppenheimer, Stephen *The Origins of the British* (Robinson, London 2006)

Paine, Thomas in *The Thomas Paine Reader* (eds. Foot, Michael and Kramnick, Isaac, Penguin 1987)

Palmer, Sue (ed.) *Play Is the Way: Child Development, Early Years and the Future of Scottish Education* (CCWB Press, Paisley 2021)

Parkinson, R.B. (ed.) *The Tale of Sinuhe and Other Ancient Egyptian Poems 1940–1640 BC* (OUP 1998)
Parrinder, Geoffrey *Sex in the World's Religions* (Sheldon Press, London 1980)
Perkins, Franklin *Leibniz and China: A Commerce of Light* (CUP 2004)
Peters, F.E. *Greek Philosophical Terms: A Historical Lexicon* (New York University Press, NY 1967)
Piggott, Stuart *Prehistoric India* (Penguin, London 1950)
Plato, *Complete Works* (ed. Cooper, John M., Hackett Press, Indianapolis IN 1997)
Polt, Richard *Heidegger: An Introduction* (UCL 1999)
Popper, Karl *Conjectures and Refutations: The Growth of Scientific Knowledge* (3rd ed., Routledge and Kegan Paul, London 1969)
Powell, Jason *Jacques Derrida: A Biography* (Continuum, London 2006)
Putnam, James *Egyptology* (Apple Press, London 1990)
Pyne, Lydia V. and Pynae, Stephen J. *The Last Lost World: Ice Ages, Human Origins, and the Invention of the Pleistocene* (Viking Penguin, London 2012)
Renfrew, Colin 1976 *Before Civilisation: The Radiocarbon Revolution and Prehistoric Europe* (Penguin, London)
Renfrew, Colin 1987 *Archaeology and Language* (Pimlico, London 1998)
Renfrew, Colin and Zubrow, Ezra (eds.) *The Ancient Mind: Elements of Cognitive Archaeology* (CUP 1994)
Roberts, J.M. *The Penguin History of the World* (Penguin Books, London 1995)
Robinson, Andrew *Writing and Script: A Very Short Introduction* (OUP 2009)
Robinson, Andrew *The Indus* (Reaktion Books, London 2021)
Rodzinsky, Witold *The Walled Kingdom: A History of China from 2000 BC to the Present* (Flamingo, London 1984)
Rohl, David *A Test of Time: The Bible – from Myth to History* (Century, London 1995)
Roth, Ilona (ed.) *Introduction to Psychology Volumes 1 and 2* (Psychology Press, Hove, East Sussex 1990)
Rothfield, Philip (ed.) *Kant after Derrida* (Clinamen Press, Manchester 2003)
Roux, Georges *Ancient Iraq* ((Second Edition, Pelican Books, Harmondsworth, Middlesex, UK 1966)
Russell, Bertrand *History of Western Philosophy* (Routledge, London 1961)
Sajama, Seppo and Kampinnen, Matti *A Historical Introduction to Phenomenology* (Croom Helm, London 1987)
Sandars, N.K. (trans.) *The Epic of Gilgamesh* (Penguin, London 1972)
Sandars, Seth L. *The Invention of Hebrew* (University of Illinois Press 2009)
Sartre, Jean-Paul 1943 *Being and Nothingness: An Essay in Phenomenological Ontology* (trans. ed. Barnes, H.E., Washington Square Press, New York 1966)
Sartre, Jean-Paul *L'Existentialisme est un Humanisme* (Gallimard, Paris 1996)
Sartre, Jean-Paul 1960 *Critique of Dialectical Reason* Volume One (*trans.* A. Sheridan-Smith, Verso, New York 2004)
Schilpp, Paul A. *Kant's Pre-Critical Ethics* (Thoemmes Press, 1998)
Simmel, Georg *On Individuality and Social Forms* (University of Chicago Press, 1971)
Simon, Bernd *Identity in Modern Society: A Social Psychological Perspective* (Blackwell, Oxford 2004)
Smail, Daniel Lord *On Deep History and the Brain* (University of California Press, London 2008)
Smart, Ninian *The World's Religions* (CUP 1992)
Smart, Ninian *World Philosophies* (*2nd ed.* Routledge 2008)

Smith, Adam *An Inquiry into the Nature and Causes of the Wealth of Nations* (George Routledge and Sons, Limited, London 1903)

Smith, Jonathan A. (ed.) *Qualitative Psychology: A Practical Guide to Research Methods* (Second Edition, Sage, London 2008)

Snell, Bruno *The Discovery of the Mind* (trans. Rosenmeyer, T.G., Angelico Press, 2013)

Solomon, Robert C. *Continental Philosophy since 1750: The Rise and Fall of the Self: A History of Western Philosophy 7* (OUP 1989)

Spencer, A.J. *Death in Ancient Egypt* (Penguin, London 1982)

Springer, Sally and Deutsch, Georg *Left Brain, Right Brain*, Revised Edition (WH Freeman and Co., NY 1985)

Starr, John Bryan *Continuing the Revolution: The Political Thought of Mao* (Princeton University Press 1979)

Sternberg, Robert J. (ed.) *International Book of Intelligence* (CUP 2004)

Suggate, Sebastian and Suggate, Tamara *Reclaim Early Childhood* (Hawthorn Press, Stroud, Gloucestershire 2019)

Sykes, Bryan *Blood of the Isles: Exploring the Genetic Roots of Our Tribal History* (Corgi, London 2007)

Taiwò, Olúfemi 'Exorcising Hegel's Ghost: Africa's Challenge to Philosophy' lecture of 21.02.97, published in *African Studies Quarterly* Vol.1 Issue 4 1998

Tanakh in Hebrew and English *published by* The Society for Distributing Hebrew Scriptures, Hitchin, Herts.

Tarnas, Richard *The Passion of the Western Mind: Understanding the Ideas That Have Shaped Our World View* (Pimlico, London 2010)

Taylor, Charles *Hegel* (CUP 1975)

Tedlock, Dennis and Mannheim, Bruce (eds.) *The Dialogic Emergence of Culture* (University of Illinois Press, Chicago 1995)

The Holy Bible *New International Version* (International Bible Society 1984)

Thomas, Nicholas and Humphrey, Caroline (ed.) *Shamanism, History and the State* (University of Michigan Press, MN 1996)

Toulmin, Stephen and Goodfield, June *The Fabric of the Heavens: The Development of Astronomy and Dynamics* (Harper & Row, London 1961)

Turner, Derek *Paleontology: A Philosophical Introduction* (CUP 2011)

Valls, Andrew (ed.) *Race and Racism in Modern Philosophy* (Cornell University Press, London 2005)

Vainstub, Daniel, Mumcuoglu, Madeleine, Hasel, Michael G., Hesler, Katherine M., Lavi, Miriam, Rabinovich, Rivka, Goren, Yuval, and Garfinkel, Yosef 'A Canaanite's Wish to Eradicate Lice on an Inscribed Ivory Comb from Lachish' in *Jerusalem Journal of Archaeology, Ben Gurion University 2*, 76–199, 2022

Van de Mieroop, Marc *A History of the Ancient Near East* (2nd ed., Blackwell, Oxford 2007)

Van de Mieroop, Marc *Philosophy Before the Greeks: The Pursuit of Truth in Ancient Babylonia* (Princeton University Press, Oxford 2017)

Van Sertima (ed.) *Blacks in Science: Ancient and Modern* (Transaction Books, London 1983)

Walker, C.B.F. 'Cuneiform' in *Reading the Past: Ancient Writing from Cuneiform to the Alphabet* (ed. Hooker, J.T., Guild Publishing, London 1990)

Watterson, Barbara *Gods of Ancient Egypt* (Sutton Publishing, Stroud, Gloucestershire 1996)

Watterson, Barbara *Ancient Egypt* (Sutton Publishing, Stroud, Gloucestershire 1998)
Whitehead, Alfred North *Science and the Modern World* (Free Association Books, London 1985)
Whitley, David S. (ed.) *Reader in Archaeological Theory: Post-Processual and Cognitive Approaches* (Routledge, London 1998)
Wilhelm, Richard (ed. trans.) *I Ching or Book of Changes* (Penguin, London 2003)
Wilson, John A. 'Egypt' in *Before Philosophy: The Intellectual Adventure of Ancient Man* (eds. Frankfort, H. and H.A., Penguin, New York 1949)
Wink, Walter *Engaging the Powers: Discernment and Resistance in a World of Domination* (Fortress Press, MN 1992)
Wood, Michael *In Search of the First Civilisations* (BBC Books, London 2005)
Wright, N.T. *The New Testament and the People of God* (SPCK, London 1992)
Wright, N.T. *The Resurrection of the Son of God* (SPCK, London 2003)

Subject/Author Index

Page numbers in **bold** indicate tables.

Nation Index